CAMBRIDGE LIBRARY COLLECTION

Books of enduring scholarly value

History

The books reissued in this series include accounts of historical events and movements by eye-witnesses and contemporaries, as well as landmark studies that assembled significant source materials or developed new historiographical methods. The series includes work in social, political and military history on a wide range of periods and regions, giving modern scholars ready access to influential publications of the past.

The British Mariner's Directory and Guide to the Trade and Navigation of the Indian and China Seas

Henry Mathias Elmore (about whom little is known) was a sailor in the Royal Navy who quit in 1783 and set out for Calcutta to be involved with the East India Company's growing trade. Elmore worked as a commander on its ships, and he decided to write this account of sailing to and within the East, which was published in 1802, in order to share his navigational knowledge and to correct earlier inaccuracies. Although much of the work consists of specific, technical directions for piloting ships around Asia, Elmore's instructions give a vivid picture of the complexities of nineteenth-century navigation and the tribulations of sailing during this time. Some of the voyages he describes include sailing around the Indonesian islands and to the Malay coast, and how to reach China from Calcutta. Elmore also includes notes about locations of valuable commodities, such as spices, tea or gold, available for trade.

T0304295

Cambridge University Press has long been a pioneer in the reissuing of out-of-print titles from its own backlist, producing digital reprints of books that are still sought after by scholars and students but could not be reprinted economically using traditional technology. The Cambridge Library Collection extends this activity to a wider range of books which are still of importance to researchers and professionals, either for the source material they contain, or as landmarks in the history of their academic discipline.

Drawing from the world-renowned collections in the Cambridge University Library and other partner libraries, and guided by the advice of experts in each subject area, Cambridge University Press is using state-of-the-art scanning machines in its own Printing House to capture the content of each book selected for inclusion. The files are processed to give a consistently clear, crisp image, and the books finished to the high quality standard for which the Press is recognised around the world. The latest print-on-demand technology ensures that the books will remain available indefinitely, and that orders for single or multiple copies can quickly be supplied.

The Cambridge Library Collection brings back to life books of enduring scholarly value (including out-of-copyright works originally issued by other publishers) across a wide range of disciplines in the humanities and social sciences and in science and technology.

The British Mariner's Directory and Guide

to the Trade and Navigation of the Indian and China Seas

H.M. ELMORE

CAMBRIDGE
UNIVERSITY PRESS

CAMBRIDGE UNIVERSITY PRESS

Cambridge, New York, Melbourne, Madrid, Cape Town,
Singapore, São Paolo, Delhi, Mexico City

Published in the United States of America by Cambridge University Press, New York

www.cambridge.org
Information on this title: www.cambridge.org/9781108045872

© in this compilation Cambridge University Press 2013

This edition first published 1802
This digitally printed version 2013

ISBN 978-1-108-04587-2 Paperback

Under the Patronage of the Hon. East India Company.

THE BRITISH MARINER'S
DIRECTORY AND GUIDE

TO THE

TRADE AND NAVIGATION

OF THE

INDIAN AND CHINA SEAS.

CONTAINING

INSTRUCTIONS FOR NAVIGATING FROM EUROPE TO INDIA AND
CHINA, AND FROM PORT TO PORT IN THOSE
REGIONS, AND PARTS ADJACENT:

WITH AN ACCOUNT OF THE TRADE, MERCANTILE HABITS, MANNERS, AND CUSTOMS,
OF THE NATIVES.

By H. M. ELMORE,

MANY YEARS A COMMANDER IN THE COUNTRY SERVICE IN INDIA, AND LATE
COMMANDER OF THE VARUNA EXTRA EAST INDIAMAN.

LONDON:
PRINTED BY T. BENSLEY, BOLT-COURT, FLEET-STREET;
AND SOLD BY BLACKS AND PARRY, NO. 7, LEADENHALL-STREET.
1802.

TO

HUGH INGLIS, Esq. Chairman;
DAVID SCOTT, Esq. Deputy;

AND THE OTHER DIRECTORS OF THE HONOURABLE EAST INDIA
COMPANY, FOR THE YEAR 1800, viz.

Sir FRANCIS BARING, Bart.

JACOB BOSANQUET, Efq.

JOSEPH COTTON, Efq.

Sir LIONEL DARELL, Bart.

WILLIAM DEVAYNES, Efq.

SIMON FRASER, Efq.

CHARLES GRANT, Efq.

PAUL LE MESURIER, Efq.

Sir STEPHEN LUSHINGTON, Bart.

JOHN MANSHIP, Efq.

THOMAS THEOPHILUS METCALFE, Efq.

CHARLES MILLS, Efq.

THOMAS PARRY, Efq.

EDWARD PARRY, Efq.

ABRAHAM ROBARTS, Efq.

JOHN ROBERTS, Efq.

GEORGE SMITH, Efq.

GEORGE TATEM, Efq.

GEORGE WOODFORD THELLUSSON, Efq.

ROBERT THORNTON, Efq.

WILLIAM THORNTON, Efq.

SWENY TOONE, Efq..

Honourable

Honourable Sirs and Gentlemen,

THE Patronage which you were pleafed to beftow on my Work, demands from me the moft grateful acknowledgements. Accuftomed to munificent and liberal acts, no praife of mine can be wanting to confirm the reputation the Honourable Court has acquired, in giving at all times its ready affiftance to bring forward whatever may tend to the extenfion of fcience or the propagation of ufeful knowlege.

In the prefent inftance, I truft that I may be excufed in obferving, that, on the fafe navigation of the Indian and China Seas, and the commerce attached to it, depends, in a great meafure, the mercantile profperity of the Company; and that I have paid the greateft attention to thofe important objects, the following fheets will afford convincing proofs.

May

May I be emboldened to hope, that, if what I have written, on a fubject of fo much moment to your concerns, fhould have the good fortune to merit your approbation, I may look forward with pride and pleafure to your future confideration and fupport?

I have the honour to fubfcribe myfelf with great refpect, Honourable Sirs and Gentlemen,

Your moft obedient,

and very devoted,

humble fervant,

H. M. ELMORE.

No. 16, *Burr Street,*
30*th March* 1802.

ADVERTISEMENT.

THE Author, confcious of his own inability, deems it neceflary to inform the Public, that thefe Inftructions were not originally written with a view of being laid before them; but, having fhewn them to fome friends, who fpoke highly of their merit, he has, with fome reluctance, complied with their requeft, of prefenting them in the fhape of a publication.

Should the leaft poffible advantage to Navigation in general (to this Country and the Honourable Eaft India Company in particular) be derived from them, he will confider himfelf amply rewarded. He could wifh, however, that this tafk had been undertaken by fome perfon more capable of performing it in the manner which the fubject deferves. And, to confefs the truth, it was chiefly to prevent thefe Remarks, Inftructions, and Obfervations from being loft, that he has, unwillingly, ventured to undertake the publication of them, under an impreffion that the experience of fixteen years actual fervice would be fufficient to ftamp their cor- rectnefs and authenticity.

The

The Author has to obferve, that he has no apprehenfion of incurring blame from any one for preferving thefe valuable Inftructions. They will difcover to every navigator the Author's own experience on fuch fubjects: and there can be very few to whom they will not impart many important facts, which they would not, perhaps, have been able to derive from another fource.

There is one circumftance attending publications of this nature, which is, that the fale of the work can never fufficiently reimburfe the Author for his labour. But this he does not regret, as he looks for remuneration from the fervices he is capable to render in the line of his profeffion. It is favourable to fociety that commercial advantage generally attends difcovery, which encourages mankind to perfevere; and it is by this means that fo many ufeful voyages and travels are given almoft gratuitoufly to the public.

The following work is fo general and extenfive, and the execution of it required fo much information, affiduity, and attention, that thofe who may be the moft inclined to encourage the undertaking will very naturally inquire, Whether the man, who thus boldly promifes, be fufficiently qualified to perform? To this the Author can only anfwer, that he had written and prepared this work during his refidence in India, and had long made the fubjects of it his peculiar ftudy. Without, therefore, arrogating any fuperiority of talents, he thinks it would be unworthy of the Patronage he is honoured with, and that

kindnefs

kindnefs expected from a generous Public, as well as deficient in duty to himfelf and to his Country, was he to permit a timid fuppofition of incapacity to deter him from doing what he deems fo beneficial to fociety in general, and to the fpeculative Britifh inhabitants of India in particular.

Under the foregoing reflections, the Author begs leave to obferve, that the politics and commerce of Afia in general, and of Hindooftan in particular, interefting in all ages to the enlightened nations of Europe, have, in the courfe of the laft century, attained a degree of importance infinitely greater than even the moft fanguine could poffibly have expected. This country in particular, by the wifdom of its legiflators, the enterprifing fpirit of its merchants, and the knowledge and intrepidity of fome diftinguifhed characters, has acquired a vaft dominion in the faireft provinces of Afia, and in the moft fertile region of the earth. Befides her late acquifitions of the Myfore country, her valuable poffeffions on the peninfula of India, and the ifland of Ceylon, fhe now holds the fole and undivided fovereignty of Bengal and Bahar; a tract of country confiderably larger than France, and inhabited by thirty millions of civilized people.

From all thefe circumftances, and particularly at the prefent crifis, independently of the work as a Directory to facilitate the navigation in the Indian Seas, the Obfervations, to which fome of the Inftructions as a guide to trade refer, are expected to be of ufe to the Commanders, Officers, and Purfers, of the Honourable

Com-

Company's fhips in general, but more particularly to the Britifh Merchants, Commanders, and Officers, of the trading country fhips.

The Author efteems himfelf extremely fortunate in being honoured with the patronage of the firft commercial body in the world; and he trufts that it will give to his work additional value, when he acquaints navigators, that a part of it was fubmitted by the Court of Directors to their Committee of Shipping, accompanied by the following Addrefs to the Court, and which received their perfect approbation.

To the Honourable the Chairman and Court of Directors of the Eaſt India Company.

Honourable Sir and Sirs,

AT the concluſion of the war in the year 1783, I quitted his Majeſty's navy, and went to Calcutta, Fourth Mate of your Honourable Court's hired packet The Surpriſe, where, ſhe being diſcharged from your ſervice, I went into the country trade, and continued until the year 1796. At this period I was appointed to the command of your Honourable Court's freighted ſhip Varuna; and having delivered the Company's cargo in this country, and returned to Calcutta, I there reſigned the command of that ſhip.

During my continuance in India I was actively employed in my profeſſion; and obſerved, with much concern, the deficiency in the printed Inſtructions for ſailing from port to port in that country.

I applied, with much care, to make remarks, write directions, fix accurately the latitudes and longitudes of ſuch places as I had opportunities of doing; and at much trouble to collect ſuch remarks,

directions,

directions, and inftructions, from the beft authorities, as would enable me to improve the then extant Directory.

I have now, with much care and application, collected a number of remarks and inftructions, which I conceive will be highly beneficial to the more ready and fafe navigating in the Indian and China Seas, particularly the Weft Coaft of Sumatra, Straits of Macaffar, Malacca, Banca, Durian, and the China Sea; as well for the ufe of the Honourable Company's as for the Country Ships.

I beg your Honourable Court will permit me to have the honour of dedicating my Remarks to you, under whofe influence they will be protected, and meet the encouragement, I truft, they will be found to deferve.

The Latitudes and Longitudes, determining the exact fituations of places in India, were fo well known to be correct, that I was told your hydrographer, Mr. A. Dalrymple, wrote to India for them, in the year 1797; but the application was never made to me, or I would readily have complied with the requeft, and trufted to the known liberality of your Honourable Court for a remuneration of my labours.

I beg leave to obferve, that my Inftructions for navigating the Indian and China Seas are allowed to be, by thofe who have ufed them, extremely correct, and of great ufe in navigating thofe feas; and I have by my own experience proved them.

Any

Any number of copies of my intended publication your Honourable Court thinks proper to order, fhall be delivered to your Secretary, from the firft impreffions.

I have the honour to be, Honourable Sir and Sirs, with the greateft refpect,

Your moft dutiful,

faithful, and obedient,

humble fervant,

H. M. ELMORE,

Late Commander of the Honourable Company's
freighted fhip Varuna.

No. 2, Gloucefter Place,
New Road, Mary-le bone, London,
December 15, 1800.

MEMORANDUM

MEMORANDUM acompanying the MS. fent in with the above Addrefs, and referred to the Committee of Shipping by the Court of Directors.

" By comparing the few plain Rules, I have the honour to tranfmit as a fpecimen of my intended Work, with thefe already publifhed, for entering the river Hoogly; or by taking the opinion of any of the Commanders of the Honourable Company's fhips who have ufed Bengal; or that of any of the Company's pilots for the river Hoogly; I ftake the merit of my Publication."

RESOLUTION of the COURT.

At a Court of Directors, held on Wednefday the 1ft of April 1801,

RESOLVED,—That this Court fubfcribe for Forty Sets of Captain H. M. Elmore's Directions for Navigating in the Indian Seas.

PREFACE.

PREFACE.

AS nations have advanced in civilization, fo has difcovery and nautical knowledge been encouraged and rewarded. The Spaniards and Portuguefe laid the foundation of our acquaintance with the Indian Ocean and the China Seas.— The French, too, have done much in adding and correcting our Navigation Charts; but the commercial world in this refpect ftands more indebted to the Britifh mariner than to any other clafs of that valuable defcription of mankind.

In proportion as improvements have been made in navigation, in the like manner has enterprize been promoted, and new fources of commerce have been difcovered.— Great pains have in general been taken to point out the advantages which may be naturally expected to flow from fuch difcoveries. But in that range which it has been the good fortune of the Author to explore, very few accounts, that are in any fhape digefted, have been prefented to the Public.

The nautical part has been hitherto given in a loofe unconnected way, unfatisfactory, and in many places erroneous. In regard to the trade, nothing has been yet faid to give the Merchants of this country any adequate idea of

its

its importance or value. Free Merchants or individual traders, proceeding to India from Great Britain, have every thing to learn; and information can only be obtained by the experience of many voyages.

The Author has it in view, in the following Work, to correct the errors of former navigators; to fix new pofitions; to point out dangers hitherto unknown; and to inftruct the unexperienced in what manner, and at what feafons, to perform his voyages in thofe feas on which he treats.

Neither are thefe the only benefits to be derived from this Publication. The Eaft India Company have, with becoming liberality, given confiderable encouragement to the country trade of India, or that which is carried on between the principal ports of Britifh India and furrounding nations to the eaftward of the Cape of Good Hope. Thefe fpeculations have been hitherto confined to the eaftern hemifphere, and to the capital of merchants fettled in that quarter of the globe. The reafon of this muft appear obvious to the moft indifferent obferver, viz. the reftrictive claufe in the Company's charter, in regard to their trade, which permits of no intercourfe, independently of that Company, between this country and thofe to the eaftward of the Cape. The expediency of this meafure, debarring *in toto* the ufe of Britifh capital, when the fcarcity of fpecie in India is confidered, is a fubject which the Author leaves to

abler

abler hands. But it has never been denied, that the moſt ſolid advantages to Britiſh India, and even to the proſperity of the Company itſelf, more eſpecially ſince the year 1780, the period when Hyder Ally's invaſion of the Carnatic threatened the exiſtence of their poſſeſſions on the Coaſt of Coromandel, have been derived from the exertions of the Free Merchants reſiding in India, under the protection of the Eaſt India Company.

The capital and ſhipping of the Free Merchants have been uniformly employed, during the moſt momentous epochs, in ſupplying the armies of the Company with proviſions in times of ſcarcity, and in tranſporting troops and military ſtores from one ſettlement to another. From their exertions additional energy has been given to operations the moſt diſtant from the reſources of government, the moſt ſucceſsful termination has crowned the general effort of all ranks and degrees; and Britiſh pre-eminence in India ſtands now unrivalled.

To multiply and encourage the Free Traders of that country becomes, therefore, a principle of political economy, conſolidating the power of the Eaſt India Company. Their ſucceſs abroad depends on the Company, and which can only be promoted by a thorough knowledge of the nature and advantage to be derived from the trade which it is meant they ſhould embrace and cheriſh.

c

The

The following remarks and obfervations will point out clearly and concifely all the facilities and vigor which can be given to the commerce in queftion. By this means it may be expected that fhoots or branches of Britifh mercantile houfes may in time be eftablifhed in the Company's fettlements, and by their knowlege, application, and capital, unite more firmly the reciprocal interefts of both countries *.

In contemplating certain minutiæ which have fallen under the Author's particular obfervation, he begs to remark, that, in the Inftructions for Navigating the Weft Coaft of Sumatra, particular attention has been paid, and much application beftowed, to find out, if poffible, every danger with which that coaft abounds. Where fo many fhoals of coral rocks exift, it cannot poffibly be fuppofed to have no other dangers than what are defcribed in this Publication; for there is fcarcely any part of India which requires a particular furvey more than the Weft Coaft of Sumatra.

The Honourable Company's fhips, from Bengal to Bencoolen, are in continual danger if they make free with that coaft. The confequence is, they are under the neceffity of

* The Author underftands that it has been recommended to the banking-houfe of Meffrs. Hammerfleys, Pall-Mall, whofe correfpondence is already fo generally eftablifhed over our own continent, to fix a branch of this concern in Calcutta, for fupplying paffengers to Europe with their circular exchange notes; and for the remittance of money by bills at fhort dates, and without rifk.

keeping

keeping a good offing until they are to the fouthward of the iflands, and then baul in to make a landfall. The lofs of the Honourable Company's fhip Foulis, Captain Blatchford, has been an additional fpur to the Author's attention, and for ufing every method to gain information of any newly-dif-covered danger which may appear to the Commanders who are conftantly trading in that quarter.

The Table of Latitudes and Longitudes, the Author believes to be as accurate as any which have been laid down; and many, which have never hitherto been noticed, are princi-pally from his own obfervations. It may be obferved in this place, that, though in the fame fhip, and with the fame inftrument, few men can be found to agree, even in the meridian altitude of the fun; fome fetting the limb clofer, fome wider than others; it therefore cannot be fuppofed but in lunar obfervations, (where every mile of error upon the inftrument, in taking the diftance of the fun and moon's, or moon and ftars' limbs, makes, when the diftance is cleared of the effect of parallax and refraction, a difference of fif-teen miles or upwards in longitude,) that every obferver, in future, will agree exactly with thofe already laid down, though at the fame time they cannot differ very widely. It was well known while the Author was in India, that he was extremely choice, and went to great expence, in chronome-ters, inftruments, &c. And he will venture to affirm, that his fhip was allowed, at all times, to be a pattern for the others in the country trade of India.

After

After all that has been done, confcious there is much more to do, he feeks his apology and confolation in the line of the Poet,

" To err is human, to forgive divine."

INTRODUCTION.

No period of our hiſtory is better calculated to elucidate the powerful effects of commerce than the preſent.

The vaſt efforts made by this country in the preſervation of the liberties of Europe, have flowed from the wiſdom of our financial regulations, the rigid application of public money, and the great and ſtill growing reſources of our commercial arrangements.

To preſerve that commerce, which has exalted the reputation and encreaſed the riches of the country to a pitch unexampled, ſhould be the ſteady aim of our legiſlators. But, as preſent poſſeſſion is not a pledge of future enjoyment, it never ſhould be forgotten, that great and unparalleled ſucceſs, in any country, excites jealouſy and envy in every other.

The powers of Europe, relieved from the calamities of a long diſaſtrous war, will now return to the habits of induſtry, and they will regard India as the moſt ample range for general commerce. The inexhauſtible reſources of that country have in all ages awakened the avidity of mercantile nations; and we behold, in India and China, productions, natural and artificial, ſufficient to ſupply the wants of all the world. To retain, therefore, our ſhare of the lucrative branch of commerce, or as much of it as our capital and ſituation entitle

title

title us to do, is the object we have in view. But, in order to do this, we must examine, not only into the interests and probable designs of surrounding nations, but into the moral principles of mankind, so far as it may regard a commercial system; since a new order of things have been established, and that the French revolution has laid a foundation for political intrigue, on a new and unheard-of basis.

It is a fact well known, that, to establish a new French East India Company, with territorial revenue, was the favourite object of the old French monarchy. To give efficacy to this measure Anquetil du Peron, a man not unknown to the literati of Europe, was dispatched by the Academy of Sciences at Paris, in order to ascertain on the spot certain facts relative to Hindooftan. The report of this writer strongly recommends an alliance between the Merhattas and the Republican government; and by this means does he propose to sap British influence and commerce in India. His details are of a complexion to disseminate revolutionary principles in trade as well as in politics, in order to allure the other nations of Europe, and to compel them, as it were, to see their own interests, in a manner best suited to the interests of France. Those principles having extended themselves over a great part of Europe, and even, in some instances, found their way into the cabinet of princes, will yet be the means of exciting great uneasiness and disorder. We have seen, under their influence, negociations carried on in a manner entirely unknown to former diplomacy; divisions of territory, of commerce and property, insisted on, under the specious pretence of the rights of nature;

6

states

ſtates and kingdoms extended or reduced according to their ſituation and the limits or boundaries which are marked on the ſurface of the globe; and combinations entered into to deprive one country of a beneficial branch of commerce, in order to enrich other leſs fortunate nations. To render theſe pretenſions more plauſible, political writers of every deſcription were employed, under the influence of the governments of Europe, to promulgate what they term the natural prerogatives of the human race.

Commercial rivality has, from the earlieſt ages, been the grand ſource of contention, and what will moſt probably again become the origin of freſh differences among the preponderating powers of Europe. "Let us (ſay the ſubtle politicians of the preſent day, as obſerved by a late writer*), examine in what manner the nations of Europe are to enjoy their natural ſhare of the commerce of the world, and particularly of India, ſo great and lucrative as it has now become. Permit us to caſt our eyes over the map of the globe, and trace, on its ſurface, thoſe lines and boundaries which nature ſeems to have preſcribed to all countries, in regard to commercial arrangements. The coaſts of Europe, from Cape St. Vincent to the extremity of the Gulfs of Bothnia and Finland, appear one great diviſion for mercantile enterpriſe and adventure; a range ſufficient for competition among thoſe nations whoſe dominions ſtretch towards the Weſtern Ocean. There is abundance of ſcope for activity and ſpeculation in the limits of that trade, which is naturally connected with the weſtern and northern ſhores of Europe, the

* Lieut. Col. TAYLOR, in his "Letters on India."

Weſt

Weſt India iſlands, the coaſt of America, the whale and other fiſhe-ries, and in the carriage of bulky and weighty articles to and from India. Let all this be enjoyed by the inhabitants of the weſtern coaſts of Spain and France, by Portugal, by the Low Countries, Hamburgh, Denmark, Sweden, and Ruſſia, and by Great Britain. But let us enquire into the ſituation, and what will be termed, by thoſe to whom it relates, the natural right of another great diviſion of the civilized world. In this they will comprehend the whole of the coaſt within the Straits of Gibraltar, including part of France and Spain, the States of Italy, Auſtria, Turkey, and Ruſſia; an ex-tent, and population, far exceeding the northern diviſion already mentioned. It will be argued that the Levant trade, or that be-tween the eaſt and the weſt by the medium of Egypt and Syria, is the natural right of thoſe countries connected with the Mediter-ranean and Black Seas; that the wants of ſo large a portion of mankind are to be attended to, and that ſeventy millions of inha-bitants ſhould not depend ſolely on the exertions of other people, while they poſſeſs within themſelves the means of commerce."— Theſe ideas are certainly alluring; and the publicity of ſuch opinions, induſtriouſly propagated, has, it may be ſuppoſed, conſiderably in-fluenced the minds of men.

The opinions of mankind are to be combated only by opinions, and are not to be overcome by brutal force. On topics of a general nature, which are daily brought under conſideration, and in which the rights of nations may be involved, or in regard to queſtions which may be agitated by foreign writers, we muſt compare,

and

and weigh one affertion againft another, and repel invidious attacks by an expofition of the fallacy of our opponents. We muft oppofe one pofition to another, fentiment to fentiment, volume to volume. The poifon contained in publications, which are carefully circulated all over the continent, by the medium of Paris, Hamburgh, Leipfic, Frankfort, Berlin, and Amfterdam, fhould be extracted by counter exhibitions, tranflated into the different languages of Europe. This is a fubject deferving the attention of Government, and daily becoming of greater confequence in the political fyftem of nations. By thefe means the bad effects of infidious reprefentation would frequently be obviated, the feeds of jealoufy be deftroyed, and the evil difpofition of defigning men be completely overthrown.

But as we cannot look forward with every care and attention, on our part, to a continual feries of fuccefs, it is proper to examine into facts and circumftances, as they may appear either applicable to this country, to thofe nations with whom we are immediately connected, or to others who may have views inimical to our own. Truth is to be obtained by comparifon: The experience of paft ages throws a light on fimilar occurrences, which are conftantly paffing before our eyes, and fairly may be prefumed to indicate what may hereafter happen from a fimilitude of exifting circumftances with thofe which have already taken place.

In this commercial age, the accumulation of money has entirely changed the fyftem of affairs. It is, in fact, become not more effential to the comfort and enjoyment of individuals, than it is to the political powers and independence of nations. In periods more

remote,

remote, the fpeculations of mankind gave way to a more animated paffion. Empires, in the early ages, reared by the alliances of tribes, were upheld by martial virtue and the energies of the human race. The Affyrian, the Grecian, and the Roman empires, were not commercial, but military and agricultural: neither were the vaft eftablifhment of the Caliphs, of Jenghis Caun, Tamerlane, or that of the Turks, founded on any other than the law of arms, fupported by conqueft and the fpoils of their neighbours. Intercourfe with commercial people, then confined to fmall ftates only, foftened the manners of mankind, and in the courfe of time drew them afide from military enterprizes. Luxury, the concomitant of riches and of trade, at length crept in, and difmembered the greateft empires of antiquity.

The Romans, a military republic, annihilated the commercial city of Carthage, becaufe they defired a participation of that commerce, which at laft ended in their own deftruction. The ifland of Sicily, the granary of the Mediterranean, in the poffeffion of the Carthagenians, attracted the avarice of the Romans, the firft nation in the world; they fucceeded in expelling the Carthagenians, and in ruining their trade: but, when imperial Rome became commercial, the Romans were themfelves affailed by the more vigorous hordes from the Euxine and the Danube *, whofe reiterated attacks they were unable to oppofe. The introduction of refinement and luxury, acting on the morals of the Roman people, proved fatal, and brought on by flow degrees the ruin of the empire. Thefe, and

* The invafion of the Cimbri, a northern people inhabiting Scandinavia, firft fhook the foundation of the Roman empire, by proving their legions not invincible: they fwept off five confular armies, till in the end they were themfelves almoft totally deftroyed by the army of Marius.

fimilar

fimilar reflections, may create in our minds many doubts of the propriety of rearing vaft commercial eftablifhments, without minute attention to thofe purfuits, which in all ages have, in the firft inftance, been the fource of national independence.

No ftate or kingdom can long exift in a fituation merely commercial. We obferve, however, that nations preferving a martial fpirit, in poffeffion of liberty and the enjoyment of civil rights, and who have not been burthened with heavy reftrictions on their commerce, for a length of time continued to affert their independency, and even to maintain a confiderable fhare of political power. Inftances, in the once flourifhing kingdoms of Syria and Paleftine, in the cities of Tyre and Carthage, in the Rhodians, the republics of Genoa and Venice, and, of a later date, in that of the United Provinces, are eafily to be found.

It is to this country a circumftance of great felicitation, that its infular fituation, the particular nature of the climate, its phyfical productions, and the boifterous element by which it is furrounded, give to the inhabitants particular energies denied to other nations, in other refpects much more fortunately placed. In fpite of the encroachments of luxury, which has within half a century wonderfully increafed, the ocean, which has nurtured fo many heroes, muft ever continue to infpire, and to give that ardour to the mind of our defenders, which is neceffary to the exiftence of maritime nations.

It may be a queftion not altogether unworthy of inveftigation, and, perhaps, may one day become of the firft importance, Whether

Great

Great Britain, fituated without the reach of foreign invafion, at leaft while defended by a numerous fleet, navigated by a brave and active race of men, may not maintain her rank among nations, without foreign alliances or diftant fettlements? But it is the fyftem of the prefent age, for European nations to derive their political independence from trade and foreign colonies; and to enjoy, according to their commerce and opulence, a proportionate fhare of importance.

The balance of power in Europe is therefore graduated by the fcale of money, which in a fmall country muft neceffarily arife from foreign poffeffions and extended commerce. Great Britain derives her confequence from the energy of a population above mediocrity, with an extenfive commerce, and great and valuable foreign dependencies. This country has been, perhaps, in thefe attainments, more fortunate than moft others; political arithmetic and the theory of commercial finance are therefore infeparable from our power, in the prefervation of which we cannot fail of feeling interefted in whatever may tend to endanger that fyftem by which our Government is upheld. On this important fubject we are, even in the midft of peace, called upon to contemplate events of the firft importance, which for a length of time muft continue to threaten the tranquillity of the Eaftern Hemifphere. Amongft thofe events, the probable downfall of the empire of the Turks, the free navigation of the Bofphorus and Black Sea, the occupancy of Egypt, the jealoufy excited in regard to our valuable India poffeffions, and the combination of thofe nations for the purpofe of obtaining a participation of the advantages we enjoy, may be comprehended.

The

The Emperor of Ruffia, aided by his allies in the fouth, will fooner or later overturn the dominion of the Turks; for, however mild and pacific the difpofition of the prefent Emperor may be, the interefts and inherent policy of that empire muft remain un-alterable. Great Britain will, probably, in fupport of the Ottoman Empire, be involved in frefh hoftilites; and the flames of war, leaving Europe in repofe, will in that cafe extend their influence to milder regions. The Mediterranean Sea, the Gulfs of Arabia and Perfia, and the Indian Ocean, will become the theatre of war.— But while, on one hand, it may naturally be fuppofed that Great Britain will, on her own element, exult in the triumph of her navy; on the other, we muft be prepared, even in the midft of peace, to meet with firmnefs thofe efforts which it may be in the power of our enemies to direct againft the moft vulnerable part of our poffeffions: for, fince the continental powers are unable to com-pete with us at fea, they will oppofe fuch other means as they poffefs; and, in proportion as they are deficient in force on one element, they will increafe their exertions where their refources may be eftimated by the contrary ratio. In this view of our affairs, the debilitated empire of the Turks, Egypt, as in fome degree a component part of that empire, and the diftracted mo-narchy of Perfia, will be found to require aid and vigour from the refources of Britifh India.

The military refources of the Merhattas and Seicks, united to thofe of the Eaft India Company and that of her numerous de-pendents and allies, will maintain againft all the world the independency of India. And if it may be yet poffible to give new intereft and animation to the ftates of Perfia, the friendfhip of that empire would contribute to the fecurity of Hindooftan, as well as increafe the confumption of our home manufactures.

The Ottoman Empire, fubverted by Ruffia, France, and Auftria, or drawn by thefe powers, whether by the operation of her hopes or her fears, from the ties of amity with us, will in either cafe add but little confequence to a continental alliance, which may have for its object any defigns hoftile to our poffeffion in the Eaft.

The political importance of Egypt has engaged the attention of Europe; but whether that country is likely to become the medium of communication between the Eaft and the Weft, or that the poffeffion of it by an enterprizing and an active people may hereafter affect our India commerce, it muft ftill be allowed, that a colony eftablifhed at any future period by a commercial rival, or by any European power whatfoever, in the centre of the antient world, on that ifthmus which connects with fo much advantage Europe, Afia, and Africa, can never ceafe to be a fubject of inquietude and fufpicion. Neither is it for the repofe of Europe, or confiftent with the juft claims of the ftates and kingdoms which comprife that quarter of the globe, that a fpot fo neceffary to all fhould be exclufively governed by any one power. It might be confidered but juftice by European nations that Egypt, which fooner or later muft be feparated from the Turkifh empire, fhould be fupported as an independent country, where the natural advantages, which arife out of fituation, foil, or climate, would, by the exercife of falutary laws, be equally difpenfed. It is, perhaps, in the nature of things, and concomitant with progreffive civilization, refinement, and general improvement, that leading nations may confider themfelves called on to eftablifh in others uncivilized, or in fuch as may have from particular caufes become degenerated, a fyftem of focial intercourfe, founded on principles of juftice and moral rectitude.

But meafures, which carry along with them whatever is gratifying to the philofopher or man of feeling, can never be fairly accomplifhed by the partial means of one country ufurping authority by the mere application of brutal force over any other. Eftablifhments of this nature, where the fituation of kingdoms are to be materially altered, can only be juftified by the general concurrence, or (if the term may be applied) by a jury of nations. Under their aufpices a neutral independent kingdom might be conftructed in Egypt as well as in Greece and other countries, where commerce, from mutual reciprocity, would find its level, and the fecurity of property be refpected. It is neceffary, for the tranquillity of Europe, that, for the prefent, Egypt fhould remain undifturbed from the views of intereft or ambition, as the period may not be far diftant when a revolution in the Turkifh empire may transfer that country to other hands. In this cafe it is evident that the fate of Egypt muft be hereafter fettled by the powers of Europe; for it would be equally unjuft that Great Britain, or any other European

nation,

nation, fhould hold the fovereignty of that ancient country, as that the French republic fhould have been fuffered to have enjoyed its poffeffion undifturbed.

It muft be allowed that the pretenfions of nations, and the civil rights of humanity, as they are connected with commerce, fhould not be entirely overlooked. But, in order to render perfect juftice, we muft examine the moral geography of the world, and recur to certain pofitions on the globe, intended, as it would feem, by Nature, for the mutual convenience of all mankind. This would be found a difficult tafk, and, perhaps, too arduous to be even undertaken. It is therefore fufficient that we fhould convince the world of the juftice of our intentions in regard to other nations; and, by perfevering in the fame honourable line of conduct which has characterifed Britifh commerce, continue to fecure to this country the trade of India, and of which the territorial poffeffion gives us the entire command. It is for this reafon that we have been reprefented " The Ufurpers of Foreign Commerce," and that we have ftudioufly combined our profperity and force in fuch a manner as to paralyfe and ftifle the principles of induftry in every other nation. We are accufed of every unfair practice, and arraigned in virulent publications, in the language of every ftate and kingdom in Europe. While fuch inflammatory writings are permitted to pafs without contradiction, they ftimulate a fpirit of prejudice and refentment between nations, and direct the minds of men to frefh jealoufies and new quarrels.

The

The prosperity of England, ever since the peace of Utrecht, has been gradually laying the foundation of envy among other nations; but it is not to be expected that, because one people are more industrious and enterprising than another, such spirit should be made the ground-work for sacrifices on the part of such people or nation. On the contrary, their example should operate as a stimulus, not only to the inhabitants, but also to the princes and rulers, of the states and kingdoms of Europe. Impolitic restrictions, imposed by short-sighted and narrow-minded governments, impede the mutual intercourse of nations, and create the evil attributed to this country, and not the liberal principles on which English commerce is conducted. To illustrate this by example, we have only to advert to the prohibitory laws of Spain and Portugal, the monopolies and restrictions in Holland, Russia, and formerly in France. It is such things as these that occasion discontent, and which the present enlightened race begin to see and to feel.

We are not, however, solely to depend on the exposition of such circumstances, to obviate all the evil consequences of which men, disaffected or envious of our success, complain. We must have recourse to national integrity and justice, and examine what is incumbent for other kingdoms to perform on their part, and then advert to what may be expected on the part of Great Britain.

On referring to the map of the world, we can distinguish those central positions which would seem intended to facilitate commerce,

e

and

and to approximate countries diftant from each other. Pofitions, which, if improved by the art and induftry of man, would convey with greater facility the merchandife of China, India, and the Eaftern Ocean, to the fhores of Europe; among them, The Ifthmus of Darien, The Ifthmus of Suez, The Cape of Good Hope, and the free paffage of the Dardanelles and the Canal of Conftantinople, appear of the greateft importance.

The Englifh, with public fpirit and liberality, have opened the ports of India to foreign nations; while the Spaniards and Portuguefe do not act in the fame liberal manner in regard to their fettlements in South America and the Philippine Iflands. Why is it that the free navigation of the Bofphorus and Black Sea is denied? Are not thefe glaring inftances of felfifh and unjuft proceedings in other nations? Why, therefore, fhould Great Britain be blamed, becaufe her exertions, being better directed, are attended with more fuccefs?

If thefe and other evils were removed, and the rights of mankind and of nations adjufted, fuch meafures would probably tend to tolerate, as far as is either poffible or practicable, univerfal freedom of commerce, by which each nation would enjoy whatever fhare their induftry, enterprife, and capital, might enable them to do.

That the foregoing important confiderations have occurred, it is not to be wondered at, when we reflect that a general convention of the nations of Europe is expected to affemble, in order to difcufs,

3

perhaps,

perhaps, fome of the very points to which our obfervations have been directed; and that in this difcuffion may be involved the interefts of Great Britain, in the very trade which is the important fubject of the following fheets.

To preferve the trade of India to this country is the ardent wifh of the Author; and he will confider himfelf amply repaid for all his labours, if the information which fixteen years refidence in India enables him to give, can in any degree augment or preferve the profperity of the Nation.

I N D E X.

Samarang

Charges

Character

ALL the lateft and moft accurate Pilots, Sea Charts, and Navigation Books, fold wholefale, retail, and for exportation, By BLACKS and PARRY, No. 7, Leadenhall-ftreet;

Where may be had,

The COUNTRY TRADE PILOT, bound in calf, price Ten Guineas.

THE

BRITISH MARINER'S DIRECTORY, &c.

DIRECTIONS

FOR THE STRAITS OF COLOGNE, IN THE STRAITS OF MALACCA.

FROM Salangore-roads in feven fathom mud, Salangore-hill bearing eaft, you fee two fmall iflands on the eaft fide of the north-fand, known by the name of Pooloo Anza (or Mud and Goofe iflands), bearing S.S.E. foutherly, the top of Parcilar-hill S.S.E. half E. and a large rock on the eaft-fand, called Poolo Boot-tool S.E. three-quarters S. diftance off fhore five miles.

Between Pooloo Anza and Pooloo Boot-tool, is a good channel of eight, nine, and ten fathom water, extending about S.E. by S. and N.W. by N. to the entrance of the Straits of Cologne, diftance from Salangore feven leagues.

From Pooloo Boot-tool there is a reef of rocks that extends a full mile off towards Pooloo Anza, which makes it neceffary (on a flood tide, which fets to the S.E.) to fteer S. by E. from Salangore-roads till you are within one mile of Pooloo Anza, which will be then the fair way in nine or ten fathoms foft mud.

From

From Pooloo Anza fteer S.E. three-quarters S. or S E. by S. which will lead you directly to the Straits of Cologne.

If obliged to work into the Straits, ftand no nearer the North-fand than eight fathoms, as it is fteep to in many places, and no nearer Pooloo Boot-tool than five fathoms, obferving to keep foft foundings, and give Pooloo Boot-tool a birth of a mile to avoid the reef; and when paft Pooloo Boot-tool, you may fteer into five or four and a-half fathoms at either fide, regular foundings and foft mud.

When ftanding to the fouthward, do not bring Pooloo Anza to the northward of N.W. and then a S.E. courfe will lead you to the Straits, as the Straits and Pooloo Anza bear S.E. and N.W. of each other, and being at the entrance of the Straits you may fteer in without fear, as it is bold to on either fide and clear of danger.

The firft Reach lies N. by W. and S. by E. and is about five miles in length, the bluff point on the S.W. fide is (for diftinction's fake) called Deep Water Point, from the great depth of water found there, occafioned by the fall from an opening to the eaftward and directly oppofite, and is called Cologne-river, as it leads to the town of Cologne.

As foon as you begin to open the fea in the fecond Reach, you may haul up at any convenient diftance from Deep Water Point, off which you will have 18, 20, and 22 fathoms, foft mud.

The fecond Reach, where we are now entered, lies S.W. by S. and N.E. by N.; but after you are round Deep Water Point the eaftern fhore is the deepeft, on account of a fand that extends nearly acrofs the Reach, and only admits of a narrow paffage not more than half a cable's length broad, and about two-thirds of a cable's length from the eaftern fhore in the mid-channel.

Being paft Deep Water Point, you will fee a fmall creek on the fame fide (namely, Weft), and on the Eaft fide another; thefe two bear N. and S. of each other: fteer directly over for the eaftern creek, which I call the Bar Creek, until about two-thirds of a cable's

length

length from the fhore, or until **Deep Water Point** bear N. 48° E.
then by following the courfe of the Strait you will crofs the bar near
mid-channel, on the top of which I have had four and a quarter and
four and a half fathoms at high water on fpring tides. The Bar is
about two-thirds of a cable's length broad; and when Bar Creek is
fairly open, bearing E. by S. half S. or E.S.E. you are on the top of
the bar, and will have the above depth of water, hard fand.

Being now over the bar, fteer directly for the fouth point of the Sea
Reach, until the north point of that reach bears W. by N. to avoid
the wreck of a large Portuguefe fhip, which bears weft from the north
point of Sea Reach, and lies on the eaftern fhore between Ann Grab
Point and the bar; when thefe bearings are on, and you are two
cables length off fhore, it is beft to keep the eaftern fhore on board
to prevent the flood tide from horfing you through the opening to
feaward (which I call Sea Reach), where there is no paffage, being
entirely choked with fand banks, left dry at half ebb.

E. half S. from the fouth point of Sea Reach is a creek, the north
point of which is called Ann Grab Point, from a grab of that name
having been loft upon it. At the fouth fide of which, about one
cable's length from the entrance and two hundred yards inland, are
three wells of excellent frefh water, of which you can fill fix leagers
in an hour; but it will be neceffary to carry buckets, as there is no
rolling-way to and from the wells; this I call Frefh Water Creek.
Sea Reach open a fhip's length, leads directly up it, and you may
water at any time of tide. Few in India know that water may be
had in thefe ftraits; but every perfon that has paffed them, knows the
great convenience of wooding there.

Paffing from the fouthward, you pafs Frefh Water Creek at two
cables length diftance, on account of the flat that runs off Ann Grab
Point; and the next creek at the fame fide is Bar Creek, where you
will get the hard foundings of the bar.

Having

Having fhut in Sea Reach, you enter the third and laft reach ; it being circular you muft fteer S.W. half S. for two miles, where you will fee the fea open to the S.W. and having run till the fea is quite open, a S.W. courfe will carry you out.

If you are obliged to turn it, as the reach is fteep to on both fides, you may ftand to any diftance you think convenient; and as you draw towards the entrance you will deepen your water from nine to feventeen fathoms regularly, and fhoal in the fame manner to feven and fix fathoms, no lefs, except you borrow too much on the fouth point of the entrance, which fide you are rather to keep the greateft diftance from, on account of the long flat point which ftretches off it.

From the S.W. entrance fteer S. by W. two miles, then S. two miles, and having fteered as many more S. by E. and S.S.E. you may direct your courfe down the Straits of Malacca about S.E. or S.E. by E. to avoid the dangers on either fide, until you come to Cape Richardo.

Being in mid-channel, at the S.W. entrance, I had the following bearings, viz. Parcilar Hill E. three-quarters S. ; the entrance of the ftraits N.E. one-quarter N. ; the fouth point of the entrance of the eaft ftrait S.E. by E. ; the weft point E.S.E. three-quarters E. ; the weft point of the true or north-weft ftrait N.W. by N. ; diftance off the neareft fhore one mile and a-half.

DIRECTIONS

TO ENTER THE STRAITS OF COLOGNE, COMING FROM THE SOUTH
EASTWARD.

COMING from the S.E. with an intent to go through the Straits of
Cologne, haul up for the land while Parcilar Hill is to the northward
of eaſt, and ſteer along ſhore in four or five fathoms, at about three or
four miles diſtance; when the hill bears eaſt, you will ſee the entrance of the eaſt ſtrait, about three miles to the N.W. of which is
the entrance of the true or N.W. ſtrait, which will ſhew itſelf
plain when Parcilar Hill bears E. one quarter S. To enter the N.W.
ſtrait, the N.W. extreme of the land being in ſight to the weſtward or larboard ſide of the entrance, obſerve the following inſtructions:

As you enter the ſtraits, if it happen to be little wind that you
cannot ſtem the tide, on the ebb endeavour to croſs the ſhoal, or at
high water, and give the weſtern points a good birth to prevent
the ebb from driving you to the northward of the extreme point
or up the opening to the N.N.W of you, which admits of no
paſſage, being full of dangers.

Being paſt the ſhoal off the eaſt point of the ſtrait, ſteer to the
N.E. till you begin to ſhut in the opening to the N.N.W. then
follow the courſe of the ſtrait, and former directions.

Be cautious in running for theſe ſtraits, that you do not go to the
northward of the N.W. point, as there is a bank of ſand ſtretching
off to the weſtward, and three miles from the point it breaks at
half tide, and is dry in many places.

Note.

Note. All through thefe ftraits, as well as the Straits of Malacca, when you fwing to the ebb the tide is half done, and when you fwing to the flood the tide is half made. If the wind will permit, you may enter thefe ftraits at any time of tide, but I would recommend at all times to have two boats on the bar. There is good anchoring ground all through thefe ftraits.

DIRECTIONS

FOR SAILING FROM POOLOO PISSANG, IN THE STRAITS OF MALACCA, TO BATTACARRAN POINT, IN THE STRAITS OF BANCA; WITH DIRECTIONS TO ANCHOR IN MINTOW BAY.

HAVING Pooloo Piffang E.N.E. you are paft the fand bank that lies off that ifland, and the paffage is then clear to the Carrimons, giving the fmall iflands, called The Brothers, which lie to the N.E. of the Carrimons, a birth of two and a-half or three miles, the ground about them being foul and rocky and unfit for anchoring.

From Pooloo Piffang fteer S.E. by E. until within four miles of the Carrimons, on account of a reef of rocks, difcovered by Captain Lindfay, that lies off the Little Carrimons N. 56° E. diftance fix miles, and when in one with Barn Ifland, bears N. 11° E. in one with Red Ifland S. 58° E. and having the N.E. point of the Little Carrimon fhut in with the north-eafternmoft of the Brothers. Steer S.S.E. half E. until you pafs the fouth extreme of the Great Carrimon, in 12 or 10 fathoms, but no nearer to the fhore, as there is a reef of rocks off that point, ftretching along fhore at about four miles diftance. I have failed within this reef, but it is by no means a fafe paffage. When the fouth point of the Carrimon bears weft, you are abreaft

of

of the middle of the reef; and when the point bears W. by N. you are to the southward of it, and should haul in S. by E. or S. until in seven fathoms, which depth, by keeping along the Sabon shore, will carry you to the westward of the Middleburg shoal, which bears from Red Island E.N.E half E. and is about midway between that island and the Sabon shore. It is a very dangerous reef of rocks, steep to on both sides, and dry at half tide.

I recommend the channel to the westward, on account of the regular foundings and good anchorage, as on the eastern side of the shoal you have 17, 20, and 24 fathoms, with great overfalls. Your foundings are no guide, and the eddies which the shoal and Red Island occasion, where the tide is seldom less than four knots an hour, may horse you on shore before your anchor gets to the ground, or takes hold. I will not say more on the preference to be given to the western channel, as it is evident, to every unprejudiced seaman, it enjoys many advantages not to be found in the other.

There is a reef of rocks about half a mile from the Sabon shore which is dry at half tide, and when in one with Sabon-hill, bears W. half N. For a sure mark to sail clear of it, keep the high land on the Malay shore over Pulo Pissang; the high land of Jahore N.W. by N. and Red Island S.E. by S. will lead you clear of it, as well as that which lies off the south point of the great Carrimon.

As you draw near the Middleburg shoal, stand no farther off shore than eight and a-half or nine fathoms, as the deepest water is not the greatest sign of safety; and borrow on the Sabon shore to five and four and a-half fathoms, where the foundings are regular and ground soft.

Having Red Island N.E. by E. and the Twins touching each other to the southward of the Red Island, you are clear to the southward of the Middleburg shoal, and should haul up for the opening between the Passage Islands, both of which you have on your left hand, or to the eastward of you; there is another flat island, longer than

either

either of the Paffage Iflands, which you leave on the right hand, or to the weftward of you, and pafs between it and the fmalleft of the Paffage Iflands, your foundings will be from 18 to 22 fathoms, very regular and foft ground. Should the wind be fcant you may fail between any of thefe iflands giving each of them a birth of a mile, as the points which projeſt from each are all rocky and foul ground.

Being through the paffage between the Paffage Iflands, fteer for the wefternmoft of the outer iflands that lies off the S.W. point of the Great Durion, called the Tombs, coming no nearer than 16 fathoms, as the point is foul and rocky. You may now fee all the Three Brothers; and be about three leagues diftance from the neareft or Round Brother. You may fail either to the eaftward or weftward of them as you chufe, both paffages being equally good; for either of which obferve the following Direƈtions:

Firft, If you mean to pafs to the eaftward of the Brothers, you muft keep E. by S. or E. and give each of the Brothers a birth of one mile and a-half or two miles as you pafs them.

Being paffed the Paffage Iflands, and the iflands off the S.W. point of the Great Durion, giving one mile and a-half birth, fteer as above, E. by S. or E. keeping to the northward of the Round Brother one and a-half or two miles; and to know when you are on the edge of the eaft bank, you will have the peak of the Great Durion N. 55 W. You muft not bring it to the weftward of thefe bearings, as the channel here is narrow and this bank dangerous, though no notice is taken of it in any former Direƈtions, nor do I believe it is generally known, many old commanders who have ufed this track being quite unacquainted with it, having generally run through with a free wind.

Being abreaft of the Little or Round Brother, the channel is not more than five miles broad; and after paffing the Brothers you are not to ftand further to the northward than to bring the peak of the Great Durion N.W. and no nearer the Brothers than 10 fathoms

thoms. A good thwart mark, is the Paffage Ifland, on with the S.W. point of the Great Durion, and open again to the weftward of the Tombs, or iflands that lie to the S.W. of the Great Durion.

Having rounded the Small Brother, fteer S.S.E. and S. by E. half E. taking care not to lofe fight of the beach on the Middle Brother from the deck, until the Great Brother bears N.W. by N.; you may then fteer S. by W for Tanjong Barroo, to avoid the overfalls on the tail of the eaft reef, which you are not clear of, while the Falfe Durion is within the extremes of the Three Brothers, or any where touching on them. You will carry from 13 to 16 fathoms in midchannel to Tanjong Barroo; but come no nearer that point than 12 fathoms, as the bank is fteep too. When the Great Brother bears N.W. or N.W. by N. you may work into any depth of water you pleafe, from 12 on the Sumatra fhore to 17 fathoms mid-channel, and 15 on the eaft fide, until you are as far to the fouthward as Tanjong Barroo, or Baffoo.

TO PASS TO THE WESTWARD OF THE THREE BROTHERS.

As foon as you are clear of the Paffage Iflands keep the Falfe Durion clofe on board, and run down mid-channel between the Round Brother and it, giving the Brothers a birth of one mile and a-half to avoid the overfalls and foul ground near them; and having the Great Brother N.W. by N. follow the former inftructions.

From Tanjong Barroo to the Calantigas the courfe is S. onequarter E. diftance 10 leagues; keep along the Sumatra bank in feven fathoms, and you will pafs between the Calantigas and the main, in mid-channel, and about four miles from the ifland.

If obliged to turn through with a fcant wind, come no nearer the ifland than nine fathoms, and ftand to the Sumatra fhore into five fathoms.

From the Calantigas to Pooloo Varilla the courfe is S.E. half E. diftance 12 leagues; you have 12 fathoms in the channel mud.

C   If

If obliged to work here with a foul wind, stand no nearer Pooloo Varilla than 14 fathoms, and no nearer the Sumatra shore than six fathoms. The channel here is five miles broad in the narrowest part.

Pooloo Varilla False bears from Pooloo Varilla N.N.W. three-quarters W. distance five leagues; close to False Pooloo Varilla the water is good, the shore steep, but the ground foul, and bad anchorage. I would therefore recommend ships to keep the Sumatra shore on board, where they may anchor when the current or tide is against them. There are regular tides all through the Straits of Durion, sometimes running strong, but often only a slack water on the flood, which is repulsed by the freshes out of the river of Jambee. The flood from the Carrimons to the Battacarran-point runs to the northward, the ebb to the southward. From Battacarran-point to Lucapera, the flood runs to the southward through the Straits of Banca, and thence runs to the eastward. The floods and ebbs from the Carrimons are well described by Mr. Nicholson.

From Pooloo Varilla to Battacarran the course is S.S.E. half E. distance 20 leagues, and over the pleasantest bank in the world, where there is not an overfall of two inches in the whole extent.— This course will carry you clear of the banks off Battacarran and Tanjong Bon, and will bring you in with Battacarran-point in six fathoms.

If obliged to work to windward in this tract, stand no farther off the Sumatra shore than seven fathoms and a-half, and work into that shore to four fathoms and a-half without fear. The tides along shore are in general strong, but in the offing scarce any tide is perceptible.

The Frederick Endrick is a rock like a point, with a narrow sand bank round it, and steep to on all sides; it bears from the highest part of Monapon-hill S. 70° E.; and from the easternmost land in sight making like an island, and commonly called in our charts Green-island; but by the natives called Poonyabang, N.E. by E. one-quarter E. dis-

tance

tance off the neareft part of Banca three leagues and a-half. As you near it, on the weft fide, you will deepen your water to 12 or 13 fathoms with overfalls; but fhips, to avoid it, fhould borrow on the bank off Battacarran-point, from four and a-half, to nine fathoms towards the rocks; with a leading wind, feven fathoms is the beft water, foft mud.

I have often run between Frederick Endrick and Banca, by which means I have faved much time. There is a very good working channel, full fix or feven miles broad, coming no nearer the Banca fhore than 14 fathoms, nor further off than to bring Poonyabang N.E. half E. on which bearings, and Monapen-hill S. 70° E. you will be fhoaling towards Frederick Endrick, and will have 18 fathoms, hard fand, and overfalls.

Between Frederick Endrick and Carangbrom is a reef of rocks, fix miles from the fhore of Banca, called Carrang Hodjee, at each end of which is a paffage; as alfo a good working paffage between the reef and the Banca fhore. To pafs either way, take the following Directions to anchor in Mintow Bay.

DIRECTIONS

TO ANCHOR IN MINTOW BAY.

IF you go to the weftward of Carrang Hodjee, ftand to the S.E. until the top of Monopen-hill bears N.E. by N. then ftand in for Mintow town; you will with thefe bearings pafs one mile and a-half to the fouthward of Carrang Hodjee in feven fathoms, hard fand; being over the bank, you will deepen to 12, 14, or 16 fathoms, and fhoal again towards the fhore to 12 or 10 fathoms. Three miles off

C 2

the

the town, which with the hill N. by E. is the beſt anchoring ground. The bank reaches from Carrang Hodjee to Carrang Bram, which lies off the point of Banca, called Tanjong Coony; it is very ſhoal towards the latter reef, and dries in many places, ſo that no ſhip ſhould attempt to paſs over the bank into Mintow-roads with Monopen-hill to weſtward of north; by keeping the hill north you may croſs the bank in three fathoms and a-half; at low water ſpring tides, your ſoundings will be hard ſand, coral, and ſhells.

If coming from the northward, and want to go into Mintow; to the eaſtward of Carrang Hodjee: keep Monopen-hill E.N.E and you will paſs between Frederick Endrick and the ſhoal of Carrang Hodjee, and may run up in a good channel of two miles and a-half broad, taking your ſoundings from the Banca ſhore, and not coming nearer the ſhore than eight fathoms. Towards the rocks is deep water, 30, 40, and 50 fathoms, and overfallsı; borrowing on the low point where the Sultan has a fort, called Tanjong Coolian, within one-third of a cable's length, then keeping a convenient diſtance off ſhore you may anchor by the former Directions.

Carrang Hodjee bears from Monipen-hill (or Peak) N.E. eaſternly; the northern extreme of it bears from the peak N.E. three-quarters E.; and the S.E. end bears when in one with the Peak N.E. half N.; the rocks are all covered at high water, and many of them ſhew themſelves at half tide.

DIRECTIONS

FOR SAILING FROM BATTACARRAN POINT IN THE STRAITS OF
BANCA, TO POOLOO PISSANG IN THE STRAITS OF MALACCA;
WITH INSTRUCTIONS FOR KNOWING THE LAND.

BEING off Battacarran-point, and bound to the northward, through
the Straits of Durion, obferve the following inftructions:

Battacarran-point is known from Battacarran-falfe by a few trees
in a clufter, not unlike the walls of a fortification or an old building;
near its extremity, befides this point, is a bluff, and the falfe point
runs into the fea by a gentle defcent, and runs off in a long flat.

Ships in this track will have no occafion to come nearer Battacarran-point than fix fathoms, and from fix to feven fathoms off Battacarran-point a N.N.W. half W. courfe will carry you up to Pooloo Varilla, diftance 20 leagues. You fhould not, however, depend
too much upon your courfe; the beft method is to coaft it, in from
five to feven fathoms, which will lead you clear of Tanjong Bon flat,
and nearly in the mid-channel from Pooloo Varilla in 11 or 13 fathoms. You muft not borrow on Varilla nearer than 14 fathoms, as
it is fteep too, but you may ftand to the Sumatra fhore to five or
four and a-half fathoms, or any depth you may think convenient, as
it is a regular flat mud bank.

Pooloo Varilla is a pretty high ifland, and may be feen from a
fhip's deck eight leagues; when it is to the northward of you, it appears like a rabbit fquatting with the head to the S.E.; and when
to the fouthward of you it makes like a faddle, with three fmall
round iflands to the S.E. and a fmall flat one to the northward;
when it is to the northward of you, making like a rabbit, the fmall

iflands

iflands are in one with it. It is faid there is frefh water on the eaft-fide; but as the ifland is much infefted with pirates I never knew any one who attempted to land there; but have heard of one commander who loft a boat and boat's crew on it. There is no appearance of a beach or landing place; the fhore is all fteep and rocky.

N.N.W. three-quarters W. from Pooloo Varilla, diftance five leagues, is a flat table Ifland, that is feen coming from the north-ward before you fee Pooloo Varilla; and as it has in the night been miftaken for Pooloo Varilla, I, for diftinction, have called it Falfe Varilla.

From Pooloo Varilla to the Calantagas, the courfe is N.W. half W diftance 12 leagues, this will carry you through in feven fa-thoms, at about four miles diftance from the Calantagas; but if obliged to turn it with a foul wind, come no nearer the Sumatra fhore than five fathoms, and off to the iflands to nine fathoms, and be careful to pay attention to the tides, which are uncertain.

The fair way between Varilla and the Calantagas is 12 fathoms, and the lead is an unerring guide. The Calantagas are five iflands, the three principal of which they take their name from, and they bear nearly N. 15 E. and S. 15 W. of each other; the centre and ex-treme iflands are the largeft, and may be feen eight leagues from' a fhip's deck: the other two, which lie between the centre and ex-treme, are round and fmall, and cannot be feen above five or fix leagues from a fhip's deck. There are two fmall rocks to the S.E. of the Calantagas, each about the fize of a large long-boat, and from their near refemblance to each other I call them the Sifters.

E.S.E. from the Calantagas is a funken rock, diftance off the foutherntmoft ifland three and a-half or four miles; but if you keep in the depth prefcribed you cannot go near it.

From the Calantagas to Tanjong Baffoo (or Barroo) the courfe is N. one-quarter W. diftance 10 leagues; this courfe will carry you clear of that point in 12 fathoms; but as you near the point it is beft

to

to keep out to 14 fathoms; then N. by E. one-quarter E. will carry you to the Great Brother in 15 fathoms, and is nearly mid-channel and even foundings. If you go to the weftward of the Brothers, keep mid-channel between them, and the Falfe Durion; but if you go to the eaftward of them, give them a birth of one and a-half or two miles, and round them in 10 or 11 fathoms. As you draw near the Small or Round Brother, deepen to 12 or 13 fathoms; but be cautious you do not borrow too much on the eaftern fide, on account of a dangerous reef already mentioned, which extends all the way to the iflands on that fide, with alarming overfalls and hard ground, When in four fathoms on this bank, I could juft fee a fmall part of the beach on the Middle Brother, off the deck, and croffed three banks of fix, eight, and ten fathoms coral before I got into the right channel again.

I have often, fince I knew this bank, worked through in the night, by fhoaling to 11 fathoms near the Brothers, and tacking as foon as I got among the overfalls. It is not dangerous to run here in the night; I have often done it; but before I was fo well acquainted as I now am, by taking too large a range to the eaftward, expecting to find deep water, I got on this bank. Our charts, as well as the Bute's track, lay down 20 and 30 fathoms as the depth of water to the eaftward; but the depth I have found is from 16 to 18 fathoms. There is no notice taken of this bank in Bute's chart, which makes me fuppofe the perfon who defcribed this place knew nothing of a bank being there; nor fhould I, had not the accident above related carried me to the eaftward.

From the Middle to the Round Brother there runs a reef of rocks, great part of which dries at half ebb; and another reef of rocks runs N.W. from the Round Brother about one and a-quarter or one and a-half mile, which makes the channel between the Round Brother and the bank narrow, not exceeding five miles broad. If obliged to turn through this channel, the beft guide is to keep the

beach

beach on the Middle Brother in fight, or not to bring the peak of the Great Durion to the weftward of N.W and ftand towards the Brother to 11 and 10 fathoms, about two and a half or three miles diftance.

After leaving Tanjong Baffoo, and having an ifland that makes like a neat's tongue E. by N. or E. the peak of the Great Durion is the firft land that appears to the northward; the next is a faddle ifland to the eaftward of the Great Durion, then the Falfe Durion, and foon after the Great Brother in one with the peak of the Great Durion bearing N. 20 W. at the fame time Saddle Ifland will bear N. four W. the peak of the Falfe Durion N. 23 W and Tanjong Barroo juft going out of fight from the deck N. 68 W. depth of water 13 fathoms, fand and fhells.

When the Middle and Small Brothers appear, they will fhew themfelves within the extremes of the Great Durion; and the Great Brother in one with the peak, as above, is a good leading mark.

The reafon of being fo particular with the bearings hereabout, is the refemblance of one ifland to another, fo that a ftranger may be eafily miftaken, and a perfon fhould be very exact in regard to thefe bearings, then no miftake can poffibly happen.

On the N.E. fide of the Great Brother is a large patch or cliff, not unlike the walls of a fortification, which fhould you lofe fight of from the deck, you may conclude yourfelf too far to the eaftward, and fhould haul over to the weftward directly, for to the eaftward you will have overfalls of three and four fathoms at a caft, and in many places fcarce three fathoms water.

While the Falfe Durion is within the extreme of the Brothers, you are not clear of the bank to the eaftward: when the Round Brother is open to the eaftward of the Falfe Durion, you are abreaft the S.W. point of the fhoal.

As foon as the S.W. point of the Little Durion fhews itfelf plain, you will fee the Tombs, or three fmall iflands that lie off the S.W.

point

point of the Great Durian, and when the largeſt or outward iſland bears N. 70 W. it will be on with the peak of Sabon-hill, (which hill now appears like two iſlands, and may be taken for the Carri-mons); that is a good long mark for leading you clear of the foul point off the Great Durian, where there are ſome rocks under water that lie along ſhore; or by giving the Durians and ſmall iſlands a birth of one and a half or two miles, you may round them without danger.

To the N.E. of the Great Durian is an opening that much re-ſembles the Straits of Durian, but admits of no channel for ſhips; the bearings of the Tombs and Sabon-hill ſhould therefore be at-tended to, as well as to obſerve not to bring the peak of the Great Durian to the weſtward of N.W.

When Sabon-hill is on with the eaſternmoſt Paſſage Iſland, it bears N. 52 W.; when the northernmoſt or ſmall Paſſage Iſland is on with the peak of the Great Carrimon it will bear N. 40 W.; when the Small or Round Brother is on with the S.W. point of Great Paſſage Iſland N. 43 W. and S. 43 E.

Being paſt the Brothers, ſteer for Paſſage Iſland, and in mid-channel you will have from 18 to 22 fathoms, mud; and by allow-ing all points of the iſlands one mile birth you will paſs clear; and being through, the following Inſtructions are to be obſerved for the Middleburg-ſhoal:

N. 63 E. from the higheſt part of Red Iſland is a ſhoal or reef of rocks about two cables length long, and reaches about half a mile off the iſland; this makes the paſſage between Middleburg-ſhoal and Red Iſland very narrow, and having deep water cloſe to the reef, makes it a leſs ſafe channel than between the Sabon-ſhore and the Middleburg. The long mark for going between the Middleburg and the Red Iſland, is to keep the peak of the Great Durian S.E. half S.; or the northern Paſſage Iſland in one with the peak of the Falſe Durian.

For

For a thwart mark, if obliged to work through this channel, you muſt not bring the Falſe Durian open above a ſhip's length to the weſtward of the Paſſage Iſlands; no nearer Red Iſland than one-half or three-quarters of a mile, on account of the reef that runs off it. When you have got a ſmall rocky iſland with a tree on it (which I call the Cap and Feather, from its reſemblance to one) open to the ſouthward of the Twins, you are then clear of the Middleburg to the northward, and may ſtretch over for the Sabon-ſhore.

When the northernmoſt of the Twins is ſhut in behind Red Iſland, you are clear of the Middleburg-ſhoal to the ſouthward; when the Middleburg-ſhoal is on with Sabon-hill it bears N. 68 W.; when the northernmoſt Twin is open a ſail's breadth to the northward of Red Iſland, you are clear to the northward of the reef of Red Iſland; when the reef was on with the northern extreme of Red Iſland, it bore N. 50 E.; and when in one with the Cap and Feather to the N.E. of Red Iſland, it bore N. 52 E.

The leading mark on the Middleburg-ſhoal is both Paſſage Iſlands in one, and the paſſage between the S.W. point of the Little Durian and the ſmall Paſſage Iſland open, and the whole of the Great Carri-mon open to the eaſtward of Sabon-point.

To go clear of the Middleburg-ſhoal, I would recommend the channel along the Sabon-ſhore, as it is the ſafeſt and broadeſt. As ſoon as you are through the Paſſage Iſlands haul to the Sabon-ſhore, until the eaſternmoſt or Sabon-point is on with the eaſt peak of the Little Carrimon, and the S.W. point of the Little Durian is ſhut in with the ſmall Paſſage Iſland, and the paſſage between the Paſſage Iſlands is fairly open; then ſteer N.N.W. along the Sabon-ſhore in five, ſix, ſeven, or eight fathoms, ſoft mud, until Red Iſland bears E. by S. and the Twins open with each other to the northward of Red Iſland; then ſteer N. by W. or N. until you deepen your water to 10 or 12 fathoms, by which time you will ſee the high land of Johore on the Malay ſhore to the eaſtward of the Little Carrimon bearing N.W. by

N.:

N.; fteer directly for it fo as to fall in with the Little Carrimon four or five miles diftance, and avoid Lindfay's Reef by going to the weft-ward of it, and the reef that lies off the fouth-point of the Great Carrimon.

When the peaks of the Great and Little Carrimon are in one, haul over for Pooloo Cocob, to avoid the foul ground off the point of the Brothers; and having got hold of the eaft bank, keep in 15 fathoms, foft mud; and pafs Pooloo Piffang at the diftance of three or four miles.

DIRECTIONS

FOR LINGIN RIVER, AND SOME ACCOUNT OF BANCA AND PALAMBANG, WITH THE TRADE THEREOF.

WHEN going to Lingin from Pooloo Taya, do not bring Taya to the weftward of fouth till paffed the latitude of the Ilchefter-fhoal, and you may ftand towards the Egolitee Iflands, within one mile and a-half, foundings fometimes hard, at other foft, with overfalls, from 14 fathoms on the weft fide to fix towards the ifland; but no danger that I have feen or heard of. To know the river's mouth, fteer right in for the high land to the eaftward of the peak, which will carry you in between two fmall iflands that lie about one mile and a-half from the fhore; and oppofite the river's mouth there are many fmall iflands in fhore. But by following thefe Directions you cannot mifs the river. To anchor, bring the extremes of Lingin, and the iflands to the fouthward of it, to bear from E. to S.S.W. half W.; Pooloo Taya S. by E. half E.; the Peak N.W. one-quarter N. in 10 fa-

D 2

thoms,

thoms, mud; and fend your boat in between the iflands. Here is a fale for opium, from 50 to 100 chefts; for which you will receive tin, pepper, gold, and rattans in return. The inhabitants are all pirates; it is therefore neceffary to be well armed, and conftantly on your guard.

The ifland of Banca, perhaps, contains the firft tin mines in the world; there are annually from 40 to 60,000 piculs fmelted and exported. It is the only export they poffefs. They have gold and filver on the ifland; but the Sultan will not fuffer the mines to be worked.

The Sultan and alfo the Dutch refident live at the oppofite fhore, at Palambang on the ifland of Sumatra. With the Dutch refident, perhaps, fomething may be done. In cafe he fhould decline trading, you muft endeavour to find out the agents of the princes of Banca, and thofe of the Caranga (or prime minifter), who have always carried on an illicit trade, in oppofition to the Palambangers and the Dutch, with whom the Sultan has contracted for 30,000 piculs of tin annually.

Some Dutch cruifers are ftationed here, under pretence of protecting the Sultan and enforcing his laws; but it is, in fact, a piece of Dutch policy, to prevent his trading with any other nation. You may have as much accefs to the Datoo, at Mintow, as you pleafe, by the obfervance of certain ceremonies, which the commanders of the Dutch cruifers expect from ftrangers, and which are well underftood.

The price of tin, in a great meafure, depends on the number of fhips who are in want of it; the price in 1789 was from 16 to 18 Spanifh dollars, and fcarcely to be had. The pecul is $133\frac{1}{3}$ pounds, generally weighed with a dotchin or wooden fteelyard. A cold chiffel is as neceffary to be ufed in the purchafe of tin, as Spanifh dollars are to pay for it. The Chinefe, who are the moft accomplifhed rafcals upon the earth, have taught the Malays to put iron

fhot

shot and stones into the middle of the slab, and then sell it as current merchandise. I have, myself, detected some of them at these tricks. Presents are more necessary here than in any part of the eastward, as it is the only way to get any thing done. The principal people on Banca are, Abange Lemon the chief, Abang Tavye, Abang Vanoos, Abang Myle, Hodge Alley, and Rajah Mahomed. At Palambang is the Coranga Japootra and his three sons, Kayagus, Abdulla, and Somille: his agents are, Aboo, Samodin Bazar, (alias Cheeks), Samoodin Catchill (alias Jarragon Lannen); these are the principal tin merchants.

It is not worth while carrying any trade to Banca, as nothing will secure you tin but Spanish dollars; and they are not fond of taking ducatoons.

Palambang sometimes furnishes a little indifferent pepper at 12 to 14 dollars per picul, and a few rattans from Jambee; these are not always to be had. They have some gold, but it is not an article of trade.

Yre Mass is a tolerable place for tin; it is at the north end of Banca, and you deal chiefly with the captain China man.

DIRECTIONS

FOR SAILING FROM BATTACARRAN, THROUGH THE STRAITS OF BANCA.

HAVING Monopen-hill E. by S. half S. in seven fathoms, soft ground, on the bank off Battacarran-point, you are then abreast of Frederick Endrick; shape your course to keep mid-channel, and avoid the shoals between Battacarran-point and the fourth point of

Sumatra,

Sumatra, as in many places they reach three leagues off fhore, and fhould not be approached nearer than fix or five fathoms, in which depth you will have fand and mud, and fometimes fhells.

The reef off Carrang Hodjee on the other fide is equally danger-ous, having deep water clofe to in many places, as 25, 20, 18, and 16 fathoms. When the peak of Monopen-hill bears N.E. the centre of Carrang Hodgee is in one with it; when the top of the hill bears N.E. three-quarters E. the weft end of Carrang Hodgee is on with it; and when the top of Monapen-hill is N.E. half N. the eaft end of the reef is on with it; 12, 10, or eight fathoms water is the beft water in this channel; and you can haul to the northward as circumftances may require.

Being paft the fouth wafh of Salt-river, which is the firft after paffing Battacarran-point, keep along the edge of the mud bank that lies off Palambang-river; this is the fecond after paffing Battacarran, in nine or eight fathoms, until you are abreaft the third or Falfe-river; then haul off and deepen to 11 or 12 fathoms: and when the ifland in Falfe-river is open in the entrance, and you fee the appear-ance of a paffage at each fide of it, you will, perhaps, get a caft on a lump of fand, with fix fathoms on it; but you muft not be alarmed as there is no lefs, nor will you get a fecond caft: you muft not in-creafe your foundings to more than 14 fathoms, as there is a reef off Carrang Bram to the eaftward of you, lying off Tanjong Cooney, whofe S.E. end when in one with Monopen-hill bears N.W. half N. and its bank reaches to the reef off Carrang Hodgee already mentioned.

Being paft the Falfe-river haul to the eaftward, and do not come nearer Salfee-river which is the fourth and laft you meet between Battacarran-point and the fourth point. Come no nearer the fhore than 10 fathoms, as the bank is as fteep to as a wall, and round the fourth point at two and a-half or three miles diftance, and come no nearer it than eight fathoms, mud; keep along the Sumatra fhore at

two

two and a-half to feven miles off fhore, in 10 to 14 fathoms, foft, until you are clear of the third point, which you may round within one mile and a-half, or in 11 or 10 fathoms; and being abreaft of it, fteer over E. or E. by S. for the Great Pula Nanka, till you deepen your water to 15 or 20 fathoms; this you will do pretty quickly, and will have ftiff clay foundings, and fometimes red clay and fhells. Keep now down about mid-channel, to avoid a mud bank that lies to the fouthward from the third point about 10 miles and near four miles from the fhore; keeping fix miles off the Sumatra fhore, until you raife the fecond point plain, will carry you down in regular foundings from 16 to 18 fathoms; as you near the fecond point bor- row towards it, and round it at four miles diftance.

It is faid there is a fhoal of fand and coral about one-third channel over from the Banca fhore between the firft and fecond points. I have enquired of the Dutch cruifers who are ftationed here, but they know nothing of its exiftence. I have ftood acrofs, working up thefe ftraits from fide to fide, and never found it   I have had overfalls as I neared the Nankas, and foul ground under Parmaffang-hill; but as it can anfwer no good purpofe to keep the Banca fhore on board, I recommend fhips to keep on the Sumatra fide, and not exceed two- thirds channel over, or even one-half channel, and you may coaft it from the fecond point to the firft, from two to fix miles diftance from Sumatra, in 10, 12, 16, or 18 fathoms, foft mud and regular foundings.

As you near the firft point haul in for it, and being abreaft of it about two or three miles you will fee the little ifland called Lacapera, bearing S.S.E. or S.E. by S. You fhould, after rounding the firft point, keep in towards the Sumatra fhore at three or four miles diftance, four or four and a-half fathoms, mud, taking care to haul to the weftward if you get hard foundings; and to haul to the eaftward if you fhoal your water, and keep muddy ground from five to four and a-half fathoms off, to any water you think proper along the
Sumatra

Sumatra mud bank, always obferving to take your foundings from that fide. Having Lacepara E.N.E. haul off to the eaftward, and give Lacepara-point a good birth of eight or nine miles in five fathoms, foft ground. The beft water in the narroweft part the mid-channel is four and a-half fathoms at low water fpring tides.

Coming from the eaftward, and having paffed Lacepara-point and Lacepara, by hauling into the Straits at too great a diftance from the Sumatra fhore, you will fhoal fuddenly from fix and a-half fathoms foft, to four fathoms hard, with overfalls from three to five fathoms, then three fathoms again, Lacepara bearing S.E. half E. diftance feven or eight miles; haul immediately over for the Sumatra fhore, and deepen to fix, feven, and eight fathoms, foft mud.

Note. When in the overfalls, and hard ground, Mount Par-maffing was open to the eaftward of the firft point; and when we had feven fathoms foft, one and a-half or two miles from Sumatra had all the Mount fhut in over the firft point. I therefore conclude that due obfervance of the above remark, of keeping Parmaffang-hill fhut in with the firft point, will carry you clear of a danger that fhould be carefully avoided.

DIRECTIONS

FOR SAILING FROM LUCEPARA, AT THE SOUTH ENTRANCE OF THE STRAITS OF BANCA, TO TANJONG SALATAN, THE SOUTH POINT OF BORNEO.

HAVING rounded Lucepara, by the foregoing inftructions, and being clear of the fhoals in feven, eight, or nine fathoms foft ground, fteer S.E. by E. or E.S.E. till you deepen to 18 fathoms, and keeping

ing in latitude 4° 16' to 4° 22' S.; and between 18 and 24 fathoms, you will have even ground and foft foundings, until you come on the bank off Tanjong Salatan, you will then fhoal gradually, and have hard foundings. I make Tanjong Salatan to lie in latitude 4° 12' S.; and longitude by fun and moon 114° 36' 15" E. of Greenwich. Keep between 12 and 14 fathoms, and you will round the point; at about four leagues diftance you will have very even foundings, fometimes ooze, fand, and fhells, with mixtures of gravel and coarfe fand.

DIRECTIONS

FOR SAILING FROM TANJONG SALATAN TO PASSIER, ON THE EAST COAST OF BORNEO; WITH SOME ACCOUNT OF THE STRAITS OF MACCASSOR.

FROM Tanjong Salatan fteer eaft, and pafs to the northward of Monaveffa; this ifland bears from Tanjong Salatan E. by S. diftance 56 miles, and lies in latitude 4° 22' S.

Coming on the bank off Tanjong Salatan, and in 12 fathoms, you will fee the high land over the point called Goonong Ratoos, or the Hundred Mountains, bearing N.E. by E. diftance 15 or 18 leagues, making like two large round iflands; but as you near it, and within the diftance of 12 leagues, it appears like a large faddle ifland; fhould it be night, or thick weather, keep between 12 and 15 fathoms, until you fee the fouth end of Pooloo Lout, which bears from Monaveffa N.E. one-quarter N. diftance 12 miles, and lies in latitude 4° 11' S. But before you run this length you will fee another fmall ifland, called Dwalder, which bears from Monaviffa E.N.E.

half

half E. Keep mid-channel in this track, having regard to the currents or tides, that set strong in and out of the Straits of Lout, that you are not set on the S.E. island off Pooloo Lout, nor on the bank off Dwalder. You may borrow towards the island off Pooloo Lout should the wind be scant, with the greatest safety, and keep between 13 and 16 fathoms, mixture of coral, rotten stones and shells, and sometimes sand. When the south point of the S.E island off Pooloo Lout bears N.N.E. half E. you first begin to soften your soundings, first with shingly sand like steel filings, then sand and mud; and as you stretch to the eastward you will have soft mud and regular soundings.

Being in 16 or 18 fathoms, and five leagues to the eastward of Pooloo Lout, steer N. till you see four small islands, called The Ampats, which at first rising will bear about N. and may be seen from a ship's deck about four leagues.

You have now to chuse whether you will go to the eastward or the westward of the Ampats; if to the eastward do not come nearer them than 22 fathoms; and if to the westward, not nearer than 19 fathoms, as they lie in the stream of 20 or 21 fathoms; nor to Poo loo Lout nearer than nine or 10 fathoms, soft ground.

Being past the Ampats, keep six leagues off shore, to avoid the shoal and sand banks in the deep bay you will have on your larboard bow and beam, until as far to the northward as 3° $0'$ S.; and then haul in for the land till you see the entrance of a large river to the westward of you, keeping in from 12 to 16 fathoms, soft ground.

As soon as you see the entrance of the large river fairly open, haul up for the northernmost point of it, giving it a birth of two or three leagues; but do not on any account increase your distance to more than six leagues, on account of a dry sand bank and reef of rocks that lie in latitude 2° $27'$ S.; and bears from the north point of the large river N. 74° E. and S. 74° W. This is a dangerous shoal, and your soundings at night are the only sure guides you can go by. From 12 to 16 fathoms is the best track; and should you have overfalls haul

directly

directly to the weftward. In approaching the banks you will have overfalls, from 17 to 19, 20, 25, 30, 15 and 13 fathoms, or lefs; at other times you may have deep water, about 15 or 18 fathoms; and next caft fcarcely three fathoms, coral and fhells.

Being paft this bank keep in fhore from 12 to 14 fathoms, till Tanjong Lapar bears W. to avoid a bank of coral and rocks that bears E.S.E. from the point, diftance four leagues, and two dry fand banks that lie E. from the point, diftance three leagues. The latitude of this point, Tanjong Lapar, is 2° 8' S.; and the latitude of the bank of coral rocks 2° 10 S.

Having Tanjong Lapar W. or W. by S. diftance four, five, or fix leagues, in 12, 14, or 16 fathoms, fteer N. by E. not coming under 10 fathoms until you are in latitude 1° 45' S.; then fteer in W. fhoaling gradually to five fathoms, mud. You will now fee the entrance of a large river, called, by the Malays, Paffier Lama (or Old Paffier), bearing W.N.W.; but fteering along fhore S.W. or S.W. by W. will bring you fair into Paffier-roads, in five or four and a-half fathoms at low water. As you near Paffier-river you muft keep a very good look out for the entrance, as it is not eafily difcerned. Having feen it, come to in four and a-half or four fathoms at low water; having the river's entrance W. by S., the extremes of the land to the northward N. half E.; the entrance of Paffier Lama N.W. by W.; the fouthern extreme, (which is Tanjong Lapar Falfe) S.W.; diftance off the neareft fhore four leagues.

The only certain method for a ftranger to find Paffier-river, is to run into the latitude of the roads, and anchor in the depth of water prefcribed. I obferved feveral times here, and invariably found the latitude 1° 49' S.; the entrance of the river bearing S. 75° W.; the extreme of the land from Tanjong Lapar Falfe, S. 22° W. to N. nine E.; the entrance of Paffier Lama N. 51° W. diftance off fhore four leagues at low water: the entrance of Paffier Lama is in latitude 1° 43' S. and has fix fathoms clofe to the N. fhore, fix or feven miles within the entrance.

DIRECTIONS

DIRECTIONS

FOR GOING INTO, AND UP PASSIER RIVER.

Being in latitude 1° 49' S. and Lapar Falfe bearing S.S.W. and the northern extreme N. half E. anchor in four and a-half or four fathoms, mud. Four leagues off fhore you may fee from the maft head fome fifhermen's huts on the north fide of the river. Let your boat leave the fhip at low water and flack tide; fteer in W. or W. by S. till fhe is over the flat at the entrance of the river; and then run in directly for the fifhermen's houfes. The fifhermen will, in all probability, endeavour to prevent your boat going up, till they try whether they cannot purchafe for themfelves or not. Your boat is not to pay any attention to them, but proceed for the river; to go up which obferve the following Directions:

Paffier-river contains 16 reaches, and has five other rivers join it. The firft river you leave on your right hand; the next three on your left; and having paffed the fifth, which you leave on the right hand, you are within half a mile of Paffier, which confifts of about 300 houfes, moft of which are wretched beyond defcription; and here the king and court refide.

It flows in Paffier-roads on full and change days at five hours; and the tides rife and fall nine feet perpendicular: the flood runs to the northward, and the ebb to the fouthward.

PASSIER, WITH THE TRADE, AND HOW TO CHUSE THE ARTICLES OF EXPORT.

Confidering the fituation of this place, the air is tolerable, being refrefhed every morning by cooling breezes from the fea, otherwife

the

the heat would be infupportable. Thefe parts, neverthelefs, are very unhealthy, as they lie in a flat for many miles, are encircled by woods, and are annually overflowed. When the waters retire, a muddy flime is left on the furface of the earth, which the fun fhining upon with perpendicular rays, occafions thick fogs, which in the even- ing turn to rain, with cold chilling winds, off the land, fo that the air at this time is very unwholefome. Another circumftance that contributes to this, is the great number of frogs, and other ver- min, left on the mud, which being deftroyed by the heat of the fun, produce an intolerable ftench.

In April the dry feafon begins, and continues until September, during which time the wind is eafterly between the fouth coafts of Borneo and the ifland of Java; but from September to April the winds are wefterly, attended by violent ftorms of thunder, lightning, and rain; thefe ftorms are fo continual, efpecially on the fouth coaft, and at Banjar Maffeen, that it is thought very extraordinary to have two hours fair weather in the courfe of the twenty-four.

Exclufive of rice, which is very plentiful, the produce of this coun- try is benzoin (or frankincenfe), mufk, aloes, pepper, caffia, and long nutmegs; alfo various kinds of fruits, excellent maftic, and other gums, particularly dragons blood, which is finer here than any other part of the world; honey, gold-duft, and camphor.

The exchange for the produce of this place is fimilar to the other parts of the Malay coaft, viz. opium, guns, mufquets, piftols, gun- powder, lead in pigs and fheets, iron and fteel in narrow bars, hangers, knives, fciffars, and other cutlery, cloths, chints, carpets, fpectacles, looking-glaffes, fpy-glaffes, clock-work, &c.

It may not be improper to obferve that the people of this place are arrant cheats; they have cut off feveral fhips by treachery, and are ever ready to take advantage of an unguarded moment. In their barter they are unjuft, particularly in weights and meafures; they make compo- fitions to imitate fome of the moft valuable articles, particularly bars of gold; which is fo artfully done that unlefs they are entirely cut

through

through the deception cannot be difcovered: and he thinks himfeif the moft ingenious who commits the greateft fraud.

This being the cafe, it becomes neceffary that the captain of the veffel, who is generally the fuper-cargo on thefe occafions, fhould be extremely cautious in examining the articles of export, which he either purchafes or receives in return for his cargo.

The following rules will materially affift in preventing thofe frauds which at Paffier, and generally on the coafts of Malay and Borneo, are very commonly practifed.

Benzoin, or benjamin, is the concrete refinous juice of a tree growing in the Eaft Indies and in North America. Benzoin is in drops and lumps; the former is feldom or never met with; the latter is compofed of fmall grains, of a colour inclining to white or yellow, with a purple caft on the furface; it is very inflammable, and dif-fufes a fragrant fmell while burning. It is gathered in the following manner: when the benzoin trees are fix years old, the natives of the iflands of Borneo, Sumatra, and Java, cut them in feveral places under the large branches, in an oblique direction, quite into the wood: the benzoin which flows from thefe wounds is white and foft at firft, but by degrees becomes harder and acquires a darker colour on the furface by being expofed to the air.

In order to be of a good quality, this gum fhould be extremely clean, of an agreeable fcent, very refinous, and intermixed with many white tears; that which is very brown, black, and without fmell, is to be rejected: the mafs fhould be broken quite through, to fee that it poffeffes the neceffary qualities.

Dragon's blood is a rofin, obtained from a kind of palm-tree; it is either in oval drops wrapped up in flax leaves, or in larger and gene-rally more impure maffes, compofed of fmaller tears.—It is externally and internally of a deep dufky red colour; and when powdered it fhould become of a bright crimfon; but if it be black it is worth

very

very little. It eafily melts over the fire, and is inflammable, diffufing a fingular, and not a difagreeable fmell.—When broken, and held up againft a ftrong light, it is fomewhat tranfparent.—It has little or no fmell or tafte; what it has of the latter is refinous and aftringent.— The dragon's blood in drops is much preferable to that in cakes, which latter is lefs compact, refinous, and pure than the former.— Several artificial compofitions coloured with true dragon's blood or other materials, have been put off inftead of this article. Some of thefe diffolve like gums in water, and others crackle in the fire, without proving inflammable; whereas the genuine dragon's bloody readily melts and catches flame, and is fcarcely acted on by watery liquors. It is moft prudent to purchafe only the drops, rejecting the impure maffes.

Mufk is the excrementitious blood of a quadruped about the fize of a goat, which is either naturally fecreted and afterwards collected by human induftry, or contained in the fmall bag of the animal when killed at a proper feafon. The fort moft efteemed is that from Tonquin, in China; an inferior fort is brought from Agra and Bengal; and a ftill worfe from Ruffia.

This drug is a dry, light, friable fubftance, of a dark colour, with a purple tinge; its tafte is fomewhat bitter, and its fmell too ftrong to be agreeable in any quantity.—We meet with it in grains, which feel unctuous, fmooth, and foft, and are eafily crumbled between the fingers; thefe grains are in a bladder or fkin, about the fize of a pigeon's egg, or larger; each bladder containing from two or three drachms to an ounce in weight. The genuine bags of mufk are fo fcented as to offend the head when applied clofe to it. The cavity containing the mufk is generally about three-quarters of an inch long and half an inch wide. The whole external fubftance is membranous rather than flefhy, and its aperture is guarded by a fphincter mufcle: the inner membrane, immediately inclofing the mufk, is full of blood-veffels all over; and towards the orifice of the bag feveral

veral glands are diſtinguiſhable in it, ſerving for the ſecretion of this perfume.

Muſk ſhould be choſen of a very ſtrong ſcent, in the dry and found natural bags of the animal, not in the factitious ones, made of ſkins ſewed together, which may be diſtinguiſhed by the cloſeneſs and length of the hair on the latter kind of bags; theſe factitious ones having more and longer hair than the genuine, and that generally of a paler colour.

A ſmall quantity of muſk, macerated for a few days in rectified ſpirit of wine, imparts a deep colour, and a ſtrong impregnation to the ſpirit. This tincture, of itſelf, diſcovers but little ſmell, but on dilution it manifeſts the full fragrance of the muſk; a drop or two communicating to a quart of wine or watery liquors a rich muſky ſcent. The quantity of liquor which may thus be flavoured by a certain known proportion of muſk, appears to be the beſt criterion of the genuineneſs and goodneſs of this commodity.

Few drugs are more liable to ſophiſtication than muſk; it is adulterated on the ſpot with the animal's blood, which acquires ſo ſtrong a ſcent of it, after drying among it, that it may paſs alone on the unſuſpicious for real muſk. This fraud may be diſcovered by the largeneſs of the lumps or clots, as the blood dries to a harder and firmer ſubſtance than the genuine muſk; it is ſometimes mixed with a dark coloured friable earth, this appears to the touch of a more crumbly texture, and harder as well as heavier than the genuine muſk; but this deception is beſt diſcovered by burning a ſmall quantity; in which caſe, muſk adulterated in this manner, leaves a large and heavy remainder. The genuine, or even that mixed with blood, either evaporates or leaves only a few white aſhes. When muſk begins to decay, it is a practice in the Eaſt Indies to put it into a bag full of needle-holes, and hang it in a neceſſary-houſe but low enough to touch the filth: others keep it wrapped up in linen, well moiſtened with rank urine.

Pepper

Pepper (black) is the fmall, round, aromatic fruit of a trailing plant, which flourifhes on the coaft of Malabar, and in the iflands of Java, Sumatra, and Ceylon. It is not fown, but planted, and great care is required in the choice of the fhoots. It produces no fruit till the end of three years; and then bears fo plentifully the three or four fucceeding years, as frequently to produce two crops in a year; the bark then begins to fhrink, and the fhrub declines faft, fo that in twelve years time it ceafes to bear.

Black-pepper is to be chofen of a pungent fmell, extremely acrid and hot to the tafte, in large grains, firm, found, and with few wrinkles; but it will always have fome, which are occafioned by its being dried in the fun. Care fhould always be taken that the largeft grains have not been picked out, as is fometimes done.

White-pepper is diftinguifhed into common and genuine; the latter is very feldom met with, and approaches nearly to the properties of the black-pepper, the nearer the better. The common white-pepper is weaker and worfe in all its qualities than the black, being nothing more than that fort difcerpticated by maceration in water, as bits of the dark-coloured fkin have fometimes been obferved upon the grains, when in Europe. In choofing it regard fhould be had to the ftrength of its qualities, its foundnefs and firmnefs, and particular care fhould be taken that it has not been dyed white.

Long-pepper is the fruit of an Eaft Indian plant, of the fame kind with that which produces the black-pepper; which fruit is gathered unripe, and dried: it is of a round form, about an inch and a half in length, nearly the fize of a large goofe-quill, have numerous minute grains difpofed round it in a kind of fpiral direction. The whole fruit is of a brownifh grey colour, of a texture not very firm, and it eafily fhatters to pieces by a blow; it is light, and when frefh broken has a difagrecable pungent fmell.

Long-pepper is to be chofen in large full pieces, frefh, not broken, dufty, not worm-eaten; and fuch as after tafting, leaves a very lafting

F

heat

heat in the mouth : when too long kept it is worthlefs, as it becomes rotten and dufty.

Maftich.—A concrete refin, obtained from the lentick-tree, by tranfverfe incifious made in the bark about the beginning of Auguft ; it is in fmall yellowifh white tranfparent drops of a refinous and rather aftringent tafte, with a light agreeable fmell, efpecially when rubbed or heated ; in chewing it firft crumbles, foon after fticks together, and becomes foft and white like wax. It is to be chofen clear, of a pale yellow colour, well fcented, and brittle : fuch as inclines to black, green, or is dirty, muft be rejected : when free from impurities it totally diffolves in rectified fpirit.

Camphor, or camphire, a folid, unctuous, concrete, that is procured by boiling the branches and other parts of the tree which produces it. It has a fragrant fmell, and a fomewhat bitter, aromatic, pungent tafte; accompanied with an impreffion of coolnefs. A fpecies of camphor is likewife found, naturally concreted into little grains, in the medullary part of the camphor-tree. Specimens of this (in Europe) are only found in the cabinets of the curious. The Indians diftinguifh two kinds of camphor, a finer and a coarfer; the latter is the Japanefe kind, before mentioned, procured by boiling: the former, produced in Borneo and Sumatra, is fo highly valued by the natives, that it is very rarely to be met with in Europe. The Japanefe value this fort fo much, that for one ounce of it they will give five or fix of what they make: and the Chinefe value it fo highly as to give 35 lb. for 16 ounces.

The tree, whence the Japanefe procure their camphor, is a fpecies of bay-tree, which grows to a large fize. They cut the root and moft tender fhoots into fmall pieces, which they put into large iron or copper kettles, placed over a moderate fire; to thefe kettles they adapt earthen heads of a conical fhape with a rifing hollow neck, in which the camphor is received as it rifes : when the procefs is over, they knead this matter with their hands into cakes, which are what

we

we call rough camphor; thefe cakes incline to a brown or grey colour, and are compofed of fmall grains, mixed with fome impure matter; they are not very heavy nor very compact, but eafily crumble to pieces; if thefe cakes be tolerably pure, they will, when fet on fire, burn away and leave but few afhes, the fewer the better. The beft package is an iron-bound cafk, lined with tutanag, to prevent evaporation; into this the camphor fhould be clofely preffed. This crude camphor the Dutch purify by pulverifation and farther fublimation, when it receives the appellation of refined camphor: it is in hollow, round, thin cakes, of the fame form with the head of the veffel they were fublimed in: thefe cakes are compofed of a delicate pure refin, perfectly clear and white, very bright and pellucid, moderately compact in texture, fomewhat fat to the touch, foftening and growing tough under the teeth. This refined camphor has a fmell and tafte of the fame kind with the rough, but more acrid; a fmall piece of it will inflame the whole mouth, on chewing, and imprefs a fenfe of coldnefs at the fame time: when pure it is more volatile than any other of the vegetable refins; infomuch that it will fly off wholly, by degrees, if expofed to the air: when fet on fire it burns quite away, without leaving any refiduum. The duties and charges render it unprofitable to bring home any refined camphor; the unrefined being eafily purified.

The Aloes of this place are tolerably good, being the infpiffated juice prepared from the flefhy-leaved plant of the fame name: there are, however, three forts, which we fhall defcribe, and thereby enable the captain or fupercargo to diftinguifh between good and bad.

Aloe Socotrina, brought from the ifland of Socotora, in the Indian Ocean, wrapt in fkins, is of a bright furface, in fome degree tranfparent, of a yellowifh red colour, with a purple caft when in the lump, and of a golden colour when reduced to powder: it is hard and friable in winter, fomewhat pliable in fummer, and foftens between the fingers: its bitter tafte is accompanied with an aromatic flavour,

F 2

but

but not fufficient to prevent its being difagreeable; this fmell is not very unpleafant, and is fomething like myrrh. To try its purity, boil four ounces in a quart of water, and it will diffolve into a dark coloured liquor: if adulterated the impurities will remain undiffolved. If in the package of this drug there fhould be any mixture of rubbifh, it will be more advantageous to cleanfe it in India, the duty being paid by weight, and purity much advancing the price. The packages fhould not weigh more than 150 or 200 pounds, if not more than 100 it will be better. The purchafer fhould calculate his lofs on the fkins, &c. at double the real difadvantage : and the infide of the package fhould be greafed, to prevent the aloes from fticking.

Aloe Hepatria is produced in other parts as well as in the eaft. The beft is ufually imported from Barbadoes, in ground fhells; an inferior kind in kits, and a ftill worfe in cafks; this kind is generally darker coloured and lefs clear than the Socotrine, and generally more compact and dry, though fometimes quite foft and clammy, particularly the cafk fort, its tafte is intenfely bitter and naufeous, without the aromatic flavour of the Socotrine, and its fmell is much ftronger, and more difagreeable. If any of this fort be brought from India, care fhould be taken that it be not liquid; a circumftance that leffens its value in England confiderably.

Aloe Caballina, Cabaline or Horfe Aloes, is eafily diftinguifhed from both the preceding, by its ftrong rank fmell; in other refpects it nearly agrees with the hepatic, and is not unfrequently fold in its place; it is fometimes prepared fo pure and bright, as to render it difficult for the eye to diftinguifh it from the Socotrine; but it is quickly difcovered by the ranknefs of the fmell: fhould this alfo be diffipated by art, the aromatic flavour of the finer aloes is a fufficient criterion. But it will not be profitable to bring either caballine or hepatic aloes from India.

Long Nutmeg and Caffia.—The long nutmeg, obtained in Borneo, is the falfe nutmeg; of which fome account is given under the arti-

cle

cle nutmeg, when treating of fpices in general. Of the caffia it is to
be obferved, that it much refembles cinnamon in appearance, fmell,
and tafte. It is brought to us in a kind of tube, into which it naturally rolls itfelf up in drying; thefe are fometimes of the thicknefs of
the ordinary tubes of cinnamon, and of the fame length; but ufually
they are fhorter and thicker, and the bark itfelf alfo thicker and
coarfer; it is of a tolerably fmooth furface and brownifh colour, with
fome of red, but much lefs fo than cinnamon; it is of a lefs fibrous
texture and more brittle, of an aromatic fmell and tafte, truly of the
cinnamon kind, but the fmell weaker, and the tafte much lefs acrid
and biting; it is diftinguifhed from cinnamon by this want of pungency, and yet more by its being of a mucilaginous or gelatinous
quality when taken into the mouth and held there fome time: there
is fome that inclines to a yellow, and fome to a brown colour, but
thefe varieties depend on accidents that do not at all affect its value.
It is to be chofen in thin pieces, of an agreeable bitter and aromatic
tafte; and the beft is that which approaches neareft to cinnamon
flavour.

This bark, when good and frefh, diffolves in the mouth, on chewing, into a kind of flime; powdered and boiled in water it renders a
confiderable quantity of the fluid fo thick and glutinous as to become
of the confiftence of a jelly on cooling.

The tree which produces the caffia-lignea is a different fpecies of
the fame genus with the cinnamon-tree; it is feparated from the
branches of this tree in the fame manner as cinnamon: they take
off the two barks together in autumn or fpring, and feparating the
rough outer one, which is of no value, they lay the inner bark to
dry, which rolls up, and becomes what we call caffia-lignea.

DIRECTIONS

FOR SAILING FROM PASSIER TO BANJAR MASSEEN.

BEING in Paffier-roads, and bound to the fouthward, Laper Falfe bearing S.S.W. or S. by W.; the northernmoft extreme of the land N. half E. or N,; and the extreme of Paffier-river W. S.W. half W. the ebb tide fetting to the fouthward, confequently at high water will be the beft time to weigh, as you will carry a whole tide in your favour. The courfe out of Paffier-river is E. by S. or E.S.E. nine or 10 miles; you will deepen your water regularly to 15 fathoms, from which depth fteer S.E. until you are in 18 or 20 fathoms, and then a S. by E. courfe will carry you clear of Lapar Falfe in 14 or 16 fathoms.

When Tanjong Lapar Falfe bears W. fteer S. having regard to the tides and currents, which are very uncertain in this track, and almoft continually changing; a due attention to your lead is almoft the only unerring guide. Continue a fouth courfe, and you will fhoal towards Lapar-point to 15 and 13 fathoms, mud and fand; but on no account come under 12 fathoms, in which depth you will be about five leagues diftance from the point.

The reafon for keeping fo great a diftance, is to avoid two fand-banks that lie E. of Tanjong Lapar, and a bank of coral rock on which the Jane floop, Capt. H. Glafs, was a-ground, and had only five feet water on the S. fide of it.—Tanjong Lapar then bore W. N.W. diftance four leagues; and their latitude (obferved when a-ground) was 2° 11′ S.; under the gangway were five fathoms, under

the

the stern were 10 fathoms. This proves the above caution necessary, as the bank is steep to.

Lapar-point is easily known by a large tuft of trees that are divided nearly in the center, and appear like a large open gateway.

The distance from Lapar False to Tanjong Lapar is about 10 leagues, and you will have a mixture of mud, ooze, sand, shells, and coral.

When Tanjong Lapar bears N.N.W. steer S.S.W. half W. keeping from three to five leagues off shore in soft ground from 12 to 16 fathoms, until you are beginning to rise the north-point of the large river, which at first making will appear to be the S.E. extreme of the land, borrow on this point to two or three leagues, but do not increase your distance from it to more than five or six leagues until it bears W.; by which means you will avoid the banks and overfalls, already mentioned, that bear N. 74° E. and S. 74° W. from the north-point of that river, and in latitude 2° 27' S.; distance from the point of the river to the bank about eight leagues.

Having the river fairly open, and the point bearing W. steer S. until the N.E. end of Pooloo Lout bears S. by W. or S.S.W. keeping in soft ground from 16 to 18 fathoms, and when the N.E. point of Pooloo Lout bears W. you will see the Ampats (or Four Islands) in the offing, bearing S. by W. or S. by W. half W.; distance six leagues. If you go to the eastward of those islands, come no nearer them than 22 fathoms; and if you go to the westward, come no nearer than 19 fathoms, as they lie in the stream of 20 and 21 fathoms, and are bold to on all sides.

The mid-channel, between the Ampats and Pooloo Lout, is the best track with a leading wind, and in it you will have 16 to 14 fathoms, mud, ooze, and fine sand.

When the Ampats bear E.N.E. and you are in 16 fathoms, steer S.W. three-quarters S. until a small rocky island, which is the eastern-

most

moft off the fouth end of Pooloo Lout, bears W.; then haul gradually to the weftward, and round the Rocky Ifland at two or three miles diftance between 20 and 16 fathoms. The Rocky Ifland and the Dwalder bear N. 44° E. and S. 44° W. of each other. The diftance from the Ampats to Rocky Ifland is 12 leagues; the foutherumoft of the Ampats lies in latitude 3° 41′ S.; and the northernmoft in 3° 38′ S. and longitude 116° 27′ 15″ E. of Greenwich. Rocky Ifland is in 4° 7′ S.; bearing from Dwalder, as above, diftance 12 miles. Dwalder is in latitude 4° 16′ S.

Having rounded Rocky Ifland, fteer W. and you will pafs the S.E. ifland off Pooloo Lout, and the fouth end of Pooloo Lout at the diftance Rocky Ifland was from you when it bore N. as they all bear E. and W. of each other. The diftance from Rocky Ifland to the S.E. ifland is four miles; and from the S.E. ifland to the S. end of Pooloo Lout the diftance is 13 miles.

There is a large high ifland which you will fee to the W.S.W. called in our charts Monaveffa; and by the Dutch, Pooloo Lout Catchell: it bears from Rocky Ifland W. by S. one-quarter S. diftance 18 miles: it bears from the S.E. ifland off Pooloo Lout S.W. one-quarter W. diftance 16 miles; and from the fouth end of Lout S.W. one-quarter S. diftance 12 miles. Should you fhoal or get hard foundings, borrow on the ifland off Pooloo Lout to two miles diftance, as the north is the beft fide of the channel. Between Dwalder and Pooloo Lout the foundings are 12, 14, to 16 fathoms, mixtures of fand and mud, fhells, gravel-ftones, and rotten ftones; there is one fmall fpot of fhining black fand, like ink-fand or fteel-filings.

Should you be obliged to turn through this place, be careful not to bring the ifland of Dwalder to the weftward of W.S.W. as there is a bank of coral runs off the eaft point of that ifland, and reaches nearly to the Brothers.

Continue

Continue fteering weft, having regard to the currents, and keep between 12 and 17 fathoms mud and fand, and you will round Tonjong Salatan in 12 fathoms. As you near Salatan your foundings will be hard fand and gravel, with black fpecks like beaten pepper.

If bound to Banjar Maffeen, keep the point of Salatan on board, diftance three leagues, from nine to feven fathoms, till Tonjong Salatan bears N. half W. it will be then in one with the centre of Pooloo Dattoo. Endeavour now to keep in 12 fathoms, to avoid the overfalls off Pooloo Dattoo, till that ifland bears N.E. then fteer N. or N. half E. and keep the eaftern fhore on board in eight, feven, or fix fathoms, till you fee the entrance of Banjar river; then fteer fo as to bring the eaft point of the river N. three-quarters E. keep it on thefe bearings till you rife the weft point of the river, and come to at the foot of the bar in fix fathoms foft mud.

Care muft be taken that you do not miftake the eaft for the weft point of the river, as the eaft point makes like a low ifland, and you will run fix or feven miles before you rife the low land that joins it to the other part of the coaft; you will nearly, at the fame time, fee the weft point of the river.

Be careful to keep foft foundings in all this track, by hawling to the eaftward or weftward; for where there are hard foundings there are coral rocks, fome of which are not many feet under water. The above track of eight and fix fathoms, and a conftant attention to the lead, is the beft guide.

The flood here fcarcely makes any current, it only makes a flack water, but the ebb runs ftrong, occafioned by the frefhes from the river.

Tombanjou, or Tômbornio, is in latitude 3° 45' S. To anchor in the roads keep in feven fathoms mud, till the flag-ftaff bears E. half S.; run in for the fort, and come to in four and a-half or four and a quarter fathoms; diftance off the river's mouth two and a-half

G

or two miles. Here your boats may get water almoſt at the fort gates, and make a trip with eaſe every 24 hours. There is plenty of fowls and ducks to be had here, and fiſh, both freſh and ſalt, equal to any in India.

In watering in this river, or for boats going in or out, attention ſhould be paid to the tides; as there is a ſhallow bar to croſs over which a boat cannot float though light, or empty, until after firſt quarter flood, nor after laſt quarter ebb: and ſhould it be neceſſary to endeavour to drag the boat over the bar, by getting out, care ſhould be taken that the people have ſhoes on, and not barefooted, as there is a poiſonous fiſh or prickle (the inſect is not known) which wounding the people in the feet, brings on an immediate ſwelling in the leg, with violent inflammation; ſhortly cauſing, from the violent inflammation and pain, delirium and death, no antidote being hitherto known for its cure, even by the natives; who will not go into the water, upon the bar, for any conſideration.

DIRECTIONS

FOR SAILING FROM BANJAR MASSEEN TO BATAVIA.

In latitude 4° 0′ S. there is a bank of hard ſand; when on it, in three and a-half fathoms the high ſaddle on Tanjong Salatan will bear N.E. one-fourth E.; diſtance about 15 leagues.

To avoid this bank, do not reduce your latitude under 4° 10′ S. till you riſe the low land of Tanjong Salatan from the deck, then keep the eaſtern ſhore on board, as before directed, in eight or ſix fathoms mud; and by this means you will go clear of the banks and over-

falls

falls on the weſt ſide of the channel, where there are many, and their ſituation not known.

Leaving Tombanjou, ſteer S. by W. or S. half W. between 16 and ſix fathoms, until you near Pooloo Dattoo; do not come nearer this iſland than nine fathoms; and being in latitude 4° 10′ S. ſhape your courſe for Carramon Java, the latitude of which is 5° 54′ S. longitude 109° 33′ 30″ E. of Greenwich, and bears from Tanjong Salatan S.W. by W. half W. diſtance 103 leagues.

The reaſon of running to the ſouthward, ſo far as 4° 10′ S. is to avoid a bank of dry ſand, on which Capt. Lindſay had nearly run aground, in latitude 4° S.; he had from 16 to three and a-half fathoms on the edge of the bank, and could juſt ſee the iſland of Borneo from the deck, bearing N.E. one-fourth N. diſtance 14 or 15 leagues.

From Carrimon Java ſhape a courſe for Boomkin's Iſland or Pooloo Racket, which bears from Carrimon Java W. half S. ſo as to go without the reef of rocks that lie without that iſland two and a-half or three leagues, many of which are above water. The latitude of this reef is 5° 57′ S. and when in one with Pooloo Racket, bore S. 30 W. you have 26 fathoms one and a-half or two miles off it, and you ſhould not come nearer. Pooloo Racket lies in latitude 6° 1′ S.

From Pooloo Racket ſteer W. or W. ſoutherly for the little iſland Edam, which will bear, when on with Bantam-hill, S.W. by W. Paſs this iſland at any convenient diſtance, not leſs than two cables length.

DIRECTIONS

DIRECTIONS

FOR SAILING THE NORTH-WEST COAST OF BORNEO, FROM PI-
RATES-POINT TO THE RIVER AND TOWN OF BORNEO.

FROM Pirates-point, which lies in latitude 7° N. to Batoomandee,
Wafhed-rock point, are feveral bays, where fhips working up and
down the coaft may anchor fafely, and get water from the fhore.
In the chart is one namelefs point, almoft half way between the two
points already mentioned: it is very well reprefented, with a bay to
its fouthward; many fharp pointed black rocks peep above water off
this point; but they may be approached within a quarter of a mile;
and there is good landing to leeward if the monfoon allow; with
large plains and plenty of deer. Juft to the fouthward of Batoomandee is a commodious bay, at the mouth of Pandaffan-river,
which has a good bar: farther on is the bar of the great river of
Tampaffock, on which at times the furf breaks very high: next is
Abia-river, the bar of which is fmooth, the ifland of Ufookan lying
before it; and will admit a veffel of 14 foot water in the fprings: the
paffage is to the northward of Ufookan; the ifland proving at low
water a peninfula; leaving, confequently, no paffage between it and
the main. Between this ifland and Ambong harbour a bay opens,
where is good riding in the north-eaft monfoon.

Ambong harbour is large and commodious, having good depth of
water, with a button-like ifland, well laid down at the entrance of
it: keep that ifland on the right hand and you will come into a fine
harbour on the fouth fide clofe to fome falt houfes. From this harbour, proceeding fouthwards, you pafs the mouths of the two rivers
Salaman

Salaman and Tawarran, and approach Dallid-point. From this Kaitan-point bears S.W. by W. five miles, and Mancabong river runs between Kaitan-point, which is bold and bluff. When it bears eaftward of fouth, and not before, coming from the northward, you will open four iflands, the firft pretty high, called Pulo Pangir, keeping either clofe to it, or in mid-channel between it and the land next to the fouthward of it, which is the proper Pooloo Gaya.

Pooloo Gaya is an ifland fix or eight miles round, and being very near the main land, appears from the fea to be part of it. The channel which feparates it from the main is faid to have deep water; but that which Capt. Forreft paffed, in a boat, was full of rocks. It is impoffible to mifs the paffage into the above bay if the fhip be kept to the fouthward of Pooloo Pangir, between it and Pooloo Gaya. The next ifland to the northward of it is Pooloo Udar Smaller; the next to it Little Udar, ftill fmaller; the fourth and fmalleft is named Pooloo Priu, thefe three are almoft joined to the fourth and fouthernmoft by reefs of rocks, with an intricate channel between Pooloo Pangir and the next to the northward of it. N.E. of Pooloo Pangir runs a reef, on which a China junk was loft many years ago; her rudder funk in three fathoms water, upon coral rocks. In the N.E. part of this bay is faid to be a good harbour, and with a fmooth bar, as difcharging itfelf into it a river called Labatuan. To the fouthward of Labatuan is Inanan, which has alfo a fmooth bar, but it is very fhallow. Patatan lies to the fouthward of Pooloo Gaya, and entirely out of the bay; its bar is fmooth, but likewife fhallow. Three or four miles up the river Patatan ftands the town, the houfes about a hundred, fronting the water. Above the town are many pepper gardens, belonging to Chinefe, in a delightful country. Further down the coaft is Papal-river, the banks abounding with cocoa nut trees, in fo much, that during the floods many nuts are driven to fea. Steering on from Pooloo Gaya, S.W. by W. you approach Pooloo Tiga, and the point of Keemanees. Pooloo Tiga is fo

called.

called, as confifting of three iflands, pretty clofe, and of a gentle flope, each having an even outline, and a fine white beach: they bear from Keemanees-point N.E. by N. two leagues; this point makes a bay to the eaftward of it, fo deep that from feven fathoms water, muddy ground, the point bears N.W. by N. with fmooth water. During the S.W. monfoon, at the point of Keemanees appears a rock, like a houfe, with a bufh or two at the top; it terminates a very rocky point, at the diftance of a mile off, which is but two fathoms water: it muft not therefore be approached. A dry fand bears from it, W.N.W. about fix miles. Pooloo Tiga lies in latitude 5° 36'. From the rocky point of Keemanees, Pooloo Labuan bears S.W. about fix leagues. The proper paffage towards Borneo-river is without this ifland; within is fhoal water, two and a-half and three fathoms, fandy ground; there may, however, be deeper water. The ifland Labuan, beheld from the N.E. forms the femblance of two hummocs. A remarkable rock like a two-mafted veffel, lies W.S.W. of it, at fome diftance from the Borneo fhore: keep mid-channel, between Labuan and this rock, fteering S. In this channel you will fee low land right a-head, not unlike a clipped hedge. A little way in land to the right, is a peaked hill; when this hill bears W. or to the northward of W. haul in for the channel which goes by Pooloo Mara, a low ifland, bearing from Labuan S.S.W. 10 miles. To the northward of Pooloo Mara runs a fpit of fand three or four miles; be fure to keep within it, in foft ground; as on the fpittle fea often breaks very high; the channel is then clofe by Pooloo Mara, which muft be left on the right hand; hence many fifhing ftakes extend towards the river's mouth, having the appearance of fo many mafts.

Pooloo Chioming (Glafs Ifland) bears about W. by S. eight miles from Pooloo Mara, keep in foft ground; but here it would be proper to get a pilot, or at leaft to anchor and explore the channel. In paffing Pooloo Chioming you muft keep clofe to the ifland, leaving

4

it

it on the left, to avoid an artificial bank of coral rocks, piled, doubtlefs, for fome purpofe. It dams up the water a little, and is vifible at
low tide. From Pooloo Chioming it is about 10 miles to the town of
Borneo, in a S.W. by W. direction, round a fmall ifland. Being up
with this ifland, which you muft leave on the right, appears a branch
of the river, from the left or S.E.; keep to the right, and finifh the
mile to town, whither can come up junks of fix hundred tons.

DIRECTIONS

FOR SAILING INTO BATAVIA ROADS FROM THE NORTHWARD.

HAVING paffed the ifland of Edam, run in to bring Batavia
church fouth, then fteer S. half W. for the roads, and anchor in
fix fathoms, the church S. three-fourths E. diftance off the entrance
of the river two and a-half or three miles.

DIRECTIONS

FOR SAILING INTO BATAVIA ROADS FROM THE SOUTHWARD TO GO TO THE EASTWARD OF THE LABYRINTH OR THOUSAND ISLANDS.

BEING to the fouthward of Pooloo Baby, fteer E. by S. and
E.S.E. for Pooloo Lacky or Maneater's Ifland in foundings from 15

to

to 10 fathoms, and round Maneater's Ifland at two miles diftance, taking care not to come under five fathoms near that ifland ; then fteer E. half S. or E. by S. for Middleburg, coming no nearer that ifland than 10 fathoms, or nearer to the beacon on Oujong Java than eight fathoms. In this tract you have eight and nine fathoms, till you begin to haul up from the Middleburg (clofe to which is deep water) for Onrooft, then fteer for the wefternmoft crane on Onrooft; and being abreaft of it, fteer fo as to give Kyper's Ifland a birth of half a mile. Being clear of Kyper's Ifland, fteer S.E. by E. for Ryland's Beacon, or S.E. half E. for the fhips in the roads ; then come to in fix and a-half or fix fathoms, the church bearing S. half E.

SOME ACCOUNT OF BATAVIA AND SAMARANG.

Immediately on your arrival your firft vifit fhould be made to the Shabunder, to whom you fhould give a true invoice of your goods, (opium excepted) ; the whole of which fhould be reported to him, and offered for fale to the Company.

As this article is a monopoly of the Company's, care fhould be taken how you proceed. The Shabunder will tell you what day the Council meets, and if you think proper you may report your own cargo, and petition for the Council's permiffion to difpofe of it. The Council will perhaps take all your opium at 500 rix dollars per cheft, or may perhaps order you out of the roads; in this cafe re-courfe muft be had to fmuggling. While you are delivering your cargo you muft fign a certificate for the behaviour of your officers and people, at the forfeit of your life, that you, nor none of your crew, will fmuggle opium or fpices, directly or indirectly ; for which reafon you are to follow thefe rules : viz. you muft firft find out whether the Fifcal or Shabander have any opium of their own on their hands; if they have you can do no bufinefs, as they will

keep

keep too good a look out, and have armed cruifers near you; but if they have hone, you may fucceed by offering to deliver any quantity at any of the iflands for them. The beft and only fafe men (befides thefe) to deal with, are their underlings; viz. the Bofs at Onrooft; the Chinaman that farms the duties and lives at the Boom; the Whipper-in at Edam; and the Vizvis at Kyper's Ifland.

If the Company take your opium they will offer you paper in payment; but if you find they are much in want of it, you muft endeavour to make them pay you in cafh; which, if they do, they will offer rupees; but the offer of rupees is a certain indication of their being in want of it, and you muft infift on having Spanifh dollars; at all events you fhould not let them have opium without paying half cafh.

If you arrive early at Batavia, agree with the Cafhier, or the Shabundar, to difcount all the paper you may receive at the then difcount. The difcount of the year 1789 was from 18 to 25 per cent.; but by agreeing as above, I got all my paper difcounted at 18 per cent.; for as foon as the Macao fhip arrives, or any Englifh fhips, the difcount immediately rifes. Paper being only payable at the caftle of Batavia, it is of no fervice any where elfe.

If you fucceed in fmuggling, the real fpecie will be paid. You will fometimes get pepper and fome tin at Onrooft; the former is generally from 12 to 16, the latter from 18 to 22 dollars per pecul, to be paid in cafh. If fpices are to be had, pay one Spanifh dollar per catty; or if Company's paper is taken at par for them, pay one and three-quarters rix dollars per catty, but no more. This I conceive would be a good article at China; for, as the duties are taken of teas in Europe, I do not believe the India commanders can fpeculate much in that article, and they would be glad to get fpices by way of remittance. Good cinnamon will always fetch from 12 to 14 fhillings per pound, cloves fomething more, nutmegs fomething lefs, and mace from 20 to 25 fhillings in England; fo that the commanders knowing this, will always prefer fpice to any other article:

H

moreover, the Chinefe give a reafonable profit if the fpice is good, free from infects, and well bought. The junks of China which trade to the Philippines and Celebes bring great quantities, but not fufficient for the confumption of that large empire.

Cuftoms.

The cuftoms and duties are arbitrary, and for impofitions there is no redrefs. The Company's cuftoms are generally eight per cent. the Weighing-mafter one, the Hotel one-half, and the Cafhier one-half per cent. The Adminiftrator, or warehoufe-keeper, has one ducatoon for each package that is landed, whether great or fmall.

Exports.

Tin and pepper are fometimes to be had.
Arrack procurable at all times.
Sugar fometimes from the Company only.
Rice is to be got at moft times, but at a high price.

By applying to the people before mentioned you may be able to fmuggle fome Japan copper, cordage, canvas, and fpices; this muft be done privately, as it is contraband trade.

The relations of amity being again eftablifhed among the powers of Europe, and our conquefts in the eaftern archipelago about to be reftored to the Dutch, we fhall foon behold the whole trade of the Moluccas in the hands of that induftrious people. The French, perhaps, by fecret treaty, will obtain, on favourable terms, fome participation. Notwithftanding of this, and that we fhall be deprived of that lucrative branch of commerce, the country fhips of India who frequent the eaftern feas, will at all times be able, by indirect means, to obtain fome fpices, either from the natives or from the Dutch themfelves. It is therefore not improper to give fuch inftructions in the choice of fpices, as may prevent impofition in the purchafe of them.

The

The Nutmeg and Mace.—The male nutmeg is moſt eſteemed by us. The fruit of the male ſpecies is fleſhy, much like an apple, and has only one cell, which contains the nut. The fruit of the female, or ſecond ſort, differs, it being pear-ſhaped; the nut likewiſe is larger, and the outer covering opens only at bottom. This nut, incloſed in a red ſkin, which is the mace, or as it is often, though improperly, called, the flower of the nutmeg, fills the hollow as completely as a walnut does its fleſhy coat; the mace only covers the nut in part in ſeveral wavy ſtripes or patches, the traces or marks of which plainly appear on the nutmeg itſelf, after it is made clean for ſale and uſe, by being ſhaked about in a bag, or ſome other proceſs, ſo as to hull or huſk it, and bring it to the ſtate in which we ſee it and the mace. The outer ſhell, in ripening, opens firſt on one ſide, and diſcovers the nut covered with its mace: afterwards the bottom opens, and the fruit falls out. The mace is prized much above the nut itſelf, as being more aromatic. The fleſhy outer covering has a ſharp or eager taſte, which is diſagreeable to Europeans, but it is eaten with pleaſure by the natives.

There are two ſpecies of pigeons who live on nutmegs, but probably it is only this outer or fleſhy ſubſtance that affords them any nouriſhment; for as to the nut itſelf they void it whole, and ſo little altered by paſſing through the digeſting organs of the bird, that it is no way impaired in its vegetative powers. Hence it happens that theſe birds flying from one place to another, and from iſle to iſle, multiply the nutmeg-tree wherever they frequent. The coat of the third ſort (the falſe ſort, or that which is not aromatic) is wrinkled or ſhrivelled, and is never bigger than an hen's egg. The nut which it contains is elliptical, and leſs than the former ſorts and much more taper; it has no aromatic flavour or taſte, but is like to that of our nuts: the mace which envelops it is of a dull red; the leaves of the tree are commonly a foot long.

The Mace is a thin, flat, membraneous ſubſtance, of a lively red-

diſh

difh yellow faffron-like colour, enveloping the nutmeg. The mace, when frefh, is of a blood-red colour, and acquires its yellow hue in drying, which operation is performed in the fun, upon hurdles fixed one above another. This fpice has a pleafant aromatic fmell, and a warm, bitterifh, pungent tafte: it is of an oleaginous nature, abounding with the fame kind of oil as the nutmeg, but thinner and in a greater quantity. It is to be chofen frefh, rough, oleaginous, of a fragrant fmell, and of a bright reddifh yellow colour. The ftate it is in when packed up fhould be particularly attended to: if it be too dry it will be broken, and lofe much of its fragrance; if too moift, it will be fubject to decay and breed worms.

The Clove plant is a fhrub, which grows in the Molucca iflands, in a pyramidal form; its leaves ftand oppofite, are pointed at each end, fmooth, and waved at the edges, and are held on by a red foot-ftalk about an inch long; this foot-ftalk is the moft aromatic part of the whole plant, the clove itfelf not excepted. The flowers grow in bunches at the extremity of the branches, fupported by a calyx divided into four, and confifts of four petals of a bluifh colour, veined with white, round at top, and concave; thefe petals adhere to the calyx as well as the ftamina, which are numerous. The piftil, furmounted with a ftyle and terminated by a ftigma, lies concealed at the bottom of the calyx, and becomes an oviform fruit, of a reddifh colour, which contain a fingle lodge, and generally has two almonds. The bark, roots, and leaves, are all aromatic; it delights and fucceeds only in moift fituations.

The firft fpecies of falfe clove, that is not aromatic, differs from the foregoing only in its leaves, which in this fpecies are mounted on long foot-ftalks, rounded off at their upper extremities, and of a pale green colour: the whole tree is void of any fragrance, and its clove is very bitter.

The fecond fort of falfe cloves differs from the foregoing only in its calyx, which is in four divifions, exceedingly long and pointed at

I   its

its bafe: the tree refembles the laurel: the extremities of its numerous branches are loaden with a prodigious quantity of flowers,
which change from white to green, and finally grow red and
hard, in which ftate they are denominated cloves. When gathered
the clove becomes of a deep brown, affuming a dark yellowifh caft
as it dries.

To gather the cloves, the boughs of the tree are ftrongly fhaken,
or they are beaten down with long reeds, into large cloths fpread
to receive them: they are afterwards either dried in the fun or in
the fmoak of the bamboo cane. The ungathered cloves that efcape
notice or are purpofely left, continue growing till they are about
an inch in thicknefs, when they are called mother-cloves, and
falling off, produce new plants, which do not bear in lefs than eight
or nine years. The Dutch preferve thefe while frefh by way of a
fweet meat. To be in perfection the clove muft be full-fized,
heavy, oily, and eafily broken, of a fine fmell and hot aromatic tafte,
fo as almoft to burn the throat; the colour fhould be very dark, and
when handled it fhould leave an oily moifture upon the fingers. While
frefh, the clove affords a very fragrant, thick, reddifh oil, upon fimple
preffure.

The Dutch often diftil parcels of cloves to the lofs of nearly half
their fubftance; they then dry and mix them among thofe that are
frefh, from which the impoverifhed ones extract part of their virtue;
by this mixture the purchafer is more readily decoived: but when
the cloves are examined, thofe which have once loft their virtue always continue not only weaker than the reft, but a much paler colour; and whenever they look fhrivelled, having loft the knob on
their top, and are light and pulverable, it affords good reafon to fufpect that this has been the cafe. The Dutch fell them by weight;
and knowing they become confiderably heavier by imbibing water,
a very unfair advantage is made of it.

When a quantity of cloves are ordered, the bags are hung over a
veffel

veſſel of water a certain time, and an addition of ſeveral pounds weight is thus made. In the ſpice iſlands, a bag of cloves in one night's time will attract ſo much moiſture that it may eaſily be ſqueezed out.

The valuable iſland of Ceylon being now become, by treaty, an appendage to the Britiſh empire, and the Dutch in conſequence deprived of the trade in cinnamon in that quarter, we ſhall forbear, in this place, making any remarks on the choice or quality of that ſpice, leaving it to come under the head of Britiſh Exports.

Arrack is ſpirituous liquor, bought at Batavia or Malacca. This is a branch of trade of which the Dutch have almoſt deprived the Portugueſe, the art of making it being transferred, for the moſt part, from Goa to Batavia. The beſt arrack in Batavia is ſold for about fifteen-pence the gallon.

The Goa arrack is made from a vegetable juice called Toddy, which flows, by inciſion, from the cocoa tree. The Batavia arrack is made from rice and ſugar. There is likewiſe a ſhrub from which arrack is made. The manner of making the Goa arrack is this: The juice of the trees is produced, by the operator providing himſelf with a parcel of earthen pots, with bellies and necks like our ordinary bird bottles: he makes faſt a number of theſe to his girdle, and any way elſe that he commodiouſly can, about him: thus equipped he climbs up the trunk of a cocoa-tree, and when he comes to the boughs, he takes out his knife, and cutting off one of the ſmall knots or buttons, he applies the mouth of the bottle to the wound, faſtening it to the bough with a bandage: in the ſame manner he cuts off other buttons, and faſtens on his pots, till the whole number is uſed: this is done in the evening, and, deſcending from the tree, he leaves them till the morning; when he takes off the bottles which are moſtly filled, and empties the juice into the proper receptacle: this is repeated every night till a ſufficient quantity is produced, and the whole being then put together is left to ferment, which it ſoon does. When the fermentation is

4

over, and the liquor or wash is become a little tart, it is put into the still, and a fire being made, the still is suffered to work as long as that which flows from it has any confiderable tafte of fpirit. The liquor thus procured is the low wine of arrack, and this is fo poor a liquor that it will foon corrupt and fpoil if not diftilled again. To feparate fome of its phlegm, they therefore immediately after pour back this low wine into the still, and rectify it to that very weak kind of proof fpirit, in which ftate we find it. The arrack we meet with, notwithftanding its being of a proof tafte, according to the way of judging by the crown of bubbles, holds but a fixth and fome-times but an eighth part of alcohol or pure fpirit; whereas our other fpirits, when they fhew that proof, are generally efteemed to hold one half pure fpirit.

SAMARANG.

I know little of this place but from report. It is efteemed the beft part of the north-eaft fide of Java for trade; and from its vici-nity to the Celebes, I imagine it would be the moft probable place to get fpices at, or the firft quality of birds nefts, of any port I either know or have heard of. A good bird's neft is about the fize of a fmall China tea-cup, almoft as white as writing-paper, and as tran-fparent as ifinglafs, a very few downy feathers hang about it, and this is the only kind you ought to take. The price depends in a great meafure on the quantity for fale; but as it is a rare article, you feldom get them for lefs than 10 or 12 Spanifh dollars the catty. And at China they fold, in 1789, for 24 Spanifh dollars per catty.

The common black neft may be got anywhere to the eaftward; they are full of feathers and dirt, and will coft from five to feven Spanifh dollars per catty; they are not always a certain fale at China.

The bird which forms this neft is a kind of fwallow, the upper part

of

of whofe body, including the head and tail, is of a dark colour, and the under part is white; its head is fmall, its bill fhort, thick, crooked, light-blue, and fhining; its legs are fhort and flim; the wings are long, extending beyond the tail. Thefe fwallows frequent the high rocks, where they build their nefts.

Thefe nefts differ from each other in fize, thicknefs, colour, and weight; their diameter is commonly three fingers breadth on the top, and their perpendicular depth in the middle feldom exceeds an inch. The fubftance of thefe nefts is white, inclining to red, fomewhat tranfparent; their thicknefs is little more than that of a filver fpoon, and their weight is from a quarter to half an ounce; they are very brittle, and have a fhining gummy appearance internally when broken: as the induftry of the bird applied the matter which com-pofes the neft in fmall glutinous pieces at intervals, the neft feems wrinkled, or flightly furrowed on the furface. This defcription muft be underftood of thofe nefts that are dry, and have been fome time kept; while they are attached to the rocks or other places they are more pliable, larger, and heavier.

Thefe nefts are compofed of an animal fubftance, which the birds procure on the fhore when the fea ebbs. They fix on a kind of ftar-fifh of a gelatinous confiftence, of which each conveys a bill full to the place deftined for its neft, applying it by threads one over the other at feveral times, and flying backward and forward till the work is completed.

Some perfons affert that the birds get the glutinous matter from oyfters, or other fhell-fifh that abound in thofe feas. It is not improbable that thefe fwallows procure the materials for their nefts both from the ftar-fifh and fhell-fifh, their ftrong crooked bills demonftrating their capability. A neft bears three denomina-tions, head, belly, and foot; the latter is yellow, dirty, and has many feathers in it, being the part which fticks to the rock; the belly is yellow, but free from dirt: the head is white and tranf-

parent,

parent, and twice as valuable as the feet: A neſt ſhould be choſen dry and very brittle; if moiſt it will be tough and pliable, the foot and belly may, with pains, be made head, by picking the feathers and waſhing the dirt out, and laying them in the dew on moonſhiny nights, which will whiten them by degrees; but if the ſun come to them they then grow yellower and ſpoil.

You are on this coaſt liable to be attacked by pirate buggeſs prows, and ſhould be prepared accordingly. If you are obliged to go to Borneo to get rid of your opium, on your return, if after July, call at Samarang again, the ſpice ſhip generally touches there in her way to Batavia, and you may perhaps pick up ſome.

ACHEEN.

The cuſtom at Acheen is, on your arrival, to go immediately on ſhore, taking all your ſamples of goods you have to ſell; and enquire for Dattoo Karkune, and Noquada Po Sallee, the Shabundar or Har-bour-maſter. The latter can do any thing with the king. Shew your ſamples to them, and agree about the prices. It is not neceſ-ſary to pay your reſpects to the king, until you have agreed to ſell, and are ſworn, which is a formal ceremony, performed by the king's people, and adminiſtered by your taking his knife or creaſe in your hand, and ſalemming with your face to the eaſtward, lifting the creaſe at the ſame time.

You pay no duties on any ſales made to the king. On all pur-chaſes of gruff goods, ſuch as brimſtone, beetel, areka or beetel-nut, rattans, benzoin, horſes, camphor, &c. the king's duties are ſix per cent. The other petty duties for the Dattoo, Shabundar, Toquadar or Aſſay-maſter, amount to three pence halfpenny or four pence per cent. But whenever you purchaſe from, or ſell, to the king, be ſure to agree with the Dattoo (or king's merchant) to be free of all duty, or he will impoſe it upon you for his own emolument.

I

The

The prefents at Acheen are large, if you do bufinefs. To the king fhould be given

A long fhawl,

A piece of gold-end fine muflin,

A carboy of rofe water,

A pair of gold flippers,

A piece of fine coffas,

A piece of fine baftas,

A fmall barrel of gun-powder, and a handfome fufee, if you have arms to fell.

To the Dattoo (or king's merchant), and Shabundar, your prefents muft be, in proportion, very genteel: for the king, profeffing him-felf to be a foldier, does not affect to be troubled with merchandife, but leaves the traffic to thefe two men; with whom you will find it your intereft to be upon good terms; and fee them, after your firft prefent, with trifles occafionally.

Thefe men are fond of parade and attention; it will be therefore neceffary, whenever they pay you a vifit on board, to falute them, on receiving them, with three guns; and the fame at their departure: indeed, this is expected by every man upon the Malay coaft who holds any rank or appointment under the king, wherever you are.

They weigh all their weighable goods with a dotchin or wooden fteelyard, except gold, which is weighed with a pair of fmall Chinefe fcales, and a buncal generally made of lead, and often covered with a thin brafs cafe; but it will be neceffary you have a dotchin and fcales to check theirs by.

It will be abfolutely neceffary to have a Tochadar * (or affayer) to try your gold (if paid in that metal), and to have the king's chop or feal upon it; and beware of impofition.

* On this fubject, attend to what is hereafter mentioned in regard to the Touch Needles of China.

Never

Never carry more goods on fhore than you have orders for, at one time; and as you fell them off receive the returns, and give no credit on any account; for if you give credit, even to the Dattoo, you will probably lofe them.

Houfes are always ready for hire; but if your fales are made to the king he furnifhes you with a houfe, gratis, till his payments are finifhed; after which time you muft hire the fame, or fome other, from the Dattoo; for which you will pay from one to two buncals, of gold for the feafon, or while you ftay there. A buncal of gold is valued at twenty-four Spanifh dollars.

I would advife, in all cafes, to be particularly careful of your fhip while in the roads; for the Acheenefe are connected with the people and pirates on the Pedir coaft; and if they find you unguarded will give them information, and you may thereby lofe your fhip.

You run no rifk on fhore but of fire, though it may be proper to have, befides your fervants, two or three Seapoys or Europeans with you; and particularly if you have any quantity of goods unfold, it will be alfo neceffary to keep fire arms in your houfe; and the fhew of being always prepared to repel, may be the caufe of preventing an attack.

Good betel-nut is procurable here, of which the following account will be neceffary:

Araca, or Areka, the Betel-nut, with the leaf, which is chewed with it.—Areka is a fruit univerfally fought after throughout the eaft, from the Indus on the weft, to the empire of China; but it is not a commercial article in Europe.

The areka is the produce of a tall thin tree of the palm kind. The fhell which contains the fruit is fmooth without but rough within, refembling the cocoa-nut, and being about the fize of a green walnut; the kernel is near the fize of a nutmeg, much refembling it externally, and having, when cut in two, the fame veiny appearance; in the centre of the fruit, while it is foft, is contained a greyifh and

almoft

almoſt liquid ſubſtance, which hardens as the nut ripens. When ripe and freſh this fruit is aſtringent but not unpalatable, and the ſhell inclines to a yellow colour. The chief uſe made of areka is to chew it with the leaves of betel, mixing therewith a chalk called chunam, and ſometimes other perfumed compoſitions. The betel-leaf is univerſally uſed with the nut; it is produced at all entertainments and viſits among the natives, and even to Europeans, ſome of whom, eſpecially the Portugueſe, have adopted the habit. The preparation muſt neceſſarily conſiſt of three ingredients, the betel-leaf, the areka or betel-nut, and chunam; for wanting any of theſe, that deep red colour, which reſults from their mixture in maſtication, would alſo fail. The betel-leaf is ſomething like that of a laurel, and grows upon poles like the hop; this leaf is full of large fibres, which, with the middle one, are generally ſtripped off by the finger-nail; it has a hot biting taſte, not unpleaſing to thoſe who are uſed to it.

The chunam is only burnt lime, made of the fineſt ſhells: it is kept in gold, ſilver, and metal boxes, and muſt be moiſtened for uſe. The catechu, chewed with the betel-leaf and chunam, is the decoction or juice of different aſtringent trees, but particularly from the areca or betel-nut: it is improperly called Terra-japonica, or japan-earth; and is the inſpiſſated juice of an Eaſt Indian tree of the palm kind. We meet with this ſubſtance in regular flat cakes, ſhewing a ſmooth, brown, ſhining ſurface on breaking, in the beſt ſpecimens, and being frequently mixed with ſand and other impurities to the quantity of an eighth part. There is a finer kind, rarely to be met with, compoſed of fine thin flakes, lying regularly over each other, and quite pure. This drug is known by ſeveral names in India, rhaath, cate, catechu, &c. It is prepared from the decoctions and juices of different aſtringent trees; but the moſt eſteemed is that prepared from the areka, which ſort is chewed with betel and chunam. Catechu has little or no ſmell, and a ſweeter aſtringent taſte than moſt ſubftances of that clafs. The finer kind readily melts in the mouth, the coarfer more flowly with a burnt tafte and gritty. The degree of purity this drug poffeffes, may be known by diffolving it in water: if perfectly pure it will be totally diffolved; if otherwife, the impurities will remain behind.

Catechu is dry and pulverable; externally of a reddifh colour; internally of a fhining dark brown, with a flight caft of red: the deepeft coloured, heavieft, and moft compact, is accounted the beft.

DIRECTIONS

FOR THE COAST OF PEDIR.

FROM Acheen-roads to Tanjong Batoo the courfe is N.E. three-quarters E. diftance 16 miles. In this track there is no danger at half a mile from the fhore but what is above water. The fmall ifland of Pooloo Malour, which lies between Pooloo Way and Tanjong Batoo, bears N.E. from Acheen-roads, and is remarkable, by having a fingle cocoa nut-tree like a flag-ftaff, and flag on it, and is fteep to on the fides all round. Having rounded Tanjong Batoo, haul up E.N.E. and E. by N. for Tanjong Batoo Pootie, which is remarkable for a large white rock, like the ridge of a houfe off it; and being abreaft of it, haul up eaft E. by S. and E.S.E. for Pedir-point. In all this track there is no danger at half a mile diftance off fhore; nor on any account exceed four or five miles off fhore, for the bank is fteep to, and the currents uncertain; fo that fhould you lofe your anchorage and meet with calms, which you will more frequently do a little way off than clofe in fhore, you may lofe in a few hours

ι   all

all the advantage you have gained in as many days. I therefore advife keeping within this diſtance. Having run five leagues from
Batoo Pootie-point, you will juſt begin to raife a remarkable buſhy
tree on the extreme of Pedir-point; and being clofe up with the
point, will fee to the S.E. of it a clump fomewhat flatted at the
top; clofe to the above there is a tree which has a round buſhy top,
and the contraſt is too ſtriking to be miſtaken. Being abreaſt of
Pedir-point, ſteer S.S.E. or S.E. by S. for Pedir-roads, and anchor
with the Golden Mount (a high peak like a triangular haycock) W.
half N. Mount Opkin will ſhew under and to the northward of it,
and though a high mount is much lower than the Golden Mount,
and will bear W. three-quarters N. or W. by N. Bring Pedir-point
to bear N.W. or N.W. half N. and anchor in 10 fathoms. The river,
though a very blind one, will bear S.S.W. or S.W. by S. and has a
houfe at the extreme point. Boats at low water or fpring tides cannot come acrofs the bar at Pedir; and, on account of a heavy furf, it
is neceffary to wait for the firſt quarter flood to go in, and out again
before half ebb. On the neaps, boats can go in and out at any time
of tide.

Pedir is a place of fome confequence, and exports great quantities of pepper and beetel-nut; the former of which is brought from
places of lefs note, and the latter they cultivate and export themfelves; which makes the trade on this coaſt go under the name of
the place.

PEDIR.

The principal trade of this place and the coaſt to Battabarra, is
areka (betel-nut), pepper, gold-duſt, canes, rattans, bees-wax,
camphor, and benjamin (or frankincenfe). The foil is fertile, and
well watered with rivulets: but in the low land, next the fea, are

bogs

bogs and marſhes, which produce only reeds, rattans, and bamboo canes.

The animals here are horſes of a ſmall breed, buffaloes, goats, oxen, and hog-deer. There are ſeveral roots and wild animals in the woods and mountains, as tigers, elephants, rhinoceroſes, monkies, wild hogs, and ſpotted deer. There are alſo in this place guanas, alligators, porcupines, ſerpents, ſcorpions, and other venomous animals; and Sumatra is the only iſland in India where bears are to be found. There are all ſorts of poultry, particularly ducks and fowls.

DIRECTIONS

FOR SAILING FROM PEDIR TO GINGAM.

THE courſe is S.E. three-quarters E. diſtance eight miles, a good bold coaſt; but in the mid-way between Gingam and Pedir a point off a river, called Cula Pedir, runs out a good way; but you may ſtand to four fathoms on it without danger; you ſoon deepen, croſſing it either way; and in Gingam you have deep water cloſe in ſhore. There is nothing remarkable to diſtinguiſh the river by, except the houſes, which are pretty cloſe to it, and the round tree on Pedir-point being juſt in ſight from the deck.

DIRECTIONS

FOR SAILING FROM GINGAM TO AYRELABOO.

THE courſe is S.E. half E. diſtance five miles, and may be known by ſome cyprus trees on the eaſt point. This is an inconſiderable place, being ſo near Gingam, from which place the Ayrelaboo people export the moſt of their produce. In Gingam-river, turning up a creek on the ſtarboard or weſt ſide, is a place of ſome trade called Boorong; the principal man is the Shabundar (Meora Marean), who does the Raja's (Comajo's) buſineſs.

DIRECTIONS

FOR SAILING FROM AYRELABOO TO MURDOO.

THE courſe is S.E. by E. half E. diſtance ſeven leagues, a bold coaſt and free from danger. The river at Murdoo is very blind, and only to be known by a large tree on the point, and a few ſtraggling ſheds and houſes. There are two caſcades in appearance, that ſhew themſelves plain in the rainy ſeaſon, but appear like a path between the valley in the fair ſeaſon; it is in reality the ſame ſtream of water, but appears like two falls, as the ſight is interrupted by the trees.

DIRECTIONS

FOR SAILING FROM MURDOO TO SAMERLANGAN.

THE courfe is S.E. by E. diftance four leagues; this is alfo a
bold coaft. Samerlangan lies quite in the Bight, Oujong Raja-
point making one and Murdoo-point the other extreme.

DIRECTIONS

FOR SAILING FROM SAMERLANGAN TO PASSANGAN.

HAVING rounded Oujong Raja, fteer E. or E. one-quarter N.
taking care not to come under eight fathoms any where in this
track: the diftance is eight leagues from Oujong Raja. Paffangan
may be known by the river appearing to run directly through the
point, and empties itfelf to the eaftward. This is the firft river
that runs to the eaftward: you will find a very great furf upon the
point, as if a reef run off a long way; but two cables length from
the break there is no ground thirty fathoms. You anchor to the eaftward of the river; in 17 fathoms, Paffangan-point (a very bluff one
formed by a grove of cyprus trees) making one, and Pongafs-point
making the other extreme of the low land. From thofe roads you
will fee the Golden Mount, appearing like a high fugar-loaf ifland,
bearing W. one-quarter N. diftance nearly 20 leagues.

DIRECTIONS

FOR SAILING FROM PASSANGAN TO TELISAMOWAY.

THE courſe is E. one-quarter N. diſtance ſix leagues. On firſt raiſing Teliſamoway-point it makes it like an iſland; but as you near the extreme of the point you ſee a grove of ſtraggling cyprus trees; the land near the ſea, and that within the trees which border along the beach, is of a tolerable height. On the extreme of Teliſamoway-point is a ſmall ſquare cluſter of trees which makes it ſomewhat re-markable.—As you near the point, you will open the bay and ſee the houſes and Bazar; hawl round the point at a convenient diſtance keeping the ſhore cloſe on board; anchor in 10 fathoms, the point and N.N.W. half W. and the town S.W. by W. off ſhore half a mile.

DIRECTIONS

FOR SAILING FROM TELISAMOWAY TO COURTAY.

THE courſe is N.E. by E. one-quarter E. diſtance four leagues. By this courſe you will round the bay in regular ſoundings, and ſee the houſes in Courtay-river very plain; anchor in five fathoms, with the river's mouth open. There are two rivers, Teliſamoway and Courtay; but the exports are very inconſiderable, as they are all under one government, and the inhabitants dare not trade without leave from the Raja of Courtay and Teliſamoway, who does every thing to engroſs the whole trade; and being abſolute is much dreaded.

4

DIRECTIONS

DIRECTIONS

FOR SAILING FROM BATTACARRAN-POINT TO POOLOO AURO, TO AVOID THE DOGGER BANKS.

BEING clear of Frederick Endrick, and off Battacarran-point in feven fathoms, fteer N. 10 leagues, and then N. half E. 10 leagues will lead you fair in mid-channel between the Seven Iflands and Pooloo Taya. Steer N. by E. or N.N.E. until five leagues to the eaftward of it; thence fteer N.E. by N. to crofs the line in 19 or 20 fathoms depth of water, and continue this courfe till in latitude 0° 30′ N. in order to avoid the Dogger Banks, which you may fafely round in 24 or 25 fathoms foft; but you muft not come nearer than 23 fathoms, as they are fteep to in many places.

Having made your latitude good 0° 30′ N. and in 25 fathoms, fteer N.N.W. till in the latitude 1° 0′ N.; and then fteer N.W. by N. till you fee Pooloo Auro; this courfe, if you do not fteer to the northward of it, will lead you fair for Pooloo Auro in 36 fathoms, diftance off four or five leagues.

DIRECTIONS

FOR SAILING FROM POOLOO AURO TO BATTACARRAN-POINT,
TO AVOID THE DOGGER BANKS.

FROM Pooloo Auro, diſtance four leagues, ſteer S.E. by S. till in
latitude 1° 0′ N.; then S.S.E. until you have made 1° 10′ eaſt meridian diſtance from Pooloo Auro; from this ſteer S. or S. half W.
till in the latitude 0° 25′ or 0° 20′ N.; from whence ſteer S.W. by S.
croſſing the Line in 19 or 20 fathoms, this will lead you fair up to
Pooloo Taya, which you will ſee bearing W. by S. or W.S.W. from
ſix to ſeven leagues diſtance, if the weather is not hazy.

Should you increaſe your depth of water from Pooloo Auro to
more than 22 fathoms, ſteer more to the ſouthward and weſtward;
but ſhould you have leſs than 25 or 24 fathoms, haul to the ſouthward and eaſtward, till you are to the ſouthward of 0° 25′ N.
This is a good track, either night or day, and may be run with ſafety
in any weather. After croſſing the Line you will decreaſe your water
to 19 or 20 fathoms, and to 14 or 15 fathoms off the S.E. point of
Lingin, which, if clear weather, you will ſee at ſeven or eight leagues
diſtance; and from that to 12 or 13 fathoms off Pooloo Taya. From
Pooloo Taya ſteer S. by W. or S. half W.; 20 leagues will carry you
on the bank off Battacarran-point, giving Frederick Endrick a good
birth; from which follow my former Directions for entering the
Straits of Banca, and going round Battacarran-point.

Our charts lay down a great many more iſlands to the northward
of Banca than do really exiſt: there is nothing between the ſeven

iſlands

iſlands and Frederick Endrick: and if you coaſt Banca between 15 and 18 fathoms, you may paſs to the ſouthward of Frederick Endrick and ſave much time. Follow my former Directions to paſs between it and Carrang Hodjee.

DIRECTIONS

FOR SHIPS, WHICH HAVING LOST THEIR PASSAGE THROUGH THE CHINA SEAS, AND MEAN TO PROCEED BY THE EASTERN PASSAGE TO CHINA: OR FOR SHIPS FROM CHINA OR OTHER PORTS IN INDIA, WHICH ARE BOUND TO EUROPE, AND MEAN TO SAIL THROUGH SOME OF THE STRAITS TO THE EASTWARD OF JAVA, AND THEREBY TO AVOID THE ENEMIES CRUISERS.

THE ſhorteſt track for ſhips returning from the China ſeas with any of the above intents, is to follow the Directions for making Tanjong Salatan. When you are four, five, or ſix leagues to the eaſtward of Pooloo Auro, ſteer S.E. to make the iſland of Victoria, diſtance from Pooloo Auro 35 leagues. Victoria lies in latitude 1° 39′ N. The ſoundings in this track are 30 fathoms, white and grey ſand. The iſland is covered with wood; on the S.W. ſide is a ſmall bay or creek; and S.E. by E. diſtance three leagues from it, lies a ſmall white iſland.

From getting ſight of Victoria, you ſteer to the ſouth-eaſtward to make St. Julians, which bears from Victoria S.E. by S. diſtance 18 leagues, and lies in latitude 0° 49′ N. You may coaſt this iſland at three or four miles diſtance. Being clear of this place, ſteer for the iſland of St. Barbes, which bears from St. Julians

S.E.

S.E. by S. 16 or 17 leagues. Sailing in this direction, you fee to the eaftward a number of iflands that lies about 13 or 14 leagues to the northward of St. Barbes ; they are all high, but the northernmoft is the higheft. The ifland of St. Barbes, which is under the Equator, is high, and at firft making it appear like two iflands, the extremes being higher than the center, particularly the N.E. end, which much refembles a barn.

The ifland of St. Barbes is about three leagues in circumference, the greateft extent is from N.W. to S.E.; the N.W. point terminates in a peak, and, almoft adjoining to it, are two fmall rocks. You may anchor to the S.E. of this ifland in 25 fathoms, and get wood and water.

From St. Barbes you fteer S.E. by S. to make Suratoo or the Quoin, and Carimetia; thefe are two iflands, with many to the fouthward and eaftward of them, laying off the S.W. part of Borneo. The foundings you will find going this track are 26, 24, and 22 fathoms; and as you near Suratoo the water fhoals to 20 and 18 fathoms. ·It is reckoned 24 leagues from St. Barbes to Suratoo, on a S.S.E. one-quarter E. courfe. Be cautious if you approach Suratoo at night, that you do not fall in with the N. or N.E. fide of it, or between the ifland to the fouthward and eaftward of it and Carimetia, where are many dangers.

Carimetia is an ifland very high and woody; it has a peak in the middle, which is generally cloud-capped, and about two and a-half leagues in length and one league in breadth ; it is about 18 or 20 leagues from the river Succadana, on the W. coaft of Borneo. From the S. point of Carimetia there runs a bank to the S.W. about one mile and a-half, or one mile.

Suratoo is W.S.W. of Carimetia, and between them is a fufficient paffage, where a fhip might run through if neceffity obliged her, when fhe muft borrow on the Suratoo fide ; but it is much better to pafs outfide to the weftward of all.

Thefe

Thefe iflands are all inhabited, and you may wood and water on the weft fide of Suratoo, and get plenty of ftock; fuch as fowls and buffalo. Thefe are procurable on a fandy plain, at the bottom of a mountain of a moderate height. You will anchor in 10 fathoms, muddy ground, in latitude 1° 43' fouth.

Bringing Suratoo to bear weft of you about two leagues, you fteer to the fouthward and eaftward to make Pooloo Mancap, which lies in latitude 3° 3' fouth.

Six leagues to the S.E. of Suratoo you have 18 fathoms ouze, but foon afterwards find 17 fathoms fand, then 16 fathoms fand and ouze. In this track you fee many iflands to the eaftward, and you muft be cautious not to go further to the weftward than 20 fathoms, on account of a bank which Captain Clement was on in the Walpole, lying 10 leagues S.W. of Pooloo Mancap. It is necef-fary alfo not to come nearer Pooloo Mancap than 14 or 16 fathoms; 15 and 19 is the beft track.

Pooloo Mancap lies on the extremity of a bank which extends about fix leagues S.S.W. from Borneo; it fhould not be approached too near, on account of the irregularity of its foundings. The tides are ftrong between Suratoo and Pooloo Mancap, for which reafon you muft be careful to guard againft their effects, particularly dur-ing the night.

Ships bound to Europe through any of the ftraits to the eaftward of Java, fhape a courfe, after being clear of Clement's Shoal, for Carrimon Java; which lies in latitude 5° 54' S. longitude 109° 33' 30" E.

Thofe who are going the eaftern paffage to China may, after paffing Pooloo Mancap, fteer S.E. by E. or E.S.E. till in lati-tude 4° 12', or 4° 15' S. then fteer eaft; and having made Tanjong Salatan, follow any one of the former inftructions for going to the northward or fouthward of Monavifa, and fo through the Straits of Macaffar.

DIRECTIONS

FOR SAILING FROM BATAVIA THROUGH THE STRAITS OF MACASSAR: WITH SOME REMARKS ON THE BRIDGWATER'S JOURNAL *.

LEAVING Batavia road, and having the little ifland Edam bearing north, fteer E.N.E. 60 leagues; then fteer E. by N. to the latitude of 4° 15' S. from which fteer due eaft. Keeping in this latitude you will get fight of the Point Salatan, and about two leagues off will have nine fathoms water; under which water you muft not near the Point, as it fhoals fuddenly to five fathoms. The latitude of Tanjong Salatan is 4° 12' S.

Having the faid point north 9, 10, or 11 fathoms, you will coaft Borneo. Steering E. by S. 23 leagues, will bring you in fight of a high-peaked ifland, called Monavifa, which you leave on your larboard hand at two miles diftance; but you may pafs on either fide of it. When it bears north you will have 16, 17, or 18 fathoms water.

In the wefterly monfoon, in the months of December and January, the currents fet ftrong to the E.N.E. between Borneo and Java.

From the ifland of Monavifa you fteer E.N.E. half E. feven or eight leagues, which will bring you in fight of three fmall iflands called Dwalder and The Brothers; the northern one is Dwalder, and the two fouthern ones The Brothers. You may pafs to the north-

---

* The Author having feen a Journal of the Bridgwater through this track, apprehends that the land has been miftaken by that fhip in paffing; and as this Journal may fall into the hands of others, he judges it proper to notice the fame.

ward or fouthward of Monavifa; I paffed to the northward in the foregoing direction. Between Monavifa, Dwalder, and the Two Brothers, is a very good channel of 12 fathoms, clay and mud; when paffed you will deepen to 20 and 21 fathoms, clay and mud The latitude of Dwalder is 4° 16' fouth, and the Brothers 4° 24' fouth, bearing from each other N.N.W. three-quarters W. and S.S.E. three-quarters E.

When among thefe little iflands, Captain Parker of the Bridge-water obferves, " That you will fee the N.E. part of Great Pooloo Lout bearing N.W. by W. and N.W. [I think Captain Parker muft mean the S.E. end of Pooloo Lout, as the eaft fide of that ifland could not be open to him in this fituation], and the northernmoft part N. by W. When you are paft Dwalder and the Brothers, the current begins to run N.E. by E. and N.E. Under Great Pooloo Lout lies three large iflands and one fmall one; but thefe iflands lay clofe in fhore off Pooloo Lout, and on the north fide. [Captain Parker muft here mean the fouth fide, as at this time he had the fouth end of Pooloo Lout, bearing N. by W. al-though it was the northernmoft part of that ifland which he could then fee.] Therefore the S.E. of Pooloo Lout will be known by a fmall rocky ifland lying a little off from the point. From Dwalder fteering N.E. by N. 10 or 11 leagues, will bring you in fight of three fmall iflands, called the Alikeones. [Thefe iflands are four in number, and by the natives called Pooloo Ampats (Ampat fignifies four in Malays), from their likenefs and number.] Their latitude is 3° 39' fouth; which three iflands you leave upon your larboard hand at the diftance of one or two miles. [You may pafs on either fide of them, having no danger but what fhews itfelf; and good water, foft mud or clay foundings. Thefe iflands fhew my conjectures to be right, in fuppofing Captain Parker to have taken the fouth end of Pooloo Lout for the N.E. and N. end.] The depth between Dwalder and the three Alike-ones, on a N.E. by N. courfe, is 14,

L

15, 16, 17, 18, and 19 fathoms, clay ground. Here the currents begin to set N.E. and N.E. by E.

" From these islands, if possible, keep the depth from eight to 14 fathoms, coming no nearer the Borneo shore than eight fathoms, nor off more than 14 fathoms, until you are in the latitude of 2° 10' south, then you are past all the dangers on the coast of Borneo. In 16 or 17 fathoms from the three Alike-islands are two sand banks that are even with the water's edge. [These I have already particularly described. Off the Great River their latitude is 2° 27' S.]

" From 2° 10' south you will, upon an E.N.E. course, for a while have 14, 16, and 18 fathoms; but in 1° 50' south, in sight of Borneo, you will have 22, 25, and 30 fathoms; and in latitude 1° 20' south, 10 leagues off Borneo, you will find 28, 30, and 35 fathoms, clay and mud; in 0° 4' south, you will have 45 and 50 fathoms 12 leagues off Borneo. The land hereabouts is very high, and may be seen a great way. In 1° 0' N. you will see the coast of Borneo. distant six or seven leagues; and the N.W. part of the coast of Celebes, bearing E. half N. a great distance off, and no soundings. [In this situation I suppose the Bridgwater to be in longitude 118° 50' E. and clear of the Straits of Macassar, properly so called.]

" From latitude 1° 0' N. we steered N.E. 24 leagues, and observed in 1° 33' N. we found the islands of Banca and Zangier in latitude 2° 15' and 2° 20' N. [This island of Banca is not reckoned any of the Sunda islands.]"

DIRECTIONS

FOR NAVIGATING THE WEST COAST OF SUMATRA.

The N.W. monsoon generally blows very hard from October to Jannary, and in some seasons, though not frequently, from September,

ber, which makes it very difficult to fail againſt it. In anchoring ground theſe winds do not always blow ſo hard, nor of long continuance to the northward of the Line, neither are they ſo frequent.

The S.E. monſoon is reckoned to blow in April, but ſeldom blows hard till the beginning of July, and then continues blowing till September, and in ſome years till October. In theſe three months, when you have freſh gales, you have no land winds; at other times you will have fine S.W. winds in the day, and northerly winds by night; however I have known very fine weather on this coaſt from the 15th of December to the 10th of February; but this was to the north of the equinoctial.

DANGERS.

It is ſaid that all the ſhoals on this coaſt are white coral, and by keeping a good look-out may be ſeen a mile off; but this is a miſtake, as there are many ſhoals of black rock, and ſcarcely to be ſeen, being ſix feet under water. The northernmoſt of theſe dangers that I know of, where ſhips have occaſion to be, is at Paſſage Iſland; which iſland lies in 2° 23′ north, and on which the Nelly got aground though ſhe drew but 10 feet water, but immediately got off again. I ſhall in theſe directions give the beſt account I can collect from all the journals and accounts I have ſeen and heard of.

TO FALL IN WITH THE LAND.

If you intend to touch at Tapanooly, it is common, and indeed neceſſary, to fall in with the land to the northward of the iſlands, that is about Labon, in latitude 4° 8′ north, and longitude 96° 5′ eaſt of Greenwich, where you have good anchoring ground; but if

bound

bound direct to Padang, I think you had better make Sumatra about the Line; as you have no occafion to go more to the northward, you will make more difpatch, and prevent much trouble. The reafon I advife falling in with the land here is, becaufe it is a very good roomy channel, and may be eafily known; whereas further to the northward or fouthward you may entangle yourfelf with the iflands. Make Pooloo Batoo, a low long ifland, off the S.E end of which lie three fmall iflands; give thefe a good birth of four leagues, and ftand in for the land. You will, if clear weather, fee Mount Ophir,* being a very high peak mountain like a fugar loaf; and you will fee four fmall iflands that lie in and off Ayre Bungy Bay. In this paffage you may find great overfalls and rocky ground; I never was through; only what I have found in other inftructions, and to be certain, would advife you to keep your boat ahead. For more minute particulars I refer you to the inftructions following from Natal to Pedang.

DIRECTIONS

FOR TWO PASSAGES.

THERE are two paffages, the one called the Outward, for which I fhall refer to the Directory; and the Inner, which I think the beft, as you may judge your diftance better, and cannot over-run your port; although this is not fo roomy, it is abundantly made up by good anchoring ground. Here, indeed, in the night-time you often cannot fail with a fair wind, while in the outer paffage you may run night or day, there being little or no danger.

---

* This mountain is elevated 13,842 feet above the level of the fea, and may be feen 120 miles. Near to it is a volcanic mountain, not much inferior in point of heiglit.

ANNA

ANNA LABOO.

This place lies in latitude 4° 8' north, (by Captain Kirton, by whofe directions I am principally guided), and may be known by a high fpot of trees that appears at firft making like an ifland, and on which the king hoifts his colours. You may ftand here along fhore from two and a quarter to five leagues diftance, there being no danger. Between this and Banjack there is a fmall bold ifland, in latitude 3° 16' north, called the Cocoas; however you may not fee it, as it lies 12 or 14 leagues off the coaft of Sumatra, in longitude 96° 52' eaft of Greenwich. Pooloo Banjack may be eafily known, being the next ifland you fee with a peak on it; and this peak you will fometimes fee before any other part of the ifland, and as you draw in with it you will rife two other hummocks. Steer about fouth, and you will fee Pooloo Sago; this is a low ifland. Between Banjack and Paffage Iflands there is no paffage. Keep thefe two iflands on your ftarboard fide, and off Sumatra 18 miles.

DIRECTIONS

FOR SOOSOO.

CAPE FELIX lies in latitude 3° 48' north, from which Soofoo bears E. half S. diftance four or five leagues. As this is a neceffary land-fall, obferve the land about the cape is low and even; you may coaft it a mile from the fhore and no danger. To anchor in Soofoo Roads bring Cape Felix to bear W. half N. the fouthern-

moft

moſt extreme of Sumatra S.E.; the houſes of Sooſoo N.E. by E.
diſtance off ſhore two miles and a-half, and from Sooſoo-river three
miles, in 24 fathoms, ſoft ground and clear anchorage. In this bay
is much foul ground and rocky bottom, with overfalls from 24 to 10
fathoms. In fine weather, by chooſing a clear birth with your boat,
anchor in ſix, ſeven, or eight fathoms, a mile from the river. Here
are ſometimes large quantities of pepper to be had for gold-duſt; the
Acheen-duſt is the beſt.

PASSAGE ISLAND.

Paſſage Iſland is a low ſandy iſland covered with trees, one of
which conſtantly appears above the reſt, and may be ſeen in clear
weather four or five leagues off the deck; I have ſeen it at Sinkel,
which is ſeven leagues diſtance. The coaſt forms a deep bay, called
Bancongter, on which are ſeveral Malay ports. When in ſight of
Paſſage Iſland keep about eight miles off Sumatra, until you bring
the iſland to bear S.E. by S.; then ſteer directly for it, until you are
three-quarters or one-half mile from it; then ſteer along it to avoid
a dangerous reef of rocks lying half way between the iſland and the
main, and which extends along Sumatra from N.W. to S.E. near
three leagues. It was here the Nelly ſtruck, as aforementioned.—
There are two paſſages, one between the ſhoal and Sumatra. But
I would adviſe keeping the iſland on board, as above; there is no
other iſland to deceive you. The dangers off the iſland may be ſeen
from the maſt-head beſt, where an officer ought to be ſtationed
while running through this channel, as the dangers, being white
rocks, may eaſily be ſeen; but you cannot ſee the reef without the
weather is remarkably fine. When you are in this paſſage you will
have various depths, 10 or 12 fathoms, rocks. If you keep the iſland
on board, as above, you will not have leſs than 10 fathoms. Its latitude is 2° 23′ N.; and the latitude of Pooloo Sago 2° 24′ N.

ADVICE.

ADVICE.

All feamen muft fee the impracticability of paffing **Paffage Ifland** with a foul wind or hazy weather: and coming from the N.W. I would advife anchoring in 20 fathoms, (for under that depth the ground is foul), and wait for fine weather.

Mr. Herbert's charts of this part of the coaft are very good with regard to bearings and diftances; but we differ widely in our account of the latitudes.

SINKELL.

Leaving Paffage Ifland, fteer S.E. by S. but nothing to the eaft-ward; or keep the ifland N.W. by N.: but by no means bring it to the weftward of that, or you will entangle yourfelf in the fhoal be-fore mentioned. When you have run about 10 miles, and find your-felf in 16 or 17 fathoms foft ground, you may keep away a point if you are bound to Sinkell. By the time you have failed three or four leagues, as above, you will fee the N. point of Sinkell-river, being a low point covered with Palmyra trees.—In the mouth of the river lies a fmall ifland covered with tall trees, and which may eafily be known as fuch at the diftance of four leagues.

SINKELL, ON THE WEST COAST OF SUMATRA.

On your arrival here, you will fend your boat well manned and armed up the river, with your linguift, or fome perfon who can fpeak the language of the natives. About half way up the river towards the town you will fee a fingle houfe, belonging to the Sha-bundar. To this man you may declare your bufinefs, and he will fend exprefs to the merchants: you need not therefore proceed any further, but wait an anfwer, and conform to his directions.—For a fmall prefent, which is neceffary and expected, he will give you

informa-

information of what is moft in demand, and what goods the merchants wifh moft to difpofe of. I need not tell you the goods you ought to affect to have leaft of and a reluctance to fell, as well as thofe you ought to make a favour to receive, although they may be the very goods you moft want.

The merchants will foon come on board, and, upon fhewing your mufters, will fettle the prices.

Be careful to be prepared to repel an attack, and fuffer none but the head merchants to come on board, and none with arms or offenfive weapons.

The prices being fettled you will have boats on board daily with their exports, principally benzoin and camphor.

Benzoin is bought by the tompong (or piece), and ought to weigh 20 catty, each catty to weigh 56 ounces avoirdupois; and for camphor, 56 ounces troy weight.

You are generally paid for your goods in belly and foot; but the head you frequently pay dollars for. The three qualities of this article (benzoin) are denominated in the fame manner as birds nefts and camphor, viz. Head, the firft quality; belly, the fecond quality; and foot, the third or worft quality, being of little value.

Their accounts are made up in tales, fooccoos, and fatallies, viz.

4 fatallies make 1 fooccoo.

4 fooccoos make 1 tale, equal to 4 Spanifh dollars.

Obferve that the head camphor be clean, free from duft or pieces of wood; that it be flaky, white, and clear, like cryftals of faltpetre. The belly will be fmall, and have a yellow or brown tint, but tranfparent; the foot will look like dirty black rofin with fhining particles in it; the more of them the better. You fhould break the cakes of benzoin and examine it carefully, for they will adulterate it, as well as the wax: and I truft this caution will fuffice for all the Malay coaft.

The exports are chiefly benzoin, camphor, wax, and gold.

The imports, iron in flat bars, opium, fwivel-guns, mufkets, gun-

powder,

powder, ſtick-lack, long cloth white and blue, ſalampores ditto, ſmall looking-glaſſes with gilt frames, kinkcobs, carpenters tools, red and yellow taffaties, gurrias, and Bandana handkerchiefs.

POOLOO LACCOTTA.

This place lies S.E. of Paſſage Iſland ſeven or eight leagues: keeping along ſhore S.E. will bring you near Pooloo Lacotta, a ſmall bold iſland ; N.W. from which, diſtance three miles, is Bird Iſland, a ſmall ſandy iſland to which a number of birds reſort. You may paſs it at one mile and a-half diſtance. You do not ſee this iſland above ſeven or eight miles off; it is about nine leagues diſtance from Sinkell. If it is night and you think you draw near the iſlands, keep your lead going, and as you near them you will deepen from 38 to 40 fathoms; then keep S.E. or S.E. by E. not coming under 27 fathoms; but if the wind will not permit you to haul in for the main, as above directed, you had better bring to for the night.

POOLOO CARANGUA.

When you haul in for the main land you will ſee a ſmall iſland covered with trees, called Pooloo Carangua; ſteer towards it, and round it to the ſouthward, at two or three miles diſtance.

TO ANCHOR IN BAROOS.

Bring the iſland Carangua to bear W.N.W. three miles; the flag-ſtaff of Baroos.N.N.E. five or ſix miles, and lay in 10 fathoms, mud.

BAROOS

Produces the beft camphor of any place on the coaft of Sumatra. The inhabitants have benzoin and gold. The imports are the fame, with the addition of wearing apparel and houfehold furniture, for the Dutch refident there.

Goods proper here, in addition to the former account, are white beads, Pulicate handkerchiefs, chints with large flowers and red ground, white dungarric, falt, rice, ghee oil, a few metal watches and gilt-hilted fwords. The proportion of buying camphor and benzoin fhould be as follows:

$$66\tfrac{1}{3} \text{ lbs. Dutch, head,}$$
$$33\tfrac{1}{3} \text{ d}^\circ \quad \text{d}^\circ \quad \text{belly,}$$
$$25 \text{ d}^\circ \quad \text{d}^\circ \quad \text{foot,}$$

125 lbs. Dutch, equal to one pecul.

MENSELAR.

S.E. by E. from this place lays Stawkan ifland, diftance about feven leagues, and is the only ifland between Menfelar and the main. Menfelar needs no defcription, being a high large ifland, between which and the main is a channel of about four leagues wide, and may be failed through at difcretion, either night or day. The courfe from Stawkan ifland to Battaboora-point, a bold point, though not fo high as the fouth part of the bay, is E. by S. half S. about fix leagues.

TAPANOOLLY, AN ENGLISH SETTLEMENT.

This point makes the north part of Tapanoolly-bay. Going in here you will be nearly abreaft of the bay before you fee it; but keep

within

within about four miles from Sumatra, and you will fee the houfes and the flag-ftaff. Steer right in for the middle of the bay, round Battaboora-point, at about two cables length diftance, and go round either end of Ponchun Cacheil you pleafe, giving it a birth of about two cables length.

MARKS FOR ANCHORING.

Bring the hill on which the colours are hoifted to bear S. by W. half W.; the Refident's houfe S. by W.; and bring up in feven and a-half fathoms, foft ground; and moor with a rope to a large tree on the ifland; you are then land-locked. The latitude of Tapanoolly is 1° 44' N. and longitude 99° 33' E. of Greenwich.

SUGAR-LOAF ISLAND.

From Ponchun Cacheil fteer S.S.W. fix leagues for the Sugar-loaf Ifland, which you may pafs on either fide; but it is beft to go to the northward of it, for there is faid to be a fhoal of coral rocks, on which the fea feldom breaks, lying S.E. about four miles diftance from it.

REEF.

You may pafs the Sugar-loaf two miles diftant without danger; as you draw near fteer to the fouthward, until you have 24 or 25 fathoms, mud; and you muft get thefe foundings before you bring the ifland to the weftward of north, in order to avoid the danger of the reef abovementioned, which, when you are paft, fteer for

POOLOO

POOLOO ILLY.

This is the next ifland you fee, and bears from the Sugar-loaf S.S.E. three-quarters E. diftance feven leagues; keep between 21 and 26 fathoms, and you may pafs this ifland at four miles diftance, and will have from 20 to 17 fathoms. From Pooloo Illy ftand along fhore towards the

ZEHLODYS.

Thefe are three iflands covered with trees; diftant from Pooloo Illy about eight leagues. You do not perceive thefe to be iflands till you are well up with them, or till you are within four leagues of them. They muft not be approached nearer than 12 fathoms, and if it is day-light five or fix miles birth is fufficient. They are encom-paffed with dangers, and thefe dangers continue as far as Carra Carra-point.

THE SYRENS SHOAL.

S. half E. of them lies a dangerous fhoal of rocks, in many parts of which there are only five or fix feet water, on which the fea often breaks. The fnow Syren ftruck upon this reef in the day-time, fhe drew but 10 feet water; the weather being favourable fhe got off, but was much damaged. The fouthernmoft of the Zehlodys bore from her S. half E. three or four leagues.

TO GO CLEAR OF THE SYRENS SHOAL.

As this fhoal extends three leagues off the main, you fhould be very cautious in paffing it. I would advife keeping the outer Zehlody N.E. by N. or at leaft not to bring it to the northward of N.N.E. until you are certain of being paft all thefe fhoals. When abreaft of

it,

it, at two miles diftance, you will have 19 or 20 fathoms, foft and regular foundings.

NATALL-HILL.

You will now fee Natall-hill open with Carra Carra-point. This hill may be eafily known by having low land on each fide of it; it is bare of trees, and appears barren. When it bears S.E. by E. it appears like a gunner's quoin; and when the outward Zehlody bears N.E. by N. diftant two leagues, Natall-hill bears S.E. juft rifing out of the water: you muft then take care to fhut it in with Carra Carra-point before you come under 18 fathoms, foft ground; when you may ftand towards Carra Carra-point without fear.

NATALL.

The method of trading here is much the fame as at Sinkell, only as well as benzoin and camphor you receive gold, from 20 to 21 Spanifh dollars per tale. As the gold is generally duft, care fhould be taken in proving it before you make your bargain, as it is frequently fo adulterated as not to be worth more than 16 or 17 dollars per tale. Aquafortis is the beft mode to prove it; or if you have none, you may try it with fpirits of hartfhorn, by putting a fmall quantity of the gold-duft well mixed up on clean paper, and drop a few drops of hartfhorn upon it; if there are iron-filings in it the paper will be turned brown or black; if brafs-filings or pin-duft, the paper will immediately turn green.

Imports the fame as at Sinkell.

CARRA CARRA-POINT

May eafily be known, by a high flat hill, opening at both ends, with a fmall peak towards the fouthernmoft high part, from which Carra Carra-point runs into the fea.

THE REEF, OFF CARRA CARRA-POINT.

While Carra Carra-hill bears S.E. by E. you may haul in and round the point, coming no nearer than four miles, for off this point is a reef of black rocks, on which, in eight fathoms water, you will have the following bearings; the tall palmira-trees on Carra Carra-ifland N.E. northerly; the flag-ftaff of Natall E.S.E.; and the fouthernmoft extreme of Pooloo Timong S. half E. diftant from the ifland one mile and a-quarter or one and a-half. The fea often breaks on thefe rocks.

When the fwell is great the break on this reef may be feen two miles, but when there is no fwell you cannot fee them; there are feven fathoms, mud all round.

TO GO CLEAR OF THE REEF.

There is a channel between Carra Carra-point and the reef; by keeping two or three miles off the point you will go within it. I would advife the outfide paffage; and after you are in 14 fathoms, bring Natall-hill to bear E.S.E. but nothing to the fouthward; and round Carra Carra-point at four miles diftance, but no lefs; then fteer right in for the hill, or fomething more foutherly, and when Carra Carra-ifland bears N.E. by N. you are clear of the reef.

I

THE SHAFTSBURY REEF.

There is another reef on the other fide of you, on which the Shaftfbury was loft: the channel between thefe two reefs is two and three-quarters or three miles wide. The bearings of the laft mentioned reef are as follows: Carra Carra Ifland N. by E. three-quarters E. diftance fix or feven miles; Natàll-hill E by N. half N.; and Durian-point S.E. by E. half E. There are other channels and dangers, but this is the one commonly ufed. Coming from the northward there is no fhelter from the N.W. winds, neither can you clear the land either way, and the whole bay appears like a breaker; it is therefore neceffary to have good anchors and cables. When you come into 14 fathoms, as above directed, and ftanding in, you will gradually fhoal to five or fix fathoms; and after you are within the Carra Carra Shoal, fteer to the fouthward, fo as to bring the flag-ftaff E. half N. by the time you are in five fathoms; then come to an anchor.

POOLOO TIMONG.

Leaving Natall-roads, for Pooloo Timong watering place, run into 14 fathoms, foft ground; and do not come under that depth, until Pooloo Timong bears from E.S.E. to E. by N.; then fteer in for the north part of the ifland, not far off which you will find 10 or 12 fathoms. When you come into fix fathoms it may be proper to fend your boat to lie on the outer edge of the coral bank that lies round this ifland. At this, and fome other places, at the diftance of three cables length off, you have fix fathoms clofe to the rocks; fo that from this depth your foundings are no guide. There are fome reefs to the northward of Durian-point which the fea breaks on when it blows hard from the weftward. When your veffel is abreaft the boat, let her go round, keeping on the outer edge of the reefs,

and

and follow her, in the veffel, in fix or feven fathoms, and at the diftance of two or three cables length from the boat. When the body
of the ifland bears W. half S. bring the extremes S.W. by S. and
N.W.; then moor in fix fathoms, foft ground, about a quarter of a
mile off fhore. The watering place will then bear W. of you; it is
a well, in low ground, and is very wholefome good water. You
may know the fpot by the fmall white fandy beach. Here is alfo
good wooding, and, in general, fhelter from the wind and fea; but
when otherwife, weigh and run round, ufing the fame precautions as
before.

AYER BUNGY.

From Pooloo Timong to Ayer Bungy fteer about S.S.W. rather
keeping the ifland on board, you will have five or fix fathoms, foft
ground; but by going towards the main you will have 10 fathoms.
Steer as the winds permit, and when clear of the eaft-point of this
ifland, fteer along fhore in various foundings and foft ground, until
you approach Oujong Lalloo, which is the third point from Pooloo
Timong. To the S.E. of this point are feveral fpots of coral rock,
very dangerous, being three or four miles off fhore, and not very well
known.

PRINCE HENRY'S SHOAL.

The Prince Henry anchored here, in the evening, in 17 fathoms,
hard ground. It blowing hard in the night fhe parted two cables
in foul ground; then ftood in for Ayer Bungy E. by N. and E.N.E.
and had 17, 18, 10, 14 fathoms, hard; then eight fathoms, foft, and
immediately ftruck on a fhoal of coral rocks, on which fhe lay two
hours, and knocked off her rudder. They found the water fhal-
loweft next the main, and the leaft water on the fhoal nine feet, and
had

had the following bearings in this depth: the weſt-point of Pooloo Timong, Pooloo Pankeel S.E. by E. half E. off Oujong Lolloo four miles.

TWO PASSAGES.

The firſt directs you coming from Timong. When you are within ſeven or eight miles of Oujong Lolloo, keep within one and a-half or two miles from the main, till you are to the eaſtward of the ſaid point; in which track you will have five or ſix fathoms, ſoft ground, and regular ſoundings; by which you may judge your diſtance off ſhore; and be very cautious not to deepen towards the ſhoal.

THE INSIDE PASSAGE.

When Oujong Lolloo is to the weſtward of north, ſteer up boldly for Pooloo Pankeel, and you will deepen gradually, and have ſoft ground. When you approach the iſlands, which are ſteep to, ſteer in mid-channel between Pooloo Tingo and Pooloo Pankeel, you will have 10 or 11 fathoms, ſoft ground, and regular ſoundings; and you may, if you pleaſe, round Pooloo Pankeel, and go between it and Pooloo Toolore; but be careful of the reef, which is very dangerous, though there is a good paſſage between it and the iſlands.

TO ANCHOR IN AYER BUNGY-ROADS.

When clear of theſe iſlands, ſteer towards the flag-ſtaff, which you will ſee on a bluff point or hill, cloſe to the north-end of which is the river where your boats land. The bearings for anchoring are the flag-ſtaff W. by N.; the body of Pooloo Bauby W. by S.; the ſettlement and river E.N.E. half E. diſtance three miles, in four and a-half fathoms, clear ground.

N

THE OUTWARD PASSAGE.

The other is a good paffage, by keeping along fhore in feven fathoms, foft ground, till you come near the iflands; then fteer fo as to pafs mid-channel between the ifland and the main; you muft borrow neareft Pooloo Bauby, which is the largeft ifland in the bay: there is a fand lies N.E. of it diftance one mile.

If you do not mean to go to Ayer Bungy, I would prefer the paffage from Natall to Pooloo Timong; and being abreaft that ifland, haul over for Pooloo Batoo; for almoft mid-way between Pooloo Batoo and the main is a large fpot, on which the foundings are very irregular, from 20 to five fathoms, and from 15 to four fathoms, hard coral rocks. We had nothing under four fathoms; but as the fhoal is large there may be lefs on it. We ran three miles N.W. before we cleared it. Off the S.E. end of Pooloo Batoo are three iflands, and from them about four miles is a dangerous fhoal; fome of the rocks appear above water. When the rocks are in one with the middle iflands, they bear S.S.W.; and we paffed them at three miles diftance, in 24 fathoms, hard ground.

A NEW PASSAGE.

There are many different tracks from Pooloo Batoo to Padang, but there ftill appears a better than thofe before mentioned: the one I mean is to the outfide, or to the weftward of all the fhoals, and to fall in with Pooloo Toojoo, keeping the ifland clofe on board, and to pafs to the northward of it: in this track you will have no foundings. When paffed Pooloo Toojoo, fteer for Pooloo Leema, and keep it pretty clofe on board, at one and a-half or two miles diftance on the ftarboard fide; and when clear of it, fteer for Pooloo Piffang, under which you may anchor in feven or five fathoms.

POOLOO

POOLOO TOOJOO.

Pooloo Toojoo is the northernmoſt of all the Padang iſlands. The following are the beſt Directions for the inſide paſſage to Padang:

POOLOO TOOLORE REEF.

Being clear of Pooloo Batoo, and the ſmall Sugar-loaf Iſland off Pooloo Lolloo, (called Batrabar), if bound to the Padang, give all the aforeſaid iſlands in Ayer Bungy Bay a good birth of at leaſt five leagues, and paſs them in 18, 19, or 20 fathoms. Take care not to come nearer than five leagues, or 19 fathoms water. Off the ſouthernmoſt of theſe iſlands (called Pooloo Toolore), to the S.E. of which, diſtance four leagues, lies a reef on which the ſea breaks. When in eighteen fathoms, ſoft ground, this reef was about three miles diſtance; I therefore conclude that 20 or 21 fathoms is near enough.

OUJONG MASSONG.

As you run down you will raiſe Oujong Maſſong Hills, being three in number, one of them making conſiderably larger than the other two. When theſe hills bear E.S.E. you are near a ſhoal of black rocks, that cannot be ſeen at any diſtance from the maſt-head.

A SHOAL.

The Prince Henry, in fine weather, run over this ſhoal, but knew nothing of it till they ſaw the rocks under her bottom; they then had the following bearings: Oujong Gading N. by W. half W.; Oujong Lolloo N. by W. the northernmoſt land in ſight made

like

like an ifland, N.W. half W.; a fmall hammock (taken for the true
point) about two leagues to the northward of Oujong Maffong Hills
Eaft; the largeft of the Maffong Hills E. by S.; the trees of the
low land juft in fight from the deck, diftance five or fix leagues.

SOME ACCOUNT OF THE SHOAL.

This fhoal is about two cables length long, and nearly round; on
the middle are faid to be three fathoms, and on the edge feven or eight
fathoms, and clofe to the edge of the fhoal 20 fathoms, fand, and
directly 21 fathoms, mud; thefe foundings are all round the fhoal;
and you may pafs it to the northward or fouthward which you pleafe.
If you pafs it to the fouthward, bring the largeft of Maffong Hills to
bear Eaft, and you are then paft it: you will now haul in for the
main until about three or four miles diftance in 17, 18, or 19 fathoms.

ANOTHER SHOAL.

In the Luconia they faw another fhoal which they judged to be
off fhore fix leagues, and bears from Oujong Maffong S.W. by W.
They faw the fea break very high on it, but were not near it. It appears from thefe obfervations to be a continued chain of fhoals, from
Ayer Bungy to Padang, with many good channels between them; a
good look-out is therefore neceffary.

POOLOO TOOLORE.

There is a good paffage between thefe fhoals, efpecially if you are
obliged by contrary winds to turn it, having good anchoring ground,
and your foundings are to be depended upon. From Ayer Bungy-
roads fteer within two miles of the main, and do not exceed this

diftance

diſtance abreaſt Oujong Gadding, but keep from five to eight fathoms, ſoft ground; and be particular if you ſail with a leading wind
in the night: if you turn to windward it muſt be by day, you may
then borrow on the ſhoals to 12 fathoms; and as you get two or
three leagues to the S.E. of Toolore Iſland, into 15 or 16 fathoms,
ſhape your courſe for Oujong Maſſong, guarding againſt the reef before mentioned.

Note.—You here paſs between Pooloo Toolore and the main, and
all the ſhoals ſhew themſelves by day; there are four inner ſhoals between the northernmoſt and Toolore. Theſe ſhoals are the narroweſt
part of the channel, which is three and a-half or four miles wide.
When abreaſt of Oujong Gadding and its bearing N. half W. the
ſhoal will bear S. half E.

PASSAMAIN AND TICCOOSE ISLANDS.

The Oujong Maſſong Hills may be ſeen from the ſouth-eaſternmoſt
ſhoals if clear weather. Do not go too deep into Paſſamain-bay.
You may paſs within a mile of Ticcooſe-iſland, and anchor on either
ſide of the outward iſland. If it is blowing weather, ſteer down in 16
or 17 fathoms, ſoft ground. Round Oujong Maſſong in 17 or 18
fathoms, and ſteer toward the outward Ticcooſe-iſland; they are
three in number; and when you are paſſed the Ticcooſe Iſlands,
keep your depth of water, if neceſſary, until you are either five or
ſix miles off Pooloo Caſſiqua.

POOLOO CASSIQUA.

This is a ſmall ſandy iſland, with a pretty high beach. You muſt
not mind your courſe, but ſail by your ſoundings: if you turn it, keep
a good look-out, and ſtand in with the main to 12 fathoms, and out
again to 18 fathoms, taking care to keep ſoft ground; but if you find

it

it hard, tack again immediately; as there is no **hard ground but near**
a fhoal, of which there are numbers both within and without you.

MR. HERBERT'S CHARTS.

Mr. Herbert's Charts of this coaft are the beft I have feen or know
of, confidering they are general ones.

PRIAMAN ISLAND.

When you are in 17 or 18 fathoms, foft ground, and five miles off
Caffiqua, fteer for Pooloo Toojoo, until you deepen your water to
35 or 40 fathoms: you are then clear of the dangers of Caffiqua and
Priaman's Iflands, which are three in number, but only two of them
to be feen till you are well up with them.

POOLOO TOOJOO, POOLOO LEEMA, AND POOLOO PISSANG.

Being up with Pooloo Toojoo, fteer for Pooloo Leema, and from
thence to Pooloo Piffang; you may pafs Pooloo Leema on either fide,
but to the weftward of it is beft, as there is a reef of rocks that run
off the N.E. end of it at a league diftance, and has 40 fathoms clofe
to it. Off the weft-point there is no danger.

POOLOO SATOO.

Steer for Pooloo Satoo, a fmall high ifland flat at the top; pafs it
in fhore, but be careful of a reef of rocks that runs S.E. half a mile
off.

POOLOO DOOA.

Or you may go between it and Pooloo Dooa, a small island to the southward, as may be most convenient. Here you may plainly see Pooloo Piffang, a small island in shore of you, within which you lie to transact your business at Padang.

PADANG.

You may now see the flag-staff, on a hill close to the sea, a little to the northward of Pooloo Piffang. Here all vessels go round that are going into the river; one mile within the entrance of which lies the town of Padang.

The land to the northward of Padang is low towards the sea, and mountainous up the country.

TO ANCHOR IN PADANG-ROADS.

Having passed Pooloo Satoo, as above directed, steer for Pooloo Piffang without fear, and round it at either end. To a stranger I would recommend the S.E. end, as most roomy, giving the island a birth of a quarter of a mile. There are 13 fathoms close to, decreasing gradually as you round it. When you see the stone wharf, bring it W. by N. and anchor in five fathoms, at half a mile from the island; but if you choose to be nearer the island you may have six or six and a-half fathoms; and are well sheltered from the westerly winds.

TO TURN TO WINDWARD.

If obliged to turn, be careful not to fall in with the shore, near the island of Caffiqua or the Priamans, near which are many shoals and

I   rocks,

rocks, both above and under water. The fhoals of Caffiqua lie
N.E. half N. and S.W. half S. nearly of the ifland. When you are
between Pooloo Caffiqua you may ftand further in, but as you near
the Priamans keep well toward Pooloo Toojoo, on account of a dangerous reef South from the ifland: about three miles from the off
fide of which reef you will have 25 fathoms, foft ground; which
depth continues to within half a cable's length of the fhoal; and at
low water many fpots of the fhoal are dry. When paffed this danger,
you may make more free with the fhore, and ftand into 12 fathoms,
mud, keeping a good look-out. When you are paffed Pooloo Lema
you will fee Pooloo Carong in the bottom of the bay (to which Mr.
Herbert gives no name). Do not come near this ifland, as there are
many dangers about it; and fome of them run into deep water to
the fouthward. The fafeft way is not to ftretch above two-thirds
channel over between it and Pooloo Satoo, off the N.E. point of
which is a fmall rock at fome diftance. When paffed Pooloo Ca-
rang and Pooloo Satoo, you may make longer boards; taking care
not to approach the bight to the northward of Padang, in which
are fome dangers: then bring Pooloo Dooa W. by S. but not to the
weftward of it, on account of fome fhoals to the S.E. of it towards
Lacrone ifland; there is a fhoal right off Padang-hill or flag-ftaff
which runs off as far as Pooloo Piffang, and almoft to it; but there is
a good channel between it and the north-end of Pooloo Piffang. To
enter the channel, bring the ifland well to the eaftward, and round
its north-end at a cable's length diftance; you will have 9 and 10
fathoms abreaft of the rocks, which are fteep to. As you round the
ifland you will fhoal your water to eight, feven, fix, and five, fathoms,
foft ground; this is the leaft water towards the ifland: but towards
the main is lefs water and hard ground. As you round the ifland
you will fee the wharf; and having brought it to bear W. by N.
anchor: the flag-ftaff on Padang-hill will bear N. by E. in fix or

fix

fix and a-half fathoms, foft ground: here you may moor, being well fheltered from the N.E.

N.E. from Pooloo Leema, diftance two or three miles, is a reef with 40 fathoms clofe to it. I have already mentioned this paffage; but as the prefent Directions are extremely good, I do not hefitate to venture a repetition, with fome obfervations

FOR MAKING THE QUICKEST PASSAGE FROM OUJONG LALLOO TO PADANG.

When Pooloo Batraba bears N.E. and you want to make the quickeft paffage, fteer directly over for the fouthwardmoft iflands off Pooloo Batoo, fteering about South till they bear N.W.; then fhape your courfe fo as to make Pooloo Toojoo: leave it on your left hand, and ftand for Pooloo Annam, and fo for Pooloo Ampat. Stand on between Pooloo Satoo and Pooloo Dooa and towards Piffang, and take care not to get between Pooloo Dooa and Pooloo Tiga, for there are feveral rocks ftretching from one to the other: if there is a channel it is unfafe and intricate; but if you are bound direct for Moco Moco, fteer without thefe inner iflands. There is a channel 12 or 14 leagues wide between them and the inner iflands, and no danger. Keep three or four leagues without the inner iflands, and make Indrapore-point, left you fhould over fhoot your port.

IMPROPER IN CONTRARY WINDS.

There is no anchorage in this paffage, therefore it is not to be recommended in contrary winds, as currents generally fet with them.

O

FROM PADANG TOWARDS THE SOUTH-EAST.

Leaving Pooloo Piffang, fteer for Pooloo Babeck, leaving it to the eaftward, and keeping it pretty clofe on board, on account of a fhoal that lies mid-channel between it and Pooloo Lacrone: this fhoal is the more dangerous as the fea feldom breaks on it. There is a paffage between it and Lacrone; but you muft keep either ifland clofe on board in fair weather; and if you have to touch at Pooloo Sinke, from Pooloo Babeck fteer for Pooloo Pergamy, leaving it to the eaftward, and ftand in for Pooloo Mufquito, which you muft leave to the weftward, and ftand off till you get five or fix leagues without the iflands, having care you do not entangle yourfelf at night; thus ftand in for Indrapore-point.

A DRY BANK.

There is a fmall dry bank that lies N.W. 10 or 12 miles from Pooloo Mufquito; and S. by E. near the fame diftance from Pooloo Toojoo, it may be feen one and a-half or two miles in the day-time, but at night you cannot poffibly fee it. Round Pooloo Babeck to the eaftward or weftward, keep within Pooloo Pergamy, Telery, and Mana, leaving them to the fouthward. This is a bold deep paffage, but narrow; you have foundings from 30 to 40 fathoms all through in mid-channel.

Over from Jerregall-point, and right oppofite to Pooloo Manna, is a high rock, very fteep and rugged, which you may leave on either hand. The deepeft water and beft channel is to the fouthward. If you go between it and the main, keep the rock on board, as a reef projects from the main one-third channel over towards the rock. If you have a fair wind you may go without Pooloo Pergamy, and fall

I

in

in with Pooloo Manna; fteer for Baby Catchill, leaving the two iflands in fhore, which you may near if neceffary, and pafs on either fide of them.

AYER BAZAR AND POOLOO SINKO.

From thence ftand for Ayer Bazar, which leave to the S.W. and when abreaft of it you will fee Pooloo Sinko bearing N.E. which may be known by the flag-ftaff ftanding on a little round hill; keep it on your larboard bow, and run into 12 or 13 fathoms, where you have good anchorage.

In going on fhore in your boat, leave the ifland on your left hand, and in rounding you will fee a wharf to land at.

POOLOO RINGIN.

Leaving Pooloo Sinko fteer along fhore from 23 to 25 fathoms, taking care not to borrow on the fhore, off which run many fhoals. When you draw near Pooloo Ringin, edge towards it, keeping two-thirds channel from the main, on account of a large reef of coral rocks that lays between it and this ifland. When Pooloo Ringin bears S.W. if you want to go to

AYER RAJA

fteer E. by S. and E. which will bring you near it: it is difficult to find it, as the flag-ftaff is four miles in land. Go no nearer than eight fathoms, with Pooloo Ringin bearing W. half N.; the flag-ftaff will then bear eaft of you, and you will be two miles off fhore.

BAD

BAD LANDING.

I would not advife your anchoring here, as you cannot clear the land fhould it blow hard, and you will ride very badly. It is dangerous to fend your boat into the river, as at low water the fea breaks very high upon the bar.

Leaving Ayer Raja, fteer for Indrapore-point, keeping two leagues off fhore. The courfe is S.S.E. half E. diftance feven or eight leagues; you pafs about four miles off fhore. When abreaft of it you may know it by a grove of trees higher than the reft: when paft it, as you bring it to the N.W. it fhews itfelf as a low point, with the aforefaid grove of trees on its extremity.

There are no more iflands between Indrapore-point and Marlbrough; Pooloo Ringin being the fouthernmoft, and at three or four leagues off a clear coaft. But it is neceffary for fuch as touch at the different fettlements to keep in anchoring ground.

MOCO MOCO.

From Indrapore to Moco Moco, the courfe is nearly S.S.E. diftance 11 or 12 leagues. But your beft guide, as well here as every other part of the coaft, is your foundings. Keep from 14 to 20 fathoms with a fair wind; nor further off than 30 fathoms, for fear of being drove out of foundings and anchoring ground. Standing in fhore do not, on any account, come under 10 fathoms; for if you do, it is probable you may cut your cables and loofe your anchors in foul ground, which you are liable to meet with every where on this coaft.

LAND AND SEA WINDS.

Between Indrapore-point and the Straits of Sunda the following Directions may be taken as a general rule for turning to windward and for anchoring, from hence to Manna-point.—Stand off to 20 or 30 fathoms in the night, and in again by day to 10 or 11 fathoms, all foft ground. In turning you muft anchor in 30 fathoms, and ftay till 10, 11, or 12 o'clock for the fea wind; then weigh, and ftand in fhore till you are in 10 or 11 fathoms, and anchor till the land winds come off, at fix, eight, or perhaps twelve, o'clock at night, and fometimes not till four or fix in the morning: this often happens in both monfoons, and then does not vary above three points from the monfoon winds: at thofe times the day winds are fteady from N.W. or S.E.

WORKING ALONG SHORE:—

it is then impoffible to beat along fhore; at other times you have the land winds from N.N.E. to E.N.E. a leading wind; at five, fix, or feven o'clock in the evening you may edge away to 25 or 30 fathoms, fo as to be in that water by eight or nine the next morning, at which time the land wind being done, come too with a kedge or ftream anchor, to prevent the currents horfing you back, and wait for the fea winds, which fet in as above. With the firft of thefe winds you ftretch along fhore, but towards night edge away into 10 or 11 fathoms, fo as to get the firft of the land wind. There is always a calm between land and fea winds, it is therefore neceffary to have handy anchors to work.

MOCO MOCO FORT.

About four or five leagues to the northward of Moco Moco, is a remarkable gap in the tall palm trees, by which you may know when you draw near the fettlement. To the fouthward you will fee two points of land, which are formed by the woods; between them is clear level land, on which is Moco Moco Fort. When you come abreaft of the fort you will fee the Englifh colours. Bring the flag-ftaff to bear E. by N. and anchor in 10 fathoms, foft ground. Here you muft wait for a boat from the fhore, as your own cannot land without great danger. W.N.W. from Moco Moco, diftance four leagues, lies a fhoal; in blowing weather the fea breaks on it, and on which there is faid to be two and a-half fathoms. About two or three leagues to the fouthward of Moco Moco is a reef of foul ground, that runs five miles to feaward, with irregular hard found-ings, and in many places fcarce four fathoms on it. The beft way is to keep between 25 and 30 fathoms, till you find you can carry your foft muddy ground to 10 fathoms; you may then depend on being clear of it, and may run along fhore to Marlbrough, the coaft being entirely clear, and good anchoring ground all the way, not coming under 10 fathoms till you have fight of

RAT ISLAND,

which is a fmall ifland covered with cocoa-nut trees. To the north-ward of Marlbrough are feveral high mountains; and at feven or eight leagues diftance, coming along fhore, you may fee the Sugar-loaf: ftand towards Ra Ifland to 10 or 12 fathoms mud. There is a reef runs from the ifland W. and W.N.W. five miles; as you approach it, give it a good birth while it is to the S.E. of you.

MARLBRO

MARLBRO' BAY.

Then fteer for Pooloo-point, which is a bluff point to the S.E. until the ifland bears S.W. and the Sugar-loaf N.E.

TO ANCHOR IN BENCOOLEN BAY.

You may anchor here in from eight to twelve fathoms, mud; but fhould you be too near Rat Ifland, you will find fandy ground with rocks and mixtures.

NORTH BREAKERS.

In coming in do not come nearer the main than eight fathoms, as the North Breakers do not fhew themfelves in fine weather.

CAUTION.

It is not cuftomary for country fhips to moor here, as the roads are quite expofed to the N.W. winds, which fometimes raifes fuch a fea as to render it almoft impoffible to ride; and if thefe gales fet in, the veffel will of courfe be under the neceffity of leaving two anchors behind inftead of one. When there is reafon to expect one of thefe gales, do not attempt to ride it out unlefs it fhould be night.—

BUT TO RUN FOR POOLOO BAY,

If day-light, flip your cables and fteer fouth, until you have paffed the Black Rocks, which lie half way between the roads and point. If the weather is not very bad the rock fhews itfelf; but when it blows

hard

hard the channel is quite a break. When you are fure which is the low point that forms the bay, you will fhoal gradually to eight fathoms: as you approach it fteer round the point at one cable's length; keep in this depth till you fairly open the bay, then luff up to the ftarboard till the point bears N.W. or N.N.W. in fix or feven fathoms, mud; here you are fheltered from all winds and weather. In going in do not anchor too near the S. or S.W. fide of the bay, on account of fome coral rocks under water, running two or three cables length.

POOLOO BAY.

This is a fine bay, but the country round it is very fickly: fhould it have happened that you have loft all your anchors you may

RUN ON SHORE AND NOT HURT.

But you muft, for this purpofe, luff clofe round the point, and keep along the weftern fhore, till you fee a tree which you think ftrong enough to hold you, then get your haufers ready and run your veffel in fhore without fear, and make faft, waiting for fupplies.

BLACK ROCKS.

There is no danger between Fort Marlbro' and Pooloo Bay; but to the northward of the rock, which lies in nine or ten fathoms, on which the fea generally breaks, there is a good channel, which lies between the Black Rocks and main, above a mile broad, with fix, feven, or eight fathoms. This channel is not much ufed, as the outer channel is more roomy, and 12, 13, or 14 fathoms carries you two miles without the rocks.

DIRECTIONS

DIRECTIONS FOR KNOWING THE LAND.

From Pooloo-point (the firſt bluff point you ſee in the roads to the S.E. or S.E. by S. of you) to Sandy-point, the land is very low, and runs N.E. and S.W. At a cable's length diſtance from the ſhore are eight and nine fathoms; and the ſame depth a mile off.

IMPROPER TO RUN FOR POOLOO BAY IN THE NIGHT.

This renders it very unſafe for a ſhip to run for Pooloo Bay in the night, or in thick weather, when you cannot ſee the land or the low ſandy point, on which you are liable to run. If obliged to leave Bencoolen roads in the night, I think it beſt to run out to ſea. The diſtance to Pooloo Bay is four or five leagues.

TWO PASSAGES.

There are two paſſages out of this road, occaſioned by a reef of rocks that bears from Pooloo-point S.W. by W. diſtance three or four miles; and from Rat Iſland S. by E. and S.S.E. diſtance three miles. The foul ground extends three miles, and a heavy ſwell breaks full a mile in length. At the S.E. end of this reef are 21 fathoms, ſoft ground, not more than one mile and a-half diſtance; and from that to 17 and 18 fathoms, hard, cloſe to the edge of the reef. The leaſt water ſaid to be on this reef is two and a-half or three fathoms, coral.

If you are coming from ſea, bring Rat Iſland N.E. by N. or N.N.E.; ſteer right for it till you are within one and a-half or two miles, then edge away to the eaſtward, and ſo round the iſland to Marlbro' Road, ſhoaling quick in ſoft ground. If coming along ſhore

P

from

from the S.E. and have got to the westward of **Buffaloe-point**, which lies S.E. by S. two or three miles from Pooloo-point, (and which will be seen S.S.E. when you are at anchor in 10 fathoms, just open with Pooloo-point) haul into 14 fathoms, or between that and 16 fathoms, sandy ground, before Pooloo-point bears to the eastward of north. Marlbro' lies in latitude 3° 46' south, longitude 102 east of Greenwich.

FURTHER DIRECTIONS FOR THE WEST COAST OF SUMATRA.

Note. By the inner passage on the coast of Sumatra is meant that from Pooloo Banjack to Indrapore-point.

PASSAGE ISLAND.

If you come from the northward, and would sail between Pooloo Banjack, Passage Island, and the main, which is the best way, you must get in with the Sumatra coast a little to the northward of Pooloo Banjack, or in latitude 2° 39' north. Pooloo Banjack is known by a peaked hill, resembling a sugar-loaf, on the N.W. end of it, and has a chain of islands to the north-eastward. But the innermost and easternmost is Passage Island, lying in latitude 2° 26' north, and makes like a punch-bowl turned upside down; which may be seen at the distance of four or five leagues. There is no other island to the eastward of this, and which you must leave on your starboard-side. Between this and the main is a dangerous shoal of coral rocks, with about three fathoms on it. On passing Passage Island, by no means bring it to the westward of S.W. nor to the southward of S. by W. half W. until you enter the channel, or you will run upon the above mentioned shoal. This passage is about one mile and a-quarter broad, and the course through is S. by W. and S. three-quarters W.

7   When

When Paffage Ifland and Pooloo Banjack are in one, bearing S.W. by W. half W. (which is the bearing of the fouthwardmoft fhoal) you are paft all fhoals, and may pafs Paffage Ifland at the diftance of a quarter of a mile. Obferve not to bring Paffage Ifland to the eaftward of N.E. for off the S.W. end are a number of rocks and fhoals at a great diftance, with eight or ten fathoms water between them.

SINKELL.

When you are about a league paft the ifland, you may fteer S.E. for Sinkell-river, but beware of the fhoals that are all the way betwixt this ifland and Sumatra.

By no means bring Paffage Ifland to the weftward of N.W. for S.E. one-quarter E. diftance 10 miles from the ifland, lies a reef of black rocks. You fhould therefore fteer S.E. by S. until you are in fight of the mouth of the river Sinkell, which is known by two fharp points of land, with thick groves of fmall pine trees growing on them; between which points the river empties itfelf into the fea, and may be feen five leagues off.

To anchor in the roads, bring the mouth of the river to bear E. three-quarters N. in 17 or 20 fathoms, mud; diftance from the river two miles.

BIRD ISLAND.

From Sinkell-roads to Bird Ifland, the courfe is S.E. by E. diftance 10 leagues. On this courfe you may venture to run (in thick rainy weather), but on no other with fafety; for between Sinkell-roads and Bird Ifland this coaft is very dangerous and full of rocks and fhoals.

N. B. Mr. Herbert's charts are very good for this part of the coaft.

P 2

Bird

Bird Ifland (fo called from the number of birds that frequent it at different times of the year) is a flat fandy fpot, partly covered with a green fod, and has 30 fathoms within a quarter of a mile of it. S. half E. and N. half W. from Bird Ifland is

POOLOO LACOTTA,

an ifland well covered with trees, and may be feen five or fix leagues off; therefore, by feeing Pooloo Lacotta, you may know where to find Bird Ifland, which lies to the northward of it.

POOLOO CARANGUA.

From Bird Ifland to Pooloo Carangua (off Barroofe) your courfe is E. or E. by S. eight leagues. To the fouthward of the ifland there is good anchorage when the body bears N.W. by W. diftance one mile. If you are unacquainted at Barroofe, you had better wait for a Sanipan to conduct you to the fhore; otherwife you may run a rifk of lofing your boat, as there is generally a great furf on the bar.

POOLOO SOKEEN.

From Pooloo Carangua to Pooloo Sokeen the courfe is S.E. by E. diftance fix leagues. Between Pooloo Manfelar and the ifland of Sumatra is very pleafant failing, by reafon of good anchorage from five to twenty fathoms; nor is there any danger but what is feen above water. Towards Manfelar is deep water.

From Pooloo Sokeen to Battaboora-point the courfe is E.S.E. half E.; this is the wefternmoft point of Tapanooly-bay, off which runs a fmall ridge of rocks, about a mile from the S.E. part. After you are round this point you will fee the Englifh fettlement of

TAPANOOLY,

on a fmall ifland, in the bottom of the bay on the N.W. fhore, diftance two and a-half or three miles. There is no danger all round
this ifland, without a cable's length diftance.

Ships that have a cargo to difpofe of, go round and anchor to the
eaftward, the body of the ifland bringing it to bear S.W. by S. in eight
fathoms, mud; and have a rope to the fhore to fwing by. Here the
tides rife fix feet perpendicular.

SUGAR-LOAF ISLAND.

From Tapanooly to Sugar-loaf Ifland the courfe is S.S.W. diftance
fix leagues. It is beft to pafs without this ifland, for S.E., diftance
four miles from it, lies a fhoal of coral rocks, which will oblige you
to ftand into 24 or 25 fathoms, before you ought to bring the ifland
to the weftward of north.

POOLOO ILLY.

From Sugar-loaf Ifland to Pooloo Illy the courfe is S.S.E. one-
quarter E. diftance feven leagues. If you pafs this ifland four miles
in the offing, you will have from 17 to 20 fathoms, muddy ground.

POOLOO ZELODY.

Seven leagues to the northward of Pooloo Illy lie the Iflands of
Zelody, which are three in number. There are feveral dangers about
them, therefore you muft pafs about four miles from the outermoft
in 20 or 21 fathoms, foft ground.

THE

THE SHAFTBROOK SHOAL.

S.S.E. diftance three and a-half or four leagues from Pooloo Zelody, is a large and dangerous fhoal of rocks, which in many places has only five and fix feet water. You muft not bring the outermoft ifland to the weftward of north, until you are paft it; you will then fee Natal-hill bearing about fouth-eaft, which you muft not fhut in with Carra Carra-point, nor come within 18 or 19 fathoms, foft ground, until Carra Carra-point bears S.E. by E. you may then haul in and round it, not coming nearer than two and a-half or three miles of the point, on account of a reef of rocks under water, which runs two miles off. One mile and a-half off the fmall ifland of the fame name, bearing S.W. by S. from the point, and when you get Natal-hill to bear E. S.E. you are three miles diftance from Carra Carra-point.

TO AVOID THE SHAFTBROOK AND CARRA CARRA SHOAL.

Come not under 14 fathoms, foft ground, till you bring Natal-hill between E. by S. and E.S.E.; then you may fteer directly for it, keeping off Carra Carra-point two miles and a-half. When abreaft of it, (by thefe Directions) you will fhoal your water gradually to fix or five fathoms.

TO ANCHOR IN NATAL-ROADS.

Here you may anchor, bringing the hill a little to the northward of eaft, and the town E. half S. This road lies open to the wefterly winds, which blow very hard fometimes.

The bearings, when at anchor in Natal-roads, are, the town to bear E. half S.; Durian-point S. by E.; Carra Carra-point N.N.W.

three-

three-quarters W.; Natal-hill E. one-quarter N.; and Pooloo Ti-
mong-paffage juft open, bearing S. three-quarters E. off fhore two or
three miles, in five or five and a-half fathoms, foft ground.

The bearings of the Shaftbrook-fhoal are the higheft part of Natal-
hill, bearing E. by N. one-quarter N.; Durian-point S.E. by E. half
E. off Carra Carra-point five or fix miles.

BETSEY GALLEY'S SHOAL.

The bearings of the fhoal off Durian-point, commonly called
Betfey Galley's-fhoal, are, Natal-hill N.E. by E.; Point Racoul E.
three-quarters N.; Durian-point S.E. half S.; Pooloo Timong S.E.
by E.; Carra Carra-point N. by W. diftance off Durian-point one
mile and a-half; leaft water fix feet. Come no nearer the fhoal than
feven fathoms, nor nearer the main than three or four fathoms.

OUTER SHOAL OF NATAL-ROADS.

The bearings for the outer fhoal of Natal-roads are, Natal-hill E.
half S. diftance 12 miles; Carra Carra-point N.E. by E.; Pooloo
Timong S.S.E.; extremes of the land to the northward N.; leaft
water known to be upon this fhoal 16 feet. This fhoal is nearly
round, and about three-quarters of a mile broad: you muft beware
of it coming from the feaward.

DIRECTIONS

TO SAIL FROM NATAL TO THE SOUTHWARD, THROUGH THE INNER CHANNEL.

Be sure you enter the channel with the following bearings, viz.: Carra Carra-point N.N.W. and the outer point of Pooloo Timong S. half E. When Durian-point bears S.E. by E. half E. you are then clear of the shoals, and may stand into deeper water at pleasure.

To sail from Natal to sea through the great passage, bring Natal-hill E.S.E.; then you may steer W.N.W. but nothing to the westward of it, till you are five leagues from Natal settlement, and the extremes of the main, and islands included, bear N. and S.S.E.; you will then have 14 or 15 fathoms water: with this depth and bearings you may alter your course with safety. If bound to the northward, steer the opposite course you came, (by the foregoing Directions): but if to the southward, steer S.S.W. and S. as your soundings direct, observing to keep in 14 or 15 fathoms.

TO SAIL INTO NATAL-ROADS, THROUGH THE INNER-PASSAGE FROM THE SOUTHWARD.

Bring Durian-point S.E. by E.; and when in 13 or 14 fathoms water, steer directly in for the road, till you bring Carra Carra-point N.N.W. which keep till you are fairly past Point Racoul: being then clear of the shoal, steer so as to bring Natal town E. half S. or E. three-quarters S.; and anchor in five or six fathoms, soft ground.

TO

TO SAIL FROM POOLOO TIMONG FOR AYER BUNGY.

When you are abreaft of Pooloo Timong, fteer along fhore to the S.E. and you will have variable foundings, but foft mud, till you approach Oufong Loolo, which is a bluff point, and the third from Timong, lying half way between it and Pooloo Baubie. To the S.E. of this point are feveral fmall fhoals in feven fathoms water; the leaft water on them is fix feet, and are three miles off fhore. Between the main and thefe fhoals is a good channel; to fail through which, when you come within feven or eight fathoms off Oujong Loolo, keep within one and a-half or two miles of the main, until you are to the eaftward of the above point. Your foundings this way are, three, four, and five fathoms, foft ground; by which you may judge your diftance off fhore; and take care you do not deepen your water towards the fhoals, nor without five fathoms. When you have the point to the weftward of north, you may keep along fhore in feven fathoms, till you approach pretty near

POOLOO BAUBIE,

which is the largeft and innermoft of all the iflands lying off Ayer Bungy; then bring it to bear S. of you, and keep its N.E. fhore on board, at the diftance of half a mile, in order to keep clear of a dangerous fhoal or fand-bank lying N.E. of Pooloo Baubie, and dry at low water; it is in length one-third of a mile. About a cable's length from the ifland are four or five fathoms, foft ground; but within this is a fhelf of coral rocks.

Q

POOLOO TULLORE.

To fail from hence to the S.E. keep the main on board at the diftance of two or three miles, as there is good anchorage all the way, keeping in five or feven fathoms, until you are abreaft of Ou-jong Gadong-fhoal, and another of coral rocks lying off Pooloo Tul-lore, which is the foutheafternmoft of all the iflands lying off Ayer Bungy. When abreaft of this fhoal, the Oujong Gadong will bear N. half W.; and the fhoal S. half E. When you are through this part, (the fhoal off Pooloo Tullore bears fouth wefterly), you will fee another dangerous fhoal bearing S.S.E. one-quarter E. diftance five or fix miles, which you muft pafs to the eaftward, at the diftance of two or three miles. Your courfe towards it is nearly S.E.; and on approaching it you will deepen your water gradually from eight to 16 fathoms, foft ground. There are four fhoals, in all, off Pooloo Tullore, which are in a N.W. and S.E. direction.

OUJONG MASSONG.

When you are paft thefe fhoals, fteer for Oujong Maffong, known by three little hills on the main, called, the Three Brothers, which may be feen in clear weather from the foutliernmoft fhoal. Be careful you do not get too deep into Paffamain-bay, as it is not well known. You may pafs the ifland Ticcoos at a mile diftance, and anchor on either fide of the outermoft ifland. If blowing hard from the weftward, fteer down in 17 or 18 fathoms, foft ground. Round Oujong Maffong in the fame depth; and then fteer towards the northend of

TICCOOS ISLAND

till you come within five or fix miles of Pooloo Caffiqua. The lead

will

will be the fureft guide, and you muft then run directly over to Pooloo Tayo, until you deepen your water to 35 or 40 fathoms. You are then clear of the fhoals of Pooloo Caffiqua, and the Priaman iflands; but beware of that lying off Pooloo Toojoo N.W. five or fix miles. Then fteer for Pooloo Leema, and from thence to Pooloo Piffang, paffing Pooloo Leema on your left hand; for from the N.E. part runs a reef of rocks, that has 40 fathoms, within two or three miles of them. After you are paft Pooloo Leema, fteer for Pooloo Satoo, paffing either between it and the fhore, or Pooloo Dooa, a fmall ifland to the fouthward, according as you have the wind. From hence you may plainly fee Pooloo Piffang, under which you muft lie while you tranfact your bufinefs at Padang, and will fee the flag-ftaff ftanding on a fteep hill to the northward of Piffang.

POOLOO PISSANG

is a fmall ifland clofe in with the main; you may pafs its N.W. end a good cable s length off. On the N.E. fide is a wharf or pier running into the fea, clofe to the end of which is 13 fathoms: off here you may anchor; the pier-head bearing W. by N.; the flag-ftaff bearing S. by E.: after this you may coaft it, about three or four miles off the main, all the way to Indrapore-point. Your courfe to Pooloo Lacrone is S. by W. half W. diftance four leagues. Leave Pooloo Lacrone about one mile and a-half to the weftward of you, but do not exceed that, on accоunt of a dangerous fhoal lying near mid-channel between it and Pooloo Piffang.

POOLOO MANNA.

There is another fhoal between Pooloo Lacrone and Pooloo Babeck. When abreaft of the former, haul in for the main; and pafs

the

the latter on your larboard-fide, and Pergamy and Pooloo Tellery on your ftarboard, diftant from the firft one mile and a-half, and from the other half a mile. After paffing thefe iflands, run through a narrow channel, formed by the fmall iflands to the eaftward of Pooloo Manna, which is a good and fafe paffage about one mile broad, particularly the north-end, where there are 30 fathoms water. We went through this paffage in the Swift, and paffed clofe to the eaftward of a large rock, lying half a mile to the northward of Pooloo Manna, and had feven fathoms within 15 yards of it.

From Pooloo Manna, fteer for Baubie Catcheel, and leave it on your ftarboard hand: then fteer for Ayer Baffar and Ayer Catcheel; thefe alfo leave on your ftarboard hand, and Baubie Baffar on your larboard fide.

AYER BASSAR.

To anchor in Ayer Baffar: bring Pooloo Sinco and the flag-ftaff to bear E. by N. three-quarters N. diftance from Ayer Baffar one mile and a-half.

POOLOO SINCO.

To anchor in Pooloo Sinco-bay: bring Pooloo Sinco N.W. by N. in 10 fathoms, foft ground.

For the reft of the paffage to Indrapore-point, confult Mr. Herbert's chart, which is very good.

From Indrapore-point the coaft is tolerably clear of danger; nor are there any iflands till you come to Rat Ifland.

S.W. by S. from Moco Moco three or four leagues, are irregular foundings, and in fome places no more than four fathoms, rocky ground.

7

W.S.W.

W.S.W. four or five leagues from the fame place is a fhoal, whereon the fea has been feen to break in hard gales of wind.

MOCO MOCO.

The direct courfe from Indrapore-point to Moco Moco is S.S.E. 11 or 12 leagues. This place is known by a large gap in the tall palm-trees that grow along the beach. A little to the fouthward of this is another gap, formed like two points of land: on this place is the fettlement of Moco Moco.

TO ANCHOR AT MOCO MOCO.

To anchor here, bring the fort to bear E. or E. by S.; and the large gap in the trees to the northward of E.N.E.

Note. In failing either up or down this coaft in the monfoon, it is much the beft to keep in fhore, and never ftand off further than 25 fathoms, nor come under eight or nine fathoms, on account of the land winds, which you will have but little of feven leagues off the land; and within feven fathoms, it is not fafe to venture.

OF

THE COAST OF MALAY,

DURING THE

LATTER PART OF THE SOUTH-WEST MONSOON.

NAVIGATORS bound from Tringano to the fouthward, generally fhape a courfe fo as to pafs three or four leagues to the eaftward of Pooloo Capas, tempted by a fhift of wind from the N.W. which generally leaves them before they can weather the ifland. When they find themfelves in deep water, and a rapid current fetting to the N.N.E. and a heavy fwell to beat againft, few veffels are equal to the tafk, and they can only fucceed at the expence of their ground tackling. I therefore think it would be more advifeable not to leave Tringano before the end of September; and fecondly, to take the advantage of the land and fea breezes, and to work down along fhore between Pooloo Capas and the main. From what I experienced of the coaft, it appears every where fafe within two miles of the fhore; I fhould therefore attempt the paffage without hefitation. The Malays affirm there is no danger on this coaft till after the 15th of October, when the equinoctial gales, or fhifting of the monfoon, may be expected: they begin from the weftward, veering round to the

N.E.:

N.E.: they reckon three diftinct gales previous to the fhifting of the monfoon, hard, harder, and hardeft.—Prudence would dictate to beware even of the firft: indeed, nothing but extreme neceffity ought to induce any one to remain at Tringano after the equinoctial; previoufly to it there is generally a great deal of threatening weather, but no danger.

From Tringano to Packanga-river the coaft lies S.S.E. with a fine fandy beach, which may be approached with the greateft fafety within two miles, gradually decreafing your foundings to eight fathoms, fand. At that diftance, as you approach towards Packanga-river, you will fee fome black rocks in fhore; they join with the beach, and there are five fathoms half a mile without them. The north-point of Packanga-river is a bluff head, on which the furf breaks very high; it is bold to. I anchored very near to it feveral times, in nine and a-half or 10 fathoms, mud and fand. There appears to be a chain of communication under water, between this point and Pooloo Brala. I worked between them four or five days without gaining above two or three miles, and then had foundings of coral rocks, 17 and 18 fathoms; 17, 18, and 19, mud; foul ground 19, 19 and a-half; fand 20 and 22 fathoms: at this time I fuppofed myfelf to be diftant four or five leagues from Pooloo Brala. To the fouthward of it, I faw a black rock diftant about two or three miles; and to the northward of it feveral others, not laid down in the charts. I therefore think it would not be prudent to approach it nearer than 21 fathoms on the weft-fide. From the fouth-point of Packanga-bay, to two or three leagues to the fouthward of Tanjorain-bay, the coaft lies nearly north and fouth; the high land bordering clofe to the fea forming a number of fandy bays.—That of Tanjorain is very deep, it is therefore beft to anchor abreaft of it in the night, with a fcant wind; for by chance you may be deceived by your foundings, and get embayed before you are aware of the miftake. At fun-fet I was about eight or nine miles off fhore, and made nearly a S.W. by

S. courfe

S. courfe good (12 miles) till 10 o'clock, when I anchored, and found myfelf at day-light about fix miles to the fouthward of Tan-jorain-bay, it bearing W. by N. in 15 fathoms, clay. During the laft hour's run I had deepened one fathom and a-half, although run-ning into the bay. This remark may appear trivial to fome people; others may think with me, that every thing that tends to promote the fecurity of navigation is of confequence. Thus far the fhore continues bold to two or three leagues. To the fouthward of Tan-jorain-bay the hills recede in land, and the coaft becomes very low, and covered with fmall trees. The foundings alfo change from clay to fand. How far the bank ftretches out to fea I know not; the general track is in about eight or nine fathoms. In ftanding in with the land you have frequent overfalls of one or two fathoms, owing to the bottom being formed in ridges coaftway. In feveral places where I have fent my boat to found, I have always found the found-ings decreafe very regularly to the back of the furf; and I believe the fhore may be approached to fix fathoms with fafety. N.E. and S.W. from Packanga-river, about 10 or 12 miles each way, are two re-markable fhoal fpots, on which, veffels coming from the offing will fhoal fuddenly from ten to feven fathoms, coarfe fand and gravel: they are of no great length or breadth, and within the one to the fouthward are nine fathoms; and it is moft likely the cafe with the other. They appear to be thrown up by fome extraordinary agi-tation of the fea.

In latitude 3° 32′ N. lies Packanga-river, formerly a place of fome note, but which has long fince fallen to decay, owing to its being dependent on Rhio, where moft of the eaftern trade was carried till it fell a facrifice to the revenge of the Dutch, Packanga is very conveniently fituated for trade, having a fine deep water river, deep enough at the mouth to admit veffels of 100 tuns burthen. The fouthernmoft of its two mouths has the deepeft water, and has a fpit of fand, projecting from the fouth-point of it one and a-half or two

miles

miles into the fea. To the northward of this fpit, in fix fathoms water, foft ground, the fpit bearing S. half W. and Pooloo Timoan S.E. the weft extreme of Packanga-river S.W. one-quarter W. diftance off fhore two or three miles, veffels will find good anchorage.

Note. The produce of this place is gold-duft, tin, and rattans. S.E. one-half S. diftance 29 miles from Packanga-river, lies the little ifland of Varilla: it is a rocky mafs crowned with a few bufhes, and may be feen five or fix leagues, in clear weather. To the N.N.E. of it, diftance about two miles, is a ledge of rocks above water. E. half N. diftance about nine or ten miles from it is a fhoal of coral rock, on which the General Elliot anchored. By founding, with their boats, and by their run, they judged it to be about three miles in length, north and fouth; and half a mile in breadth, eaft and weft; and the leaft water they found on it was fix fathoms, coral rocks; and had the caft before they came on it 18 fathoms, at the fame time I was half way between them and Pooloo Varilla in 13 fathoms and a-half; the ifland bearing W. one-quarter S. diftance about five miles.—I anchored with thefe bearings and foundings for the night. Next morning I ftood for Pooloo Varilla, and found regular fand foundings the whole of the way, except in fome fpots had black mud, as the General Elliot had without us. This fhoal lies nearly in the track of veffels bound to Tringano and Siam, as laid down in the chart: but they have no bufinefs under 25 fathoms until they near Pooloo Brala.

In returning to the fouthward, I paffed between Pooloo Varilla and the main: when it bore Eaft, diftance about four miles, had nine fathoms and a-half, coarfe fand. From hence I worked, as winds permitted, to go without Pooloo Timoan; found the foundings in general very regular and good; but very threatening weather, and a ftrong current fetting through the iflands to the S.W.

Veffels bound to India through the Straits of Malacca may go within

R   the

the iflands Timoan Piffang and Pooloo Aura, Pooloo Tingy and the main.
I have been well informed the paffage is fafe, all the dangers being in
fight; and no veffel has any bufinefs to run in the night. I left Pooloo
Aura the 10th of October (bound to the fouthward), had blowing weather, with a hollow fwell from the S.W.; the wind very fcant, fo that
I made no better than S.E. half E. courfe good. The fecond and third
days little wind, with pleafant weather, and the fwell abated, (which
rifes and falls as quick as the wind); foundings from 26 to 31 fathoms, blue clay; the current fhifting pretty regular, from S.E. to
S.W. twice in 24 hours. The third day I faw the ifland of St.
Victoire, which I found very correctly laid down in Mr. Dalrymple's
charts of the China Seas. Shortly after I faw the ifland of St.
Julians, which is further to the eaftward feven or eight miles than
it is laid down in the fame chart. To the eaftward of it we could
juft difcern another ifland. Thefe iflands may be feen very plainly
in clear weather 10 or 11 leagues. From the 13th to the 16th
made nearly a fouth courfe about 50 miles, being obliged to anchor
frequently on account of the currents, and the wind ftill hanging to
the S.W. with frequent calms. From the 17th to the 21ft, the
wind began to favour us, by veering from S.W. to S.E.; the 18th
we made Lingin-peak, which I am pofitive may be feen 20 leagues.
The foundings I have experienced in this track does not at all agree
with the account in the Englifh Directory, as there is no fuch deep
water to the eaftward as it lays down.

I have frequently found a difference of feven or eight fathoms,
as may be feen in my track. As I came to the weftward I obferved
the fame kind of ftinking fcum which I had feen in July.

Pooloo Taya may be feen in clear weather from the maft head
15 leagues, as I have experienced in my run to and from it. To the
fouthward of Lingin I faw a range of hammocks, ftretching to the
E.N.E. which I conceive to be part of Lingin ifland. To the weft-

ward

ward I also saw several of the islands which form the N.E. side of the Straits of Durian; Pooloo Taya bears S.E. half S. From Lingin-peak I saw them in one, when six or seven leagues from Pooloo Taya, in 14 fathoms, sand and shells.

The Seven Islands lie a little way further to the eastward of Pooloo Taya than they are laid down in the charts. The northern-most island has three or four rocks or islets detached from it, but no other danger to the westward of it that I saw. When it bore E. by S. I am pretty certain I saw breakers to the E.N.E. from the mast head; they therefore must bear nearly N. from the Seven Islands, distance five or six miles. When I passed to the eastward of these islands, in the month of July, I saw a shoal bearing N. by E. from them eight or nine leagues. A good look-out ought therefore to be kept in crossing the north of their meridian. To the southward of the Seven Islands are laid down several islands that do not exist; for the only islands to the northward of Banca are those Seven Islands, which are improperly called Green Islands: they stretch along the coast eight or nine leagues N.E. and S.W.; so that they may easily be supposed to form a part of the north-side of Banca, whereas, in reality, they are separated, having a good channel within them. Any person happening to fall to the eastward, may coast them with safety in 15 or 17 fathoms, sandy soundings. This track will carry him clear of some rocks that lie a little to the northward of them.

SOME ACCOUNT OF THE MANNERS AND CUSTOMS AT TRINGANO.

At Tringano the fame ceremony is to go through as at Succadanna, with regard to your firft vifits, &c. (viz.) When you arrive, your firft vifit muft be made to the king's Dattoo (or merchant), who will introduce you to the King and all the male part of the royal family. It is the cuftom here (as at all other eaftern ports) to give a prefent at your firft audience, which you muft proportion according to the rank of the people. The King's prefent fhould not be lefs than the value of 50 dollars; the Raja's about 30; and the Shabundar and Agent about 20 each: thefe are the only prefents abfolutely neceffary to be given at this place. It will be proper to vifit the Dattoo after you have feen the royal family; a little attention to him may be of fervice in the courfe of your bufinefs, as he can give you every information as to the markets.

You will find the King much more of a courtier than the King of Succadanna; and he will treat you with much more refpect: Mannally, his brother, is perhaps as good a black man as you can meet with; is a good merchant, and punctual in his agreements. I cannot fay fo much for the young King, or Prince of Wales, or the king's Dattoo, Nafferdeen; the former is a fool, and the latter a knave in all his dealings: but your own good fenfe will point out your intereft, in keeping on a good footing with thefe people, and all who are particularly in high power.

Cuftoms.

5 per cent.—when paid.
200 Spanifh dollars anchorage—when paid.

To

To avoid thefe duties you muft make a bargain, and ftipulate that you are to be free from all duties, which is the only way to get off.

Pepper they have in great abundance; of tin they fometimes get a fmall quantity from Banca: they have gold of a finer quality than at Momparva; but the fame precaution muft be taken as at Succadanna, viz. to have the king's feal on it, and he to be anfwerable for the quality, &c. &c.

Price of Exports.

Pepper for cafh 14½ Spanifh dollars, per pecul of 133⅓ lbs.
Tin   do   18   do   do   do
Gold 19 Spanifh dollars per tale weight of 1½ Spanifh dollars, or 380 Spanifh dollars per catty of 30^{ds} weight.

All goods are weighed here with a dotchin, except gold.

DIRECTIONS

FOR SAILING FROM MADRAS THROUGH THE STRAITS OF MALACCA TO CHINA.

In failing from Madras I would, by all means, advife you to go through the Sombrero Channel, that being an open and clear one, at leaft fix leagues wide, and bold to on either fide, from one mile to the fouthward of Paffage Ifland, to two and a-half on the north fide.

By going through the Sombrero Channel, you not only cut off a great deal of ground, but always find a current fetting ftrong to the

eaft-eastward, which continues at a little distance from the Malay shore all the way to the sand heads.

Having passed the Sombrero Channel, shape your course for Pooloo Jarra, and from thence S.S.E. towards the sand heads, which course will carry you to the northward of the Arroes, and bring you on the north-sand, on which you will shoal your water very fast. Be not alarmed should you get into ten or even eight fathoms; but haul to the southward, and keep in 13 fathoms; this will carry you towards the two and a-half fathom banks without danger, even should you not see the Arroes. From this, adhere to Mr. Nicholson's directions, which are exceedingly good, as far as Mount Formosa; but when you are that length, you will find Mr. Nicholson mentions a four fathom bank; let this be no obstacle to your standing over it. Should you have a working wind, and gain any advantage by so doing, you may depend on it, there is nothing will bring you up on any part. The shoalest part is with Mount Formosa North, and Pooloo Pissang East, four fathoms, hard sand at low water spring tides.

Having passed Pissang, follow the Directory as far as Pedro Branco; recollecting, at the same time, that should you be becalmed, and the tide making against you between Barn Island and St. John's, there is a good bank of 16, 17, and 18 fathoms to anchor on, and about midway between them and a little on the north side.

REMARKS ON A SHOAL, ON WHICH THE SULTAN STRUCK.

A.M. weighed with the flood-tide, wind S.W. by S. and worked to windward far over to the Malay shore. At half past 10 o'clock struck on a bank, backed all sails, wore round, and anchored in 14 fathoms, soft mud: bearings, when aground, as follows, The northern-most point of the Little Carrimons W.S.W. half W. about five or

fix

fix leagues; the fouth-end of Barn Ifland and the Rabbit and Coney open S.E. diftance eight miles; Tree Ifland S. half E. feven miles; Tonjong Bolus W by N. five leagues. Sounded round the reef with two boats; one of the boats anchored on it in three feet water, rocks and fand: the other boat rowed round the reef, and had the above bearings and foundings. On the courfes fteered as follows: W. S.W. half W. one mile; and had 1, 2, 3, 4; 5, 6, 7, 8, 9, 10 fathoms, N.W. one-quarter of a mile, S.E. one-quarter of a mile, and S. one-quarter of a mile.

The above reef Mr. Nicholfon lays down tolerably well and exact, but much nearer the Malay fhore than it really is. I am convinced it is more than fix or feven miles from the Malay fhore, and much in the fair way of fhips with a working wind. It is alfo very dangerous, as you can fee nothing of it at high water until you are aground upon it. At low water it is dry, and appears a dangerous reef of rocks, having 10, 8, 7, 6, fathoms, and one-third of a cable's length diftance fand and mud; and its extent does not exceed one cable's length. We got on it at high water, hove off, and did not weigh till it was dry; and examined it with the boats as before expreffed.

Note. In working up and down you muft not bring Barn Ifland to the eaftward of S.E. by S.; nor bring the northernmoft part of the Carrimons to the fouthward of W. half S. five or fix leagues, or you will be very near this reef.

Having rounded Point Romania, by Mr. Nicholfon's directions, and being bound to China, fteer from the reef off Point Romania N.N.E. till you are in the latitude $5° 20'$ N. or $5° 30'$ N.; this courfe will carry you within four leagues of Pooloo Auro, then fteer N.E. by N. and obferve, that when in the latitude of Pooloo Condore *to heave* too and *found.*—If your depth of water fhould be 52, 55, or 57 fathoms, you may depend on it Pooloo Sapata will bear from N. by E. to N. by E one-quarter E.; and by continuing the

I   fame

fame courfe, will carry you within fix or feven leagues of Pooloo
Sapata.—This I have found by experience of feveral runs, with little
variation: however, it fometimes happens that fhips are benighted
before they fee Sapata; fhould this be your cafe when in latitude
9° 30' or 9° 35' N. heave too and found: if you have no ground 100
fathoms, haul up north, and run five miles; then if no ground 100
fathoms, haul in N.N.W. for five miles; and fhould you get ground
85, 90, or 95 fathoms, mud and fand, you may depend on Sapata
bearing about N. half W. or N. by W. diftance four leagues. Then
fteer E.N.E. 10 or 12 miles, and haul up N.E. by N. or N.E. half N.
to get foundings on the Macclesfield Shoal. But fhould you be paff
ing Sapata between the 1ft and 15th of September or later, I would
recommend you to fteer N.E. till in latitude of 16° N. then N.N.E.
fo as to be about 5° 30' or 5° 40' E. of Sapata, by the time you are
in the latitude of the north part of the Scarbrough Shoal; then fteer
North till in latitude of 20° 30' N. keeping a good look-out for the
Pratas Shoal; then N. by W. till in the latitude of 21° 30' N. when,
if no land is feen, you may be affured you are to the eaftward. However I would recommend you to found in this latitude, and if you
have ground at 50 or 55 fathoms, the Lema Iflands will bear about
N. or N. half W. of you.

Recollect the tide between Parcelar Hill and Cape Richardo
fets nearly N.N.W. half W. and S.S.E. half E. as Mr. Nicholfon
mentions.

REMARKS ON A VOYAGE TO CHINA.

The proper feafon to leave the Malabar coaft for Canton is from the
1ft of April to the middle of May, by which means you will have fufficient time to ftop in the Straits of Malacca to purchafe tin, pepper,
beetle (areka) nut, rattans, fea fwallow, (called, beach de mar by
the

the Portuguefe; and trepong, by the Malays) and birds nefts; all of which, if well laid in, will nett a handfome profit at Canton.

The articles of trade from Bombay and the Malabar coaft, are chiefly cotton, pepper, fandal wood, putchick, fhark fins, olibanum, elephants teeth, rhinoceros horns, pearls, cornelian ftones, and beads.

When you make the land, and are near the Ladroon, ·a Chinefe pilot will come on board, to carry you into Macao-roads, and bring the fhip to an anchor. The pilot will then go on fhore to report to the head Mandarine, at Macoa, of what nation you are. Should there be any women on board, application muft be made to the bifhop and fynod of Macoa, for leave to put them on fhore, as they will not be permitted to go to Whampoa in the fhip.

As foon as the Mandarine at Macoa is fatisfied in all his inquiries, he orders off a river pilot, who never comes on board until you have laid 24 hours in the roads *, and brings a chop (a licence) to pafs the Bocca Tigris (the mouth of the Canton river), and carries the fhip to Whampoa.

The captains and fuper-cargoes are allowed, as a great favour, to wear a flag in their boats, which paffes them without ftopping to be examined at the different hoppo houfes; but all other boats muft ftop to be fearched, and have their chop examined. Some com-manders who have lent their flags to others, have, by fuch abufe of the indulgence, been deprived of it for the feafon.

Canton is about 15 or 16 miles from Whampoa; and in that dif-tance are five hoppo, or chop houfes, which to call and ftop at are very troublefome, particularly if in hafte to town; for this reafon the indulgence of the flag ought particularly to be attended to.

* I have frequently weighed and run up to Linting, to anchor under fhelter of that ifland, in the event of a tuffoon coming on. It was the more neceffary for me to do this, as I was always a late fhip to China, never arriving before the latter end of Octo ber, and fometimes not before November; for the trade upon the Malay coaft requires you to ftay as long as poffible.

S

The

The day after your arrival at Canton, the Cohong, or directors of the Chinese Hong merchants, will wait upon you *. To these merchants you give a manifest of your cargo. When one of them, who becomes security for your performance of the customs of the port, carries the manifest to the head Tontiff (generally called, John Tuck), to regulate the Emperor's duties, which, however, the importer knows nothing of; as the customs and duties are paid by the purchasers. He afterwards summonses a meeting of the Hong merchants; the manifest is laid before them, and they fix a price upon your goods; with which you must be contented, as no other merchants but the Cohong are allowed to purchase.

There are two hoppo (or custom-house boats) stationed to each ship, one on each side; and when you are delivering your cargo they attend, and weigh it all before it is put into the boats which convey it to Canton; where it is again weighed, to see if the weights agree with that taken on board, which is seldom or never the case, on account of the embezzlement, which invariably happens, by the boatmen, between the ship and Canton, for the Chinese exceed greatly the watermen upon the Thames in filching and chicanery.

If you come to market early, and expect other ships to arrive soon after with the same kind of articles your cargo is composed of, I would advise you to take the Hong merchants first offer, provided it is nearly the price you expected, as probably, by your refusal, they will leave you, and perhaps not return or see you for eight or ten days, well-knowing that you cannot dispose of your cargo to any others: and that from Canton you have no market left to choose or go to.

* The Company of Hong Merchants consist of twelve, who are particularly licensed by the government; and the government are security for the performance of their contracts, engagements, and payment of their debts; though the government seldom perform the guarantee, and never fully.

After

After you have agreed about the prices, money, and time of payment, which will be fettled at feven mace two candereen per head, or Mexican dollar, you muft infift upon the payment being made in one month from the delivery; for if you are a late fhip, fome of your own payments may become due before you are in cafh, or have affets in hand to retire them.

Having effected the fale of your cargo, the Hong merchant furnifhes you with a chop to deliver your cargo, and fends boats down to Whampoa to receive it, in fuch numbers as you pleafe to order, though they feldom exceed three boats (or chops) per day, being as many as they can well attend to during bufinefs hours, which is generally from ten in the forenoon till two in the afternoon.

I would recommend to have two or three of the fhip's company in each boat to prevent plundering; for although the boats are clofe covered and locked up, yet thefe Chinefe watermen are fo very dexterous at the trade of embezzlement, that, in defpight of your greateft care, they will fteal a great deal, particularly tin. I have experienced this article changed in the boats, and fmall flabs fubftituted in lieu of large ones. I fuffered feverely once at Calcutta by the fame kind of dexterity, of my owners Sircars, who changed the large for fmall flabs of tin: I was obliged to pay for the deficiency, although my chief mate made affidavit that the tin was weighed, and delivered to the Sircar with the owners weights and fcales the fame it was purchafed by.

You have no occafion to hire warehoufes at Canton for the receipt of your cargo, as it is weighed and carried off immediately upon landing. Here the Emperor's as well as the Hong merchants' clerks or writers attend, check the weights, and take the account of the delivery. They are very fair in the weighing of your cargo, being done by Englifh weights, and weights of fifty pounds (inftead of fifty-fixes, or half hundreds); and afterwards reduced to cattys, by

multiplying

multiplying by three, and dividing by four; and then reduced to piculs, by dividing the product by one hundred.

When there are ships which have not been measured at Whampoa, the head Mandarine sends word to the Hong merchants, appointing a day to go down the river for the purpose of measuring the ships; which is put off until there are six or more ships waiting, (for the Mandarine will not go down in the early part of the season to measure a less number than six). The Hong merchant informs you, through your linguist, the day the Tontiff means to go down; when it is expected all work shall be suspended, and the commander of the ship, supercargo, and officers will attend dressed; and the Hong merchant, by (the Comprodore *) sends tea, sweetmeats, &c. for his (the Tontiff's) entertainment on board. The boat in which the Tontiff is carried, is distinguished from his attendants by a yellow flag, which is the Imperial colours; and as soon as he comes in sight of the ships at Whampoa, a boat with an officer is sent off from each ship which is to be measured to attend him. Some years ago the ships used to salute him, but that ceremony is dispensed with since an accident happened in the Lady Hughes in 1785, by one of the wads from her guns killing a Chinese; for which the gunner of that ship (according to their laws) was strangled.

As the ships invariably strip their rigging, to examine (or overhaul) at China, care should be taken, before the Tontiff comes on board to measure, to have the after wedges of the foremast knocked out, the stay taken off, and the mast wedged from the foreside close against the after-part of the partners; the mizen-stay or tackles should be kept on, all the foremast wedges knocked out, and the mast boused and wedged close forward to the foreside of the partners.— The reason of this is, that they measure from the centre of the foremast to the centre of the mizen-mast, for the length: and close

* The House Steward.

abaft

abaft the mainmaft, from outfide to outfide, taking the extreme for the breadth.

They multiply the length by the breadth, and divide by ten, which, they fay, gives the fhip's meafurement; and charge according to her rate, whether firft, fecond, or third rate, deducting twenty per cent. which the Emperor allows: but feven per cent. is again added to make it touch, that is, equal to fine pure filver: from which calculation there is no appeal; nor is your fhip properly reported and entered until after this ceremony is gone through.

The rates of fhips are generally allowed after this meafurement, viz. Seventy-four covids, of fourteen and a-half inches long, and twenty-three covids broad, are called firft rates.

Second rates are under feventy-four covids long and twenty-three broad, to feventy-one covids long and twenty-one covids broad: and all under feventy-one covids long and twenty-one covids broad are accounted third rates.

The duty on firft rates are feven tale, feven mace, feven candereen, and feven cafh per covid.

The new teas and china-ware feldom arrive at Canton before the beginning of November; this is almoft an unerring rule to guide you in the purchafe of your teas; for be affured all that are offered before this time are the remains of the old ftock from the former feafon.

In purchafing your goods for a returning cargo, you are at liberty to buy, where and of whom you pleafe, though the beft teas are always to be had from the Hong merchants; and in making your bargains never omit fettling the exchange at which you pay your dollars; for though you receive them from the Hong merchants at feven mace two candereen, you pay them away at feven mace five candereen, for teas, filk, mufk, tutenague, fugarcandy, and foft fugar, lacquered-ware, &c. &c. &c.; by which you fave four and one-fixth per cent.

The

The Emperor's prefent, from fhips of all defcriptions, whether large or fmall, as fixed in 1754, and is now become a certain claim or cuftom, is one thoufand nine hundred and fifty tales, exclufive of the meafurement duties.

The general Exports for the India Market—are

tutenague, china-ware, hartall (a yellow paint, inferior to gumbooge), tea, filks and fattins of all forts, velvets, ribbons, artificial flowers, hams, paper, thread, copper (white and yellow), china-root, ftockings, fugarcandy, allum, camphor, quickfilver, dammer, fugar, redlead, vermilion, lacquered ware, furniture, toys, &c. &c.

The general Imports I have already mentioned—in addition to which may be added, cardemums, fago, teapoy (or mother of pearl), fhells, turtle-fhells, glafs of all defcriptions, broad-cloth, kerfeys, hats, fcarlet-cloth and cuttings, furs of all kinds, fpices of all kinds, and bullion.

Coins.

10 cafh, make 1 candereen,
10 candereen, make 1 mace,
10 mace, make 1 tale.

Weights.

10 candereen, make 1 mace,
10 mace, make 1 tale,
16 tale, make 1 catty,
100 cattys, make 1 pecul of $133\frac{1}{3}$ lbs. avoirdupois.

4

Long Measure.

10 punts, make 1 covid, of 14½ inches Englifh.

Having faid thus much of the cuftoms and ufages at Canton, I fhall clofe the account with a few more remarks for the guidance of the merchant adventurer and trader.

In making your filk contracts * follow thefe

Rules:—

Find out who are the merchants of credit and proper to be trufted; but get every thing from a Hong merchant, if poffible, as they fhould be punctual to a day in their delivery. The agreement ftipulates the length, breadth, colour, and weight (in tales) of each piece; but all this they will comply with, and deceive you, if you do not ufe the utmoft circumfpection.—For this reafon it is better to pay a little extraordinary to a merchant on whom you can depend, than run a rifk of loofing a great deal, and be difappointed in your expectations on the fale.

It is neceffary to be exact in defcribing the colours; for which purpofe the filk merchant will fhew you feveral bundles of fewing filks, of various colours; from which (befides naming the colour) you can choofe, and fhew it him.—Particularly requeft that the filks may be all bright colours, and gloffes; that the whites be all per-fectly white (or colourlefs), and not a dead cream colour, (which they frequently are); that the blacks be not an iron (or rufty) colour, but jet black; and when you attend to pack them, examine each piece carefully, and let it be on a very dry and hot day.

---

* Becaufe they are never to be got ready, or good. It requires feventy days to get plain, and ninety days to procure flowered filks to be made.

Teas

Teas yield the greateſt profit of any article exported from China; but it is requiſite to pay as much attention to them as to your ſilks: and to be cautious in chooſing your merchant of whom you purchaſe, that he is a man of character: but, as I before obſerved, make all the purchaſes you poſſibly can from a Hong merchant.

If you put your tea in cattys, have them ready ſeaſoned, but pack no tea in ſingle cattys, and in double cattys put only thirty-two or thirty-three ounces; ſo that what is ſhort of two cattys pays for the empty catty. I would recommend to a ſmall adventurer to buy or lay in only the very beſt ſort of teas, ſuch as pekoe, gunpowder, hyſon, and padrae ſouchong, which will always find a ſale, when coarſer teas will not go off.

Tinſel and copper of all deſcriptions are prohibited, and all of which you purchaſe muſt be ſmuggled on board: the fees for doing which reduces the profits ſo much as to make it ſcarce worth the trouble. If you purchaſe tinſel, which is made up in rolls of one catty each, you muſt contract for the number of leaves or ſheets to be in each: I believe forty leaves are the general number: if you do not agree accordingly they will make the leaves thicker, perhaps, from twenty-five to thirty-five leaves, which will reduce your profits on the ſale. As thoſe thick pieces are not ſo valuable, I would recommend that you agree for forty-five or fifty leaves to the catty; and even pay a little extraordinary for it.

The china-ware proper for the India market are chiefly cruddled plates, and ſneakers (pint baſons) of the ſame ſize, ſtrength, and fineneſs; plates of the ſame ſort without ſneakers; bowls and diſhes, either with or without four flowers on the outſide. There are a ſort of plates and ſneakers all white, as ſtrong as the cruddled ones, and they are cheaper than the cruddled: no other china will ſuit the native markets, except the dragon china, but that is from fifteen to twenty per cent. dearer, and the breakage will be near as much; whereas the breakage on cruddled china ſeldom exceeds five per cent. and the mer

chant

chant allows you two per cent. for breakage, which is deducted from the price of all china-ware, for the accidents that may happen in conveying it on board, from Canton to the ship.

The china-ware proper for the Europeans tables are, the best stone china, whole long sets, tea sets, and an extra quantity of flat plates, dishes, and sneakers. Choose your china of a brilliant and deep blue, and purchase by a muster (or sample), rejecting all which are of an inferior quality.

I trust the foregoing advice, with very little experience, will be a sufficient guide to the Chinese market; for there can be no fixed prices, as there is not any market in the world which fluctuates so much as that of Canton.

As China, from the vast extent of the empire, is a principal market for almost all the produce of India, it may not be thought superfluous to give some account of the people, their dress, and customs.

In general the Chinese are of the middle stature, their faces broad, their eyes black and small, and their noses rather short and flat.— The women have little advantage of the men in point of beauty: the only thing for which they are remarkable is the smallness of their feet, which are swathed up when they are young to make them so; this appearance is much esteemed by the Chinese, but highly disgusting to an European, as the ankle is thereby rendered thick and disproportionate, and they totter as if in continual danger of falling as they walk; notwithstanding all these disadvantages, the Chinese women think nothing so ignominious as to be said to have large feet; on which account they hold the Tartar women in great contempt, who suffer their feet to grow as nature has formed them.

The men pluck the greatest part of their beards out, by which their faces are rendered remarkably smooth, and gives them an effeminate appearance.

Upon the crown of their heads they wear a single lock of hair, (shaving all the rest) which they plait, and artfully join to it false

T

hair

hair until it touches the ground: the length of the lock is allowed to be a great ornament.

They leave the nails of their little and third fingers growing to an enormous length, to fhew they are not employed in manual labour.

The dreffes of the men and women differ very little: the chief difference is, that the women wear a collar to their fhirt, or inner garment, and the men's are cut round (without a collar), like a woman's fhift.

In fummer their dreffes are light, and calculated to the heat of the climate: at this feafon all wear fans, upon which their almanack or other memorandum is written, either for bufinefs or amufement.— In winter they wear warmer cloathing; and even furs, which are highly in demand, particularly thofe of the fea-otter, beaver, and feal-fkin.

They are ceremonious to an extreme, and appear very polite and affable; but thefe exterior accomplifhments are only a cover to their duplicity and fraud: they excel every nation upon earth in cheating and deceit, as well towards each other as to ftrangers.

I fhall here give a caution to thofe who may be interefted. When at Whampoa, and preparing for fea, the Comprodore, who attends and fupplies your fhip, fhould put your ftock on board a week or ten days before you fail, as every thing is fold by weight in China, except eggs and milk. They mix falt with the food of all the live ftock, and then give them water in abundance to drink to make them heavier; and it frequently happens that more than one-third of the ftock dies. The Chinefe eat every thing, whether it dies, or is killed: the ftock thus dying, and thrown away, is picked up by them and eaten. For thefe reafons the ftock fhould be on board at leaft three days before they are weighed, or received from the Comprodore.

Theft, in this country, is punifhed before a Mandarine, either by
flogging

flogging or cutting off the lock of hair, the lofs of which is reckoned the greateft mark of infamy.

To fum their character up in a few words, the Chinefe are the moft faithlefs, deceitful, cowardly, and thievifh fet of people in the world.

Europeans at Canton are not permitted to enter the city, but are confined to the fuburbs.—The hongs, or factories, in which they refide, are not unlike long courts, having no thoroughfare, or outlet, at the inner end; and generally contain from four to five factories, or feparate houfes, in each hong. They are built on a fine quay, and have a broad parade in front; the promenade is railed in, and generally called the Refpondentia Walk, where all the European merchants, commanders, and officers of fhips meet after dinner, talk of bufinefs, and form parties for the evening. This, in my opinion, is the moft fociable part of the world, where Europeans of all nations meet, divefted of ceremony; but never forgetting etiquette and good breeding.

This country is well fupplied with fifh, of which the great numbers of rivers, interfected by inumerable canals, and the induftry of their fifhermen, furnifhes them with a great plenty of both the frefh and falt water kinds.

They have, befides, great numbers of gold and filver fifh, which are kept in large ftock ponds, as well as in glafs and china vafes, for the infpection of the curious.

Thefe induftrious people have a mode of making paper from the bamboo, which forms a great article of their export.

The tea plant of China, of which fome-account is hereafter given, with their china-ware, furnifhes the Chinefe with their principal articles of export, for which they receive from this country, as well as other nations of Europe, and the Americans, large quantities of filver bullion, and money; having the balance of trade much in their favour.

Ginfeng, of which the Chinefe are fo fond, and of which they

T 2

have

have the higheſt opinion, as a panacea for all diſorders, was once an article of great eſteem and value among them, and that of their own growth ſtill bears a great price, though they have been latterly ſupplied with large quantities of it by the Americans, with whom it is a natural produce in great abundance; and they now participate with us a large proportion of the China trade.

There are many drugs and vegetables in China of a medicinal quality, particularly rhubarb, china-root, ſnake-root, and ſarſaparilla.

They have tobacco alſo in great plenty, which they manufacture after a peculiar manner.

Their principal Exports—are

tea, china-ware, gold (in bars), ſugar, ſugar-candy, rhubarb, chinaroot, ſnake-root, ſarſaparilla, leather, tutenague, japan copper, varniſhed (or lackered) ware, drugs, leaf-gold, gold-thread, utenſils made of (white and red) copper, caſt-iron, ſilk (raw and wrought), thread, &c. &c.

China produces white-copper, of which beautiful metal they make various utenſils, which are ſmuggled out of the empire, the exporting of copper being prohibited.

It produces grain of every kind in great abundance, excellent oranges, grapes, figs, pomegranates, and many other fruits.

Few countries are better ſupplied with horſes, oxen, hogs, buffaloes, poultry, and game of every kind.

The muſk-cat is alſo found here in great numbers, which carries that valuable perfume in a kind of bag under its navel. This perfume is a valuable article of commerce to the Chineſe.

With reſpect to birds, they have eagles, cranes, ſtorks, peacocks, pheaſants, ſwans, geeſe, ducks, teal, widgeon, ſnipe, curlew, partridge,

tridge, and all other game, except the woodcock, which I never could fee or find.

The golden pheafant of China is not only remarkable for the beauty of its plumage, but for the delicacy of its flefh, which, on account of its flavour, is as much fought after by the epicure, as the bird is by the curious for its fingular beauty.

Before taking leave of China, it will be proper to mention their method of affaying gold; and alfo a defcription of fome of the chief articles of export and import which have not been already noticed in this work.

Chinefe Touch-needles. Thofe who are accuftomed to the infpection of gold varioufly alloyed, can judge, nearly from the colour of any given mafs, the proportion of alloy it contains, provided the fpecies of alloy be known. Different compofitions of gold, with different proportions of the metals which it is commonly alloyed with, are formed into oblong pieces, called needles, and kept in readinefs for affifting in this examination, as ftandards of comparifon.

The ftandard gold of Great Britain is of twenty-two carats; that is, it confifts of twenty-two parts of fine gold, and two of alloy. The Chinefe reckon by a different divifion, called touches, of which the higheft number, or that which denotes ftandard gold, is one hundred; fo that one hundred touches correfpond to our twenty-four carats; feventy-five touches to eighteen carats; fifty touches to twelve carats, and twenty-five to fix: whence any number of the one divifion may be eafily reduced to the other. The proportion, in the compofition of the feveral needles, are adjufted in a regular feries, according to the carat weight: the firft needle confifts of fine gold, or of twenty-four carats; the fecond of twenty-three carats and a half of fine gold, and half a carat of alloy; the third, of twenty-three carats of fine gold to one carat of alloy: and fo on, the

gold

gold diminifhing, and the alloy increafing, by half a carat in each needle, down to the twentieth càrat; all below this are made at difference of whole carats; half a carat being fcarcely diftinguifhable by the colour of the mafs, when the proportion of alloy is fo confiderable. Some make the needles no lower than to twelve carats, that is, a mixture of equal parts of gold and alloy: others go as low as one carat, or one part of gold to twenty-three of alloy.

Four fets of thefe needles are commonly required; one in which pure filver is ufed for the alloy; another with a mixture of two parts of filver and one of copper; the third with a mixture of two parts of copper to one of filver; and the fourth with equal parts of the two; to which fome add a fifth fet, with copper only, an alloy that fometimes occurs, though much more rarely than the others. If needles fo low as three or four carats can be of any ufe, it fhould feem to be only in the firft fet; for in the others the proportion of copper being large, the differences in colour of different forts of copper itfelf will be as great as thofe which refult from very confiderable differences in the quantity of gold when the copper is nearly equal in quantity to the gold, very little can be judged from the colour of the mafs.

In melting thefe compofitions, the utmoft care muft be taken that no lofs may happen to any of the ingredients fo as to alter the proportions of the mixtures.

The colours are beft examined by means of ftrokes, drawn with the metals, on a particular kind of ftone, brought chiefly from Germany, and called, from their ufe, a touch-ftone; the beft fort of which is of a deep black colour, moderately hard, and of a fmooth but not polifhed furface; if it be too fmooth, foft gold will not eafily leave a mark upon it; and if rough, the mark proves imperfect; if very hard, the frequent cleaning of it from the marks, by rubbing it with tripoli or a piece of charcoal wetted with water, gives the furface too great a fmoothnefs; and if very foft it is liable to be

fcratched

scratched in the cleaning. In want of the proper kind of stone, moderately smooth pieces of flint are the best substitutes: the more these approach in colour to the other the better.

The piece of gold to be examined being well cleaned in some convenient part of its surface, a stroke is to be made with it on the stone, and another close by it, with such of the touch-needles as appears to come the nearest to it in colour; if the colour of both, upon the stone, be exactly the same, it is judged that the given mass is of the same fineness with the needle: if different, another and another needle must be tried, till one be found exactly corresponding to it. To do this readily practice only can teach.

In making the strokes, both the given piece and the needle of comparison are to be rubbed several times backward and forward upon the stone, that the marks may be strong and full, not less than a full inch long, and about a tenth or an eighth of an inch broad: both marks are to be wetted before the examination of them, their colours being thus rendered more distinct: a stroke which has been drawn some days, is never to be compared with a fresh one, as the colour may have suffered an alteration from the air; the fine atoms left upon the touch-stone being much more susceptible of such alterations than the metal in the mass. If the piece be supposed to be superficially heightened by art in its colour, that part of it which the stroke is designed to be made with should be previously rubbed on another part of the stone, or rather on a rougher kind of stone than the common touch-stones, that a fresh surface of the metal may be exposed: if it be suspected to be gilt with a thick coat of metal finer than the internal part, it should be razed with a graver to some depth, that the exterior coat may be broken through: cutting the piece in two is a less certain way of discovering this abuse; the outer coat being frequently drawn along, by the sheers or chisel, so as to cover the divided parts.

The metallic compositions, made to resemble gold in colour, are

readily

readily known by means of a drop or two of aquafortis, which has no effect upon gold, but diffolves or difcharges the marks made by all its known imitations. That the touch-ftone may be able to fupport this trial, it becomes a neceffary character of it not to be corrofible by acids; a character, which fhews it to be effentially different from the marbles, whereof it is by many writers reckoned a fpecies. If gold be debafed by an admixture of any confiderable quantity of thefe compofitions, aquafortis will, in this cafe, alfo difcharge fo much of the mark as was made by the bafe metal, and leave only that of the gold, which will now appear difcontinued, or in fpecks. Silver and copper are in like manner eaten out from gold on the touch-ftone; and hence fome judgment may thus be formed of the finenefs of the metal, from the proportion of the remaining gold to the vacuities.

It has been obferved that hard gold appears on the touch-ftone lefs fine than it really is. It may be prefumed that this difference does not proceed from the fimple hardnefs, but from the hardnefs being occafioned by an admixture of fuch metallic bodies as debafe the colour in a greater degree than an equal quantity of the common alloy. Silver and copper are the only metals ufually found mixed with gold, whether in bullion or in coin; and the only ones whofe quantity is attempted to be judged of by this method of trial.

The Chinefe are extremely expert in the ufe of the touch-ftone, fo as to diftinguifh by it fo fmall a difference in the finenefs as half a touch, or a two hundredth part of the mixture. The touch-ftone is the only teft by which they regulate the fale of their gold to the European merchants: and in thofe countries it is fubject to fewer difficulties than among us, on account of the uniformity of the alloy, which there is almoft always in filver; the leaft appearance of copper being ufed in the alloy gives a fufpicion of fraud. As an affay of the gold is rarely permitted in that commerce, it behoves the European

trader

trader to be well practifed in this way of examination. By carefully attending to the above directions, and by accuftoming himfelf to compare the colours of a good fet of touch-needles, having the finenefs marked on each, he will be able to avoid being impofed on, either in the touch itfelf, or by the abufes committed, of covering the bar or ingot with a thick coat of finer metal than the interior part, or of including maffes of bafe metal within it. A fet of needles may be prepared for this ufe, with filver alloy, in the feries of the Chinefe touches. Or the needles of the European account, may be eafily accommodated to the Chinefe by the following table, calculated on the principles already explained.

It may be obferved, that the gold fhoes of China have a depreffion in the middle, from the fhrinking of the metal in its cooling, with a number of circular rings, like thofe on the balls of the fingers, but larger: the fmaller and clofer thefe are, the finer the gold is faid to be. When any other metallic mafs is included within, the fraud is difcoverable at fight, by the middle being elevated inftead of depreffed, and the fides being uneven and knobby. But the fame kind of fraud is fometimes practifed in the gold bars, when it is not difcoverable by any external mark.

U *TABLE*

TABLE of Correspondence between the European and Chinese Divisions representing the Fineness of Gold.

Carats.		Touch.	24ths	Carats.		Touch.	24ths	Carats.		Touch.	24ths
24		100	0	16		66	16	8		33	8
23¾		98	23	15¾		65	15	7¾		32	7
23½		97	22	15½		64	14	7½		31	6
23¼		96	21	15¼		63	13	7¼		30	5
23		95	20	15		62	12	7		29	4
22¾		94	19	14¾		61	11	6¾		28	3
22½		93	18	14½		60	10	6½		27	2
22¼		92	17	14¼		59	9	6¼		26	1
22		91	16	14		58	8	6		25	0
21¾		90	15	13¾		57	7	5¾		23	23
21½		89	14	13½		56	6	5½		22	22
21¼		88	13	13¼		55	5	5¼		21	21
21		8-	12	13		54	4	5		20	20
20¾		86	11	12¾		53	3	4¾		19	19
20½		85	10	12½		52	2	4½		18	18
20¼		84	9	12¼		51	1	4¼		17	17
20	Are equal to	83	8	12	Are equal to	50	0	4	Are equal to	16	16
19¾		82	7	11¾		48	23	3¾		15	15
19½		81	6	11½		47	22	3½		14	14
19¼		80	5	11¼		46	21	3¼		13	13
19		79	4	11		45	20	3		12	12
18¾		78	3	10¾		44	19	2¾		11	11
18½		77	2	10½		43	18	2½		10	10
18¼		76	1	1 ¼		42	17	2¼		9	9
18		75	0	10		41	16	2		8	8
17¾		73	23	9¾		40	15	1¾		7	7
17½		72	22	9½		39	14	1½		6	6
17¼		71	21	9¼		38	13	1¼		5	5
17		70	20	9		37	12	1		4	4
16¾		69	19	8¾		36	11	¾		3	3
16½		68	18	8½		35	10	½		2	2
16¼		67	17	8¼		34	9	¼		1	1

Method of bringing several Touches of Gold into one.

Let the finenefs of each fort be multiplied by its particular weight, and let their products be added together for a dividend; then make the divifor, by adding the weights together: the quotient will be the finenefs, or touch.

Example.

10 tale	94 touch	940
10 —	92 ——	920
——		——
20		)1860(93 touch of the whole.
		180
		——
		60
		60
		——
		..

Tea is the leaf of a fmall fhrub growing in China, and alfo in Siam and Japan. The dealers in this article diftinguifh many kinds, which, however, are all leaves of the fame tree, and may be reduced to the three general divifions, ordinary green teas, finer green teas, and bohea.

The leaves of the common green tea are fomewhat fmall, crumpled, much twifted, and clofely folded together in drying: the colour is a dufky green, and the fmell agreeable. The leaves of the fine green tea are larger, lefs crumpled and twifted in the drying, and more lax in their folds; of a paler colour, but more blooming, approaching to a blue-green. All the ordinary green teas give a

ftrong

ſtrong yellowiſh-green colour to boiling water, and the fine green teas give a pale-green, or light ſtraw-colour.

Bohea tea conſiſts of ſmaller leaves than either of the others, and thoſe more crumpled and cloſely folded. Its colour is dark, inclining to black.

The ſhrub that produces tea ſeldom riſes higher than five or ſix feet. It is much branched and ſpreading: the leaves are oblong, pointed at the ends, and ſerrated at the edges. Theſe leaves are collected generally in April and May, and the young ones, taken from the new ſhoots, are ſeparated from thoſe gathered off the old branches. Upon ſuch diſtinctions as theſe, and on ſeparately gathering full grown and only budding leaves, are founded the different qualities of our tea.

After gathering, the leaves are dried, and ſeparated according to their ſize, &c. Bohea tea is gathered before the leaves are perfectly opened, and is made to undergo a greater degree of heat than green, to which its colour and peculiar flavour are in a great meaſure owing.

Rhubarb is an oblong tapering root, growing plentifully in China and Tartary, and likewiſe in Turkey and Ruſſia. The oriental rhubarb is in pieces of four, five, or ſix inches in length, and three or four in diameter at the top. It is of a ſmooth even ſurface, moderately heavy, but not hard; externally of a yellow colour, with an admixture of brown; internally variegated with lively reddiſh ſtreaks, forming a marbled appearance when cut; the yellow is the ground colour, and the red is diſpoſed in ſhort irregular veins, much in the manner of the darker-coloured nutmegs.

The Chineſe are very careful in their manner of drying it; they take up the root only in winter, or early in the ſpring, before the leaves begin to appear. They cut it into ſuch pieces as they think

proper,

proper, and lay it on a table in a fhady place, turning it once or twice a day for two or three days; after this they ftring the pieces on a cord at a diftance from one another, and then hang them up in a fhady place, where they may dry leifurely. It is by this management the rhubarb is rendered fo firm and folid as we find it; for, if it were hung up to dry at once in a warm airy place, it would become light and fpungy. They fay alfo, that if the root be taken up in the fummer, it is not only light and of little value, but that it has nothing of the reddifh marbling, which is one of the great characters of its goodnefs.

Sometimes the rhubarb-root is cut down the middle, and afterwards divided into pieces of four or five inches in length, which appear flat, and dry better than the round. For fome time paft flat rhubarb has fold confiderably better than round of the fame goodnefs.

Rhubarb is not fo often adulterated as damaged. To be good it fhould be particularly dry and found: if it be wet or rotten it is worthlefs. By long keeping it frequently grows mouldy and worm-eaten: and fome of the more induftrious artifts are faid to fill up the worm-holes with mixtures, and to colour the outfide of the damaged pieces with powder of the fine rhubarb, or with fome cheaper materials. The marks of its goodnefs are, the livelinefs of its bright nutmeg-colour when cut, its being firm and folid, but not flinty or hard, its being eafily pulverable, and appearing, when powdered, of a bright yellow colour, mixed with a flight coat of red. On chewing, it fhould impart a deep faffron tinge, and not prove flimy or mucilaginous in the mouth: it fhould yield a fine yellow colour on being infufed a few minutes in water. Its tafte is fomewhat acrid, bitterifh, and rather aftringent. Thofe pieces which appear green or black when broken through the middle, fhould be rejected.

Ginfeng.—This plant was formerly thought to grow no where but in China and Tartary, but it has been difcovered in North America,

particularly

particularly in Canada and Pennſylvania, whence conſiderable quantities have been exported. On comparing theſe with the Chineſe ſpecimens, no material difference could be obſerved in quality or appearance, except that the Chineſe, in general, were rather paler-coloured externally, and internally ſomewhat whiter. It is aſſerted that the American roots have been received in China as the true ginſeng, though without the ſuppoſed advantage of their method of preparing it. And it will probably render the importation of the coſtly Chineſe ſort unneceſſary.

The plant dies yearly; and the age of the root may be known by the number of ſtalks it has ſhot forth, when the marks of them are fair and intire: but very old roots not being much eſteemed, the people who gather this commodity have the precaution to cut off ſome, or even all theſe knobs, before they dry the root. The natives themſelves are ſo nice in this particular, that they will not uſe an imperfect root, nor any one but what has evident marks that the upper knob is the real head, not having more than one or two under it.

After the ginſeng is gathered, it is waſhed and ſcoured, then dipped in ſcalding water, and prepared by the following proceſs. A ſort of yellow millet is put into a veſſel with a little water, and boiled over a gentle fire: the roots are laid over the veſſel upon ſmall tranſverſe pieces of wood, being firſt covered with a cloth, or having ſome other veſſel placed over them. This gives them the colour admired by the Chineſe. When the roots are dried, they muſt be kept cloſe, in ſome dry place, otherwiſe they are in danger of corrupting, or of being deſtroyed by worms.

Ginſeng is to be choſen ſound and firm: if the worm be in it the root is worthleſs. It ſhould be moderately heavy, not very tough, but ſuch as will ſnap ſhort, and afford an agreeable ſmell. It ſhould be carefully packed, ſo as to be kept extremely dry. It

6

would not be imprudent to cut the roots through, as the Chinese frequently introduce a piece of lead to increase the weight.

The *Bezoar* is a medicinal stone, to which extravagantly-efficacious qualities were formerly attributed, but which latterly has been more lightly esteemed. It is produced in the stomach of an animal of the goat-kind, inhabiting the mountains in different parts of Persia. It is of the size of our common deer; and its coat of hair is of a grey colour inclining to a rusty brown. The head is shaped like that of our goat; the horns are near three feet in length when the creature is full grown; they are strait, and, in that part which is near their insertion on the head, they are annulated, or marked with circular risings; and all the other part is black, smooth, and glossy. The tail is near a foot in length, and is covered with hair of the same colour with that on the rest of the body, but considerably longer. The legs are very strong, and covered with short hair. The creature is very nimble, and jumps about upon the rocks like our goat.

Beside the Oriental, there are German, and other bezoars, which are less valuable. The genuine Oriental bezoar is commonly of an oval form, and between the size of a hazle-nut and a walnut: if larger, it is more valuable; if smaller, of no value. This stone is externally smooth and glossy, and composed of several shining coats, like an onion, inclosing either a powdery substance, or a nucleus, round which they are formed. The colour most valued is a shining olive or dark-green; but there are some whitish, some grey, and some of a dull yellow. Purchasers should be careful in choosing this drug. The real bezoar has little smell, and no taste. It should be as large as possible: the very small pieces should be intirely rejected, as they are most commonly increased in quantity with factitious substances resembling them.

When a red-hot needle, on entering the bezoar, occasions it to fry

and

and fhrivel, it is not genuine: if it only throw off a fmall fcale or cruft, without entering, it is good.

If, on rubbing it over paper, previoufly fmeared with chalk or quick lime, it leave a yellow taint on the former, or a green one on the latter, it is a good ftone.

If the bezoar, after foaking five or fix hours in luke-warm water, remain unchanged, in weight, colour, or confiftence, it is genuine. Nor fhould it appear fenfibly acted upon by rectified fpirit any more than by water.

The powder, after agitation with water or fpirit, fubfides uniformly and totally, leaving no greenifh matter diffolved in the liquors, as thofe powders do in which the bezoar-tincture has been imitated by certain vegetable matters.

China-Root is produced in China and in the Eaft and Weft Indies; but the qualities of the produce of the two former are the beft. It is an oblong, thick, jointed root, full of irregular knobs, of a reddifh brown colour on the outfide, and of a pale red within. The Oriental root is confiderably paler and harder than the Weft Indian.— When cut, it exhibits a clofe, fmooth, gloffy, furface. It fhould be chofen large, found, heavy, frefh, of a pale red colour internally. While new, it will fnap fhort, and look glittering within: if old, the duft flies from it when broken, and it is light and reeky. It is of no value if the worm be in it.

Gamboge. This is the concrete refinous juice of certain trees growing in Cambodia and other parts of the Eaft Indies. It is in cakes or rolls, externally of a brownifh yellow, internally of a deep red or orange-colour. It has no fmell, and when firft chewed, makes but little impreffion on the tafte; but, after remaining fome time in the mouth, difcovers a confiderable acrimony. If this drug

be

be wetted and rubbed upon the nail, it gives a curious bright lemon-colour; by which, and its appearing smooth and clear from impurities, it is known to be good. The small cakes or rolls are most profitable in London.

Ginger is plentifully produced in the East and West Indies. This root spreads itself near the surface of the earth; and, when arrived at maturity, it is dug up and dried, either in the sun or an oven.

Ginger should be chosen new, dry, well-fed, not easy to break, of a light brownish green-colour, resinous within, and of a hot pungent taste.

Ginger, green or preserved, will retain its flavour several years.—The East and West Indies furnish this commodity: and the West Indian kind is here preferred. The best is in small and somewhat transparent lumps, of a pale yellow colour: the inferior sort is more opaque and browner, being fibrous or stringy when broken.

Tamarind. The fruit of this tree is a pod, somewhat resembling a bean-pod, including several hard seeds, together with a dark-coloured vivid pulp.—This pulp is connected with the seeds by numerous tough strings or fibres; and these are freed from the outer shell. The Oriental sort is drier, darker-coloured, and has more pulp than the West-Indian. The former is sometimes preserved without addition of sugar, of which the latter has always an admixture. Red, brown, and black, are brought from the East-Indies and China: of these the black is the best; the more pulp the better.

Turmeric, a small root of an oblong figure, usually met with in pieces, from half an inch to an inch or two in length, and about an inch in circumference. Its surface is uneven and knotty, and the longer pieces are seldom strait. It is not easily cut through with a knife; heavy, hard to break, and of a glossy smooth surface when it

X

is

is cut through. Its external colour is a whitifh pale gray, with a faint yellowifh tinge: internally, when broken, it is a fine, bright, pale, unmixed yellow, when the root is frefh: by keeping, it becomes reddifh, and at length is much like faffron in the cake; it fpeedily gives a fine yellow tinge to water, and the fame colour to the fpittle when chewed. It is eafily powdered in the mortar, and, according to its age, makes either a yellow, an orange-coloured, or a reddifh, powder. It has a kind of aromatic ginger-like fmell, and a warm, bitterifh, difagreable tafte. The curcuma roots fhould be frefh, thick, heavy, and hard to be broken. This root is produced in China and Bengal: the former fort is moft valuable. Cafks are preferable to bags for packing it, the leaft damp rendering it ufelefs.

Elephants Teeth are valuable in proportion to their fize and foundnefs. The ftrait white teeth, without flaws, and not very hollow in the ftump, but folid and thick, are the beft.

> The beft weigh 50lb. (or upwards) each.
> The next ——— 40lb. (or upwards) each.
> The third ——— 30lb. (or upwards) each.
> The fourth——— 20lb. (or upwards) each.
> The fmaller are of little value.

Grains of Paradife, called, by fome, Greater Cardamums, are angular, rufty-coloured feeds, fmaller than pepper, and apparently refembling cardamom-feeds, from which, however, they differ in their properties. Thefe feeds poffefs fomewhat of the cardamom flavour, joined with the heat and pungency of pepper, while frefh and round.

Ebony is plentifully produced in Cochin-China and the ifland of Ceylon. If it be found, black, heavy, and without white wood, it will be fufficiently ufeful for moft purpofes.

Canes,

Canes, called Dragon's-Blood, muſt be found, taper, ſupple, and clouded, the more ſo the better; the middle joint muſt be thirty-ſix inches long, and the top and bottom joints eight or ten more.

Canes, called Japans, or Wangees, muſt be pliable, tough, round, and taper, the knots being at regular diſtances.

Canes, called Rattans, muſt be found, well glazed, full four yards long, not ſmaller than the little finger, and of a pale yellow colour.

Canes, called Walking Canes, to be of any value, muſt be found, heavy, tapering, twenty-eight inches long in the joint at leaſt, and the more clouded the better. Canes thirty-ſix inches long in the joint and upwards, are moſt in demand.

Cayelac, a ſweet-ſcented wood, which grows in the kingdom of Siam. The Siameſe and Chineſe burn it in their temples. It is a part of the commodities exported from Siam to China.

Tutenague is formed into blocks of about twenty pounds each. There is no difficulty in buying it, only to ſee that it be free from droſs.

Lacquered-ware and china muſt be purchaſed at diſcretion, faſhion varying their value.

Coral is in great demand in China: the beſt of which is brought from Europe, particularly from Italy and Turkey.

Candied nutmegs, mixed ſweetmeats, candied oranges, hams, preſerves, and pickles, are to be procured cheap in China; as alſo rice, and grain of all ſorts, which are ſold by weight, and not by meaſure, as in other countries.

Bird of Paradiſe. This bird is a native of New Guinea and the Iſlands in its vicinity. Theſe iſlands abound with many ſpecies of birds equally as elegant for ſhape, and as brilliant in the luſtre of their colours.

The

The bodies of the dead birds of Paradife ferve for ornament to their chiefs, who wear them faftened to their bonnets by way of aigrette: but in preparing the fkins they cut off the legs. The Dutch, who trade on thefe coafts, buy them in this condition, and carry them to China, Perfia, Surat, and other places in India; where they fell them exceffively dear to the rich inhabitants, who wear them as aigrettes in their turbans or helmets, and adorn their horfes with them. Hence thefe birds are fuppofed to have no feet; that they fleep fufpended by the two long hair-like feathers which adorn their tail; and laftly, that they hatch their eggs by carrying them under their wing. The Dutch have given a credit to thefe idle tales, which by throwing an air of the marvellous over the object of commerce, was likely to fet it off and enhance its value.

Sago. The Sago-trees, in the Molucca iflands, grow wild in abundance, and are thirty feet high, and fix in circumference: the woody bark is about one inch thick, and covers a multitude of long fibres, which, intermixing with one another, form a cover to a mafs of gummy meal. When the tree is ripe, and ready to give its farinaceous fubftance, the extremities of its palms are covered with a white duft, which tranfpires through the pores of the leaves.—Then the Malay cuts it down by the root, divides it into feveral logs, and fplits them into quarters; takes out the mafs of meal that is on the infide, which adheres to the enveloping fibres; dilutes it in common water, then ftrains it through fine linen, in order to feparate it from the fibres: when this part has loft fome of its moifture, by evaporation, it is thrown into earthen moulds of different fhapes, and left to harden and dry; is a wholefome food, and will keep good many years, for common ufe: they only dilute it with water, but fometimes they boil it. They have alfo the art to feparate the flour of this meal into fmall grains: thus prepared, it is thought proper for old and fick perfons. It is an excellent remedy for thofe affected

with

with weak lungs. When it is boiled in fair water or broth it forms a white jelly, very agreeable to the taſte. The Dutch call it the Bread-tree. It has been found on Madagaſcar, where it is called Raphia.

The Sago (or libby-tree) has, like the cocoa nut-tree, no diſtinct bark that peels off, and may be defined a long tube of hard wood, about two inches thick, containing a pulp or pith, mixed with many longitudinal fibres. The tree being felled, it is cut into lengths of about five or ſix foot; a part of the hard wood is then ſliced off, and the workman, coming to the pith, cuts acroſs (generally with an adze made of hard wood called an ubong) the longitudinal fibres and the pith together, leaving a part at each end uncut; ſo that, when it is excavated, there remains a trough, into which the pulp is again put, mixed with water, and beat with a piece of wood; then the fibres, ſeparated from the pulp, float a top, and the flour ſubſides. After being cleared in this manner by ſeveral waters, the pulp is put into cylindrical baſkets made of the leaves of the tree, and it is to be kept ſome time: theſe baſkets are generally ſunk in freſh water to keep it moiſt.

One tree will produce from two to four hundred weight of flour. I have often found large pieces of the ſago-tree on the ſea-ſhore, drifts from other countries. The ſago, thus ſteeped in the ſalt-water, had always a four diſagreeable ſmell. The leaf of the ſago-tree makes the beſt covering for houſes of all the palm kind; it will laſt ſeven years. Coverings of the nipa, or common attop, ſuch as they uſe on the ſouth-weſt coaſt of Sumatra, will not laſt half the time. When ſago-trees are cut down, freſh ones ſprout up from the roots.

We ſeldom, or never, ſee ſago in Europe but in a granulated ſtate. To bring it into this ſtate from the flour, it muſt be firſt moiſtened, and paſſed through a ſieve into an iron pot (very ſhallow) held over a fire, which enables it to aſſume a globular form. Thus,
all

all our grained fago is half baked, and will keep long. The pulp or powder, of which this is made, will alfo keep long, if preferved from the air; but if expofed it prefently turns four. The Papua oven, for this flour, is made of earthen-ware; it is generally nine inches fquare, and about four deep: it is divided into two equal parts, by a partition parallel to its fide; each of thefe parts are fubdivided into eight or nine, about an inch broad: fo the whole contains two rows of cells, about eight or nine in a row. When the cell is broad, the fago-cake is not likely to be well baked; I think the beft fized are fuch as would contain an ordinary octavo volume upon its edge: when they are of fuch a fize, the cakes will be properly baked, in the following manner: The oven is fuppofed to have at its bottom a round handle, by which the baker turns the cells downward upon the fire: when fufficiently heated, it is turned with the mouths of the cells up; and it then refts upon the handle (which is now become the bottom) as on a ftand.

Whilft the oven is heating, the baker is fuppofed to have prepared his flour, by breaking the lumps fmall; moiftening it with water, if too dry, and paffing it once or twice through a fieve; at the fame time rejecting any parts that look black, or fmell four: this done, he fills the cells with the flour, lays a bit of clean leaf over, and with his finger preffes the flour down into the cell; then covers all up with leaves, and puts a ftone or piece of wood at top to keep in the heat; and in about ten or twelve minutes the cakes will be fufficiently baked, according to their thicknefs; and bread thus baked will keep, I am told, feveral years. I have kept it twelve months, nor did vermin affect it in that time. It may not be amifs to mix a little falt with the flour.

The fago-bread, frefh from the oven, eats juft like hot rolls. I grew very fond of it. If the baker hits his time the cakes will be nicely browned on each fide. If the heat be too great, the corners of the cakes will melt into a jelly, which, when kept, becomes hard,

horny,

horny, and flinty; and if cut fresh proves insipid : when properly baked, it is in a kind of middle state, between raw and jellied.

A sago-cake, when hard, requires to be soaked in water before it be eaten, it then softens and swells into a curd, like biscuit soaked ; but if eat without soaking (unless fresh from the oven) it feels disagreeable, like sand in the mouth. No wonder then if agriculture be neglected in a country, where the labour of five men, in felling sago-trees, beating the flour, and instantly baking the bread, will maintain a hundred !

The sago-bread intended for immediate use need not be kept so long in the oven as what is intended for sea use, which may be said to resemble biscuit.

I have often reflected how well Dampier, Funnel, Roggewein, and many other circumnavigators might have fared, when passing this way in distress for provisions, had they known where to find the groves of sago-trees, with which most islands here in low latitudes abound; Morty, near Gelolo, especially. Fresh bread, made of sago-flour, and the kima (a large shell-fish like a cockle,) would have been no bad support among the Moluccas. The kima is found in abundance, of all sizes, at low water, during spring tides, on the reefs of coral rocks. From experience, I prefer the fresh baked sago-bread to our wheaten-bread; and the kima stewed, is as good as most fish, nor does one tire of it; but it must be stewed some time, or it will not be tender. Its roe will sometimes weigh six pounds; the fish altogether, when cleared of the shell, weighing twenty or thirty pounds.

Neither is the kima cockle the worse for being large. Sometimes the kima in the shell may endanger staving a small canoe getting it in. The best way is to put a stick under water into the gaping shell, which then closes, and holds fast: then drag, or lift it towards the shore, and stab it with a cutlass: it dies immediately, and can be taken out. Small kimas, about the size of a man's head, are very

good :

good: they will keep long alive if wetted frequently with falt-water.

Large fhips, navigating thofe feas, muft naturally dread the reefs of rocks, which might produce fo much good to them, if in diftrefs for provifions: but to profit from them, they muft hit the time of low water fpring-tides. The vaft fleets of Mangaio boats that fet out from Soloo and Mindano, to cruife among the Philippine Iflands againft the Spaniards, truft to the reefs of rocks, which may be faid to furround all thofe iflands, producing them fifh for their fubfiftence, as they only lay in rice or fago-bread.

The account given of the fago-tree fhows how eafily the inha-bitants of thefe countries may find fubfiftence. They have alfo, all over the Moluccas, and on New Guinea, the rima, or bread-fruit, which is the chief food of the inhabitants of Otaheite, in the South Sea; where (according to Doctor Forfter's curious computation) ten or twelve perfons live eight months upon the produce of an acre planted with this tree. I fhall therefore endeavour to fhow how many perfons may live on an acre planted with fago-trees, which growing more upright, and the roots not fpreading fo much, will confequently take up much lefs room than the rima-tree.

I fhall allow a fago-tree to take up the room of 10 feet fquared, or 100 fquare feet. Now, the contents of an acre are 43,500 fquare feet, which being divided by 100, allows 435 trees to grow within that fpace: but to give ample room, I fhall fay 300 trees only. And fuppofing that, one with another, they give 300 weight of flour: then three trees, or 900 weight, may maintain one man for a year; and an acre to be cut down would maintain 100 men for the fame time. Now, as fago-trees are 7 years a growing, I divide 100 by 7, which will then allow 14 men to be maintained for a year, on the produce of one-feventh part of an acre: immediately, or on the pro-duce of a whole acre progreffively cut, one-feventh part at a time, allowing frefh trees to fprout up.

Before

Before quitting China, I beg leave to inform the reader, that the people of that country are extremely good at making all kinds of wearing apparel. Gentlemen, therefore, proceeding to China, need not overstock themselves with cloaths, as they will be able to procure many in that way very reasonable.

Tailors Charges, at Canton;—as regulated by Mr. PEGUE, *Chief Super-cargo.*

	Tale	Mace	Can.	Cash				
For making a coat - - -	1	4	0	0				
Pockets, buckram, and lining -	0	5	5	0				
18 Buttons, at 8 cash each - -	0	1	4	4				
					2	0	9	4
For making a waistcoat - -	0	4	5	0				
Pockets and lining - -	0	2	0	0				
Buckram - - -	0	0	2	0				
Taffety to line the skirts -	0	4	3	0				
18 Buttons, at 4 cash each -	0	0	7	2				
					1	1	7	2
For making a pair of breeches -	0	3	0	0				
Pockets, lining, (waistbands) and buttons	0	1	2	0				
					0	4	2	0
For making a plain shirt - -	0	4	7	0				
Ruffled ditto - - -	0	2	2	0				
Cap - - - -	0	0	2	0				
Stock - - - -	0	0	3	0				
Short drawers - - -	0	0	6	0				
Hemming a handkerchief -	0	0	2	0				

Shoes are made in China, and also very good stockings.

Y

A PLAN

A PLAN

OF A

VOYAGE,

FROM

CALCUTTA TO THE MALAY-COAST AND CHINA.

THE firſt thing neceſſary for this voyage is to procure a ſhip about four hundred tons, pierced for eighteen or twenty guns, carrying them under cover. She ſhould have the good qualities of ſailing faſt, and carrying a large cargo, as well of dead weight as of gruff goods: under which head, I reckon pepper, rattans, &c. &c. which require much room for ſtowage.

The ſhip, in addition to the neceſſary ammunition for her guns, muſquets, and piſtols, ſhould have a box containing fifty hand granadoes in each top; together with an arm cheſt, containing muſquets and ball cartridge: that if boarded by the Malays, or pirate Lanoons, and driven from the deck, your crew may be able, from the tops, to drive them off with their granadoes and muſquets: the officers and people at the batteries below will prevent the enemy from getting poſſeſſion of the inſide of the ſhip.

Having

Having a ship every way suited to the purpose, the commander, being generally super-cargo, or executive agent, upon those voyages, should have two rooms or apartments built upon the orlop-deck, which should be so contrived, that they could at all times be kept well aired and ventilated, by scuttles in the sides of the ship: and windsails, for carrying his opium, which should not be kept in the hold, being at all times too hot; but more particularly so after any pepper is taken on board, on the coast. These rooms ought to be dunnaged, with battons of two and a half inches high, and scuppers in the wings, to let the water (if any should by accident come through the scuttles, or leak into the opium rooms) run off the deck before it could accumulate so as to damage the opium. These battons should be nailed athwart the deck, or at right angles with the keel, so as to admit the water to pass from side to side without interruption as the ship rolls. The least opposition it meets with, to check the momentum given it by the motion of the ship, will make it splash up, wet the opium chests, and if it does not damage the opium, will inevitably rot the skins in which the chests are enveloped, to the great detriment of the sale of that article.

We shall now suppose the ship is ready, armed, stored, manned, and victualled for twelve months. The commander ought to be well supplied with boats, viz. a good fast-sailing long-boat, as large as the ship could possibly stow; a second boat, or pinnace, to stow in her, also as large as possible; a third boat to turn bottom up over the former two; a yawl, to hang upon one quarter; a good paddling canoe, for dispatch upon the other quarter; and a gig, or light fast rowing boat, to hang over the stern.

The long-boat should carry two (at least) or four chambered swivels, of three pound calibre; the second boat two; and third boat one; with grape, canister, and langrage shot sufficient for them. Each boat should also be armed with a sufficient number of pikes, cutlasses, pistols, musquets, and bayonets, with an arm-chest to con-

tain

tain them; and a magazine for the neceffary ammunition. Thus, with fix boats, crews for the three firft fhould be carried, exclufive of the number of men abfolutely neceffary for working or navigating the fhip. This number of men fhould be taken on board as fepoys, in the following proportion: Suppofe the firft, or long-boat, carries ten men and a cockfwain, which in all boats is generally a tindal; the fecond boat, eight and a cockfwain; the third boat, or cutter, fix men and cockfwain; making the aggregate twenty-feven men, or one havildaur (or ferjeant), two naigs (or corporals), two drummers and a fifer, and twenty fepoys. Thefe people are, in general, good, fteady, careful men; and their fenfe of honour, as foldiers, makes them ever upon the alert; they are confequently, at all times, a check to the treachery of thofe with whom you deal; and the mifchief which in confequence await all men and fhips trading to the eaftward; as well as trufty men to fend in the chops (or boats) which carry your cargo from Whampoa to Canton.

Thus having the fhip ready ballafted with rice, a little wheat and gram (a kind of vetch), and in condition to receive her cargo by the middle of December, about which time the Company's firft opium fales commence. She may be fuppofed to take on board five hundred chefts of opium, or upwards, with a proportion of piece goods, and from twenty to forty thoufand Spanifh (head) dollars in fpecie.

Having a fair wind fhe will foon be clear of the pilot, and ought, as a firft fhip, to run for Junkceylon.

If fhe expects other fhips to follow her foon, fhe ought not to wait to fell her rice; but take fuch tin and elephants teeth as are ready for her, in barter for opium and piece goods; referving her dollars. This is the firft place fhe will find her boats ufeful in caufing difpatch.

Having finifhed here, no delay muft be admitted in this active voyage. The next port is Pooloo Pinang; where, if the Company's opium is not arrived, fhe will fell from fifty to one hundred chefts,

at,

at, perhaps, fifteen to thirty per cent. profit, for dollars and tin. If rice or piece goods are in demand, she may sell here; but the time must not be procrastinated: she may sell her wheat and gram, and go on to Salangore.

The business of this place may, or ought to be, done in two days; and from hence go on to Malacca (through the Straits of Cologne).

Here she should sell her rice, wheat, and gram; though selling the wheat is not an object, as it will find a readier sale at Batavia.

At Malacca, if she is the first ship, there is no doubt of selling one hundred chests of opium; the amount sale of which, and the rice, will be paid in dollars: this will be a good supply, with the specie, from Calcutta to proceed through the Straits of Durian to Lingin-river; where the Linginees will have collected some tin, pepper, and rattans, from the month of September until this time.

Opium will bear a better price here than at Junkceylon, Pinang, Salangore, or Malacca; though they will not take more, perhaps, than twenty chests; and the remaining cargo you receive must be paid for in Spanish dollars: they may take a few piece goods; but the sale is uncertain.

From Lingin run over to Palambang, in the Straits of Banca; and while your long-boat goes into the river (for water) send accounts of the ship's arrival to the governor of Palambang; the fishermen will send accounts to the sultan s minister (the Carangue), and others of the natives. In the meantime the ship should run into Mintow-roads, as well for shelter, as to inform the Banca people of your arrival. Whatever tin they have ready, which at this time of the year is in general pretty considerable, they will sell, and deliver it to you immediately, (for they are remarkably quick at business). You must pay them in Spanish dollars, except about ten chests of opium, which is as many, at this early part of the season, as they will venture upon.

As your business will be soon done here, run into Palambang-
roads,

roads, to pick up your long-boat; and if the governor means to do any thing, you will, upon the third or fourth day, have accounts: but fhould he not be prepared to deal with you, you may advance him what cafh you have, or he may want, opium, &c. until you return, for you have no time to lofe. You will now proceed without lofs of time to Batavia.

Immediately upon your arrival at Batavia, wait upon the Sha-bundar, and deliver him a manifeft of your cargo, referving twenty or thirty chefts of opium for the private dealers; for which, if you fell, you will receive Spanifh dollars, nutmegs, cloves, mace, pepper, and tin.

Having fpoken already of the trade of Batavia*, I will now purfue the voyage, leaving the reader to refer to the trade of that place for further information.

The principal object now in view is to realife dollars. If you cannot fell your opium at Batavia for dollars, you have no alternative but to go on to Banjar Maffeen, and thence to Paffier. Should you fail of a fale at thefe places, you muft return, and try upon the weft fide of Borneo, at Succadanna, Pontianna, Mumparva, and Sambafs, where there is no doubt but you will find a fale for the remains of your opium: for which, as well as for the articles necef-fary for your China cargo, you will be paid in gold.

Having finifhed at Batavia, Banjar Maffeen, Paffier, Succadanna, Pontianna, Mumparva, and Sambafs, crofs over for Lingin-river again, from thence to Banca and Palambang; and go again (if necef-fary to fell your gold and procure Spanifh dollars) to Batavia; which having done, return to the Straits of Banca, and continue collecting tin and pepper, until the Company's fhips pafs through the Straits for China, which generally happens in Auguft.

Having met the China fhips, who always carry fpecie (in Spanifh dollars,) put out as much of your cargo, as you think convenient, on

* See Page 48, &c.

board

board of them, for Canton; agreeing with them for the freight, which is ufually two per cent. for tin, and four per cent. for pepper; and take, upon the cargo depofited, as a guarantee, as much of their fpecie, payable at Canton (upon Refpondentia), as you think you fhall have occafion for to finifh your purchafes, and fill up your cargo again, preparatory to your going to China. For this loan of Spanifh dollars you ufually pay fix per cent. payable one month after your arrival at Canton.—This is an object of confequence to the commanders of the European fhips, who, without trouble, rifk, or delay, clear twelve per cent. upon the value of the cargo they receive on board, which is feldom lefs than one lack (or one hundred thoufand Spanifh dollars), or twelve thoufand Spanifh dollars, equal to three thoufand pounds fterling, for freight and ufe of money for three months.

Your bufinefs being finifhed with the European fhips, you are to confider whether there is time to run over to Mumparva, Succadanna, or Sambafs again: if not, keep about the Straits of Banca; going to Lingin oecafionally, until the 10th or 15th; but by no means exceed the 20th of September in the Straits of Banca.

Having finifhed your feafon in the Straits, leave them, and run to Tringano, where take on board whatever is ready; tin, pepper, rattans, wax, or beetlenut, and make the beft of your way to China.

It being now very late in September, or probably the early part of October, when the fouth-weft monfoon is nearly done in the China feas, it may not be inapplicable to give fome advice about fecuring your paffage to China, which cannot be done againft the ftrong currents, which at this feafon begin to fet out of the great Pacific Ocean, through the Straits of Formofa, and to the S.W. down the China Sea.

Leaving Tringano, fhape a courfe for the fouth-end of Pooloo Condore: and having paffed it, fteer for Pooloo Sapata, by Mr. Nicholfon's Directions: and having feen Pooloo Sapata, keep on that

I tack,

tack, (fhould the wind be againſt you,) on which you can make
moſt northing, until you are in the latitude of 11° 30′ N.; keep then
ſtanding to the N.E. as I believe you are to the northward of all the
ſhoals: but if the wind will admit of your making more northing, follow Mr. Nicholſon's Directions for making Goat Iſland, and work
up the weſt coaſt of Luconia, as far as Cape Bajadore; from whence
ſtretch over for the coaſt of China, taking care to allow the Pratas
a good birth, as they are a dangerous chain of rocks and ſhoals, and
cannot be diſtinguiſhed any great diſtance from a ſhip's deck.

Along the weſt coaſt of Luconia, from September to June, there
is a current (or rather a counter eddy, from the great current which
ſets to the S.W. down the China Sea) ſetting to the northward:
and from September until April, upon the ſame coaſt, you have land
and ſea winds; all which aſſiſt a ſhip very much in going to the
northward and ſecuring her paſſage to China; which ſhe can never
ſucceed in making (at this late ſeaſon) in the middle of the China
Sea; except by a great chance, as ſome ſhips did in the year 1787,
who, upon the change of wind after a heavy tuffoon, ſteered direct
for the Ladroon, and got in; but, had they had twenty-four hours
further run, they would either have been obliged to ſtretch over for
the weſt coaſt of Luconia, or have gone to winter at Hainan. Inſtead of ſteering directly for the Ladroon, had they ſteered over for
Cape Bajadore, they muſt have been aſſured of their paſſage, let the
wind change as it may. I therefore recommend the cautious navigator to make the coaſt of Luconia (if late in the ſeaſon); and
though it may delay his voyage a day or two, it ſecures him a paſſage
and good landfall without riſk or anxiety.

Having cleared the Pratas, and made the coaſt of China, ſteer for
Pedro Branco, and paſſing to the ſouthward of it, run for the Great
Lema, and paſs to the northward of it; then ſteer for the iſland of
Linting Fora, and if late in the evening, or night is coming on,
anchor under the lee of it, and wait for day-light to run into Macao-

7   roads;

roads; weigh at day light, and pafs under the Peak of Lantou, between it and Longfhitoa, fteer over for Macao-town, and anchor in any convenient depth of water, or diftance off the entrance to the town you think proper. In all probability you will have pilots applying to you before you are near Linting Fora; if fo, I would advife your having one, as the fum you pay for his fervices is trifling, (ten to twenty Spanifh dollars), and you have the ufe of his boat to go to Macao, which is fafer under his management than any of your own boats.

Having now brought you to Macao, follow the former Inftruétions for going up to Whampoa and conduéting your bufinefs at Canton.

For your returning cargo to India, your price current, and Calcutta commiffions, muft be your guide; and you muft be diligent to endeavour to get difpatched from China early in November, to get to Calcutta, if poffible, before Chriftmas-day; where your men, lafcars, for manning your fhip, which requires from one month to fix weeks to effeét, fhould be ready impreffed, and your eaftern cargo prepared for going on board, that if you mean to follow the eaftern trade, you may be able to purfue the rout prefcribed in the foregoing fheets.

In this Plan I have given a great deal of ground for a fhip to run over; it will be therefore neceffary to calculate your time, which muft be fuited to the feafons and change of the monfoons, otherwife you will not be able to perform the engagement, and in confequence, inftead of a faving, will make a confiderable lofing voyage for thofe interefted in the concern: it muft therefore appear obvious, to every judicious merchant, that the executive agent, on a voyage of fuch extent and importance, fhould not only be a very aétive perfevering man, but a man of knowledge, intimately acquainted with the nature of the winds, currents, and trade of the Malay còaft and places to the eaftward, as well as adding the abilities of an able navigator to his other qualities.

Z

The

The ship being completely ready for sea, with all her cargo on board except her opium, (the Company's first sale for which is usually between the 20th of November and 8th of December: suppose we say the sale commences the 15th of December, that we might not be too sanguine in our prospects), and say that article is cleared, and put on board the 17th of December.

This being a favourable season, with fresh N.E. winds and clear weather, (the fogs not coming on in the river Hoogley before the latter end of January or beginning of February,) the ship ought to put her pilot out on the 25th of December, (which is allowing a great while,) and ought to be at Junkceylon on or before the 3d of January: leave that the 8th and be at Pooloo Pinang the 11th, or say the 12th, (which is allowing rather too much time,) as she will meet with dispatch here. She must sail (out of the south channel) the 15th of January, and ought to be at Salangore the 18th; leave that the 20th, and arrive at Malacca the 25th of January. As her own boats will carry her ballast on board (having three constantly employed) from Red Island, and the shore boats (which are to be had in great numbers) will take her rice, wheat, and gram, on shore, she ought to sail the 1st of February; be at Lingin (going through the Straits of Durian, as there is no trade at Rhio since the Dutch took possession of that island and place) the 3d or 4th, and leave it the 7th. She will be at Palambang the 8th or 9th of February, at Mintow the 10th, and back to Palambang-roads the 11th. She will sail for Batavia the 12th, and arrive there the 15th or 16th of February. Her stay at Batavia should not exceed one month, as by this dispatch she will be certainly the first opium ship there, being able to do her business quicker, and with more dispatch, at the several ports she stops at, than the vessels who go down the west coast of Sumatra (who have more places to touch at, less trade, and more detention) and through the Straits of Sunda to Batavia.

We

We fuppofed, in the Plan, that the opium would not fell at Batavia: and we have in confequence loft a whole month, which brings us to the 16th of March. The fhip muft now run for Banjar Maffeen, where fhe will arrive the 25th of March, and leave it the 1ft of April. She will be at Paffier-bar the 7th; allow her to be here until the 20th, and be again (if neceffary) at Banjar Maffeen the 25th. She will have a fhorter paffage from Paffier to Banjar Maffeen, than from Banjar Maffeen to Paffier, on account of the monfoon changing at the full moon in March: fay, fhe leaves Banjar Maffeen the 1ft of May; fhe will be at Sambafs, Pointanna, Momparva, and Succadana, until the 10th of June: fhe will be again at Lingin the 20th of June; at Banca and Palambang the 25th of June. Sail, if fhe has any gold or opium left on hand, (if fhe has not, fhe may keep in the Straits of Banca,) for Batavia on the 5th of July, arrive the 15th, fay the 20th, do her bufinefs, and fail the 1ft of Auguft. She will be in the Straits of Banca the 5th of Auguft, ready to intercept the Company's fhips for China; and follow the former part of this Plan. The lateft time of continuing in the Straits, collecting tin and pepper, being now arrived, viz. the 20th of September, you leave the Straits of Banca; and on the 24th you will arrive at Tringano. The feafon being far advanced, and probably other veffels having juft failed, there will be little delay in fhipping off any cargo that might be ready: you will therefore fail from Tringano the 29th of September, but fay the 1ft of October. Take the eaftern range prefcribed, and you will get to Canton by the 25th of October, or at fartheft the 1ft of November. You fhould be particularly cautious at this feafon of the year, in thofe feas, to have your fhip well prepared for bad weather; your boats, booms, &c. &c. well fecured and frapped, by the time you get the length of Pooloo Sapata: and be particularly guarded againft the prognoftic of a tuffoon, by obferving if the fun fets red, and tinges the clouds of the fame colour; in the weftern quarter parti cularly, if this appearance is on the 17th, 18th, 19th, or 20th day

of

of the moon's age. By being prepared in this manner, in the year 1790, I faved my fhip, from fuffering any lofs; when a very fine Danifh Eaft-Indiaman, and the largeft I had ever feen at Canton, came in totally difmafted, having loft every ftick, bowfprit not excepted; and fuffered fo much in the gale, that fhe was condemned at Whampoa as unfit for further fervice. Many of the Bombay fhips fuffered in the fame gale, particularly the Surat Caftle, and Shaw Byramgore.

Upon comparing accounts with the Guftavus's (the Danifh Eaft-Indiaman's) reckoning, I could not be more than ten or twelve leagues diftance, to the eaftward of her.

By difpatch, your fhip may leave Whampoa the 20th of November, and arrive at Calcutta, by taking the infide paffage to the weftward of the Paracels, (as hereafter defcribed), by Chriftmas-day.—The paffage has been made in twenty-five days, including two days delay at Malacca, and three days at Pooloo Pinang. But having taken the longeft round, and allowed more than fufficient time for the fhip to make her paffages; with the precaution to carry the fhip from port to port, by taking the advantage of the feafons, and making her carry a fair wind all round the whole track; I think I have made fufficient allowance for her detention at each port to enable her to perform her voyage in the time I have mentioned.

It muft be allowed it is an active, bufy, as well as a dangerous voyage; and much, or the whole of the fuccefs of it, refts upon the knowledge, vigilance, and induftry of the executive agent.

DIRECTIONS

FOR ENTERING THE STRAITS OF MALACCA FROM THE CHINA
SEA, THE ANCHORAGE AT POOLOO AURO, AND SAILING
THROUGH THE STRAITS.

THE proper bearings for anchoring at Pooloo Auro, which moft
fhips do who make the ifland in the morning, are Pooloo Timoan
fhut in with Pooloo Piffang, bearing N.W. diftance nine leagues,
Pooloo Tingey (or High Peak Ifland) W. by S. eight leagues, and
the extremes of Pooloo Auro from S.E. half E. to N.W. half N.—
The watering place will then bear N. by E. and your diftance off
fhore half a mile.

If you have a frefh breeze, weigh from Pooloo Auro about eleven
or twelve o'clock at night, fo as to be 10 or 12 leagues from it by
daylight. The courfe, after being clear of the ifland, is S. by E. to
avoid a funken rock, which bears fouth from the body of the ifland
about feven leagues, until the ifland bears N. half W. You have generally a current fetting from the China feas, and runs about S.S.E.
one and a-half or two miles an hour. With thefe bearings, and 12
leagues from Pooloo Auro, you will (if clear) fee Bintang-hill bearing S. by W. about 14 leagues diftance; ftand on, until Bintang
bears S.S.W.; upon which bearings you may fteer down with
fafety. Should you bring Bintang-hill to bear S. by W. half W. or
S. by W. you will have overfalls, and irregular foundings, from 17
to 13 and to 7 fathoms. The fhip Shaw Ardifeer run down for
Bintang-hills, keeping them in one, bearing S. by W., and fhoaled
among overfalls to feven fathoms; but, by hauling off, deepened to

17 fathoms

17 fathoms immediately; and then hauled round the reef off Point Romania, the rocks off the Point bearing W. by S. She kept that fhore on board, not coming under 14 fathoms.

It is frequently foggy or hazy, and you cannot fee Bintang-hills. Though you have loft fight of Pooloo Auro, keep between 20 and 26 fathoms, foft ground, until you fee the hill; for fhould you bring Barbacet to bear S.W. by S. or S.W. you will find it difficult to get to the weftward, on account of the current. Should you fee the low land about Barbacet-hill, you will have under 20 fathoms, and will fhoal faft towards the fhore; edge to the fouthward, until you deepen your water again, and have nearly loft fight of the low land, which you will do about fix and a-half or feven leagues off, and will then have Bintang-hill bearing S.S.W. You may run until Barbacet-hill bears W. by S.; and if in 20 fathoms, haul up until you fhoal your water, for you may then confider yourfelf on the edge of the bank ; and when you have brought Barbacet-hill to the northward of weft, you will have 13 or 14 fathoms; and diftance from the low land of Bintang nine leagues. You may confider yourfelf now, to the fouth-ward of the bank; and may haul up W.S.W. and W. by S. When you have brought Bintang to bear S. half W. five or fix leagues, Pedro Branco may be feen bearing S.W. by W. one-quarter W. dif-tance four or five leagues, your depth of water 19 fathoms, and Barbacet-hill W. one-quarter N. fix leagues. When Bintang-hill bears S. in 24 fathoms, Pedro Branco will bear S.W. diftance three leagues.

There is a fmall hill near Bintang-hill; when in one, they bear S. half E. You may pafs Pedro Branco in 18 fathoms, and from thence keep mid-channel. If obliged to turn to windward, ftand no nearer the fouth fhore than 13 fathoms, and towards the rocks off Romania-point to any diftance you pleafe, until you come up to Johore-river. When you come up with the point (of Johore-river), do not come nearer on that fide than 15 fathoms, until you have

paffed

paffed two red ftrands on the weft fide of the river, for there is a fhoal lies out from them. When the rocks off Point Romania bear N. by E. half E. diftance five leagues, St. John's ifland will bear W. by S. half S. You may pafs this ifland at any diftance you pleafe. From hence to Barn Ifland your courfe is W. by S. In the midway, for fix or eight leagues, you will have 14 or 16 fathoms.— If you cannot get through before night anchor upon this bank; for off of it you will have deep water, 40 or 50 fathoms, and even 60 fathoms, with foul ground. There are feveral fmall rocks on the fouth fide, juft above water, which you will avoid, by keeping mid-channel.

When St. John's Ifland bears N.E. by E. three leagues, Barn Ifland will bear N. half W. diftance four leagues; then you will per-ceive feveral openings; but Barn Ifland and the True Paffage is known by two fmall rocky iflands, with a few trees on them, (at the fouth end of it,) called The Rabbit and Coney, or the Paffage Iflands. They appeared before the year 1781 like rabbits fquatting: but fome trees, which formed like ears, were cut down by the mafter of a French privateer. Leave thefe iflands on the ftarboard hand (or north fide) of you; and Red Ifland on the larboard hand (or fouth fide). The Paffage Iflands (or Rabbit and Coney) are fteep to. If running in the night, and cannot keep clofe to Barn Ifland in 13 or 14 fathoms, you had better come to an anchor, for fear of being fet upon Tree Ifland. In the mid-way between Barn and Tree Ifland, you will have 25 fathoms water. If you get fo far to the fouthward as to fhoal to 15 fathoms, you will be very near Tree Ifland, and fhould haul over for Pooloo Oular (or Snake Ifland). If Barn Ifland bears E.N.E. half E. from you, diftance off fhore two or three leagues, Green Ifland and the rocks will bear from S.W. by W. half W. to W. by S., diftance five miles; and the northern Carrimon will bear W. one-quarter S. fix or feven leagues, and you will have 25 fathoms water.

6

When

When you come up with the two iflands of the Carrimons, (called the Two Brothers,) or when they bear weft of you fix leagues, you will fee Pooloo Coccob N.W. half W.; it is eafily known, being a low flat ifland and always green; towards the N.W. extreme Tanjong Bolus will bear N.W.; the high land of Pooloo Piffang N.W. half W.; Tree Ifland S.E. half E.; and Barn Ifland E. by S. diftance three or four leagues.

Do not come nearer Pooloo Coccob than 17 fathoms, as that is very near the fhore; and before you can go about, you will be in 15 fathoms. You may ftand to the S.W. till you are in 12 fathoms, and then go about. After you have paffed Pooloo Coccob, you may ftand into what water you pleafe upon that fide, until you are to the weftward of Pooloo Piffang. When paffed Pooloo Piffang, if you ftand to the weftward two or three leagues, you will fhoal your water very faft. Come no nearer than 10 or 12 fathoms, then ftand in fhore until you bring Pooloo Piffang to bear S.E., then you will be in feven fathoms, and have the tree open. If you bring Pooloo Piffang to bear S.E. by E. you will fhoal your water very quick, and deepen again for two or three cafts. You fhould not come under eight or nine fathoms while you have fight of Pooloo Piffang, nor bring it to the fouthward of S.E., for between Formofa and Pooloo Piffang are great overfalls. Pooloo Piffang is fteep to, and you will have 10 or 11 fathoms half a cable's length from the fhore. Keep Pooloo Piffang E.S.E. and you will lead down in the beft part of the channel. From Mount Formofa to the Water Iflands the coaft is bold to; Mount Formofa bearing E. half S., Mount Morra N. half E. off fhore three leagues, in 18 fathoms water, you will fee the Water Iflands bearing N.W.; they are fteep to, and muft be all left upon the ftarboard hand (or to the northward) to go into Malacca-roads; where you may anchor in 8, 7, 6, or 5 fathoms, the church bearing N. by E.

From Malacca-roads to Cape Richardo, the courfe is N.W. by N.
diftance

diſtance 10 leagues; depth of water from 16 to 24 fathoms from two to ſeven miles off ſhore. There is a bank with three or four fathoms water on it, about three or four miles off, and rocks above water about a mile and a-half off. Near the Cape the tides run very ſtrong N.W. and S.E. the ſoundings are uneven with overfalls from 15 to 30 fathoms. From Cape Richardo the courſe is N.W. by W. depth of water from 25 to 16 fathoms; and, when to the N.W. of the bank that lies four leagues N.W. from the Cape, and only three miles off ſhore, ſteer more northerly for Parcellar-hill, which will, when bearing N.E. by E., be on with a ſmall bank of gravel, having 13 fathoms on it, within and without which is deep water. When you have brought the hill to bear E. one-quarter N., E. half N., or E., edge over to the weſtward, and keep the bearings on from E. one-quarter N. to E. half S., which I have, by repeated croſſing, found the beſt marks and evenest depths of water in the channel.— This channel is between the North and South Sand Heads, and in it the tides run very ſtrong, eſpecially the ebb, which runs longer W.N. W. than the flood, which ſets about E.S.E. When you are half over, if the weather is clear, you will get ſight of the Round Arroe, bearing W. one-quarter S. ſeven or eight leagues; Parcellar-hill will bear E. half S. 9 or 10 leagues; ſtill ſtanding to the weſtward, you will ſoon ſee the Long Arroe, and the ſmall rocks which lie about it.— When this is ſeen, you are to the weſtward of all the ſands, and in mid-channel. Between the rocks and the ſands is deep water, from 30 to 50 fathoms; and cloſe to the rocks 15 and 16 fathoms, ouzey ground. On the ſand ſide you frequently ſhoal ſuddenly to 10 fathoms; though I would adviſe keeping along the weſtern edge of the north ſand, for the benefit of anchoring in ſhoal water. When the tide was againſt me, I have run upon the weſt ſide of the north ſand, in ſeven to five fathoms, very even ground, and never had an overfall of more than a quarter of a fathom at a time. The tides flow Eaſt and Weſt at the Arroes, and ebb longeſt and run much

A a

ſtronger

ftronger than the floods, particularly in the N.E. monfoon; for though there is no regular monfoon in the Straits of Malacca, the quantity of water thrown into them from the China Sea in the N.E., and from the Indian Ocean and Bay of Bengal in the S.W. monfoon, muft affect the tides greatly in the different feafons; confequently the tides are more regular in the S.W. monfoon. (Times are divided in India by the N.E. and S.W. or dry and wet monfoons.) Being clofe up with the Arroes, and clear of the fands, fteer N. by W. half W., or N. by W. three-quarters W. for Pooloo Jarra, which bears from the Arroes N. 10° W. diftance 25 leagues, which ifland you may pafs on either fide, it being deep water clofe to. I would recommend keeping to the eaftward of it, as you will be lefs liable to calms along the Malay fhore than in the middle of the Straits, or on the coaft of Sumatra, where you are alfo expofed to violent fqualls, and perpetual thunder, lightning, and rain.

From Pooloo Jarra to Pooloo Perah, the courfe is N.W. by N. diftance 42 leagues, the depth of water, 40, 30, and 20 fathoms; but do not go near Pooloo Perah, but keep to the eaftward, (it lies W. N.W. half N. or N.W. by W. half W. diftance from Pooloo Pinang 20 leagues,) as you will be lefs liable to calms, and fteer for the Pooloo Laddas; and being clear of them, fhape your courfe for your deftined port.

The former tracks that were ufed by fhips paffing through the Straits of Malacca, were along the Sumatra fhore; but experience proves to us that it is not only the moft dangerous, on account of lightning and fqualls, but alfo moft fubject to delay, from calms and currents. Along the Malay fhore you have regular tides, few calms, fcarce any fqualls, and none very fevere, with regular land and fea breezes; all which advantages are more than fufficient, I imagine, to induce every perfon, in charge of fhips, to take the track along the Malay fhore. For further information I give the following

DIRECTIONS

DIRECTIONS

FROM THE NICOBARS THROUGH THE STRAITS OF MALACCA.

THE fouth end of the Nicobars lie in latitude 6° 48′ N.; from whence fteer E. by N. for Pooloo Boutan; the fouth end of which lies in latitude 6° 30′ N.; from thence fteer to go between Pooloo Perah, lying in latitude 5° 30′ N. and the fouth end of Pinang lying in 5° 18′ N. Pooloo Boutan is a large high round ifland, with feveral fmall ones near it. The Laddas are high rugged iflands, running in ridges from the mountains to the fea, with beautiful vallies between them. Pooloo Perah is a barren rock, as high as a very large fhip's hull, and may be feen fix or feven leagues. On the north fide is a white patch, like a boat's fail. From between Pooloo Perah and Pooloo Pinang, (which is a high ifland covered with trees,) to the very fummit, fteer S.E. by E. half E. for Pooloo Jarra, in latitude 4° N. the diftance is about 42 leagues. From Pooloo Jarra fteer S. by E. three-quarters E. for the Long Arroe, lying in latitude 2° 20′ N. the diftance is about 25 leagues. Between the Arroes and Parcellar-hill is the channel (to crofs over): between the north and fouth fand-heads the breadth of the channel is about four leagues in the wideft part. The Arroes bearing S.W. you will fhoal gradually to the fouthward, and towards the rocks to 16 fathoms; I have been as clofe as feven fathoms, ouzey ground; but this is clofer than can anfwer any purpofe, except to avoid, or intimidate an enemy lefs acquainted with the navigation of thefe Straits. Thofe rocks lie about a league to the N.E. of the Long Arroe.

Standing over to the eaftward you will deepen to 20, 30, 40, and 50 fathoms; you will again fhoal regularly to 30 fathoms. and then

have

have overfalls upon the weft edge of the north fand; fometimes 20,
25, 15, and, perhaps, 10 or 12 fathoms: it will again deepen to 15
fathoms, with overfalls to 22 and 25 fathoms. Mr. Nicholfon's
Directions are fo very clear, that I need not fay any more than what
has been already obferved in crofting this channel. The flood-tides
fet S.E. by S., and ebb N.W. by N. between the fands and the
Malay-fhore.

The channel between Parcelar-hill and the fands is not above four
leagues broad, the foundings irregular, from 15 to 30 fathoms.—
Parcelar-hill bearing N.E. by E. and two leagues off fhore, I had
foundings on a fmall gravel bank, 13 fathoms only, and deep water
all round it.

From Parcelar-hill to Cape Richardo the courfe is S.E. half S.
diftance four leagues; but the coaft and the edge of the fouth
fand lie S.E. half E. or S.E. by E.

About N.W. from Cape Richardo lies a fhoal, upon which a large
Portuguefe fhip ftruck in the year 1790, but by keeping Cape
Richardo S.E. by E. half E. and Parcelar-hill N.W. half W. you
will go to the fouthward of it, in 12, 15, or 20 fathoms. Cape
Richardo lies in latitude 2° 17′ N.; a moderately high bluff, not
unlike Mount Dilly (on the Malabar coaft), though not near fo high,
with a fmall rock (or ifland) near it, and projecting its bold head
into the channel, fo as to form a bay on each fide of it. Being
about a league off the Cape, (this being the narroweft part of the
Straits to the northward of Malacca,) you may fee the low land of
Sumatra from the deck. The tide flows off Cape Richardo nine
hours full and change, and rifes about 12 feet perpendicular; the
foundings very uneven, having overfalls from 17 to 30 fathoms.

The courfe from Cape Richardo to Malacca-roads is S.E. by S.
but attention muft be paid to the tide, as it throws very much off
fhore; the depth of water 16 to 24 fathoms. A S.E. by E. courfe

(well

(well fteered), diftance 10 leagues, will carry you into nine fathoms in Malacca-roads.

The outer Water Ifland and Cape Richardo bear N.W. three-quarters W. and S.E. three-quarters E. of each other, diftance 12 leagues.

Being bound to the fouthward from Malacca, you muft go to the weftward of all the Water Iflands. One mile from the outward one you will have 20 fathoms water. From hence fteer S.E. or S.E. by S.; or if obliged to work to windward, you may ftand toward Sumatra to 15 fathoms, and in fhore again to 20 fathoms. You will have fome cafts of 30, 35, or 38 fathoms mid-channel.

I have already, in my former Directions, referred to Mr. Nicholfon's Inftructions for failing through thefe Straits, and have always found them very fafe; and upon which you may borrow, if you are fure of your fhip, in a working wind.

DIRECTIONS

FROM NARCONDAM TO RANGOON-BAR

From Narcondam, make your courfe good about N.E. by N. till you get in 12 fathoms water; then fteer N.N.E. and N. in for the land; but let the tides be guarded againft, and the foundings your guide.

The tides to the weftward of Barague-point run W.N.W. and E.S.E. and your water will fhoal very quick (fhould you be to the weftward of the Point in 20 fathoms, fand and mud) into eight and
a-half,

a-half, feven, and fix and a-half fathoms, hard fand; but in the proper track you will have fand and mud only.

China Buckeer is a high grove of trees very confpicuous, there being no fuch other, in appearance, on the whole coaft: it reprefents a long low barn, at the diftance of about two leagues and a-half, bearing N. by E. which is the beft land-fall you can make.

After bringing it to bear W. by S. or W.S.W. you will fee the Elephant-grove, which forms the weft fide of Rangoon-river; on the eaft fide are feveral palmira trees. Bring the Elephant to bear N. by W. or N.N.W. and you will have, at high water neap tides, fix fathoms and a-half: with thefe bearings and depth of water, come to an anchor, and fend your boat to Rangoon for a pilot.

The foundings to the eaftward of the Bar are ftiff mud; the tide fets S.S.W. and N.N.E.: when you find this to be the cafe, do not come under 12 fathoms; but get to the weftward as faft as poffible on the ebb-tide; and be guided by the tides and foundings till you alter the foundings to quite foft mud, and the tides fet N.E. and S.W.; then you may fafely fteer in for the land, where your foundings will fhoal very gradually, until you are in fix and a-half or feven fathoms water, and can fee the land from the maft-head; fteer then into about five fathoms and a-half, and do not come under; but this fhould depend on the fhip's draft of water, as no hard foundings are found until you have lefs than four or three fathoms water, which is much nearer than you have any occafion to come, as in five fathoms you diftinguifh every object with your glafs. The latitude of Rangoon-bar is 16° 28' N.

FURTHER DIRECTIONS

FOR PEGUE—WITHOUT A PILOT.

IF your obfervations for latitude are not to be depended upon, the beft way is to make the ifland of Norcondam, and run from it, fo as to make 2° 10' eafting: by the time you are in 15° 20' N., then if you are under 12 fathoms, you may be certain you are well to the weftward of the Bar: run to the northward until you fhoal to fix fathoms (low water), and if you can then afcertain your latitude within five miles, and are near 16° 20' N. you are ftill well to the weftward of the Bar, and may fteer along fhore N.E. or N.E. by N.; and if on this laft courfe you do not fhoal your water, you are near China Buckeer, and will fee it bearing N. or N. by W. of you; it is very confpicuous, being a long thick grove of trees, ap-pearing like an ifland, and forming two rivers. Running along the fame courfe, in fix fathoms (low water) you will foon fee the weftern grove, called The Elephant, which lies on the weft fide of the river: and on the eaft fide is a long grove of palmira-trees; but the beft mark for knowing the river is the courfe above-mentioned, and your foundings; for when you deepen on a N.E. by N. courfe, a fathom or two (all at once), you are abreaft of the Bar, and may haul up immediately, in the fwafh of the river, paying attention to the tides, as the flood-tides fet very rapidly to the eaftward until it is half done. The beft channel is, to bring the two points that appear to form the river, about a fhip's length open, and fteer right up with this mark on, or fteer between five and feven fathoms water on the weftern fide: for on the eaft fide there is 10, 12, and 14 fathoms clofe

6   along-

along-fide the middle ground. As foon as you are abreaft of the weftern grove, keep the weftern fhore aboard. The channel is wide and free from danger all the way to the upper Chokey. The people who keep guard there (chokey wallahs) will inform you where it is. Take great care the tide does not horfe you to the eaftward of the channel in going over the Bar; and keep the lead going brifkly, as the track recommended is clofe to the edge of the weftern fand.

FURTHER DIRECTIONS

BY CAPT. GREAVES.

In the N.E. monfoon, coming from Bengal, it is proper to make Cape Negrais; from whence fteer for Diamond Ifland, and to round the Alguada Rocks; which, when you have done, fteer to the S.E. to fall in with Barague-point: and between the months of October and February keep, without fear, in feven fathoms upon the fands in a large fhip, and in five fathoms in a fmall one; but no nearer, as you will approach the breakers. My reafon for borrowing fo clofe upon the fand is, that you have no flood at this feafon; but, from the rivers, a continual current fetting to the W.S.W. and round to the N.W. But, between February and July, when you are round Barague-point, you will find the flood fetting N.E. by N. and the ebb S.W. by S. In falling in with Barague-point you fhould not have any dependence upon your dead reckoning, as that may miflead you, where the currents run fo ftrong; but keep your lead conftantly going, and when you deepen on the eaftern courfe and find a mixture of fhells with your foundings, you will have the river Dalla open, and will be in the latitude 15° 40′ N. or, perhaps, a

mile

mile or two more, or lefs, in 10 or 12 fathoms. From this fituation I fhall fhape no courfe, as the winds are generally very variable, and far eafterly; but you may ftand on boldly, and make the land in latitude 16° 10' N.; you will then fee China Buckeer, and will know it by a clump of trees, making like an old barn. There is a mud flat which lies off here, on which you will have three and three-quarters or four fathoms; yet, without fear, ftand on to the northward, but take care not to deepen your water to more than feven fathoms, at which depth you will have a fandy bottom, and will fee The Elephant (or weftern grove), bearing N. by W.; keep well in to the weftward in five or fix fathoms, until you fee the eaftern grove, the Grove of Palmiras, which will bear N.N.E.; the Elephant N.W. by N. or N.W. northerly, are the beft bearings to anchor: and from thence fend your boat in for a pilot, to take you over the Bar, and from thence to Rangoon.

FURTHER DIRECTIONS

FOR PEGUE BAR.

Near the Eaftern Grove, at the entrance of Rangoon-river, (or river Serian,) there appears a forked tree; and when the Elephant bears N.W. by W. half W. the forked tree N. by E. then you have the channel open; with thefe bearings on, you will fee Ental-point, about a fail's breadth open with the weftern grove (or Elephant). Thefe are the leading marks that the pilots ufe for keeping the channel, and is the beft track over the Bar. Your depth of water will be five and a-half, four and a-half, to four fathoms, obferving to borrow on the weftern fide, which is not dangerous, though you fhould un-

B b   fortunately

fortunately take the ground, which will never happen, except you fhut in Ental-point. The beft time of tide to crofs the Bar is at half-flood, when you have the *true* fet. If clofe to the foot of the Bar, I would not recommend weighing before half-flood, as you would be liable to be fet upon the middle ground, which is dangerous; to avoid which, obferve, if Ental-point opens too faft with the Elephant (or weftern grove), you had better anchor until you find the tide fet true.

Another caution to be obferved to avoid this fhoal.—As you approach it you will deepen your water, with irregular foundings, from five and fix to nine fathoms, and the next caft aground. This accident I have (fays the writer) met with frequently, in a fix-oared cutter. The tide of flood fets very ftrong over the middle ground. Should you get aground on this fhoal, you need not be under any apprehenfion of *falling* off, although fo fteep, as I have never known any veffel to do fo. The Betfey (Captain Lawrie) was aground on this fhoal (in March 1788), though he had a pilot on board; alfo the fhip Ganjaver, (Captain Jamefon); but got off again by their anchors.

FURTHER DIRECTIONS

FROM NORCONDAM TO RANGOON.

FROM Norcondam, fteer N.E. by N. until you get into 12 fathoms water; then fteer N.N.E. and N. for the land, being governed folely by your foundings.

The tides to the weftward of Barague-point run W.S.W. and E.N.E. nearly, and you will fhoal your water very quick. Should

you

you be to the weſtward of the point, from 20 fathoms, ſand and mud, ſtand into eight, ſeven, and ſix fathoms, hard ſand; but in the proper channel you will have all ſoft mud.

China Buckeer is a high grove of trees, and cannot be miſtaken, there being no other like it in appearance on the coaſt; it reſembles a long low barn. At the diſtance of two leagues and a-half you will ſee this grove bearing N. by E. which is the beſt landfall you can make. When you bring it to bear W. by S. or W.S.W. you will ſee the Elephant (or weſtern grove), which is on the weſt ſide or Rangoon-river: and upon the eaſt ſide you will ſee ſeveral high palmira-trees, which are called the Eaſtern Grove. Bring the Elephant to bear N. by W. or N.N.W. and you will have at high water neap tides ſix fathoms and a-half: come to an anchor, and ſend your boat and an officer to Rangoon for a pilot.

The ſoundings to the eaſtward of the Bar are ſtiff mud, and the tide ſets N.N.E. and S.S.W. nearly. When you find by theſe marks you are to the eaſtward, do not come under 12 fathoms, but haul out to the weſtward as faſt as poſſible (upon the ebb), and be guided by the tides and ſoundings until you get ſoft mud, and find the tides ſet N.E. and S.W.; then you may ſafely ſteer in for the land, where your ſoundings will ſhoal gradually to ſeven and ſix and a-half fathoms. When you ſee the land from the maſt-head, ſteer into five and a-half fathoms, and do not come under; but this will depend upon your ſhip's draft of water, as no hard ſoundings are experienced until you have paſſed four or three fathoms, which is much nearer than you can have occaſion to go, as in five fathoms you will diſtinguiſh every object with your glaſs. The latitude of Rangoon-bar is 16° 28′ N.

Capt. Burgoyne obſerves, That in the latitude 14° 30′ N. you will get ſoundings 42 fathoms, which is the meridian of Barague-point; and from thence ſteer to the northward, to get into 14 or 15 fa-

thoms,

thoms, and keep thefe foundings, fteering E.N.E. making allowance for the fet of the tides. After you have carried thefe foundings fome time, you will deepen quickly two or three fathoms; then you are clear of Barague-point, and may ftand in to the northward, until you fhoal to fix, or five and a-half fathoms; you will then fee the land, and be cautious to keep foft foundings, clear of the leaft fand or ouze. Should you find fand or ouze, haul out as faft as poffible, as the channel is fine foft mud. The tides to the eaftward of the Bar fets N. by W. and N., and S. by E. and S.; and high water on the Bar, on full and change days, is at three o'clock.

Between Barague and Dalla you have 27 fathoms, green mud. To the weftward of Barague you have 30 fathoms, black fand, mud, and gravel mixed.

Should you come in with the land at night, do not come under eight fathoms, but anchor until day-light. You fhould not come nearer the land than five fathoms, for, between Dalla and China Buckeer, you will fee the land very plain from this depth of water; but to the weftward of Barague you will not fee the land until you are clofe in with it. Should it be dark or fqually, I would not advife your running on the flood-tide, but on the ebb, when you can haul off to advantage, if occafion required.

China Buckeer makes like a quoin, coming from the weftward, with a bluff, or perpendicular, to the eaftward; but fhould you be making the land in the meridian of China Buckeer, you will firft fee it from the maft-head like a fmall ifland: it will keep this appear-ance until you raife the low land of the coaft. Juft at this time you will pafs two or three veins of different coloured water, which has a very alarming appearance, but muft be no bar to your northerly courfe, until you are in five, or five and a-half fathoms, when you may fteer along fhore N.E. or N.E. by E. juft as the tides affect you, which are very rapid, and rife and fall 15 feet perpendicular,

and

and at certain times of the year 18 feet; be therefore careful to allow for the fall of water when you anchor, or you may ground before the tide is done.

Captain Swain fays, Should you leave the coaft of Pedir, for Pegue, in Auguft or September, he would advife your making Norcondam; and run from thence, fo as to make 2° 10′ E. meridian diftance, by the time you are in 10 fathoms water; then fteer N. and you will foon fee China Buckeer appearing like an ifland in a river's mouth; but it is not difcernible until you are in fix fathoms. If you are to the weftward of this depth, you will not fee the land. In this depth (fix fathoms) fteer N.E. and N.E. by N. and you will fhoal to five and a-half fathoms; and when upon thefe courfes you deepen your water fuddenly to fix and a-half, or feven fathoms, and do not fhoal again on a N.E. courfe, you are at the foot of the Bar, and, if it is day-light, you will fee the weftern grove, (which is a chump of trees) bearing N.N.W.; the eaftern grove (of Palmiratrees), at the fame time, will bear N by E. or N.N.E. Between thefe two groves is the river's mouth; and the beft place to lie, (if you have rough weather), is to keep the two points, which apparently form the river's mouth, about a fail's breadth open, and you may run in until the weftern grove bears W.N.W.: here come too (in the river) in feven, eight, or nine fathoms, and wait for a pilot. Should you find yourfelf, according to the foregoing remarks, near the Bar in the night, anchor in fix or feven fathoms, muddy ground.

On my leaving Rangoon, I obferved China Buckeer, at the diftance of four or five leagues, bearing W. by N. and was then in fix and a-half fathoms water, firft quarter flood; and it then appeared (as Captain Swain remarks) like a fmall ifland, and making at that diftance like a quoin; and little of the other part of the coaft was in fight.—This is a very good mark to be obferved coming from the S.E. ward.

DIRECTIONS

FOR WORKING UP THE COAST OF PEGUE IN THE SOUTH-WEST MONSOONS.

By Captain Newton.

You fhould not permit the pilot to leave you until the Elephant bears N. by W. and in five fathoms water, except you are very well acquainted with the coaft, and know certainly your fituation.— When in five fathoms, and the above bearings, you will be nearly mid-channel; and ftretching to fea you will foon fhoal your water to four and a-half fathoms; then tack, and ftand in fhore to fix fathoms; then tack again, for by deepening your water fhews you to be approaching the in-fhore dangers. Before you come up with China Buckeer, if it fhould be night, embrace the ebb-tide, and let your fhip drive to the windward under ftayfails; and attend to your foundings to know your fhip's place.

When you have brought China Buckeer to bear W. by S. you may make your tacks to fea as long as you pleafe; but I would advife your keeping in fhore, and by anchoring occafionally, take the advantage of the tides, which run very rapid. Your approach to the fhore muft be directed by your lead, the foundings being regular until you get a fmall lump of land, called, Falfe China Buckeer. bearing N.N.W. or until you fee Dalla-river; your latitude will then be about 15° 50' N. After you bring thefe bearings on, or have this latitude, do not come nearer the fhore than feven or eight fathoms. Your foundings throughout will be ouze, until you pafs

Dalla;

Dalla; then you will have fand and fhells, which is a certain fign of approaching Barague-point; one tide's work from which point will take you clear to fea with the wind at S.W.

Trade of Pegue.

The chief exportations from Rangoon and Baffeen are, teak timber in baulks (called duggies and arties), keel-pieces, maft-fifhes, planks, and fheathing-boards: they have other timber in great abundance, but it is feldom exported; particularly an inferior kind of cedar, both red and white, called jarroll; and which is ufed there chiefly for compafs, and crooked timber in fhip-building.

Exports.

This country produces rubies, fmall diamonds, and other precious ftones; iron, copper, tin, lead, wood-oil, earth-oil, wax, dammer, (a kind of rofin, which, when tempered with oil, ferves all the purpofes of pitch, which latter cannot be ufed alone in India, on account of the heat, without being tempered with rofin or dammer), elephants' teeth, cotch, and filver. The iron is faid to be of fo excellent a quality, as to be little inferior to fteel: but Europeans, who build fhips at Rangoon (the principal port), generally carry their iron-work, ready forged, from the Englifh Prefidencies, particularly from Calcutta.

There are but few horfes or fheep here; the horfes are of the fame breed as thofe on the coaft of Pedir, Acheen, and Tellefomoy. They have oxen and buffaloes; deer are exceedingly numerous, but though they are flefhy they are not fat: poultry and hogs, both wild and tame, are very plentiful.

The females of this country are very fond of ftrangers, fo that any man during his ftay may be accommodated with a temporary help-

7   mate:

mate: hence moſt of the commanders, who trade hither, keep one of them, who are very obedient and obliging to their maſters. The wife goes to market, dreſſes the victuals, takes care of her huſband's effects, and even ſells his retail commodities for him; ſhe is, to all intents and purpoſes, his upper ſervant; and if ſhe proves falſe to him, he ſells her for a ſlave; if the contrary, ſhe poiſons him.

When her maſter quits the country, he allows her from twenty to one hundred ticcalls, for one year's ſubſiſtence; but if ſhe has no other maintenance allowed her, ſhe is at liberty at the expiration of the twelve months to chooſe another maſter.

The Imports—are

ſtick-lack, and beetle (areka) nuts, from the coaſt of Pedir; cocoa-nuts, from the Nicobars; brimſtone, from Acheen; cloaths of all kinds, and fire-arms, from the coaſt of Coromandel and Bengal; iron in bolts and bars, canvas, cordage, and ſhip chandlery, braſs-ware, cutlery, and toys; coarſe earthen-ware, from China; ſugar, kiſs-miſſes, hing or aſſafœtida, coral, beads, gunpowder, ghee, arrack, &c.

Cuſtoms.

Thirteen per cent. paid in kind, beſides preſents to the princes, miniſters, &c. which, whoever trades here, will find an advantage in making liberally.

Weights.

100 Moo are one Tual.
100 Tual — one Vis, equal to 3lb. 5oz. 5drs. avoirdupois.
150 Vis — one Candy, or 500lbs. avoirdupois.

DIRECTIONS

DIRECTIONS

FOR SAILING TO THE WESTWARD OF THE PARACELLS, FROM CHINA TO POOLOO CONDORE; AND FROM THENCE TO THE STRAITS OF MALACCA.

LEAVING Macao-roads, almoſt all ſhips take their departure from the Grand Ladroon when it bears Eaſt from them; and if the winds hang to the eaſtward, and the ſea runs high, I would by no means recommend the outſide (or eaſtern) paſſage, the inner one (or that to the weſtward of the Paracells) being much ſhorter; and by going (nearly) before the ſea, your ſhip is conſequently eaſier. On the contrary, by going the outſide paſſage, and being obliged to haul up S. by E., or S.S.E., (to prevent the current horſing you to the weſt-ward), againſt a heavy ſea, you tear and ſtrain your ſhip to pieces, and run great riſks of carrying away your maſts, ſpringing a leak, and many other diſaſters, (as was the caſe with the Bowman Yead, a new Bombay ſhip, and one of the fineſt ſhips in the country trade, in the year 1791-2), which heavy laden ſhips are ſubject to; more particularly from Canton, where ſhips take on board, and ſtow cloſe down in their bottoms, large quantities of tutenague, china, and quickſilver, which makes them roll, and pitch heavier than ſhips laden with an aſſorted cargo. As this is only a hint on the merits of the Inſide-paſſage, the more experienced ſeaman will uſe his diſ-cretion, and, doubtleſs, guard againſt the accidents which may poſ-ſibly happen. I will therefore proceed to give ſuch inſtructions as I have invariably found good in this track; together with ſuch re-marks as I have collected from the moſt experienced Portugueſe pilots, who, from the bad condition of their ſhips, are obliged to

C c

take

take this rout in general; and it is a great doubt to me if there are any exceptions.

Ships leaving China in the month of November or early in December, generally find the winds hang fo far to the eaftward, as to make it difficult to fteer high enough to get foundings on the Maclesfield-bank, which is neceffary, as well to avoid the Lincoln's Shoal, Triangles, and St. Anthony's Girdle, as to be able to correct their account, fo as to fhape a courfe for Pooloo Sapata, and thereby avoid the Andrade-rock, and other dangers thereabout.

As I do not mean to give any directions about the Outfide-paffage from China, I will not digrefs further, but confine myfelf to the merits of the Infide-paffage, and endeavour to give the beft account of it I can, as well from experience, as information.

Leaving the Ladroon, and being determined to go to the weftward of the Paracells, when the Ladroon bears Eaft, fteer South 43 or 45 miles, till in the latitude of 21° 16' N.; then fteer S.W. by S. till in the latitude of 16° 40' or 16° 35' N. which is the latitude of the north-end of the Paracells; and having made 3° 7', or 3° 10', meridional diftance, you may certainly conclude yourfelf within, or to the weftward of the Paracells, and in a fair channel. Being certain of your latitude, fteer fouth until nearly the length of Pooloo Camber Mar, or in the latitude of 14° 10' N.; then haul in S.S.W. and S.W. by S. for the land, taking care not to make it until you are to the fouthward of Pooloo Camber de Terra, or the latitude 13° 33' N. —This is the only thing you have to guard againft, becaufe of a Bay that runs deep to the weftward, and which you will find it difficult to get out of, fhould the winds hang far to the eaftward; to avoid which, keep at leaft five or fix leagues off fhore until paffed the laft named latitude; but it is neceffary to make the land about Cape Avarella, or before you are to the fouthward of 13° N.

Should it be night, and you have not now made the land, fteer a point or a point and a-half off fhore, under an eafy fail, taking care

to

to keep from two and a-half to four leagues off fhore; nor reduce your latitude under 13° 20', if poffible, before you make and fee the land plain, as the foutherly currents are very ftrong through. It is beft, if you are about making the land, to work to windward in the night, by which means the current will not have fo great an effect. I have known them run true along fhore to the fouthward, from three to four knots per hour, but not always fo violent.

Should it happen to be thick weather, which is generally the cafe, and you do not fee the land, haul up W. for it, or W.N.W. to prevent the current horfing you to the fouthward of Cape Avarella.

Having made the land, and can depend upon the latitude, the fhip's place is eafily known; the coaft lying S. by W. and N. by E. From Cape Avarella coaft it along fhore at a convenient diftance, not more than three or four leagues off, until Pooloo Cicer de Terra bears N. or N. by E.: then a S.W. by S. courfe will carry you five leagues to the eaftward of Pooloo Condore. You may borrow toward Pooloo Cicer de Terra to feven fathoms, two miles and a-half off; but you are not to expect regular foundings, as it is hard coral bottom, with overfalls.

Having run your diftance, on the above named courfe, from Pooloo Cicer de Terra, and in 17 or 18 fathoms (water), fand, you will fee Pooloo Condore at about four or five leagues diftance; then fteer S.S.W., and deepen your water to 34 fathoms by the time you have run the diftance of Pooloo Timoan; but do not upon any account deepen to more than 36 fathoms, as by keeping too far off you may near Pooloo Domar, which lies in the ftream of 40 fathoms, and near it the foundings are no guide, it being fteep to on all fides.

Being as far to the fouthward as Pooloo Timoan, and in 34 fathoms water, fteer South, and keep a good look-out for Pooloo Auro, which bears S. by E. and N. by W. from Pooloo Timoan, diftance nine leagues, from which continue your courfe, and if clear you will foon fee Barbacet-hill and Bintang-hill nearly at the fame time.

You

You fhould not near the land under 20, or at leaft 18 fathoms water, to avoid the funken rock that lies in the fair-way between Pedro Branco and Pooloo Auro, and bears from the latter South, diftance feven leagues.

Having Bintang-hill S. half W. coaft it along fhore, until Barbacet-hill bears W. half S., you will then (if the weather is not thick or hazy) fee Pedro Branco, bearing S. by W. or S.S.W. diftance three or four leagues.

Obferve not to come nearer the reef off Point Romania than 14 or 12 fathoms, nor fhould you keep further off than to bring Bintang-hill to bear S. half W., by which means you will avoid the ftrength of the current, which fets ftrong to the fouthward at this feafon of the year, and be able to fee Pedro Branco much fooner than by keeping a larger offing.

Having Barbacet-hill W. half S., and Pedro Branco in fight, bearing S.S.W. in 17, 18, or 19 fathoms water, haul into the Straits of Malacca, coming no nearer Pedro Branco than 22 fathoms, nor to Point Romania than 14, or at leaft 12 fathoms.

If there is not a probability of your getting within the Straits' mouth before night, I would not recommend to you to run, but either bring to well to the northward, or keep working to windward all night, while you have fufficient drift, as the entering of thefe Straits fhould not be attempted in the night or thick weather, when the above leading marks and crofs-bearings cannot be feen.

FURTHER DIRECTIONS

FOR THE INNER PASSAGE, AND TO KNOW THE LAND.

CAPE Avarella lies in latitude 13° N.; it is a long floping point of moderate height, ftretching to the S.E. with very high land at the back of it; a high-peaked mountain to the northward and weftward of this Cape makes it eafily known. To the fouthward of it the coaft forms feveral bays, with fome barren iflands under the main: the moft remarkable is Fifhers Ifland, being longer than any of the others, and of a moderate height. The three iflands, called by the Portuguefe Inhaatrao, for which we have no name in our charts, lie a little way to the fouthward of Fifhers Ifland: the fouthernmoft is high, in the fhape of a hay-cock; its latitude 12° 22′ N.: the others are fmall rocks.

The Aquada Iflands, fo named by the Portuguefe, are not named in our charts: they are fix in number, the fouthernmoft is high, and fhaped like the ridge of a houfe; the middle is larger and longer than thofe to the northward, and is of a moderate height. The coaft hereabouts continues high, with feveral bays. A little to the fouthward of the Aquada Iflands, on the main (near the fea), are feveral white pitches or downs of fand.

Cape Padran Falfe, or as it is called in our charts, Cape Avarella Falfe, is tolerably high hilly land, and fteep to, with a fmall ifland near its wefternmoft extremity. The land to the weftward of it is high, with a peak refembling that near Cape Avarella. The coaft here has feveral openings or bays, as well to the northward as to the fouthward of it. Between Cape Padran Falfe and Cape Padran, (called in our charts Cape Cicer), the coaft forms a deep bay, called

Foul

Foul Bay, with feveral iflands. The pitch of Cape Padran is of a moderate height, with very high land to the weftward of it from Cicer or Padran-bay; which proves how erroneous our charts of this coaft are, as they lay it down as a low flat point. A little to the fouthward and weftward of it the land is low, and continues fo to Tiger Ifland.

Pooloo Cicer de Terra lies in latitude 11° 12′ N. and longitude 108° 22′ E. of Greenwich.—It is a fmall rocky ifland, of a reddifh colour, and has fome ragged rocks, like the ruins of an old building, on the fouth end of it, and lies about three leagues off fhore. You may borrow to within two or three miles of it, in 7, 9, or 11 fathoms, there being no danger though the foundings are very irregular.

Pooloo Cicer de Mar is a pretty high ifland, in latitude 10° 31′ N. longitude 108° 30′ E.; the fouth-end is higheft, and the north-end flat.

DIRECTIONS

FOR MAKING A SOUTHERN PASSAGE FROM BENGAL TO BOMBAY, IN THE CONTRARY OR SOUTH-WEST MONSOON.

JUNE the 4th, we left the pilot in nine fathoms water, in the South Channel, fuppofing Point Palmiras to bear W.S.W. diftance feven leagues; a fmall grab-fnow and fhip in company, feveral veffels then in Bengal preparing to go to Madras and Bombay.

We ftood away to the fouthward clofe upon a wind, it blowing from the W.S.W. a frefh gale; and as the wind drew to the fouthward, we ftood in to the weftward again. Finding we fhould be in want of water, refolved to make the beft of our way to Madras, to which port we had 31 days paffage. We found, to our great fur-

prife,

prife, that fome of the veffels we left in Bengal-river had been there and failed, having, by keeping along fhore, had a 10 or 12 days paffage from the pilot to Madras. The grab-fnow which failed with us was in Madras-roads, with fome of her cargo delivered; I therefore conclude, that keeping along the coaft is a more certain method of making a quick paffage to Madras, or any of the fouthern ports, than by ftanding off to the S.E. as we did; as, from the great track of country the foutherly monfoon has to blow over, it is more than probable to expect land and fea winds, or at leaft the winds to blow along fhore fo late in the feafon. But thefe land and fea, or along-fhore winds, do not prevail off Point Palmiras, nor in the bottom of the Bay of Bengal owing to the innumerable fhoals on that coaft, and all acrofs the mouths of the Ganges as far as Chittagong, which keep fhips fo far to the eaftward to avoid thefe fhoals, that they are out of the influence of thefe winds. When they do prevail there, or when they do reach them, they are faint and nearly exhaufted).

To take the advantage of thefe winds, I would recommend the following Rules, deduced from my own experience.

Having made fufficient fouthing, fo as to be able to ftand to the weftward, though at a difadvantage, and weather the Falfe Point, to the fouthward of which there is no danger, until you are the length of the Santapilla-rocks, I would advife you to work along fhore, obferving to be well in with the land by two o'clock in the morning, about which time, or before, the land wind generally comes off (but one day's trial will guide you better than a multiplicity of inftructions). Stretching off fhore you will get a fea breeze, or rather along-fhore wind, that will carry you in with the land in good time.

As there are particular times when thofe winds do not prevail, and you may be difappointed in your expectations from what thefe inftructions promife, the working in fmooth water and a weather-

fhore

fhore will fufficiently compenfate, by eafing your veffel and pre-venting her tearing her fails and rigging to pieces. Should you be on the coaft, and not meet thefe favourable winds, you muft not be difcouraged by it, but ftretch in with the coaft occafionally, about the time they may be expected off. Indeed I would not advife you to ftand off fhore more than one degree, till you are nearly as far to the fouthward as Point Guardawar; from which ftretch to the fouth-ward, and work up to the weftward, fo as to fall in with or to the fouthward of the Armigon-fhoal. You may now depend upon favour-able wefterly winds, and will often have a fea wind as far round as S.E. or S.S.E.; with which you will foon get to the fouthward in long ftretches both ways.

You will now begin to find a drain of foutherly current, which will affift you ; but this I own is a bold affertion, and in contradic-tion to all inftructions before written on the fubject: but as late as the month of June, when the foutherly moonfoon is general all over India, it may be expected; and whoever depends upon it will not be difappointed.

The monfoon having blown along the coaft of Coromandel from the early part of April, muft at this time begin to die away, and the ftrong northerly currents which fet along the weftern fhore are now running out in the middle of the bay, and, having no vent to the northward, muft run back to the fouthward by the fhores. This is proved by the eaftern fhores of the Bay, as the waters find a paffage through the Straits of Malacca, and along the weft coaft of Sumatra.

Now, when the S.W. monfoon is general, and blowing in a diagonal line acrofs the Bay of Bengal, and having a very long range of 30 or 40 degrees in a foutherly direction, it muft force a large quantity of water into the Bay of Bengal, in a direction with the Adaman's and Nico-bar Iflands; and as the weft coaft of the Bay of Bengal may, at this time, be faid to be a weather fhore, and make a fmooth fea, it is no more than natural to conclude, that part of the great body of waters,

which

which is forced in by the foutherly winds, (after paffing the Equinox), is acted upon by the wefterly winds, partake of its influence, and are driven forceably againft the fhore of the Adamans and Pegue, from which it will be ftill forced to the northward, by the foutherly winds conftantly blowing, and find a paffage out by the coaft of Orixa, and fo to the fouthward, by the Ifland of Ceylon: add to all that has been faid that the rains which have been falling in the bottom of the Bay of Bengal for fome time, and the rivers fv elled with them, now begin to empty themfelves in rapid currents. Thefe circumftances are fufficient to convince me of the juftice of what I have advanced, and it is only neceffary for any perfon to look at the geographical fituation of Bengal Bay, and be convinced alfo. It is unneceffary to fay more on this head, but leave the difcuffion to the natural philofopher, whofe province it more immediately is; and proceed to affift the navigator with all the information my ability and experience will admit.

Leaving Madras, coaft it with land and fea breezes, and along fhore, until you come as far to the fouthward as 11° or 11° 30' N.; then ftretch away to the S.E. or S.S.E., giving Point Pedro a large birth, as you have no bufinefs to come nearer Ceylon than 8 or 10 leagues; if you are further in, you loofe the true monfoon. You will by this means carry the true monfoon in a frefh gale, from the opening between Ceylon and the Coromandel coaft, until you begin to open the fouth end of Ceylon, when the winds generally take a more wefterly direction, though not for any great diftance ; perhaps they will blow W.S.W. and S.W. for a degree or two, and you may find here a confined fea, occafioned by thefe wefterly winds and the fwell round Ceylon. Croffing that from the fouthward, ftand to the foutheaftward, with the fails clean full, for I am not partial to hugging the wind where there is good fea room, nor indeed at any time. Crofs the Line as far to the weftward as the winds will permit, only with this precaution, not to crofs the Line to the weftward of the Frier's

D d

Hood,

Hood, until you are to the southward of the Ouras, as laid down in the Oriental Pilot, particularly the Three Rocks seen by Captain Missener. Standing to the southward and eastward, you will increase your East Variation, and perhaps by the time you reach the Line, may have 2° 30′ or 2° 35′ East Variation, in which case you may safely reckon yourself in 88° 30′ or 89° East longitude from Greenwich; or 8° or 8½° to the eastward of Madras. As you near the Line, the wind will draw more to the southward; stand upon that tack you can make most southing on, giving the preference to the S.E. board.

There is now a choice of two different tracks, for making a passage to the southward with safety, independent of that laid down by Mr. Nicholson, as far as 10° S. One of these are to the southward of that large archipelago of shoals and islands, called the Basses de Chagas: and the other to the northward of these dangers.

For the better understanding of these Directions, I shall first take notice of the prevailing winds.—As the S.E. winds seldom reach to the northward of 2° S., and are even faint in the latitude of 4° S. in the months of April and May, and indeed in the early part of June; I would recommend the southern track, for ships at this time must go as far as 6½° or 7°, probably 7° 30′ S. before they get the fresh trade. In this case, I would recommend running your westing down in 7° 35′ or 7° 40′ S.; making Diego Garcia, which you cannot miss, and by that means correct your longitude, as the situation of that island is well known. Its latitude is 7° 30′ S., and longitude 72° 27′ 30″ East of Greenwich: and it may be seen in clear weather from a ship's deck four leagues.

After making Diego Garcia, I recommend your making 1½° or 2° more westing, and then steer to the northward, so as to cross the Line in longitude 65° or 64° 30′ E.; by this means you will have a leading wind, though it should hang more to the westward than at this season of the year you have reason to expect.

In

In the latter part of June I would recommend the northern track; as you will in general have fine pleasant weather with only a few squalls at times; whereas in the southern track, at this time, you have it sometimes blowing (weather) with great violence, and dark cloudy rainy weather, and all dependence upon observations of any kind rendered uncertain. The latitude of 4° 30' or 4° 45' I would reeommend as the best and most expeditious; and you have an opportunity of correcting your longitude, by getting soundings on the Speaker's Bank, which is well ascertained. Its latitude is 4° 45' S., and longitude 72° 57' E. I have doubts of the existence of Adie and Candy, as well from the accounts of several that I have seen, as what I have noticed going this passage; nor do I believe any such shoal, rock, or island, as that called Gama, to exist. I shall say something of Diego Rais, but shall proceed first to the Line. In the other track, having corrected your longitude by getting soundings on the Speaker's Bank, continue your westerly course, and cross the Line in longitude before mentioned in 65° or 64° 30' E.; by this means you avoid entangling yourself with the Banks of Cherbaniana or Padua, or labouring under the smallest apprehension of falling in with the Malabar Coast before you have made good your northing.

Having run into the latitude of Bombay, follow Mr. Nicholson's Directions for making and knowing the land, and sailing into the Harbour, or the subsequent Directions for making Bombay in the S.W. monsoon, to be certain of a good landfall.

SOME

SOME ACCOUNT OF THE ISLAND OF DIEGO-RAIS, AND THE BANKS
OF CHIRBANIANIA, AND PADONA (OR PADUA).

THE clufter of iflands, called Diego Rais, and faid to be near the
Line, I am clearly of opinion is not to the eaftward of 70° E.; neither are any of the banks, faid to be fituated about the Lacavavies, to
the weftward of 71° 30' Eaft longitude, or we muft have run over
them this voyage; for we had, both at the Line and about latitude
12° 20', feveral good obfervations of the fun and moon's limbs.—
By the Hope's track, which was only ftretching from Mount Dilly,
and could not err much in that time, the Cherbaniania, on which
fhe faw part of a wreck, lies in latitude 11° 10' N. and meridian
diftance from Mount Dilly 3° 5' W., or longitude 72° 16' Eaft of
Greenwich; this is the wefternmoft danger which was feen in this
track: and the ifland Banca Point, which is the northernmoft
danger fhe faw, (from which the Bank of Padua extends,) lies in
11° 35' N.; meridional diftance from Mount Dilly 2° 55' W., or
longitude 72° 26' Eaft of Greenwich.

Note. This is the north-end of the dangers, as they could not
fee the fouth-end from on board the Hope.

In thefe regions the Sea Cocoa-nuts are to be met with. This
fruit is a natural curiofity, and the production of the palm. Some
account of the varieties of the fruit of that tree, and of the tree itfelf,
fo ufeful to the natives of India and Perfia, may in this place prove
both amufing and inftructive.

The

The natural hiftory of the palm-tree is extremely curious. This tree flouriſhes the moſt in thoſe countries where no others exiſt, and would feem intended by nature, from its extreme abundance and variety, to ſupply the want of all others. Thoſe which bear dates are the true race of the palm. In India they do not produce that ſpecies of fruit; for, in the northern parts of that country, the only part of it where the date-tree grows, the fruit never arrives at maturity. In Africa, and all over Arabia, they are found in the utmoſt plenty; but in the former country they are ſuppoſed to arrive at the greateſt degree of perfection.

In Arabia there are feveral varieties which ſerve, according to their quality, as the food of the inhabitants and as provender for their cattle. That which is moſt fuperior in taſte and flavour is called Muxana; they are fmall, and principally reſerved for the uſe of the Sherreeffs, none being allowed to be exported from the country. The more common forts form a very confiderable article of commerce by caravans all over the three Arabias.

The palm, equally with the fig-tree, requires the aid of the male plant to bring the fruit to maturity; but it is much more prolific than the fig, and is advanced by one peculiar excellence above all other trees. The palm-tree takes no repoſe as others do, but every month in the year prefents new fruit. A cluſter of thirty or forty nuts, fometimes more, appear monthly; of which feven, or at the moſt twelve, come to perfection.

The moſt favourable climate or foil, which produces the greateſt abundance of this tree, is Aſia, particularly that part of it called India, containing the kingdoms and provinces which lie to the fouthward of the two rivers Indus and Ganges. The land neareſt the ſea ſide produces the beſt, the air from the ſea being very favourable to them.

The natives diſtinguiſh them by particular names, and reckon eight varieties, all differing in their trunks, leaves, fruits, produce,

and

and appearance, yet retain the name of Palm-trees. That which is
beſt entitled to this diſtinction is the tree which bears cocoas; of
theſe ſome are wild and ſome are cultivated; the beſt are called
barca, which ſignifies excellent. The nut is ſavory and wholeſome,
and though eaten in ever ſo great a quantity, do not ſurfeit. What
is remarkable, the ſame tree bears at the ſame time both the barcas
and the common nut.

If the roots of this tree are moiſtened by the ſea or any brackiſh
water, its bearing is much improved. Of the other ſeven ſorts, ſome
are eſteemed wild, from their fruit, ſoil, and the little manuring they
require. The tree called cajura, or brab, is the peculiar one which bears
dates. In India this tree yields no fruit, but affords a liquor which
is diſtilled and made into wine. Another ſort is named areka, from
the nut of the ſame name; another variety is called the talipot,
of whoſe leaves large umbrellas are made. This tree yields no fruit.
There is another tree of the race of palms, the fruit of which is
called the foxes'-fruit; it is unpleaſant to the taſte, and therefore
may be termed a wild date. The tree called berlim bears no fruit:
its boughs are uſed for adorning churches. The kind called maco-
meiras is without doubt a ſpecies of the palm: the fruit, in cluſters
of thirty or more, is as big as an ordinary apple when ripe, of a
date-colour, and very grateful to the taſte.

The laſt to be noticed is a ſpecies of the cocoa-nut, which are ſeen
floating on the ocean off the coaſts of Africa and Arabia, at the
diſtance of above two hundred leagues, and are therefore called ſea
cocoa-nuts; they are about the ſize of a man's head, and grow
double; the colour of the rind is black, and they are ſo much
eſteemed by the natives as a remedy for many diſeaſes, particularly
againſt poiſon, that they have been known to ſell for their weight
in ſilver.

Theſe nuts are the growth of the Iſle of Praſlin; and it is upon
this iſland only that the palm-tree is found, which produces this fruit

hitherto

hitherto known by the names of Sea-cocoa, Solomon's-cocoa, or the Maldivian-cocoa. This fruit being uncommon, its form particular, like a fcrotum, and its origin unknown, have all contributed to affign to it extraordinary properties; and to give rife to fables concerning its exiftence, as is ufual everywhere with refpect to what is unknown and fingular.

The tree which produces the fea-cocoa rifing in many parts of the principal ifland upon the border of the fea, the greateft part of the fruit falls into the water, where floating, it is carried by the wind and currents towards the Maldivian Ifles, the only part of the world where this fruit had been found before the difcovery of the Ifle of Praflin; from whence the Europeans called this cocoa, the Maldivian-cocoa, and the Maldivians, travacarné, that is, treafure. It was afterwards called Solomon's-cocoa, to give it a name correfponding to the marvellous accounts annexed to its origin. The tree that produced it being unknown, it was believed to be the produce of a plant that grew at the bottom of the fea, which came off when it was ripe, and by its lightnefs floated on the waves. There was nothing wanting to complete the fable, but to afcribe very great and extraordinary virtues to this fruit; and this was done accordingly. It was given out, and believed, and is ftill believed throughout all Afia, that the almond of the fea-cocoa has all the properties which we attribute to theriaca, and which perhaps we exaggerate, (viz.) that its outward covering is a certain antidote to all kinds of poifon. The grandees of Hindooftan ftill purchafe this fruit at a very high price: they make cups of the fhells, which they adorn with gold and diamonds, and never drink out of any other, being perfuaded that poifon (which they are very much afraid of, becaufe they often employ it themfelves againft others) let it be ever fo active cannot hurt them, if their liquor is but purified in thefe falutary goblets. The King of the Maldivian Ifles avails himfelf of this general error: his predeceffors affumed, and he referves to himfelf, the exclufive right to a

fruit,

fruit, which, being carried upon the waves and driven afhore by the wind, ought to belong to whoever picks it up. But this fea-cocoa, when it fhall be found not to be fo rare and extraordinary a production, will doubtlefs foon lofe its value and virtues, and the Maldivian monarch the tribute which has been paid him by ignorance and error.

The Ifle of Praflin is at moft but fix or feven leagues in circuit; makes part of the archipelago, known formerly by the name of the Three Brothers, afterwards by that of the Mahé, and now by that of The Sechelles. In this ifle, of fo fmall an extent, and in this ifle alone, has this cocoa (fo valued in India) been hitherto difcovered. But how comes it that it is not to be met with in the ifles adjacent? How comes it that the tree which produces it does not grow upon them? Why was it confined to the Ifle of Praflin, when that archipelago was feparated from the continent, and this part of the globe changed into a collection of ifles by an eruption of the fea? But I leave this fubject (the difcuffion of which would be long and difficult) to naturalifts, and proceed to give fome account of the tree which produces this fingular fruit.

This tree, upon an exact obfervation, has been found to be a fpecies of the latanier, or lontard, of India; it rifes forty-two feet in height, or nearly fo; its head is crowned with ten or twelve leaves in the form of a fan, about two feet high by fifteen wide, fupported by ftalks fix or feven feet long. Thefe leaves are of an oblong round form, and each lobe is bifid at top: their fubftance is firm and tough, which makes them better coverings for houfes, in the Indian manner, than thofe of the common cocoa-trees.

From the bafe of the leaves rifes a loofe fpike, commonly fix feet long and very much branched, the bafe of which is flefhy and thick; the branches are terminated by collections of female flowers, which appear to be all one calyx, compofed of feveral pieces, of five, fix, and fometimes feven divifions. The piftil becomes a round fruit, a foot

and

and a-half in diameter, the outer coat of which is very thick and fibrous, like that of the common cocoa. This fruit contains three nuts, one of which is generally abortive. These nuts are nearly round, flat on one fide, and divided lengthways in the middle half way, into two parts, which gives them a very fingular appearance. Their infide is at firft filled with a white liquor of a bitter and un-pleafant tafte: as the fruit grows ripe this liquor changes (as in the common cocoas) into a folid, white, and oily fubftance, which ad-heres to the infide of the fhell. Clufius gives a flight defcription of this cocoa, under the title of Nux Medica.

It were to be wifhed that we could difcover, by repeated trials, whether the opinion of the Indians concerning the virtues of this nut be well founded.

Every one of thefe fruit has the calyx, which I mentioned above, at its bafe, and which does not fall off even after the fruit is quite ripe.

The trunk of the tree is like that of the cocoa-tree, but in general larger, harder, and blacker.

Some plants and nuts of this tree have been tranfported into the Ifle of France, and fucceeded very well.

The tree which I have juft defcribed, appears to have been a female. Thofe who vifited thefe ifles in July, which was certainly the feafon of the fruit being perfectly ripe, met with no other. But M. Cofde, who harboured in this archipelago in October, has defcribed a part of a male catkin of this tree; which feems to fix the time of its flowering to September, which anfwers to the European fpring; and the time of maturity to June and July, which anfwers to our winter. This part of the catkin was cylindri-cal, two feet and a-half long, and four inches in diameter, covered with an infinite number of male flowers, compofed of a calyx of fix divifions, and a ftamen oppofite to each. As the male catkins have not yet been found on the fame ftems that produce fruit, it is pro-bable that this tree produces them on different individuals; fo that

this

this palm may be reckoned, as I faid before, a fpecies of the lontard; which it alfo much refembles in all its other parts.

Palm-trees have neither a thick trunk nor boughs like other trees: as they grow in height, they branch out at the top, and open to make room for others; and as the old ones fall, they leave an impreffion in the tree. The tree called macomeira (from the fruit named macoma), has the peculiarity of dividing itfelf into two trunks, when arrived at a certain height. The areka or beetle-nut tree is the talleft of the palms, and grows proportionably thick; the wood is folid and ftrong, and did it poffefs fufficient fubftance, might be converted into mafts for large veffels; for fmall veffels they are frequently made ufe of.

The foil moft congenial to the palm is, as before-mentioned, what is moiftened by the fea or falt-water. The palm-tree has, by experience, been found to thrive beft near inhabited houfes, or in low grounds, where they are fheltered from high winds, which, from their height, are prejudicial to them.

Thefe trees are produced by fowing the nuts in a bed, and covering them with earth. In a fhort time they put forth a fhoot, and, when arrived at fome growth, are tranfplanted into a place deftined for that purpofe. Thefe plants are manured at a fmall expence; they require but little water, and to the roots are laid afhes and all kinds of fhell and putrid fifh; to fome they apply mud taken out of falt marfhes, which is reckoned highly beneficial towards its fruitfulnefs: they bear fruit in five years, if planted in foft artificial beds, but without fuch aid not before feven.

The fruit of every fpecies of this tree comes forth thus: from the ftem of the palm fhoots out a twig, refembling a Moorifh fcymitar: this opens and puts forth a clufter of thirty, fifty, eighty, and fometimes an hundred nuts, about the bignefs of an hazle-nut. Few of thefe arrive at perfection; feldom more than twelve or fourteen: the reft drop off, and a new clufter fupplies their place before the firft is

6

ripe

ripe or cleared of the flower, and thus every month produces a fresh bunch. The palm-tree resembles an indulgent mother, environed by greater and smaller children, at the same time feeding these and bearing others, a rarity not experienced in other trees.

The fruit of the cocoa is productive in various ways: while the kernel is soft and full of water, the natives drink it as a sweet and pleasant beverage: when arrived to a greater consistence, like that of cream, it is eaten with spoons: and when come to maturity it is agreeable and well-tasted, but hard of digestion and unwholesome. The nut barca is the only exception, which is pleasant and harmless. The thin black rind which covers the kernel is good in medicine; the kernels separated from the rind, divided and dried in the sun, are called copra, of which excellent oil is made. Every part of the cocoa is of some utility: the outer rind, called coir, is not unlike the strong fibres of certain plants; and when well macerated and drawn into threads, affords lines and ropes large enough for vessels of any size; cables made of it are highly esteemed, as they will bear considerable stretching: and as they will not rot in salt water, they have a great advantage over cables made of hemp. The second rind, the immediate cover of the cocoa, when green, is eaten like chardons; when ripe it is very hard and thin, and is made use of in different ways; when burnt into charcoal, it admirably tempers iron, and is accordingly much approved of by artificers.

Besides the above-mentioned excellencies, the palm-tree and its fruit are productive in various other ways. The tree alone is sufficient to build, rig, and freight a ship with bread, wine, water, oil, vinegar, sugar, and other commodities. There are instances of vessels, where the bottom and the whole cargo has been from the produce of the palm-tree. The vessels are called Pangaryos, on which the natives coast the African shore, and go into the Red Sea: they do not venture far from the land, being weak, without any binding of iron, and unable to endure any stress of weather. The palm-tree

yields

yields plank, which is, however, weak and fpungy: the planks are fowed together with fine thread, made of the outermoft rind of the nut; the feams are caulked with oakum of coir; it is afterwards laid over (as is ufual) with the fat of fifh, ferving inftead of hot pitch: where nails are wanted, they are fupplied by wooden pins made of a certain fpecies of the palm-tree; the maft is alfo of the fame tree, and does not require much trouble in fitting it. Ropes of all fizes are made of coir: fails are woven of the leaves of the palm-tree called cajuras, of which facks are alfo made, in which they carry millet, &c. Bread the fame nut fupplies; when dry it is called copra; when green, named puto; which grated and put into hollow banes, is termed cufcus. The nuts when green, and before the kernel arrives to any confiftency, produce water, which is clear, fweet, and pleafant. Oil is made of copra (that is the nut dried in the fun), and ufed in great quantites by the people in India, who have no other befides this, but what is drawn from a feed called jingerly, which is much inferior, and only ufed by the pooreft clafs.

The wine requires fome pains and affiduity. When the palm-tree puts forth her fhoot, before the clufter appears, they cut off three fingers' breadths from the point, and, tying it near the incifion with a reed to prevent flitting, put the end of the fhoot into a pitcher made for that purpofe; and the fhoots weep that juice which fhould have produced cocoas. This liquor is drawn twice in the day; in the morning, that which was exuded in the night, and in the evening the diftillation of the day: the men employed in this bufinefs are called Bandarins, who, with a gourd hung at their girdle, and with a pruning hook in their hand, climb the talleft palm-trees, fome of which, particularly thofe called cajura, are of a prodigious height; they afcend as on a ladder, by notches made in the trunk of the tree, and with apparent eafe and fecurity.

In palms of a leffer fize, called the brab-tree, and of the clafs which, in Africa and Arabia, yields dates, they make a hole in the

trunk,

trunk, in which they place a cane, through which the liquor diftils; and which, if the tree affords this liquor, bears no cocoas.
This liquor is fweet, medicinal, and pleafant, and is called fura;
it is fet by the fire in large veffels to diftil as in an alembic, but
with this caution, that they continually caft cold water upon the
veffel, left, as a fpirit, it fhould take fire. This is the wine made of
the palm-tree, called by the natives arrack: it intoxicates like fpirits,
and is much more powerful when diftilled a fecond time, as it then
becomes a quinteffence. Of this arrack excellent vinegar is made, by
putting into it two or three fired fticks, or a great ftone well heated.
Sugar is made of the fweet fura frefh from the tree, which boiled
till it coagulates, becomes good fugar. The merchandife afforded by
the palm-tree, and laden on veffels, are dried cocoa-nuts, the rind
and various other commodities before-mentioned: thus the palm-
tree builds, rigs, and loads a veffel with goods and provifions, all its
own produce.

The palm is, undoubtedly, fuperior to every other tree, from the
various advantages arifing from its productions.

All places do not produce cocoas of the fame fize: they are great
or fmall, according to the nature of the climate and quality of the
foil. The coaft of Malabar being cool, and abounding with rivers
which fpring from the mountains, to whofe bafe this coaft extends,
affords fuch large cocoas, that the lanhas, (namely) young and imperfect nuts of Cochin and thefe territories, are each fufficient to
quench the thirft of two perfons. After thefe, are to be ranked
thofe of the ifland of Ceylon, where the ground is very luxuriant,
yet inferior to the foil of Malacca and the places adjoining, where
the cocoas are the largeft. Thofe of Arabia Felix are finer than any
yet fpoken of, from the goodnefs of the foil and the nature of the
climate.

The palm-tree continues flourifhing feveral years; and its age is
faid to be known by the number of marks left by the branches dropping off. Among the other ufes arifing from the produce of the

palm,

palm, may be added that of the boughs and leaves, which made up with a wick ferves as a torch, by the natives called chulé, who ufe them as a fecurity againft fnakes, when obliged to travel: they are alfo ufed when fifhing in the rivers: the leaves are made into coverings for their palanquins, which defend them from the rain and fun. Some palm-trees afford a leaf called olhas, which ferves as paper, on which they grave the letters with an iron pencil. The leaves of the cajura-tree dried remain of a white colour, which are made into light cheap hats: the bark of the poyo or the twig, being of a thicker and ftronger fubftance, furnifhes the common people with caps.

The trunk of the palm-tree being flender and difproportionate to its great height, the whole weight of the boughs and fruit being at the top, in a manner at the vertical point of the flim body, the fhock of winds would, without doubt, eafily break and deftroy this difproportioned fabric; but Nature, ever provident, has, againft this, furnifhed each bough with fwathes of the fame matter and texture as the palm-tree, and not unlike coarfe cloth or canvas: with thefe the branches are fo ftrongly fecured, as to defy the violence of the wind to injure them.

DIRECTIONS

DIRECTIONS

FOR MAKING BOMBAY IN THE SOUTH-WEST MONSOON TO BE
CERTAIN OF A GOOD LANDFALL.

The S.W. monfoon in general fets in between the 1ft of June
and the 15th, if the full or change happen near that time, with a
hard gale from the S.S.W and S.W., with dark cloudy weather and
heavy rain, which lafts for five or fix days or more. A fhip that is
bound to Bombay in this feafon of the year, fhould keep the latitude
of 18° 42′ or parallel 18° 43′ N. until fhe has foundings, which will
be 36 or 38 leagues off the coaft, at 55 or 60 fathoms; and from
that depth fhe will run 23 leagues before fhe comes under 40 fathoms; fhe will then be about 13 leagues off the ifland. About
eight or nine leagues from this ifland there is a fand bank, lying
parallel with the coaft, the north end lies in 18° 43′ N.; you will
have 36 fathoms without, 31 or 32 upon it, and 37 within. For
further defcription of this bank, confult Mr. Nicholfon's book of
Remarks. This bank being a great guide for failing into Bombay
Harbour, is the reafon I would advife a fhip to keep in that latitude.
Mr. Nicholfon mentions, in his Remarks, making an allowance of
18 or 20 miles for a foutherly current; but therein he is miftaken,
being affured, from my own experience, there is none fuch at any
time of the monfoon, but rather a drain to the northward.

When you have got under 40 fathoms, keep your lead going con
ftantly, and to know the colour of the ground, as well as the depth
of water, if you meet with fandy ground. When you have fhoaled
your water to 32 or 33 fathoms, and then deepened again, you may be

certain

certain of being upon the above bank; if not, and you decreafe your foundings from 40 to 20 fathoms gradually, you are then to the northward of it; but fhould you have no foundings of fand and mud when in 30 or 32 fathoms, then fteer E. by S. and E.S.E., which will carry you in fight of the Ifland of Kenery, bearing E. half N. or E. by N. when in 9 or 10 fathoms; but fhould it be fo hazy that you cannot fee the ifland, or any land in that depth, ftand to the northward two or three miles, and you will deepen to 11 or 12 fathoms or more, if off Kenery; or if you ftand to the fouthward you will probably fhoal to eight or eight and a-half fathoms, and may be then certain of your fituation; whereas if you fteer in 18° 50′ N. you will be confiderably to the northward, and muft look-out for Malabar-point, which is the firft land you will fee: if hazy weather, and at high water in 11 and a-half or 11 fathoms, you will not be more than three miles off fhore; and fhould you not pay attention to the tides when under 17 fathoms, you may be horfed to the northward, which will oblige you to ftand off to the weftward, whereby you will lofe a great deal of time before you can fetch Bombay. In the years 1786, 1791-2-3 and 4, the beginning of the monfoon, the wind was moftly from S.E. to S.W., under 40 fathoms, and without that depth it was at W.S.W. Should you make the Ifland of Kenery in 9 or 10 fathoms, you may then haul to the E.N.E. or N.E. by E. and keep along in feven and feven and a-half fathoms, but not under until you have fight of the light-houfe upon Old Woman's Ifland, which keep N.N.E. and N. by E. half E. until you fee the Great Carranja; bring the monaftery, that ftands on the north end, E. by N., you are then in the mid-channel, and may fteer according to Mr. Nicholfon's Directions. In keeping on this fide, and in the above depth of water, you will have a large fwell fetting you in fhore; you muft therefore be very attentive to your lead, and by fteering the above courfe, when you are to the northward of the ground of Tull-point, you will deepen to feven and a-half, a quarter lefs eight, or eight

fathoms,

fathoms, according to the time of the tide, and may be certain you are entering the Channel between Tull-fhoal and the reef off Old Woman's Ifland. And if you cannot get a pilot on board, fteer Eaft until you have Mazagon-houfe a fail's-breadth open to the eaftward of the N.E. baftion of Bombay Fort, which will carry you clear of all danger to the weftward up to the fhipping in the harbour.

Bombay is the emporium of commerce on the weftern fide of India, and is fituated in latitude 18° 58′ N., and longitude 72° 38′ E. This ancient domain * belongs to the Eaft India Company, being held in fee-fimple from the crown. It is from this circumftance, as well as prefcriptive right, unalienable. Whatever may be the fate of the territorial acquifitions of the Company in India, this poffeffion, while they are able to protect it from invafion, muft continue to the proprietors of India ftock a valuable eftablifhment. The harbour is the beft in India, and capable of containing any number of fhips, to which it affords the moft perfect fhelter. Its docks admit fhips of war of eighty guns; the yards are proportionably large, and well provided with marine ftores of every defcription.

Bombay was, very foon after the difcovery of the paffage to India by the Cape of Good Hope, anno 1498, fettled by the Portuguefe. From the excellence of its harbour, formed by a long chain of narrow iflands and the continent, it was named by that people the Buon-bahia. On the marriage of King Charles the Second with the Infanta of Portugal, anno 1662, the ifland of Bombay, and Tangiers in Africa, with 500,000 l. were the dower of that princefs. Lord Marlborough in 1663 failed from England with five fhips, to receive poffeffion of the ifland from the Portuguefe viceroy; but the obfti-nacy and bigotry of the clergy would not permit of its being de-livered, although by the king of Portugal's order, to heretics. It was

* See Letters on India, publifhed in 1800, by Carpenter, Old Bond Street.

not

not till next year, after the departure of Lord Marlborough, that Sir Abraham Shipman, the governor appointed by King Charles, was able, by means of a treaty with the inhabitants, fecuring their property and the free exercife of their religion, to obtain poffeffion. The ifland and caftle were fhortly transferred by King Charles to the Eaft India Company *for ever*. The fettlement of Bombay became about this period the feat of the Englifh power in India, to which all the other fettlements were fubordinate.

This little ifland commands the entire trade of the north of India, together with that of the Gulfs of Perfia and Arabia. It is the great mart of Oriental as well as of European commerce, and in the article of cotton alone exports yearly to China upwards of one million fterling. Befides being the centre of trade, it is a place of great importance, naval as well as military. Without a fleet to protect the trade on that coaft, the pirates which infeft it would, in a very fhort time, put a total ftop to trade; and without a military force there would be no check on the Mahrattas, or other native powers on the north-weftern fide of India. The arfenal and magazines are abundantly fupplied, and are carefully attended to.

Bombay, from its infular fituation, guarded very generally by a rocky fhore, bids fair to be the moft durable of all our eaftern poffeffions, and therefore fhould be held for the proprietors fo long as it is for the intereft of this country to preferve the independency of an Eaft India Company.

The ifland of Salfette, which is only feparated from Bombay by a narrow arm of the fea, is every day becoming of more importance. The foil is peculiarly adapted for the cultivation of indigo, fugar-cane, flax, and hemp.

Eftablifhing a flax manufactory in India, under the patronage of the Eaft India Company, is a circumftance which has frequently occurred to my mind; and therefore, in this place, I beg to remark,

that

that great quantities of fpirit, called bang *, is diftilled in India, from the leaves of a plant which grows wild; the value of the ftem is hardly known, being very little applied to the ufeful purpofes of which it is capable. In order to bring fo valuable a plant into immediate ufe and general utility, the fibrous parts might eafily be converted into yarn, capable of making fail-cloth of the fineft fabric, and in texture equal, if not fuperior, to that with which the Britifh navy is at prefent fupplied. The inferior part of the plant could be manufactured into coarfe cloth, fuch as tarpawlins, facking, &c. &c. fo that every thing would be completely worked up, agreeable to the various qualities of the raw material.

By the cultivation of this plant, it might be fo improved, that when converted into yarn by machine fpinning, it would well bear the expence of freight from India to this country, and prove a material advantage, more confiftent with the true intereft of this country than the prefent ruinous plan, of importing annually to the amount of five millions fterling in raw material, yarn, and cloth, from the Continent. Such an immenfe balance of trade, which now makes againft this country, would be thrown into the hands of the Eaft India Company, and more effectually fupport the commercial intereft of Great Britain, by producing yarn better in quality than that from the Continent, and manufactured upon that kind of principle which will make the produce from the material invariably good in ftrength and flexibility.

The ifland of Salfet, as has already been obferved, in point of foil, water, and climate, is well calculated for the cultivation of fine flax; contiguous to it, is foffile alkali †, a commodity of great value in the

---

* Bang is a fpecies of opiate, much efteemed by the natives of India. It is the leaf of a kind of wild hemp, differing very little, either as to the leaf or feed, from Britifh hemp.

† Great praife is due to Dr. Helenus Scott, of Bombay, for his Refearches in Chemiftry, and in bringing to light many important difcoveries in the natural hiftory of India, particularly on the weftern fide of that continent.

fcouring

fcouring and bleaching of yarn. This ifland, at prefent almoft ufelefs to the Eaft India Company, may be made a very confiderable
acquifition, and be the means of bringing into ufe many valuable
articles which at prefent lie unnoticed. On this new principle of
fpinning, it includes the whole extent of the linen manufactory,
from the coarfeft facking to a texture of cloth as fine as cambrick.
This laft affertion may be thought vague and erroneous by many,
yet the produce of the machinery muft certainly fubftantiate the
fact, and open a field new and unexpected; it will alfo render fail-
cloth more perfect for the Britifh navy, which at prefent is much
inferior to that of the Dutch and French.

The natives of India could manage the machinery with the greateft
facility, and the procefs of raifing, cleaning, and fpinning, would afford fubfiftence to many, now in abfolute diftrefs for want of employ-
ment. The Americans would alfo take a large quantity of thread
annually.

I need fcarcely obferve, that the canvas and cordage of this plant
have been in general ufe in the country fhipping trade of Bengal upwards of ten years paft; and Mr. Lewis of Chittagong has much
merit in bringing it to its prefent perfection, which will ftill admit
of much improvement. I had many of my fails in the Varuna made
of this material, and in a fair trial, (a winter paffage to Europe,) I
found them equally, if not of more durability, ftrong as the Englifh,
Danifh, or Ruffia canvas which I had, of the fame number or
quality.

For the European market, Bombay is an excellent place to procure gums and drugs of all forts, coffee, barilla, cornelians and
agates, and the blue and alfo the white goods of Surat. Cinnamon
and fome fpices from Batavia, and the baftard cinnamon and nutmeg from Malabar, are alfo procurable; but it is preferable to take
on board the laft-mentioned articles on the coaft, if poffible: where
may be alfo had fandal-wood, cardamums, pepper (black and white).

Almoft

Almoſt all the articles, the produce of the coaſt of Malabar, are eſſential to the China as well as the European markets, with the addition of ſharks fins for China, which are much eaten and admired by the people of that country. We ſhall now ſubjoin a few articles, procurable on the weſtern ſide of India, with inſtructions how to chuſe them.

Cinnamon. The cinnamon, of our ſhops, is a thin bark, rolled up into ſmall pipes, from the thickneſs of a gooſe-quill to that of a man's thumb, and of various lengths, the bark itſelf is alſo of different degrees of thickneſs; but commonly about as thick as a ſhilling. Its ſurface is tolerably ſmooth, but not gloſſy: its texture is fibrous and moderately firm: it eaſily breaks, and is not heavy. Its colour is brown with a mixture of red: it is of an extremely fragrant aromatic ſmell, and of a pungent but very agreeable taſte; that which is ſmall is generally reckoned preferable to the larger kind, and the long pipes are eſteemed more valuable than the ſhort; ſuch as are very thick and cracked on the outſide are ſeldom good. The Dutch having formerly monopoliſed this article, together with mace, cloves, and nutmegs, it was hazardous to purchaſe them in India.

The greateſt deceits practiſed in the ſale of cinnamon are, ſelling ſuch as has by diſtillation loſt its eſſential oil, and ſubſtituting caſſia-lignea for cinnamon. The firſt of theſe deceptions is diſcovered by want of pungency in the cinnamon; the ſecond, by the caſſia becoming mucilaginous when held a little time in the mouth, which the true cinnamon never does. When the pipes, which have been diveſted of their fragrant oil by diſtillation, are laid for ſome time among good cinnamon, they reaſſume their virtues, which at the ſame time are loſt by the good cinnamon, in proportion as they are imparted to the bad; ſo that the one cannot be diſtinguiſhed from the other without examining every pipe; but as this would be an immenſe labour, the purchaſer ſhould be careful that the perſon with

whom

whom he deals be thoroughly honeft. Our cinnamon is the interior or fecond bark of the tree which produces it. The people who collect it take off the two barks together, and immediately feparating the outer one, (which is rough and has little fragrance), they lay the other to dry in the fhade, in an airy place, where it rolls itfelf up in a tubular form.

Storax. Solid ftorax is the odoriferous refin of a middle-fized tree, bearing a filbert-like fruit, growing naturally in Afia. Two forts of this refin are commonly diftinguifhed ; ftorax in the tear, and common ftorax, in larger maffes: the former is not in feparate tears, or but very rarely; it is generally in maffes compofed of whitifh and pale reddifh-brown tears, or having an uniform reddifh-yellow or brownifh appearance, being unctuous and foft like wax, and free from vifible impurities; this is preferred to the common ftorax in large maffes, confiderably lighter and lefs compact than the preceding, and having a large admixture of woody matter like fawduft. Although the impurities of this kind of ftorax render it lefs valuable than the firft-mentioned, yet it is not lefs ufeful, nor its medical qualities lefs potent after purification, by foftening it with boiling water, and preffing it out from the fœces between warm iron plates, a procefs that is unneceffary with the former kind.

Affafœtida is a fetid concrete juice of a large plant growing in Perfia. When this plant has grown to a proper age and fize, the root is bared of earth, fkreened from the fun by the leaves that have been pulled off, cut horizontally after fome days, and again carefully fkreened; in a day or two the juice gradually rifes and accumulates on the furface, whence it is collected, and the fuperficial part of the root that has become dry is cut off, that the remaining moifture may be extracted and collected in a fimilar manner. This juice, as it firft iffues from the root, is liquid and white like milk; it gradually acquires different degrees of confiftency. It has a ftrong fetid fmell

and

and a naufeous fomewhat bitter biting tafte; the ftronger thefe are the better, as age diminifhes both.

This drug is originally in fmall drops, but when packed it forms irregular maffes, compofed of little fhining lumps or grains, which have the different fhades of white, brown, red, or violet. It fhould be chofen clear, frefh, ftrong-fcented, of a pale red colour, and variegated with a number of fine white tears. Its peculiar fcent and tafte will diftinguifh the genuine from the adulterated.

Galbanum is the produce of an ever-green plant, found in Perfia, and brought to Bombay. When the plant is in the third or fourth year of its growth it exudes drops of galbanum at the joints. The Perfians, to increafe the produce, wound the main ftem when the plant is arrived at this age, at a fmall diftance above the root; the juice flows plentifully, and is collected for ufe.

Galbanum is a gummy, refinous, rather unctuous, fubftance; fometimes in the natural drops or tears, but more frequently in maffes, compofed of a number of thefe blended together. The drops, when perfect, approach near to a roundifh or oblong figure; but they commonly lofe their form in the maffes: thefe are pale-coloured, femi-tranfparent, foft and tenacious. In the beft fpecimens they appear compofed of clear whitifh tears, often intermixed with the ftalks and feeds of the plant. When frefh and new, the maffes and tears are white, and with age change to yellow or brown.

It is almoft unneceffary to obferve, that, when the tears can be procured, they are to be preferred to the maffes or cakes. Thefe tears fhould be fattifh, moderately vifcous, and gloffy on the furface. Such as are too foft, of a dark-brown colour, and mixed with flicks or other foreign fubftances, are to be rejected. The beft cakes are thofe of a light yellow colour, of a ftrong, piercing, and, to moft perfons, a difagreeable fmell; of a bitterifh warm tafte, not very

humid

humid nor yet quite dry, being of a nature between a gum and a resin, flaming in the fire, and with difficulty diffolved in oil. The lefs dirt, chips, ftalks, or other impurities, the better. A mixture of two parts of rectified fpirit, and one of water, will beft fhew its quality, by diffolving all the pure galbanum, and leaving the im‐purities.

When its foulnefs renders it of little value, it is beft purified by inclofing it in a bladder, and keeping it in boiling water till it melts or becomes foft enough to be ftrained by preffure through a hempen cloth. If this procefs be fkilfully managed, the galbanum lofes but little of the effential oil, fome of which is generally carried off in evaporation.

Balfam of Mecca, or *Balm of Gilead*. A refinous juice that diftils from a tree growing between Medina and Mecca. It is much ufed by the Afiatic ladies as a cofmetic. The tree is fcarce; and the liquor which iffues from it fmells like turpentine, but more fweet and pleafant. That which drops from old trees is thicker than that produced by young ones, but their effects are the fame. When the liquor is not clear and tranfparent, it is not uncommonly owing to the veffels that have contained it, the balfam being no worfe in point of quality. This commodity is very liable to adulteration; and the following method is recommended to difcover the im‐pofition:

Caufe a drop or two of the liquid balfam to fall into a glafs of clear water: if the drop go to the bottom, without rifing again to the furface, or if it continue in a drop, like oil, it is a proof that the balfam is adulterated. If, on the contrary, it fpreads upon the fur‐face of the water like a very thin cobweb, fcarcely vifible to the eye, and, being congealed, may be taken up with a pin or fmall ftraw, the balfam is pure and natural.

Other modes of trial are likewife practifed. If the pure balfam

be

be dropped on woollen, it will wash out; if adulterated, it sticks to the place. The genuine, dropped into milk, coagulates it, which the spurious will not. When a drop of the pure balsam is let fall on red-hot iron, it gathers itself into a globule, whereas oil or spurious balsam runs and sheds itself all around. The genuine balsam also feels viscid and adhesive to the fingers, which the adulterated does not. If sophisticated with wax, it is discovered by the turbid colour, never to be clarified: if with honey, the sweet taste betrays it: if with resin, by dropping it on live coals it yields a blacker flame, and of a grosser substance, than the genuine.

When the balsam is too thick to be taken out of the bottle, it need only be placed near the fire, the smallest degree of heat easily liquifying it. The bottles must not be quite full, lest they should break, as this liquor is apt to rarefy.

Balsamum is the Latin name of the tree whence the balsam issues: opo-balsamum is the juice which distils from the tree, that is, the balsam; carpo-balsamum is the fruit; and xylo-balsamum is the wood. These are all useful.

Carpo-balsamum should be chosen fresh, plump, ponderous, of a hot biting taste, and smelling, in some moderate degree, like the balsam. Hypericum is sometimes mixed with it; which may be discovered by its excess in size, its vacuity, want of virtue, and peppery taste.

Xylo-balsamum ought to be in small knotty rods, the rind red, the wood white, resinous, and having a scent somewhat like the balsam.

Sandal-Wood is of three sorts, yellow, white, and red. The yellow is a beautiful wood, of a close texture and fine grain. It is usually in blocks, formed from the heart of the tree, and cleaned from the investing bark. Its colour is a pale yellow; and it is of an extremely sweet-perfumed smell, somewhat like a mixture of musk and roses. It has an aromatic taste, somewhat bitter, and agreeably pungent.

G g

Thefe

Thefe qualities, joined with foundnefs, are the characters of its goodnefs.

The white is a wood much refembling the former, and is either in long flender pieces or in chips. It is of a light colour, with a fragrant fmell and tafte; but far weaker than the yellow in all its qualities.

The red is very different, in colour and quality, from either of the preceding. It is commonly in blocks of a confiderable length, which appear to be the heart of the tree that produces it, feparated from the foft outer wood and bark. It is of a dark red colour externally, and of a fine blood-red within. Its tafte is very inconfiderable, and rather auftere. Its fmell is very trifling, and without any perfume like the other kinds.

Cardamomum, or *Cardamum*. There are three forts of cardamoms, the largeft, the middle-fized, and the fmalleft. Of thefe the two latter forts only come from the Eaft Indies, the firft being the common feed of paradife, which comes from the coaft of Africa, and is externally like the others, but particularly diftinguifhable by its hot peppery tafte. The fecond fort grows in the kingdom of Java: the pods are long, rather triangular than round, full of cornered, reddifh-brown, hot, aromatic grains. The third fort (which is that commonly in ufe) is gathered in the kingdom of Cananor, in the Malabar country. The pods, which grow on fhort ftalks, are triangular, tough, of a light-grey colour, a little ftriped, containing feveral angular, brown, fmall grains, of a hot, fpicy, aromatic tafte, and pleafant fmell.

Cardamoms fhould be chofen full, clofe, and difficult to be broken: thofe which have not thefe properties are ftale and decayed. They fhould alfo have a piercing fmell, with an acrid bitterifh tafte, and fhould be well dried, found, and large. The beft package is a ftrong found cheft, properly fecured from damp, the leaft greatly reducing their value.

A PLAN,

A PLAN,

THIS being fo well known, that it requires little from my pen to elucidate it; but as I have fpoken upon moft other fpeculations, I think it will be expected I fhould fay fomething upon it, though it is well known to every fpeculatift on the weft fide of India Proper.

The principal part of the cargo of a fhip, bound from Bombay or Surat to China, confifts of cotton (wool); for the conveying of large quantities of which commodity they have the largeft fhips that are built in India, and peculiarly adapted for the ftowage of fuch a gruff article. The commanders and officers are the completeft ftevadores of this peculiar cargo I have ever met with, and fo exceedingly quick and clever at it, that they will ftow and fcrew from fixty to eighty tons of it in a fhip's hold in one day; or from one hundred and twenty to one hundred and fixty bales, each bale containing from three hundred to five hundred weight: and by their fuperior mode of fcrewing this commodity, will put twelve hundred weight in the compafs allowed for a merchant's ton (or forty cubic feet). Some of the large fhips, belonging to Bombay and Surat, will carry upwards of four thoufand bales, which will contain about two thoufand five hundred Bombay candy, of five hundred and fixty pounds avoirdupois.

The other part of their cargo confifts of fandal-wood and pepper, from the Malabar coaft; gums, drugs, and pearls, from Arabia, Abyffinia, and Perfia; elephants teeth, cornelians, and other produce of Cambay; fharks fins, birds nefts, &c. &c. from the Maldiva and Lackadiva iflands, (which lie extended oppofite the Malabar coaft, and at no great diftance).

Ships

Ships generally load a full cargo of cotton from Bombay or Surat, including the above articles, which are only a fecondary confideration; and endeavour to fail from Bombay about the middle or latter end of May or beginning of June, previous to the fetting in of the S.W. monfoon, which invariably brings with it bad weather upon the Malabar coaft, (which, for brevity fake, I will fuppofe to take in the whole extent, from Cape St. John's, at the entrance of the Gulf of Cambay, to Cape Comerin, at the entrance of the Gulf of Manara), which the fhips fhould carefully avoid; as they are in general crank, unprepared for carrying fail, to work off a lee-fhore, being very light, expofing a great deal of top-fide (or top-hamper) to the gale, and not a fufficient hold of the water to make refiftance to the gale; confequently, their drift muft be great: and if not fufficiently ftiff to carry fail, they muft drive on fhore. Out of many inftances, this being a well known fact, I fhall only mention two fhips, viz. the Lady Hughes, which overfet, and was floated by the buoyance of her cotton (wool) cargo, until fhe drove on fhore: and the Hercules, which drove on fhore near Bancoot (Fort Victoria).

The fhips which get away early in May foon get off the coaft; and as their object is to get to Canton, and an early market, they lofe no time, but generally all arrive in the month of June or the beginning of July, and lie there, with nothing to do, (but deliver their cargo, and take in their returning cargo,) until the month of December; indeed, many fhips longer than even this time; and fome do not leave Whampoa until February.

Such a detention as this muft, unavoidably, make the expence of the voyage come much higher than it otherwife would, could it be fo contrived to get the fhip employed until the middle or latter end of Auguft before fhe leaves the Straits of Malacca for China.

For this purpofe I would propofe the following Plan to the owners of thofe large fhips, which, I conceive, would pay them well, and turn out to advantage.

6

The

The ſhips ſhould be loaded as ſoon as poſſible, after being cleared at Bombay of their China cargo; and, I think, they may be able to ſail in the early part of March: they ſhould call at Madras, and deliver one, two, or three hundred bales of cotton, or more, if neceſſary, to be carrried on freight to China, by the Company's coaſt and China ſhips; and which the commanders will be glad to take on board.

The freight has been ſo low at Madras as one pagoda per bale; and I never knew it higher than four pagodas per bale: probably the average two and a-half pagodas may be reckoned upon as a certain rule; and this is an eaſier freight than thirty to fifty (ſay the average forty) Bombay rupees per candy, the uſual freight from Bombay to China.

It becomes now a quere, why ſhould a ſhip ſail ſo ſoon; or why break up her cargo; the expences, by ſailing in June, and returning in January, becoming great enough not to expoſe her to larger charges of freight for goods ſhe might carry herſelf, and more expence for wages and victualling her crew.

I will make my anſwer to theſe two queries as ſhort as poſſible, and at the ſame time clear, to the undertaker of the ſpeculation, by ſhewing him how his ſhip may be making a profitable advantage of the time thus complained of.

The owners of theſe large ſhips ſhould have a ſmaller one (which I ſhall, if I have occaſion to mention her in future, call her Tender) fitted out at Calcutta, to take up the Plan of the Voyage I have given to the Coaſt of Pedir; and inſtead of delivering her firſt cargo upon the Coromandel coaſt, meet the large ſhip at Madras, and transſhip her firſt cargo, to fill part of the vacuum made by the delivery of the propoſed cotton. The Tender, as ſoon as ſhe is ready, ſails again with a few bales of Guzerat chints, which are always a certain ſale among the Malays, as they are fond of large flower patterns, and which the large ſhip ſhould bring with her from Bombay, and funds to prepare her fecond cargo. The large fhip may, in the mean time, run over to Prince of Wales Ifland (Pooloo Pinang), and wait the Tender's return; at the fame time collecting as much tin and pepper as fhe has funds for, particularly tin, which being a heavy article, lying low, and taking little room, fhould be kept down in the bottom as ballaft, which will prepare the fhip better to en-counter the probable gales fhe might meet with going through the China feas in the month of September. The Tender is to purfue the plan laid down for her, until after the failing of the large fhip; and then, as directed, prepare her cargo for Bengal: and follow the fame plan for the following year.

The large fhip being full from Pooloo Pinang, fhould proceed to China; and fail in all the month of November. Follow the Di-rections for a Paffage to the weftward of the Paracels, as being the quickeft; where fhe will find a current fetting to the fouthward, from fifty to feventy miles a day in her favour: and being furnifhed with Spanifh dollars (from China), go directly into the Straits of Banca, where there is little doubt of her getting four thoufand peculs of tin. She muft then return through the Straits of Durian and Malacca, and finifh her voyage at Bombay; where her tin, as well as her China inveftment, will find a ready fale for the Arabian, Perfian, Abyffinian, Guzerat, and Cambay markets.

But fuppofe this Plan to be too extenfive, and require too great a capital, I will endeavour to contract it, and fuppofe the Tender put out of the queftion.

Let the large fhip take on board, inftead of a few bales of cotton, a few bales of Guzerat chints and fome Spanifh dollars; and inftead of going to Madras, proceed directly from Bombay to Pooloo Pinang; there, if poffible, fell the greateft part of the chints (which, as I be-fore obferved, are always in demand) for Spanifh dollars. If they do not fell at Pooloo Pinang, they will find a ready fale at Malacca. She fhould now ufe every difpatch to get to Banca, going through the

the Straits of Durian; here she will sell the remainder of her chints to advantage, and buy what tin and pepper she can procure until the season for going on to Canton (as mentioned in my Plan of a Voyage from Calcutta to the Malay coast and the eastward). And following that Plan, should she find her Spanish dollars grow too short for her purchases, she may, by borrowing dollars from the Company's direct ships (from Europe to China), and delivering these ships a deposit in cotton for such loan, complete her cargo. This will clear the ship for the bad weather in the China seas, and give room for any pepper cargo she may be able to procure, either in the Straits of Banca or at Tringano.

Having got to Canton, she must again sail early and go to Banca, (a never-failing place for tin,) to procure some tin for her Bombay sales, as the former year.

These plans, I am confident, will turn to a profitable account, and pay well for the additional month or two which the ship may be employed (extra) upon these voyages, or either of them.

The new ceded country (the Mysore) is a no less beneficial one to the merchant trading to China, than to those merchants who drive a trade to Mocho, Judda, and other ports in the Arabian Gulf (or Red Sea), the Persian Gulf to Bussorah, and intermediate ports, and to the coast of Guadel and Gulf of Cambay, as it furnishes the principal goods in demand at all these markets; goods which never miss a sale, and make very advantageous returns to the speculator, particularly cardimums, pepper, and sandal-wood, which this rich and valuable country to commerce produces in the greatest abundance, and I may add inexhaustible quantities.

DIRECTIONS

FOR SAILING FROM BOMBAY TO SURAT.

BEING clear of the Prongs, and bound to the northward, you may keep along fhore in fix or feven fathoms; but do not come under that depth until you come to Mahim. You may anchor in Mahim-roads in five and a-half or fix fathoms, foft mud; diftance off fhore two and a-half or three miles, with the fort bearing E. half N., the entrance of Mahim-river E. three-quarters N., a Portuguefe church on a hill on the north fide of the river E.N.E. half E., Verfevoa fort N. half E., and Malabar-point S., in latitude 19° 6' N., where the tide flows 12ʰ 30ᵐ full and change.

Stand along fhore in five or fix fathoms, and do not come under that depth. Off Derawa there is a fhoal that runs off about two miles and a-half from the fhore. Derawa may be known by the point making very bluff, with a fort on the top of Derawa-hill, which is the northernmoft point of Salfet ifland; its latitude 19° 20' N., it is high water 12ʰ 56ᵐ full and change. By keeping the fame depth will carry you clear of all danger to Arnoll, which is a low flat ifland clofe to the main, and fortified all round. You will fee many round towers with Mahratta flags flying on them. When you are abreaft of it you muft not come under fix and a-half or feven fathoms, as there is a fhoal of rocks off it that runs a long way out to feaward; its latitude is 19° 34' N. and high water 1ʰ 15ᵐ full and change.— Between Bombay and this place are a great number of fifhing ftakes, that are laid in from 5 to 10 or 11 fathoms, but no danger near them. Between Arnoll and Derawa you will fee a very deep bay,

with

with a large town at the bottom of it, which is Baſſeen town and river, belonging alſo to the Mahrattas.

You muſt now keep out in ſeven fathoms, as under that depth the ground is foul, and bad anchorage, until you bring Panrapore-hill N.E. by E.; then haul off, and deepen to 11 fathoms, and not come under that depth, or you will find rocky ground. Stand on to the northward of Tarrapore, or until Tarrapore-fort is on with Valentine's-hill: when they are in one they bear E. by N. one-quarter N. Hereabout you will ſhoal ſuddenly from nine to ſix fathoms, or probably next caſt to three or only two fathoms, and you muſt pay attention to the lead. If you keep out in 11 fathoms, you will find the ground ſoft and even, but under that depth hard. If bound into Tarrapore, anchor in 10 fathoms and a-half, the fort bearing E., Valentine's-peak E. by N., Tarrapore-peak S.E. half E., the body of the high land over St. John's N.E. half E., diſtance off ſhore four or five miles; its latitude is 19° 44′ N. High water here full and change 1ʰ 36ᵐ.

Note. Valentine's-peak is a ſmall hill in land, and forms like a ſmall pyramid, (with no other hill like it), by which it may be eaſily known.

From Tarrapore, you ſhould not come under 10 or 11 fathoms, and ought to deepen to 15 or 16 fathoms before you bring the high mountains over Cape St. John's to bear E.N.E. The body of the Cape is very low, and can ſcarcely be ſeen in 16 or 17 fathoms, therefore you muſt ſet the body of the high land over it. Whenever you bring it to bear E.N.E. you are then entering abreaſt of the foul ground off the ſouth point of a very dangerous rocky ſhoal, with overfalls from five to ſeven fathoms at a caſt of the lead. If you keep out in 16 or 17 fathoms, until you bring the body of the high land over St. John's to bear E.S.E. ſoutherly, you are then clear to the northward of the ſhoal off St. John's, the latitude of which is 20° 1′ N., and high water full and change off the Cape

H h   2ʰ 15ᵐ

2^h 15^m. Should the wind be againſt you when abreaſt of the foul ground off the Cape, and you are working with the tide in your favour, do not ſtand nearer than 14 fathoms towards the Cape. Should the tide be done, and you are obliged to anchor, come to in 16 or 17 fathoms; you will in that depth have good anchorage; but under that depth there are many ſpots of hard ground, and you are liable to chafe your cables. When the high land over Cape St. John's bears E. by N. do not ſtand further off ſhore than 20 or 21 fathoms, as you will have from 22 fathoms, ſoft, to eight and perhaps only three fathoms, hard ſand, on the ſouth end of the Malacca-bank; and as you get to the northward, do not ſtand off ſo far.

When you are to the northward of the foul ground off Cape St. John's, you will then ſhoal your water gradually from 16 to 17 fathoms, to 12 or 8 fathoms, ſoft mud. You now ſtand towards Damaun, which is a Portugueſe ſettlement to the northward of St. John's; you will eaſily know it by the churches and town, which in general are white; it is in latitude 20° 30′ N., and high water full and change 2^h 30^m. A little in land are three hills near together, which are at the back of Damaun town; from hence you may ſtand along ſhore in ſeven or eight fathoms, fine ſoft mud, and will ſee, to the northward of Damaun, a round high hill, with a fort on the top of it, which ſtands in a plain by itſelf, having no other hill near it; at firſt ſight it appears like the crown of a hat. This is called Panula-hill, off which it is high water full and change 3^h. Hereabout you may ſtand off ſhore towards the ſand to 15 and 16 fathoms, but not farther. When Panula-hill bears from E. by N. to E. by S. coming either from the northward or ſouthward, and bringing either of theſe two bearings on, you will ſhoal your water very faſt, and from ſoft to hard ground, on a bank that runs acroſs the channel from the ſhore to the ſands, but no danger. Should you ſhoal to ſix fathoms, haul to the weſtward, and if off ſhore in 16 or 17 fathoms, haul in, and ſhoal to 10 fathoms, then

you

you will deepen your water as you ftand either to the northward or fouthward. Do not be alarmed in the night when you fhoal here-abouts, as the foundings in general are very regular, excepting this fpot. When you have fight of the fhips in Surat-roads, do not ftand further off than 11 or 12 fathoms. As you near the roads with a working wind, do not ftand off to more than 11 fathoms, and into feven fathoms towards the fhore, but no nearer either way. The Malacca-bank is a very dangerous fhoal; fome parts of it are dry at low water fpring tides, therefore do not make too free with it. This bank extends from off Cape St. John's a long way to the northward of Surat; the water is deep near it, and fhoalens very fuddenly from 18 fathoms, foft, to two fathoms, hard fand. You may anchor in any depth you pleafe in Surat-roads. The beft birth is Vaux's (or Piere's) Tomb N. half W., Domas-tree N.E. by N., Noffarree-point S.E. one-quarter E., in nine fathoms, off fhore three miles. The latitude of the roads is 21° 5' N., and high water on full and change days 4ʰ 20ᵐ. The tide in the fprings runs at the rate of three or four knots, from Bombay to Surat. You will find the tides very ftrong as you get to the northward, particularly off the foul ground of St. John's it runs in general fix knots each way; however the ebb runs longeft, fome-times feven hours, and the flood only five hours; therefore take care, by obferving either by the lead or the land; and anchor when you find the tide againft you.

DIRECTIONS

DIRECTIONS

FROM Surat to the northward, keep in 10 or 13 fathoms water, three or four miles from the fhore, which will carry you between the inner and outer fands off Swalley; the outer are fix miles from the fhore, and the inner one mile and a-half; both which are dry at low water fpring tides. When Cutcherre-tree bears E. by N., which is known by a large fingle brab-tree on a low point, keep out W. by N. until you have the following bearings on; Donda E. by N., Cutcherre-tree E. by S. one-quarter S.; then you are clear of Goolwaller-fand to the weftward; foundings from 10 to 14 fathoms: fteer N. by W., which will carry you fafe into Baroch roads, from 14 to 8 fathoms, where you may fafely an-chor, with the following bearings: Baroch-point N. by E. one-quarter E, Catchajal S.E, Peram Ifland W. one-quarter N., dif-tance from the point four or five miles, in fix fathoms at low water. The bar lies in latitude 21° 33′ N., high water on full and change days thirty minutes paft four o'clock, ebbs and flows five fathoms perpendicular, and runs fix knots per hour.

To the fouthward of the bar is Baroch-fand, which lies north and fouth: it is three-quarters of a mile long, one and a-half broad, and within 30 yards of either fide from two to three fathoms deep. Be-tween it and the inner fand (which runs from the fhore five miles, and continues as far to the fouthward as Jannier, the breadth de-creafing, and dry at low water fpring tides) is a good channel to the bar, from feven to three fathoms water, and one mile and a-half

ɪ

broad:

broad: the mark for it is Peram Ifland W.N.W.; fteer in with it until Baroch-point is N. by W. one-quarter W., then haul up for it, until you have Peram Ifland W. one-quarter N. which will carry you abreaft of the bar in three or four fathoms, at half a mile diftance.

There are two fands off Bogway, called Goolwaller and Bogway, which are dry at low water fpring tides. The former lies north and fouth, and is four miles and a-quarter long, half a mile broad, and lies off fhore from Donda fix miles and a-half: the latter lies N. by W. and S. by E., is five miles and a-half long, one mile and a-quarter broad at the north end, and at the fouth end two miles and a-quarter broad, its diftance from the fhore two miles and a-quarter; and within 20 or 30 yards of each fand are three and four fathoms water. Between thefe fands is a good channel to fail or work through in the day-time, but exceffively dangerous in the night, for you cannot depend upon your foundings; therefore in the night I would advife you to go to the weftward of Goolwaller. The channel between the fands is from two miles to two and a-half broad, and the foundings from five to nine fathoms.

From Baroch to Jumbafier keep within three miles of the fhore, in feven or eight fathoms at low water; and in working, do not ftand at any time more than two leagues off, keeping in from 8 to 10 fathoms, becaufe the tide runs fo very rapid, that in cafe of its falling little wind you would meet with great difficulty in getting in fhore again. From the fhore a flat runs off one and a-half or two miles, dry at low water fpring tides, and continues from Jumbafier to Dugum (to the northward of Jumbafier); it runs in fome places four or five miles from the fhore: clofe to it are from four to feven fathoms water.

Jumbafier-road lies in latitude 21° 49′ N., known by a pagoda on the north fide of the river, called Dieu. The mark for anchoring is the aforefaid pagoda N.E. by E. half E., Jumbafier-point E. by N. in feven fathoms low water: the dry part of the flat, half a mile diftant,

and

and from the pagoda four or five miles. With the aforefaid bearings you will have very little tide, and lie with great fafety, the north part of the flat breaking the ftrength of the tide. It is high water on full and change 48^m paft four o clock; ebbs and flows fix feet. This is a great place of trade for cotton, grain, and oil.

The diftance between Jumbafier and Gonway is fix leagues, with a channel one mile and three-quarters broad, but very dangerous, the tides running with fuch amazing velocity (foundings from feven to two fathoms) firft quarter flood. In going, keep within a quarter of a mile of the flat, in two, three, or four fathoms, until you have brought a fmall clufter of trees Eaft, then haul in for the fhore, keeping within 200 yards of it, up to Gongway-road; and when abreaft of the town you may fafely anchor, about 20 yards from high water mark, when you will ground at firft quarter ebb.— It is dry over the bay from the latitude 22° 3' N. to Cambay, at low water, fpring tides. No veffels attempt to go above Gongway, in a tide from Jumbafier, as it is attended with bad confequences; for if they cannot get into Cambay Creek they muft return to Gongway. High water at Gongway a-quarter paft five o'clock, full and change. It is five leagues from Gongway to Cambay, which lies in the latitude 22° 24' N. At firft quarter flood they always weigh and ftand over, keeping the pagoda at Cambay bearing N. by E. three-quarters E. and in working, keep it from N. by W. to N.E. by N.; the foundings are from two to four fathoms. You muft keep the fhore clofe on board until you are to the northward of Dagum, meeting with great overfalls, and the tide running fo rapid that if the veffel fhould take the ground fhe muft overfet immediately, and in all probability every foul on board perifh, which often happens through the negleft and obftinacy of the pilot.

N. B. The tide fets N.E. and S.W.

From Surat to Gogo keep (as mentioned in the Remarks) from Surat to the northward, until you get clear of the Goolwaller-fand to the weftward; then fteer over for the ifland of Peram, keeping to the eaftward in 14 or 15 fathoms to clear the reefs that run off, it being very dangerous and environed with rocks and fhoals. When it bears S.W. fteer N.N.W. (foundings from 11 to 9 fathoms) until you get the following bearings on: the body of Peram S. by E. one-quarter E., Hourah-point S.S.W., Gogo-point W.N.W.; then haul up for the body of Gogo-town, which will carry you clear of Gogo-fand. Soundings from 10 to 3 fathoms. When the following bearings are on, you may anchor with great fafety: Gogo-point W. by S., Hourah-point S. by E. one-quarter E., the houfe on Peram S.S.E. three-quarters E., diftance from the fhore half a mile, in three fathoms at low water. The town lies in latitude 21° 44' N. It is a fafe roadfted in the S.W. monfoon, where veffels may run to, in cafe of parting from their anchors in Surat-roads, it being an entire bed of mud for three-quarters of a mile from the fhore, and always fmooth water. Ships may here get fupplied with ftores and pro-vifions, and repair any damages they may have fuftained. The na-tives, who are principally Moors, build fhips and veffels from 50 to 300 tons burthen.

DIRECTIONS

FOR THE STRAITS OF BABELMANDEL AND MOCHA-ROADS.

WHEN you make Cape Babelmandel you will fee the openings and inlets appearing like the ftraits, being deep bays. Steer for Babelmandel ifland until within a-quarter of a mile of it. Your foundings will be from 28 to 23 fathoms: when entered the Straits, your foundings will be from 21 to 10 fathoms, and will again deepen as you run through to 36 fathoms; your courfe will be nearly S.W.

Note. There is a bank nearly in the middle of the Straits with fix fathoms on it, and off the north end only two fathoms on it.

From the Straits of Babelmandel to Mocha, the courfe is N.N.W. 14 or 15 leagues. Keep in foundings from 14 to 18 fathoms. The land along the fea-fide is low, but inland is mountainous. The approach to the town is known by a row of date trees, about two leagues in length, a little to the fouthward of Mocha. There are no other trees to be feen along the coaft, as it appears very barren. Come no nearer than 14 fathoms, in order to avoid a dangerous bank which encompaffes the road on the S.W. fide; it is fteep to. From 10 fathoms you will be fuddenly in two fathoms. The Succefs galley in rounding the fand-head had 13 fathoms, foft ground, and next caft had only three fathoms, hard fand. When you bring the Grand Mofque to bear E. by S. half S. you may haul round the fhoal and bring the Grand Mofque to bear E.S.E., when you may haul up for the roads, and anchor in any depth from feven to fix fathoms. the Grand Mofque E. by S. or E.S.E., the North Fort S.E. by E., and the South Fort S. by E., off fhore two and a half or two miles.

DIRECTIONS

FOR SAILING UP THE RED SEA TO SUEZ.

N.W. by N., diftance about 16 leagues from Mocha, lies the ifland of Jebbel Zeker, in latitude 14° N. Off its north end lie three fmall iflands of a tolerable height, and when in one with each other they bear W. by N. one-quarter N.; the eafternmoft fide appears to be fteep and clear of danger, bearing N. 30° W., and diftance 18 leagues from Mocha-roads. There are likewife feveral fmall iflands off the fouth end of the above ifland, the largeft of which may be feen from Mocha-roads.

N.N.E. fix and a-half or feven leagues from the north end of Jebbel Zeker lies a fhoal of fand with only two fathoms and a-half water on its fhoaleft part, but it has 17 fathoms clofe to the wefternmoft fide of it.

N. 28° W., diftance 28 leagues from the eafternmoft of the fmall iflands, to the northward of Jebbel Zeker, lies the largeft and eafternmoft of the Sabagar Iflands, in latitude 15° 2′ N. To the N.W. by N. of it are a number of fmall iflands of a tolerable height, and appears to be clear of danger.

N.W. by N. diftance 13 or 14 leagues from the Sabagar Iflands lies the ifland Jebbel Torr, in latitude 15° 35′ N., and 1° 20′ W. meridian diftance from Mocha; this ifland is clear of dangers, and may be feen feven or eight leagues. W. by S., diftance eight leagues from Jebbel Torr, lies a fhoal, whereon a French fhip ftruck and had nearly been loft.

Note. From Jebbel Torr all veffels bound to Judda take their departure; which paffage is fo well known, that I fhall only give an account of fome difcoveries lately made.

I i

In

In latitude 18° 46′ N. and 2° 35′ W. of Jebbel Torr is a fhoal whereon the fea breaks.

In latitude 20° 50′ N. and 3° 46′ W. from Jebbel Torr, lies Point Hamer, which may be feen feven or eight leagues off. Five miles to the eaftward of this point is an ifland near as big as Jebbel Torr, making like a gunner's quoin when it bears W.S.W. half S. diftance five leagues. N. by E. one-quarter E. diftance fix leagues from the above point, lies Cape Calmer, in latitude 21° 7′ N. meridian diftance from Jebbel Torr 3° 44′ W., with a reef of rocks ftretching five miles from it. And S.E. half S. diftance four leagues from Calmer, lies a fhoal of coral rocks, whereon the fea breaks; this is the eafternmoft fhoal off fhore, and lies about mid-channel over. To the weftward of this fhoal are two low iflands, and within them two large fhoals of rocks whereon the fea breaks, all of which are laid down in the charts.

Note. When you make Cape Calmer and Point Hamer they appear like two feparate iflands, the land between them being low and forms a bay.

All fhips that have made this Cape have made it fooner than they expected by 9 or 10 leagues, and imputed it to the current fetting them to the weftward, which is a miftake; for when the chart of this fea was made, the general method of marking the log-line was 42 feet to a knot, and 28 feconds to the glafs: and the prefent method is from 46 feet to eight fathoms to a knot, and the fame glafs, which makes a difference of nine miles in a hundred.

Note. As the foutherly winds feldom reach farther than the latitude of 20° N. and between the latitude of 19° 30′ and 21° the winds are moftly variable, with calms and light airs, I would advife all ftrangers bound up to Suez, fhould the wind be northerly, to ftand to the weftward in the day time, and endeavour to make the land about Cape Calmer, or in latitude 21° 30′ N., and not to go to the northward of Cape Adhat without taking a frefh departure, as you will fee all the places in the day time before you are near any danger,

particularly

particularly the high land of Adhat, which may be feen 10 or 12 leagues diftance. After you have made the land, I would advife you to keep near the mid-channel, and particularly to avoid the eaftern fhore, near which are a number of fmall iflands and fhoals, fome lying a great way off. It is moft advifeable, whether you have a fair or foul wind, to have a fight of either fhore before dark, that you may know how to fteer or ftand on each tack; and by no means to ftand to the weftward of the Parallel of St. John's ifland until you are to the northward of it, as there is a deep bay between it and Cape Adhat wherein are a number of fhoals, the fituation of which are not yet known. It is neceffary a good look-out fhould be kept, but particularly in the night time, as you have no foundings 80 or 90 fathoms near any of thefe fhoals, fome of which lie directly in your track. In latitude 21° 30', and 4° 4' W. from Jebbel Torr, is a remarkable hill, refembling a fort at the top, (which I call Fort Hill); it ftands near the fea. Between it and Cape Calmer is a deep bay, the land at the bottom of which is low. E.S.E. five miles from this hill is a rock above water fome-what like a buoy; and two miles to the eaftward of it is a fhoal with breakers (feen in the Betfy). N.E. by E. diftance feven miles from Fort Hill, are two fhoals (feen in the Terrible): there are no foundings near any of thofe fhoals. Cape Adhat lies in latitude 22° 11' N. and 4° 50' W. from Jebbel Torr; and 13 leagues to the weftward of Cape Calmer lies the Ifland of St. John's, known by a high peak on the fouth end, which may be feen 10 or 11 leagues off: the true courfe made from Cape Adhat to this ifland, was N. by W. three-quarters W., diftance 33 or 34 leagues. In latitude 24° 5' N. and fix leagues W. of St. John's, lies Emerald Ifland, which may be feen feven leagues off, lying two leagues and a-half eaft of Cape Nofe.

In latitude 24° 22' N., and two miles to the weftward of Emerald Ifland, are three fmall fhoals at a little diftance from each other, lying fix leagues off fhore (feen in the Terrible). In latitude 24° 54' N., and two or three miles Eaft of St. John's, is a fhoal of white coral

breakers,

breakers, lying S.E. by E. and N.W. by W., in breadth a quarter of a mile. In latitude 25° 8′ N. is another fhoal of breakers, feen in the Terrible, on her paffage to Suez; fhe made 30 miles meridian diftance from Emerald Ifland. Thefe fhoals lie nearly N.E. and S.W. of each other, and make this part dangerous to pafs in the night. In latitude 26° 16′ N. and 1° 2′ W. of St. John's, lie two fmall low iflands called The Brothers; they appear to be clear of danger, but cannot be feen further than feven or eight miles; the northernmoft is about half a mile, and the fouthernmoft a quarter of a mile long, and they lie eight or nine leagues off the weftern fhore. The fouthernmoft of the Jeffetanna Iflands lies in latitude 27° 6′ N., diftance two leagues off the Egyptian fhore; the northernmoft is in latitude 27° 14′ N., and they may be all feen at four or five leagues diftance. There is no danger to the fouthward and eaftward of them.

In latitude 27° 28′ N., and 13 leagues to the weftward of the Two Brothers, lies the ifland Shadwan, which is fteep to on the eaft fide, having no foundings, with 120 fathoms of line, at three-quarters of a mile diftance. This ifland is high, and may be feen 10 leagues off. Between this and The Brothers the paffage is clear, having no fhoals but what are near the fhore.

In latitude 27° 44′ N. and three leagues to the eaftward of Cape Rofs Mahomed, lies the ifland Tyrone; it bears N.E. by E. from Shadwan, diftance nine leagues and a-half: this ifland is high in the middle, flopes gradually towards each end of it, and may be feen 11 leagues off. In latitude 27° 41′ N. lies Cape Rofs Mahomed; its extreme point is very low and cannot be feen further off than five miles: but a little way from this cape is a chain of high mountains, extending as far to the northward as Mount Sinai, which are generally fet for the Cape itfelf, and are a good mark for Shadwan Ifland, as you will fee them in latitude 26° 50′ N. bearing N. by W. or N. by W. half W.; the low point bears from Shadwan Ifland N.E. half E., diftance fix leagues and a-half. Five miles to the weftward

of

of this Cape lies a large fhoal, with a rock above water on its fouth end, and by the pilots is called Beacon Rock; it bears from the N.W. end of Shadwan Ifland N.E. by E., diftance 17 leagues. Between this rock and the Cape is good anchorage. From Cape Rofs Mahomed, as far up as Torr on the eaftern fhore, are a number of fhoals, fome extending more than mid-channel over. Ships that have met with a pilot have gone through them; but I would advife all ftrangers to go to the weftward of them, where there is a good and fafe paffage about feven miles broad. But before I proceed, it is neceffary you fhould be acquainted with the diftances and bearings per compafs of the iflands and wefternmoft fhoals. N. 25°W., diftance five leagues from Shadwan, lies the ifland Jubell in latitude 27° 41′N. which is both high and fteep to, having 15 fathoms water within half a cable's length of its eaft end. One mile to the northward of this ifland is another ifland lying E. and W.; the eafternmoft part of this ifland bears from the S.E. or eafternmoft part of Shadwan N. 31° W., diftance 17 leagues. This ifland has always been fet for the north part of Jubell, and has no danger at a cable's length from its eaft end. From this ifland I took the true bearing and diftance of Shadwan and the iflands adjacent. It flows 8ʰ 30ᵐ at full and change, and the tides rife fix feet perpendicular.

The N.E. part of Shadwan (real), bears from the eaft end of this ifland, which I call Fair Ifland, N. 29° W diftance 19 miles; between which are feveral low iflands, which have been taken for reefs of rocks; they are about two or three feet above the furface at high water; for their fituation, I refer you to the chart. N.E. diftance eight miles from the ifland Jubell, and feven miles from the eaft end of Fair Ifland, lies the fouth end of the wefternmoft fhoal, on which is a large rock that is nearly covered in high fpring tides; it bears from the S.E. part of Shadwan Ifland N. three-quarters W. fix leagues and a-half; and from the N.E. of Reat, S.E. one-quarter E. diftance 19 miles under the lee of this fhoal, there is good anchorage from 18 to 20 fathoms (with the wind northerly). The rock, when in one with Mount Agarib, bears N.W. by W. a little wefterly; this is called Carrangar Shoal. The higheft part of the peninfula of Reat lies in latitude 28° N., and is clofe to the fea-fide; this is called the N.E. part. The land between this and the fouth end, which is of a tolerable height, is lower, and forms a bight, over which you will fee Mount Agarib, which is here given as a mark through the channel: that which is generally fet as the north part of Reat lies in latitude 28° 4' N.; and N.W. by W., diftance feven miles from it, is a fmall bluff, in latitude 28° 10' N. Between this and the north part of Reat abovementioned, the land is low, and forms a bay, which has made many people take Reat to be an ifland.

TO SAIL THROUGH THE WEST CHANNEL.

Being two or three miles off Shadwan and abreaft of the eaftern-moft part of it, you will fee the N.E. part of Reat bearing N.W. half W. or N.W. one-quarter W.; you may then fteer N.N.W. or N. N.W. one-quarter W., fo as to pafs Jubell and Fair Ifland at the fame diftance. And when you bring Jubell to bear S.W. one-half W. or S.W., you will have foundings at 40 or 48 fathoms, which depth you will fhoalen as you go to the northward to 17 or 15 fathoms regular foundings, and then deepen again to 35 or 40 fathoms. And when that which is called the fouth part of Reat bears W. half N., you are paft the Carrangar Shoal. And when the fouth part of Reat bears W.N.W. you will fee the low land and iflands that are be- tween Jubell and Reat abreaft of you; from which runs a fhoal, with about feven fathoms water on its outer part: this fhoal does not run out fo far as to bring the S.E. part of Shadwan and N.E. part of Reat in one. When you are paft the Carrangar Shoal the channel becomes wider.

N. half

N. half E. diſtance three and a-half or four leagues from the high land of Reat, is a bank of coral rocks and ſand, lying N. by W. half W. and S. by E. half E., about two leagues in length; it has 18 fathoms ſand on its ſouth end : and about a mile further to the northward are five fathoms, rocks; the north end ſhoalens gradually from 26 to 8 fathoms, ſandy ground. On both ſides of this bank the ſoundings are black ſand, the water ſhoalens gradually as you approach it. And when Mount Agarib is juſt open to the northward of the bluff point, in latitude 28° 10′ N., bearing W. by N. one-quarter N., you are then on the ſhoaleſt part. A good mark for going through the channel is, to keep Mount Agarib open to the weſtward of the high land of Reat, bearing N.W. three-quarters W., for when it bears N.W. by W. weſterly, it is in one with the Carrangar Shoals, and juſt on with the high land of Reat.

N.E. from the high land of Reat, in latitude 28° 14′ N. lies the town of Torr, where there is a ſafe and good harbour, formed by a ſpit of ſand running from the north part of Torr Bay. On the point of the ſpit is a beacon, whereon a light is kept in the night time when any ſhips are ſeen in the offing. It is a good mark to run into the harbour by. Cape Jahan lies in latitude 28° 34′ N., and bears from the body of the high land of Reat N. 1° W., diſtance 11 leagues and a-half. N.W from this Cape, and one league diſtance, is a ſhoal, with four fathoms water on it. When you are abreaſt of Cape Jahan you will ſee a bluff point, (which is often miſtaken for Hammum Point,) but lies five miles to the ſouthward of it. The land between them is very low towards the ſea, which makes it appear like a bay. The courſe from Cape Jahan to the Hammum Point, which lies in latitude 29° 14′ N., is N. by W. one-quarter W., diſtance 14 leagues; this is a low point but clear of danger.

In latitude 28° 42 N. on the Arabian ſhore, lies a large ſhoal partly dry; the outermoſt diſcoloured water upon it, bears from Hammum bluff point South.

I

Zephatama

Zephatama Point is very low, lying in 29° N., and bears from Cape Jahan N. 23° W., diftance 13 leagues. A little above this point, in latitude 29° 3' N., lies a fhoal of rocks, ftretching from the weftern fhore about two miles and a-half; the outer part bears from Hammum bluff point W. half S.

N. half W. from Hammum low point lies another point, called Muln Hammil Point, in latitude 29° 26' N.—From this point runs a fhoal, about one mile in length, and is dry at low water. On approaching this point you will fhoalen your water gradually from 30 to 10 fathoms, but only for a fhort diftance.

In latitude 29° 47' N. lies the fouth point of Simon's Bay, off which runs a fmall fhoal. This point bears from Hammum low point N. 8° W., diftance 11 leagues. Two miles to the fouthward of this point is a fhoal, running W.S.W. (diftance one mile and a-half off fhore.) In latitude 29° 50' N., on the weftern fhore, lies Agada Point, which is low, and has a fhoal ftretching off it three-quarters of a mile. Near this point the land is very high, and when firft feen, at the diftance of fix or feven leagues, it appears like a neat's tongue, and bears from Hammum Point N. 15° W., diftance 12 leagues.— Between Agada Point and the low land of Abdorage is a deep bay with low land to the fouthward.

Nebah is a low point in latitude 29° 55' N., and has a fhoal running off it about three-quarters of a mile, the greateft part of which is dry at low water. Juft above this point is Suez harbour, wherein you may anchor from four to fix fathoms abreaft the entrance of the river. Between the point and that before mentioned, in latitude 29° 46' N. is a deep bay, called Simon's Bay, the land in the upper part of which is very flat, and the water fhoalens from two miles below Nebah Point. Working into Suez Harbour, be careful of a fhoal that lies nearly Weft from Nebah Point, diftance two miles and a-quarter, and bears from the eafternmoft part of Suez town S. 43° W. diftance three miles and a-half.

Note. There is a good channel to the weftward of it.

SOME

SOME ACCOUNT OF MOCHO AND JUDDA, AND THE TRADE.

Mocho, the firft city we meet with in the Red Sea where European fhips call at for the purpofe of trade, is tolerably large, and exceedingly populous; the principal part of the inhabitants are Mahomedans; but there are a great many Jews, which live in the fuburbs, fome few Armenians and Perfees, all of whom are obliged to comply with the cuftoms of the Mahomedans; and they find fuch compliances convenient and profitable; as they reap great advantage from the lucrative trade they carry on from hence to moft (indeed I may fay all) parts of India.

The ftreets are tolerably large, the houfes are built of brick or ftone, confifting of two ftories, with terraced roofs; the fhops are particularly adapted to (and built for) trade, and are well filled with all forts of commodities, both of Europe and India.

The harbour of Mocho is formed by two points (or flips) of land, (on each of which is a fortification,) about three miles from each other.

The moft confiderable trade they have is coffee, which is cultivated at Beetlefackie, and allowed to be the fineft in the world; large quantities of this wholefome berry are taken into Turkey by the caravans which come from thence to Mecca, and in return, as well as this, take back all the fpices and manufactures of the whole eaftern world; many of which find their way into Europe by this circuitous rout; and hence this grateful berry, with us, gets the name of Turkey Coffee.

Having faid thus much of the berry, it may not be confidered irrelevant to this work to add here fome account of the coffee plant, and the manner that the Arabs cultivate it; particularly fo, as it is in

K k

univerfal

univerfal ufe at home, and general cultivation in our Weft India plantations.

The coffee plant grows to the height of about eight or nine feet, (not much unlike our white-thorn bufh,) the twigs grow in pairs, oppofite to each other; the leaves grow in the fame manner (oppo fite to each other in pairs alfo) and about two inches afunder, each pair from the other; both above and below, the leaves are about four inches long, and in the middle (being the wideft part) are about two inches broad; from whence they decreafe to the extremities, and end in a point; they are not unlike the bay-leaf, but neither fo ftiff, crifp, or thick.

The plant, as I obferved before, is much like our white-thorn, with a grey fmooth bark, the wood white, and very little pith.— The fruit hangs on the twigs, fometimes one, two, or more together.

Thefe plants are watered by artificial channels, and after three or four years bearing the natives plant new ones, as the old begin to decline about this period.

The berry is dried in the fun, after being carefully gathered from the fhrub, and the hufk is afterward taken off by handmills.

In the hot feafon the natives ufe thefe hufks inftead of the coffee berry, and efteem the liquor impregnated with them more cool- ing and more refrefhing than that prepared from the berry.

BEETLEFACKIE

Coin, or Money.

40 caveers are 1 Spanifh dollar.

Weights.

Weights.

15 vakia are 1 rattle.

29 vakia are 1 maund.

1 maund weighs 2lb. 10dwts. 23grs. 4decim.

10 maunds are 1 frazil, 20lbs. 6oz. 4dwts. avoirdupois.

40 frazils are 1 bahar, 814 to 816lbs. avoirdupois.

They reckon 14½ vakia, at Beetlefackie, to 1 rattle, and 2 rattles to 1 maund; in coffee, 29 vakia are 1 frazil; and to all other goods 15 vakia to one rattle: but of all kind of merchandife whatever (except jaggry, dates, candles, and iron, of which 16 vakia make one rattle) the above are the weights.

At Mocho and Beetlefackie the rattle is only ufed in the bazar.

They have great numbers of horfes, the fineft in the world, whether we confider them for fwiftnefs, beauty, fymmetry, or fagacity.

When you arrive at Mocho, the firft ftep you take fhould be to find out a good linguift, provided you have not one with you; if you have, it is natural to fuppofe he will be more in your intereft than a ftranger got there. But you ought to take a pilot to carry you on to Judda, agreeing with him for the run; which will be from fifty to one hundred Mocho dollars, for the trip there and back, befides a fuit of cloaths at Judda.

If you fell here, your filk will fetch one hundred and twenty Mocho dollars per frazil of thirty-one and a-half ufe. I would advife you to ftrike for that price, as well as for your cloves, if they offer one hundred Mocho dollars, or even ninety-five per frazil for them; and if you can get five Mocho dollars per tomaund (100 hundred bags are 82 tomaund) for your rice, I would advife you to fell it alfo; obferving, that if you do not make any fales at Mocho, you do not pay any port charges; but if you fell any thing, even one bag of

rice,

rice, you become liable to pay the whole, as if you had fold the entire cargo: but in all probability, as your fales here will be but trifling, fettle with your broker, and be very clear and pofitive with him not to pay port charges, nor prefent to the Xerif; or elfe you muft put what cargo you fell on board fome fhip in the roads, who is landing goods, and have them fent on fhore as her cargo.—By this mode you· may evade the charges, which are confiderable; though you cannot do this with your rice, for you will want it as ballaft going up to Judda.

The captain, if fupracargo (or executive agent), had better not go on fhore at Mocho, as the broker, (who will come off to the fhip as foon as fhe anchors in the roads,) or linguift, will be able to do any thing neceffary for him; fuch as fending him water or neceffaries off to the roads.

MOCHO

Coins, or Money.

The coins of this country are only carats and comaffees, which rife and fall extravagantly, according to the quantity of filver there is in them.

1 carat is 3grs. 057decim. troy weight.
7 carats are 1 comaffee.
60 comaffees are 1 Spanifh dollar.
80 caveers are 1 Mocho dollar.
121½ Mocho dollars (are efteemed) 100 Spanifh dollars.

Exchange of Gold Coins.

Venetians produce each in filver 2 dollars 25 caveers.
Touch by the fhroffs 13½ verfua.

7

Gubbers

				Dol.	Cavcers.
Gubbers	are	—	—	2	20
Gingerlys	—	—	—	1	55
Xeriffees .	—	—	—	1	50

Bars of gold from Muſſova, touch from 11 to 12 verſua.
Dᵒ   dᵒ   Moſambique   dᵒ   9 to 10   dᵒ.

Weights Troy.

			lbs.	oz.	dwts.	grs.	decimals.
16 carats, or	1 coffola	are	0	0	2	0	912
1½ coffola, -	24 carats, 1 miſcal	-	0	0	3	1	368
10 coffola, -	1 vakia	-	0	1	0	9	012
1½ vakia, -	1 beak	-	0	1	10	13	068

Avoirdupois.

			lbs.	oz.	dwts.	grs.	decimals.
15 vakias, or	1 rattle	are	1	2	0	0	0
40 vakias, -	2⅔ rattle, 1 maund	-	3	0	0	0	0
10 maunds, -	1 frazil	-	30	0	0	0	0
15 frazils, -	1 bahar	-	450	0	0	0	0

Meaſures.

1 guz   is 25 inches Engliſh.
1 covid - 19   dᵒ
40 kellas - 1 tomand, or 165 lb.

Liquid Meaſure.

16 vakias is 1 naosfia.
4 naosfias - 1 cuddy, nearly 2 gallons, or 18 lbs.

Cuſtoms.

Cuftoms.

The Englifh pay government 3 per cent. on fales.
Brokerage is 1½ per cent.
Shroffage - 1 per thoufand.

The Mahomedan merchants nominally pay government 7 per cent. cuftoms; but the impofitions of thofe who are entrufted with the receipt, take care to impofe other duties, not authorized, to the amount of 15 per cent.

Should it fo happen that the broker at Mocho cannot fend you a pilot he would recommend, obferve, that, as foon as you are as far to the northward as 20 degrees of north latitude, begin to fire guns for a pilot, viz. morning and evening, and fire two each time, at about a minute interval; taking, however, the precaution to be clofe in with the Arabian fhore at the time; and endeavouring to make them have the beft poffible report, by being double wadded and the muzzles well greafed, pointing them directly towards the fhore.

The beft pilot in Judda is Ally Eufuff, to whom for pilotage inwards you pay one hundred Judda cruz; outward, only forty Judda cruz, befides a fmall prefent, which is cuftomary in piece goods, and a bag of fine rice when he is leaving the fhip.

As foon as you anchor in the harbour of Judda, the Enubar and officers of the Bafhaw will come off, and demand a manifeft of your cargo, that is the number of packages, they do not inquire about the contents; only fay, " fo many chefts of chinaware, fo many bales of Bengal goods," &c. &c.

The only man I can or would recommend to you at Judda, is Shaik Ally, as an Arab writer, (which it is neceffary you fhould have); he will alfo ferve you as your broker.

When

When the Enubar's boat leaves you, he will leave two cuſtom-houſe officers on board, who will remain until the cargo is all de-livered and the ſhip ſearched (or jerqued), to whom, during their ſtay, there is a cuſtomary daily allowance for proviſions. In addition to theſe officers there will be a boat moor aſtern of you every night while any cargo remains on board; and do not ſuffer your own boat to leave the ſhip, except when it cannot be avoided, as the officers of government are both troubleſome and inſolent, ſtopping and ſearching your people, &c. &c.; but as ſoon as the ſhip is cleared and ſearched, this ceremony is diſpenſed with and no longer purſued, and you have a free communication with the ſhore.

Should it ſo happen that you arrive at Judda before the Hodjee (and to effect this you muſt not loſe any time at Mocho,) get per-miſſion to go on ſhore as ſoon as poſſible, and in this caſe the govern-ment will wiſh to haſten you ; ſo that there will be no difficulty in procuring the indulgence. But do not leave the ſhip until you have agreed to be allowed to chooſe your own broker and ſhroff; and have it in writing under their ſignature, or elſe they will impoſe ſome creature of their own upon you, who pay them for it. I have already ſaid that Shaik Ally will probably be your broker, and aſſiſt you in chooſing a ſhroff. If you cannot get Hodjee Hogg Sayell, who is the moſt honeſt man in the Engliſh ſervice at Judda, ſtipu-late with them alſo, that all your cargo pay the duties, charges, &c. in kind, which will amount to eight or nine per cent.; and that it be opened and examined at your own houſe (only), and by no means in the public cuſtom-houſe.

A good houſe, with convenient warehouſes and godowns, will coſt you from three to four hundred cruz for the ſeaſon.

When you go on ſhore, your firſt viſit is to the Baſhaw (or Baud-ſhaw), and afterwards to the Xeriffs; after which, and you have re-turned to your own houſe, begin to land your cargo as faſt as poſ-ſible, and arrange it in your godowns for inſpection, (taking care that

it

it comes immediately from your boats to your own houfe, and not to go near the cuftom-houfe), forting each defcription of goods by themfelves; freight and private trade promifcuoufly: and when all is afforted fend information to the government, that your cargo is ready for examination.

When the Bafhaw and Vizier come, point out to them the different parcels of baftas, &c. and tell them they contain fuch a number of pieces, of fuch and fuch goods, but be very exact as to the quantity and number in each bale ; for if they find the number agree with your account they will not open more than a bale or two of each kind; but if the number differs from your report, they will open every bale of your cargo ; this will be exceedingly troublefome, and caufe you to be fufpected in all your future dealings.

When this job of examination and fettling the cuftoms is over, (which you will find the moft troublefome of any you will meet with at Judda,) you are to make up the government prefents of piece goods; two or three pieces of each kind in your cargo, probably to the amount of four thoufand cruz: of this Shaik Ally will inform you particularly.

Thefe prefents muft not be charged to the owners alone, but in proportion to all the freighters; and your brokerage, which will be about one thoufand five hundred or two thoufand cruz, (including your Arab writer,) muft be charged in like proportions.

Your prefents being delivered, find out (among the fhroffs) what are the price of old and new german crowns, venetians, flamboles, &c. &c., gubbers, zurmahaboubs flamboles; but do not buy any zurmahaboubs, miffiree, nor gingerlys, as they do not turn to advantage: the beft guide for your direction is to have the product of thefe coins from the Bombay and Madras mints, and make your purchafes of them according to your calculation.

When you are thus far prepared the merchants will come to you, and even prefs upon you if the Hodjee is near. You need not talk of

ready

ready money, as none pay until after the Hodjee; fo that you muft make your bargains to be paid after the Hodjee and their returns from Mecca, together with the fpecie in which you will be paid, and the rate of exchange of each kind of coin: all thefe articles muft be booked by your writer, as his book is your voucher in cafe any difpute arifes, (and indeed this is the only real ufe of having an Arab writer).

The firft offer is invariably the beft; and if you can agree with one perfon for your whole cargo, you will reap a double advantage, for you will get a larger price, and lefs trouble. The time from your arrival, until the time of the Hodjee, will be very fhort; and after its arrival your goods will not fell, at leaft not to fuch a good account.

You are to be guided by the character of the merchants to whom you give credit. In this I will not pretend to guide you, as the honeft man of one year may turn out otherwife the year following; and by prefents and bribery to government may purchafe their protection; or may probably be able fo far to influence government to prohibit any others, but himfelf and his creatures, to purchafe your goods. As a guide, I can tell you what they fay of each other,—" If he has been at Mecca (or Hodjee) once—take care of him: if he has been there twice—do not truft him: but if he has been there three times—have no kind of dealing with him, for he will cheat you."

There is one thing which I cannot omit in this place. In the event of your felling the whole of your cargo to one perfon, or only one particular fpecie of goods, you ought to obferve, (as they buy them at an average price), that the proprietors of fine goods of that fpecie fhould have a proportionate advance upon their goods; and confequently the proprietors of coarfe goods fhould have fuch advance taken from the amount fale of their goods being of a worfe quality; and only fold (probably) by the demand of the other (fine) goods.

As foon as the merchants return from Mecca, which will be

L l   about

about a month, begin to collect your money, and send it off to the ship immediately as you receive it; and never, if you can possibly help it, keep any in your house: and at the same time call upon all the merchants and pilgrims, and fix upon a day for sailing: the merchants will by this means prepare their treasure freight and themselves as passengers; from whom, and the pilgrim passengers, the Captain's principal emolument arises; as he has so much a head for each, as well as so much more for his water and provisions; both of which, by custom, are allowed to him by the owners of the ship.

A further emolument of the Captain arises from insuring the freight treasure which he takes on board, and which the native merchant never objects to, although he may be a passenger on board; and will take the captain's guarantee, though not worth a sous, for lacks of dollars, if he has so much on board.

The freight of treasure from Judda to Surat, Bombay, or Madras, is generally three per cent.; the premium of insurance, as the captain can agree, from one to two and a-half per cent.; the freight of gruff goods is arbitrary, as it must be agreed upon by both parties.

Should the season be so far advanced as to make it doubtful whether your ship will be able to go to Surat, deliver her freight, and leave it before the full moon in March (or not). It would be better declining taking any Surat freight, except the merchants will allow you to send the treasure by some other conveyance from Bombay immediately upon your arrival there: if they agree to this, the additional expence must be paid by their constituent at Surat, and not by you. If you can prevail upon them to do this, it will considerably increase your freight, as they have large consignments from thence in Guzerat, Cassimbuzar, and Bengal piece goods, &c. and consequently they have large remittances to make.

Probably, if the prices of goods are low at Judda, and you do not sell at the first offer, your Arab writer will endeavour to persuade you to send them to Mecca, in hopes of their being entrusted to his care,

7   and

and himfelf with the fale at the Hodjee, and have the commiffions; they will furnifh you with very fpecious and favourable accounts of the markets, as well as bringing numbers of people to recommend them, as being well acquainted with the markets, and of the greateft integrity. But do not on any account fall into this fnare, for as certain as you fend goods to Mecca on your own account, to be fold at the Hodjee, you will be a confiderable lofer (if not lofe the whole) by the fpeculation.

The cuftoms upon your china-ware and goods will be fettled by the government, and (though it may be extravagantly exorbitant, complaint is ufelefs, as you can have no redrefs) from the account you give them, and which fhould be done by the fupracargo or purfer, in the public cuftom-houfe: as it is a neceffary form it ought to be complied with.

Your mufk and agalla-wood they will weigh in the cuftom-houfe, and probably want to open it there to fatisfy themfelves; but you muft not allow it to be done. If they want to fee the contents of your packages, let them come to your houfe; for if you open any thing in the cuftom-houfe, you may reft affured of lofing twenty-five per cent.; and you cannot poffibly help it, they are fuch expert thieves.

When they deliver you the amount cuftoms upon your gruff goods it will be ten per cent. above what the cuftom fhould be.

Upon both piece goods and gruff cargo they charge you, under the heads of Calum and Xeralphie, ten per cent. upon the amount of your cuftoms; which they call fees, for the different writers and people attached to the cuftom-houfe. By a fmall fee you may prevail upon them to take your china-ware at five per cent. without unpacking or counting, which will reduce the whole of your cuftoms to about eleven or twelve per cent.: and if the time before the Hodjee is fhort, the government will readily agree to this; but will take ten cups from every cheft of china-ware, exclufive of the cuf-

toms.

toms. What this is done for I could not find out, only that it was an old eftablifhed cuftom.

As you generally fell your china-ware by the cordge, which is twenty, in all parts of India, you are to recollect that the cordge is twenty-two at Judda.

When you fell your fugar-candy, or any thing elfe by weight, fend for the cuftom-houfe fteelyards, (as it will prevent difputes, and have the goods weighed, and delivered at your own houfe.— They make arbitrary deductions, from five to twenty per cent. for tare of the packages; therefore agree previoufly about the tare: fugar-candy is about ten per cent.; upon this account, a fmall prefent to the cuftom-houfe weighman (conveyed privately) may be advantageoufly difpofed of, as he generally fixes the tare; and, as well as his prefent, give him a few cruz and a bottle of arrack occafionally. If the Bafhaw purchafes your cargo, or any part of it, the weighman dare not fhew you the fmalleft favour in the delivery: on the contrary, you may expect the reverfe; but even in this, your prefent will not be mifapplied, as he will, for arrack and a few cruz, do all he dare to ferve you.

Infift upon your fhroff to have the weighing of your mufk; it will fave you a great deal. Mufk fells by the rattle (of four hundred drachms).

You pay one thoufand to twelve hundred cruz anchorage, with about three hundred and fifty cruz when you get on the coaft, which will be all the charges, befides the pilotage, you have to pay at Judda.

It may be now neceffary to caution you againft difputes, which will unavoidably arife, (either about your prices, your payments, your money, or your goods,) that they fhould be fettled amicably, if poffible, by your fhroff, or by merchants of refpectability; but if you are under the neceffity of referring the difpute to the government, apply to whoever has the moft weight at Judda, either the Bafhaw or the Xeriffs; but not without a prefent. If your application

cation is to the Bafhaw, go yourfelf perfonally: and if it is to the Xeriff, go to his houfe in Judda: if he is abfent, write to him to Mecca, through your Arab writer. But all this is only upon the moft urgent neceffity: for all communication with the government ought to ceafe, immediately after making your prefent and paying your cuftoms.

Having finifhed your bufinefs at Judda, which will probably be in the end of July, and able to fail by the firft of Auguft, you will probably get to Mocho the 10th; of which you fhould inform the broker before you leave Mocho to go up the Gulf (or Red Sea); and defire him to procure you all the freight he can, and have it ready by this time. The freight from Mocho to Bombay is two and a-half per cent. for treafure; and to Surat, to be delivered free of all charges to the confignee, three per cent. for gold, and four and a-half per cent for filver: by this mode you will be able to do all your bufinefs, and leave Mocho, perhaps, with full freight, by the 20th of Auguft, (particularly if it fhould be a year when there is no Company's fhip there, then there will be little doubt of your getting full of freight,) by which means you will get to Bombay in the early part of September, and have fine weather, and a whole feafon before you, to go to Surat, if neceffary

The cuftoms upon piece goods being taken in kind at Judda, the government allow the purfer and linguift the cuftoms arifing to it, of two bales, viz. one bale each; and give them leave to pick the two richeft bales in the cargo for themfelves. The captain being generally his own purfer, this alfo is one of his perquifites, as well as in his freight treafure he draws the following primage, viz. on every one thoufand two hundred and fifty cruz he has one german crown; the figning every bill of lading one german crown; every paffenger on going on board, one german crown; and on every bale, cheft, bundle, or package whatfoever of freight, twenty-five dooanies each.

A comparative

A comparative View of the relative Value of Coins with Bombay.

		Rup.	Qrs.	Rais
100	Mexico, or head dollars, will mint	239	2	74
100	French crowns (if full weight)	239	0	59
100	Englifh ditto (of which they have many)	239	2	74
100	Pillar dollars	241	3	38
100	German crowns	226	3	92
100	Duccatoons	244	1	39
100	Old abaffes *	226	3	80
100	New abaffes	256	3	0
100	Eftimates	239	2	74
100	Old Seville eftimates	242	3	70
100	Peru (or cobb dollars)	224	2	28
100	Lion dollars	193	1	4

Should you wifh to coin your filver, the above ftatement will be found pretty correct, exclufive of mintage, which amounts to about four per cent. But if your fhip is going to Madras and Bengal, it is better to fell your filver to the fhroff than coin it. One hundred ounces of ftandard filver will bring you two hundred and fifty-eight and a-half, or two hundred and fifty-nine Arcott rupees; and there being only one per cent. difference between Arcott and Madras rupees, makes it feven per cent. better thus to fell to the fhroffs than coin it into Madras rupees.

The exchange at Judda frequently fluctuates, but the general average may be taken at two hundred and fifty cruz per hundred Spanifh (head) dollars.

* There are another kind of old abaffes often mixed with the above, which are five per cent. worfe.

From

From the above statement it would be best, at making your sales, to fix both the price, or value, of your gold and silver coin (in cruz) with the merchant: in this be very exact, and observe, that gold fluctuates more than silver all over India: it would be neceſſary, therefore, before you leave Calcutta, Madras, Bombay, or Surat, to have the price current, of all kinds of coins, from the ſhroffs, in the current rupee of the place: as in Bengal the price in Sicca rupees; Madras, in Madras and Arcott rupees; Bombay, in Bombay and Arcott rupees; and Surat, in Surat and Arcott rupees: by this means you will know to a certainty what your coins will produce, and the best market for the ſale of them: add to this, large ſums are paid at Judda in gold; and a ſmall error in calculation may amount to a conſiderable ſum. And be guarded, upon the receipt of gold, not to ſuffer them to charge you one or two per cent. for what they call overweight; or if obliged to allow it them, make your eſtimate of the relative value accordingly.

The Grand Signor's cuſtoms on goods imported by the Engliſh, through his dominions, are five per cent.; however, the Baſhaw of Judda, under pretence that Judda is not named in the phirmaund for our trade, has always impoſed a great deal more: he takes four per cent. for himſelf, four per cent. for the Xeriffs, and the other impoſitions may be reckoned at four per cent. more; making the whole aggregate amount equal to at leaſt twelve per cent.

Your packages of every kind ſhould be, if poſſible, in even hundreds; for if the number exceed the hundred by a ſingle piece, you pay the cuſtom on the additional hundred. Whether this is done by the officers for their own emolument, or for the benefit of government, I could never find out: nor any redreſs for the exorbitant cuſtoms frequently laid upon gruff goods.

The

The general Imports—are

Caffia-lignum, cardimums, pepper (both long and black, or round), fandal-wood, nutmegs, cinnamon, cloves, turmerick, collembeck, benzoin (head and belly), ginger, lamp-black, fugar, fugar-candy, tin, copper, iron (bars), fteel, tutenague, fome Ballafore iron, piece goods of all kinds, filks (both raw and wrought), chints, &c. &c. &c.

The pillar and head dollar are efteemed here of the fame value, although the pillar dollar is two per cent. better than the head (or Mexico) dollar: the French crown thirteen per cent. lefs, though of equal ftandard; in which you may gain an advantage, by buying up French crowns or pillar dollars: but, if poffible, avoid taking gold (upon your own account).

The new acquifitions lately ceded to the Eaft India Company, in the Myfore, will open a new fource of wealth and commerce to the Englifh and native merchant in India, particularly from Bombay and Calicut to Mocho and Judda; the whole of the Malabar and Canary Decan, and Concan coafts, as well as the rich kingdom of Myfore, furnifhing the richeft articles of commerce for thefe markets.

JUDDA
Coins, Weights, and Meafures.

					lbs.	oz.	dwts.
1 vakia is equal to	-	(troy weight)			0	1	0
15 vakias are 1 rattle	-	-	-		1	3	0
2 rattles are 1 maund	-	-	-		2	6	0
10 maunds are 1 frazil	-	-	-	25	0	0
10 frazils are 1 bahar	-	-	-	250	0	0

All

All goods are weighed with the fteelyards, after the Turkifh manner; and Europeans as well as Turkifh merchants are obliged to reft
contented with fuch weights as the weigher thinks proper to give
them; nor are merchants allowed to weigh goods (whether bought
or fold) themfelves, but the weighman muft attend.

DIRECTIONS

FOR SAILING TO THE WATERING PLACE.

WHEN you weigh from the roads, fteer S. half W. or S. by W.
until you deepen your water to fix and a-half or feven fathoms,
you may then fteer fouth or fouth-eafterly as your lead directs;
but do not come under four and a-half or five fathoms from the
eaftern fide. Two miles below the roads is a large flat, which has
but little water on it. When you approach the Watering Place in
Simon's Bay you will deepen your water to 9 or 10 fathoms, fandy
ground, and will fee a gap in the land to the northward of a bufhy
tree that ftands near the Watering Place; when this tree is juft on
with the gap you are then in the middle of the bay, and may anchor
from 10 to 7 fathoms, but not under feven fathoms, as you will be
too near the fhoal that runs off fhore. With the tree E. half S., in 10
fathoms, there are two fmall fpots of coral about the length of a fhip,
with four or five fathoms water on them.

SHOALS LATELY DISCOVERED.

In latitude 24° 50' N., and 26 miles Weſt of St. John's Iſland, lies a ſhoal, (ſeen in the Gunjaver,) about a cable's length of which is dry.

Note. There is a dangerous ſhoal of rocks, even with the water's edge, and about 50 yards in length, lying to the eaſtward of Sabagar Iſlands, diſtance three or four miles. When in one with the northern-moſt of the above iſlands they bear N.W. by N.; and when you bring the Peak of the S.E. iſland to bear W. half N. diſtance three or four miles, the rocks will then bear N. by W one-quarter W. diſtance four miles.

EXTRACT FROM THE ROYAL ADMIRAL.

Auguſt 16, 1772, at noon, they obſerved, in latitude 20° N. and had made 49° 16' W. from Prince's Iſland meridian diſtance, when they found the water diſcoloured, but had no ground 70 fathoms. On the 18th they weighed, in order to find a paſſage between the main and the iſland, ſteering N.N.E. and N. by W., and had ſix and ſeven fathoms water for ſome time; then ſhoaled from ſeven to four and a-half gradual ſoundings; they then ſtood N.E., E.N.E. and E. until they came into three fathoms, upon which they anchored, the iſland of Mereira bearing from E.S.E. to S., diſtance two and a-half or three leagues: ſome time after the water fell two feet, and the ſhip ſtruck. At eight P.M. they found the water riſing again, which makes the time of high water 10^h 48^m in full and change. It riſes about five feet.

On the 19th they went and ſounded in the boat. N.W. by W. half a mile they had four fathoms, on which they weighed and anchored;

anchored; in that place the variation was obferved to be $5°56'$ W. On the 20th, at ten P.M. a boat with a pilot went on board, who agreed to conduct her between the iflands and the main; the boat went and founded between the fhip and the ifland, and had from four to three fathoms, then deepened gradually to 4, 5, 6, and 7, fathoms. The boat founded to the weftward, and had four and a-half fathoms for two miles from the fhip. On the 21ft, at noon, they weighed and ftood S.E. by E. towards the ifland; foundings 4, 4, 3¾, 3, 3, 3¼, 3½, and 4 fathoms, then deepened gradually to fix fathoms; then bore away E., E.N.E., and N.E , keeping in fix and fix and a-half fathoms until near the iflands; and they then anchored in five fathoms, foft mud and fhells, the ifland bearing from N.E. by E. to S.W. by S. off fhore two miles; latitude, obferved, 20° 23 ; and variation 5° 36 W. On the 25th, at two P.M. they weighed, and ftood along fhore, off the ifland, to the northward and eaftward, fteering from N.N.E. to N.E., in five, five and a-half, and five three-quarters fathoms. At three they came up with a large fand-bank, bearing N.W., above water; they entered this channel, keeping off the bank half a mile, the ifland three miles, and the main two miles; they had from four three-quarters to four one-quarter fathoms, and a caft or two fix fathoms. The ifland bearing about S.W. to N.E., one and a-half or two miles diftance, they anchored in four fathoms to found to the eaftward and weftward of the fhip, and found no lefs than three fathoms. At eight weighed and ftood N. by W. and N E. along fhore; had from five to feven fathoms, and at times three and a-half fathoms. At eleven they anchored in four and a-half fathoms, the north end of Mecca bearing from S. half W. to W.S.W., diftance three miles; latitude obferved, 20° 48' N. In going this paffage they had no lefs at low water than one-quarter lefs three fathoms.

A N

AN

ACCOUNT

OF THE

TRADE TO PERSIA,

BY

THE GULPH AND BUSSORAH.

THE Armenian, Gentoo, Perfee, and Mahomedan merchants of Calcutta, Madras, Bombay, Surat, and Cochin, carry on a large trade to Perfia, through Buſſorah, and to the Red Sea; ſupplying both Perfia, Arabia, and Turkey, with all the manufactures and rich merchandize of India: in return for which they import pearls, carpets, gums, particularly maſtic, ammoniac, galbanum, and a variety of others; pearls, a variety of wines, particularly that of Shiraz (ſo much eſteemed for its delicacy and high flavour), ſenna, nuxvomica, almonds, raiſins, dates, piſtachio nuts, and leather, together with many drugs of high eſtimation in the Materia Medica; aſſafœtida, galls, horns, and numerous other commodities; as well as ſhawls, horſes, &c. &c.; but particularly large quantities of treaſure.

This traffic being carried on by Britiſh commanders and officers, I think it comes within the limits of this work to make ſuch part

of

of it known as I have been able to collect from my own knowledge and the beft information.

The chief manufactures of Bengal, for thefe places, are, muflins,
dimities, calicoes, filks of a variety of fabrics, and gold and filver
gauzes, fugar, &c. &c.

The other general exports of Bengal are, faltpetre, opium, indigo,
rice, drugs, diamonds, and precious ftones, and a variety of grain.

From the coafts of Coromandel and Malabar, are fent to thefe
places, chints, calicoes, and a variety of fpices, particularly cardimums and pepper (both round and long), with many other valuable
articles.

BUSSORAH.

At Buſſorah is got, at a very eafy rate, a bitumen, which, in colour,
fmell, and other qualities, refembles coal-tar, and fully anfwers all
the purpofes which that valuable article is applied to, though in a
very fuperior degree; as it will remain many months under water
uninjured by the worm, which will not touch it, on account of its
fulphureous ftench, and which makes it valuable for fhips bends
and boats bottoms.

I have tried fome experiments with this bitumen (or naphtha)
and coal-tar, by paying (or fmearing) fome plank over with each
fort, both hot and cold; and found the plank done thus with coal-
tar in three months quite eaten like a honeycomb, while that
done with this bitumen remained uninjured, and was fome months
after before the worm made any impreſſion on it.

I believe there is not any part of the world where the worm is fo
deftructive, bites harder, or fooner deftroys a fhip's or a boat's bottom, than in the river Euphrates and the Perfian Gulf; for which
reafon, nature feems to provide this bitumen, as an antidote, to pre-

I

vent the deftruction which this infect would otherwife caufe, and whofe deftructive purpofes are defeated by this valuable but little known material.

This bitumen is a moft beautiful and fhining black, and makes a fhip's bends (when payed with it) appear as if they were varnifhed. Mixed with oil, it makes a beautiful black paint; but it is little ufed, on account of the intolerable ftench it emits until it is quite dry. It is worthy the attention of the navigator, and deferves to be ufed for the many good qualities which it poffeffes.

The horfes brought from Bufforah are very valuable, and the moft perfect beauties of any of their fpecies in the world (except the hoof, which is fmall, narrow, and high, in proportion to the animal). They are able to travel with great expedition, and to undergo incredible fatigue.

The articles for this market (after having your fhip well dunnaged with fhinbin, comar, and fheathing teak planks, of which they are much in want, having little timber of their own) are, iron, pepper, both heavy and light; [what is meant here by heavy pepper is, that which is well garbled, winnowed, and clean, fuch as is fit for the European market; the beft fort of which is got on the Malabar coaft. The light pepper is that which comes from the Malay coaft, Borneo, and coaft of Sumatra, which has invariably a great quantity of hufks in it, and makes it light compared to the other, not being fo well cleaned;] cotton, lamp-black, agala-wood, foofies, cuttanies, moogadooties, elatchies, fine piece goods, toffimet, algar hagar, bule tanmum, alyar bule zurry, alyar bule nunzier, alyar bule fudda, baftas and coffas of all forts, bildar fudda, bildar furry, alyar nimzeer, alyar tomumzier, chetwah corgonnah, chetwah funam, gurrumfoot mohomedfhe, cotnus faddy, of all forts, fhanbs fhelfre, fhanbs cumberbands, farrooks duftoor, fhargen, mufk, broadcloth, &c. &c.

Mahometans pay here only two and a-half per cent.; all other
nations

nations pay five per cent ; and upon gruff goods they pay six per cent.

Should the foregoing lift of goods not be known to the India fircars and merchants, any Turk, Arab, or Armenian, can explain them; as they are a lift taken from a native merchant of Buf-forah.

Immediately upon your arrival at Bufforah, ufe difpatch in going up to town, and procure boats for your cargo; for which you apply to the chief, who generally fends down boats, called dunnocks; but I would advife you to have trankeys, as they are lefs liable to be ftopped in the river, which frequently happens when dunnocks are fent.

You are next to look out for, and hire, a good houfe, with large godowns (cellars or warehoufes), which ought to be as nigh to the creek as poffible, for the convenience of landing and receiving your goods.

In choofing your broker, much caution and circumfpection is neceffary, as your whole tranfactions depend upon his being fteady to your intereft. If poffible employ a perfon who trades a little for himfelf, and is independent of any one elfe: the fame caution is to be ufed in choofing your fhroff (or banker).

Thefe people you will find very flow in tranfacting your affairs; though they will appear to be very affiduous: your fervants fhould be folely dependent upon yourfelf; and you ought not to employ any recommended by perfons whom you fufpect to be defirous of prying into or being acquainted with your bufinefs and concerns. This caution is to be obferved, otherwife your whole tranfactions will be communicated to the whole town; which, doubtlefs, will be much to your prejudice.

After you are fettled in your houfe, the merchants will come and pay you a vifit; the Turks and Armenians will be very inquifitive about your affairs; they are particularly tenacious of any flight; be

there-

therefore very complaifant in your behaviour, and treat them (particularly the Turks) with much courtefy.

When landing your cargo, the freight goods (if you have any) fhould be put in different boats from your own, otherwife it will caufe much confufion and trouble, as all the freight is carried to the gomrook (or cuftom-houfe); but your own private trade, immediately upon landing, is carried to your own houfe; for which reafon the officers on board fhould have a lift of the freight goods; and orders not to mix them in the boats with the trade, but load them feparately.

The purfer (if you have one) ought to attend at the landing place with a lift of the freight, and the marks and numbers of each package; as it frequently happens that the merchants do not know their own bales.

After all your goods are landed, you inform the Shabundar you are ready for his vifit; he will come, with his officers, attendants, writers, and fome of the principal merchants of the place; they will take an account of your goods, open a bale or two of each quality, and are fatisfied with your account of the number of bales, and quantity of pieces in each. This good opinion fhould not be abufed, as it renders the infpection extremely eafy to you. And for the gruff goods he takes the account entirely from yourfelf.

After this firft vifit he pays you another, to be informed of the prices for which you have fold your goods; and if any remain unfold they are valued, and the cuftoms and duties calculated upon the whole.

The Shabundar receives no duty upon grain; this is paid to the Murbarall: other goods either pay to the Shabundar or cuftom-houfe.

Upon exporting any goods, you muft have a permit from the Shabundar, mentioning the quantity and quality of them.

The gomrook hamauls (or cuftom-houfe porters), will not allow

your

your own hamauls (or porters) to bring your goods from the water
fide to your houfe, (as thefe people farm their place from government, and pay a large fum annually for it), for which you pay them
one mamoodie per bale, and five mamoodies per hundred maunds
(fophy). Houfe hamauls have only half that fum for their labour;
and five mamoodies per hundred maunds (fophy), for the returning
cargo.

Boat hire is two mamoodies per bale, and ten mamoodies per hundred maunds (fophy). The beft method is to hire trankeys, for fo
much per trip; the expence is fomething more; but the fafety of
your goods, and the difpatch they make, fully compenfate for it.

Prefents here are very neceffary, particularly to the Iflam (or
Bafhaw); they are generally made up in goods, to the value of twelve
or fifteen hundred cruz: but he afterwards receives the amount in
money, and the goods are returned. This makes it eafy to the merchant, as he might otherwife difpute the value of the goods.

You fhould make a proportionate prefent to the Shabundar and
his people; the Murbar's people, your broker, fhroff, linguift, and
the Bafhaw's fervants.

After your prefents are all made you vifit the Iflam, who makes
you fome trifling prefent, as a coat (or gown), fuch as is worn in
the country.

Your houfe will coft you about thirty tomands for the feafon; befides you muft have a licence to trade, which is five tomands per
annum more. Your doorwaun (or porter), thirty-fix mamoodies
per month; waterman (or beaftie), thirty mamoodies per month;
and your watchman, twenty mamoodies per month.

You fhould have Englifh weights and fcales; as their weights are
feldom juft, being only bags of ftones.

Owners of fhips, from all ports in India, allow the commanders
houfe-rent, palanquin (or carriage) hire, oil, candles, grain, fuel.
Sircars (or comprodors) pay, except at the port to which the fhip

belongs,

belongs, when no houfe-rent or palanquin hire is allowed, but every thing elfe. And this cuftom is general in India, except there is a fpecial agreement to the contrary. If they bring freight back, upon their returning voyage, the owners allow to the commander five per cent. as a commiffion for collecting it.

Weights.

					lbs	oz.
1	vakia is	—	—	—	10	19
24	vakias are	1 maund	—	—	28	8
76	d° -	1 maund feefe (or fophy)	—		90	4
117	d° -	1 cutra	—	—	138	15

A Lift of Bengal and other Goods for the Bufforah Market.

Baftas, fhaundpore.
  D° dacca.
  D° blue.
Dureas, flowered and plain.
Elatchies, maulda.
Emerties.
Hummums.
Mulmuls, muxadabad.
    D° furbetties.
    D° heatty.
    D° anundy.
    D° mahmodeatty.
    D° fevohdeatty.
Soofies.

Turmeric.
Coffaes, ordinary.
Sugar-candy.
Sugar, Bengal.
  D° Java.
Jaggary.
Benzoin.
Cloves.
Nutmegs.
Mace.
Pepper, black.
  D° long.
Rice, fine.
  D° courfe.
          Searhaudpeak.

Searhaudpeak.	Tin.
Surbands fonnarjam.	Lead.
Terendams.	Iron.
Taffeties, fine.	Copper utenfils.
Coffaes affmary.	Planks.
Lamp-black.	Stick-lack.
Camphor, China.	Ginger.

Lieutenant Colonel TAYLOR, of the Bombay eftablifhment, who, in the year 1790, croffed the Great Defert in his way to Bufforah, in charge of public difpatches, and touched at fome of the ports on the Perfian fhore during the voyage to Bombay, has mentioned the following particulars*; which are inferted in this place, in order to throw a further illuftration on the commerce of Perfia, and of the connection, which it may be in contemplation to eftablifh, between Great Britain and that once flourifhing and extenfive empire.

The author here quoted had an opportunity, during his ftay at Bufhire, of making obfervations on the prefent ftate of Perfia; and he obferves, that "The articles of commerce, with which the empire of Perfia abounds, are various; in particular, fine carpets, wrought filver, pearls, excellent tobacco, filk and cotton. The principal commodities taken in return are, Englifh broad-cloth, particularly fcarlet' and yellow. Manchefter printed cottons were fuggefted, as likely to anfwer the Perfian market, and fome of the moft brilliant patterns were felected, and fent to Bufhire, but they by no means fuited the tafte of the Perfians; for what appeared extremely handfome in the eyes of an European was difregarded by that people, and the more fimple, though perhaps not lefs elegant, patterns of their own preferred. It might be worth while to carry the experiment a little further; and it would very well repay the trouble and expence, pro-

---

* See Travels from England to India.

N n 2

vided

vided fo material a branch of our manufactures could be brought into ufe in Perfia. The experiment (which I would alfo recommend) is, to collect fome of their moft efteemed patterns, and have them printed upon fine cotton, particularly the figures which are common, or in general ufe in India and Perfia, with the moft vivid colours that can be procured; and, in fhort, by variety, and attention to their national tafte and character, induce them to become purchafers of thofe, and fuch other commodities as are the manufacture of Great Britain."

" In the beginning of 1799, an embaffy was fent, by the Governor General, by the way of Bombay, to the court of Shirauz. This miffion is faid to have had a twofold object; the one, political, the other commercial. The vicinity of Perfia to the dominions of Zemaun Shaw, and the depredations committed by that prince on the eaftern provinces of the Perfian empire, give to the Eaft India Company a well-grounded hope, that the military refources of that kingdom may, on fome future occafion, be fuccefsfully turned againft that powerful and ambitious invader, or his fucceffor; who will no doubt be guided by the fame views and interefts with the prefent prince. The commercial relations may, no doubt, be carried to a very confiderable extent. A monopoly in the hands of the Company, of Britifh woollens, Manchefter goods, metals, &c., would promote the fale of the ftaples and manufactures of Great Britain; while a free commerce would be carried on between the country traders of India and the natives of Perfia. It is computed that Perfia confumes annually of the produce of India, two crores and three lacs of rupees; and that the returns are under half that fum: confequently, the balance of trade being fent back in bullion, or coin, muft not only be beneficial to the Company, but to the European private trader in India, and to Great Britain in particular."

The wine of Shirauz, fo much efteemed by the Perfians, has never been allowed a fair trial by the European connoifeurs. A

fhort

ſhort account of it, from the ſame author, may not in this place be improper.

" The wine of Shirauz is rich, full, and generous; and when old, may be compared to the beſt productions of any country or climate. The new wine has a diſagreeable roughneſs, which age wears off.— It is to be had both white and red, but the firſt is eſteemed the moſt delicious. It is ſaid that four thouſand tons are annually made by the Jews and Armenians in the months of October and November at Shirauz. Much of it is uſed in Perſia, and the remainder exported to India, where it is diſpoſed of at a moderate price. In this country it is ſold at the immoderate rate of one guinea a bottle!"

DIRECTIONS

FOR GOING INTO BALASORE-ROADS IN EITHER MONSOON,
AND HOW TO FIND THE PILOTS.

THE entrance into the river Hoogly is allowed to be the moſt difficult of any river in India; and is the terror of ſtrangers, for want of good directions. The following plain rules will be found more inſtructive to navigators, for going into Balaſore-roads, than any I have hitherto ſeen; and what I have always found correct.

The S.W. monſoon, in the bottom of the Bay of Bengal, always brings in thick weather, with drizzling rain, and prevents obſervations (at times) for many days; by which ſtrangers are much at a loſs, and afraid to run in for Point Palmiras. I will endeavour to obviate ſuch uneaſineſs, by theſe Inſtructions, ſo as to enable any ſhip

to

to go into Balafore-roads, by night or by day, or in any kind of weather.

From Point Palmiras to Chittagong, the firſt of the foutherly winds fet in about the full moon in March, when you have light airs, veering to the eaſtward in the morning, and to the northward towards noon and in the evening. The full moon in April generally brings in the S.W. monfoon, attended with heavy clouds, ſtrong gales, and fometimes rain. It blows in general ſtrong, but more fo upon the fpring or neap tides: for when it blows hard upon the neaps, you generally have it moderate upon the fprings; and when it blows hard upon the fprings you have it more moderate upon the neap tides, as they take off. It continues with little variation until after the full moon in Auguſt; when you have often, for many days together, fair weather.

The N.E. monfoon comes on, in general, about the full moon in October, and generally with a gale of wind from the N.N.W.; it veers round to the weſtward, and breaks up in the S.W. quarter, where it blows hardeſt; then veers to the fouthward and S.E., and ends in the eaſtern quarter, with fair clear weather, and fmooth water.

Having now given a brief account of the monfoons, as they prevail in the bottom of the Bay of Bengal, and particularly in Balafore-roads, I proceed to give Directions for going into Balafore-roads, and how to find the pilots, in either monfoon.

Suppofe you are in the Bay of Bengal, without having an obfervation for many days. As foon as you reckon yourfelf to the northward of 18° N. latitude, haul in for the land, and, if poſſible, make the high land of Pondy, running in without fear, by the lead, which ought to be hove every half mile until you get foundings. There is no danger in doing fo, for there is not more than from 30 to 35 fathoms water, any where from Ganjam to Point Palmiras, at four miles off ſhore. Having got ground, keep along ſhore from 20 to

18 fathoms,

18 fathoms, until you fuppofe yourfelf about the length of Manaka-patam; then haul in for the land to 15 or 16 fathoms by day, and 18 or 20 fathoms by night; keeping the lead going.

From Manakapatam to the Black Pagoda the courfe is N.E. and N.E. by E. If it is daylight, and you are not in more than 18 fathoms, you will fee Jagranaut Pagoda although it may be hazy: haul up for the fhore, and keep between 14 and 16 fathoms until you get foundings upon the Falfe Point, which foundings will be coarfe fand, fhells, and black fpecks, like beaten pepper.

As you run from Jagranaut to the Falfe Point, you will be obliged to haul out E.N.E., or perhaps E., to keep your depth of water; and being over the Falfe Point, and in foft foundings of green mud and ftinking ouze, fteer N.E. by E., and keep between 14 and 16 fathoms water; but do not exceed 16 fathoms for fear of croffing the True Point, or Point Palmiras, without getting the foundings, which are the fame kind of ground (with little difference) as the Falfe Point; and in 16 fathoms, the Point foundings do not exceed three miles broad. As foon as you deepen your water, on the above courfe, to 22 fathoms, with fand, broken fhells, and mixtures of gravel, haul up N.N.W. for the foot of the Brace; and being in 11 fathoms water, not feeing a pilot veffel, keep under weigh, and work from eight fathoms water, into the weftward, to fix or feven fathoms on the Brace, croffing Balafore-roads in the depth of from 12 to 15 fathoms; and anchor at night in 11 or 12 fathoms, keeping under weigh all day.

Should it fo happen that you have not feen the land before you get foundings, and by running along fhore find the foundings off one of the Points; to know whether it is the Falfe or True Point obferve thefe Rules:—If by fteering N.E., N.E. by E., or E.N.E., you keep the fame depth of water (14 or 16 fathoms), foft muddy ground, you may be certain the Point you have croffed is the Falfe Point. But fhould your water increafe 3, 4, or 5 fathoms upon thefe courfes,

in

in the diftance of 3, 4, or 5 miles, with mixtures of fand, fhells, and fometimes mud and fhells, you may reft affured you have croffed the True Point, or Point Palmiras, and may haul up N.N.W. or N.W. by N. for the Brace, or Balafore-roads; and keep working as before directed.

When you fee a pilot veffel (which veffels are in general fnow-rigged, with a jigger or wringtail maft) whofe turn it is not to take charge of your fhip, they will direct you to where your pilot veffel is, who will have a red flag flying at the gaff end: fteer for him, and he will carry you to Calcutta, or fuch place as you may ride in fafety, until a river pilot comes on board to take charge of your fhip.

Coming into Balafore-roads in the N.E. monfoon, you have in-variably fine weather and fmooth water.

You fhould endeavour to keep between the latitude of 21° N. and 21° 10′ N. I think 21° 5′ N. is the beft latitude to keep in; and by fteering W., or W. by S., keeping between the depth of 8 or 10 fathoms water, having regard to the tides (which rife here, and all acrofs the fands, from Point Palmiras to Chittagong, 15 to 18 feet perpendicular) to govern your courfe. The firft hard foundings you will get, in this latitude and depth of water, will be upon the tail of Saugur Reef: by continuing your courfe and depth of water, you will foon crofs this reef, and have foft muddy foundings, at which time Saugur Channel will be fairly open. The foundings upon Saugur Reef are fine grey fand, with fhingle and fparks, like ink-fand or fteel-filings.

By continuing your courfe and depth of water, the next hard ground you come to will be the Eaftern Sea Reef; the foundings upon which are fomething brighter than thofe upon Saugur Reef: and when you deepen upon this courfe to two or three fathoms off the Reef, and have again foft muddy foundings, the South Channel will be fairly open; and a N.W. by N., or N.W. half N. courfe

will

will lead you (with a flood-tide) from eight fathoms on the Eaftern Sea Reef, fair up to the French flat buoy, (which is a red buoy).

If you are a ftranger, and afraid to run up channel, keep between eight and fix fathoms water; and the next hard foundings you get will be on the Eaftern Sea Reef; (this is alfo called the Tail of the Eaftern Brace). You will foon crofs this reef and get foft foundings again; (for the foundings in all the channels are mud). And the fourth hard foundings you get will be on the Weftern Brace; ꞏne fame ground as the Eaftern Sea Reef.

Should you not in this track fee a pilot veffel, ftand to the N.W., for upon a weft courfe you will deepen your water very faft to 12, 15, 18, 20, or 25 fathoms; and, obferve, as foon as your water deepens (as above), you have Balafore-roads open, and ought to haul up for them, as above directed; for in the early part of the N.E. monfoon, before the rivers (which form the different mouths of the Ganges) have emptied themfelves, there are ftrong currents fetting to the W.S.W. and S.W., which might, by inattention, horfe you into deep water, probably round Point Palmiras, out of foundings, and oblige you to crofs the bay, and make your paffage from the eaftward again.

You fhould (as before directed) keep under weigh all day, and work as the tide will permit, between the Weftern Brace and the Eaftern Sea Reef, from 6 to 12 fathoms water; anchoring at night in eight fathoms upon the Tail of the Eaftern Sea Reef; by which means you will keep the South Channel open, and lie in the fair way for pilots coming down that channel, which is the track generally ufed at this feafon; and they will fee you much fooner by being under weigh, than if you continued to lie at anchor.

An

An Account of some of the Articles of Produce which are generally exported from Bengal.

Opium. There are four qualities in Bengal which are exported for the consumption of the Malay coast and places to the eastward, viz. Patna, called (among the eastern people) Company's opium, being marked with their mark, thus

Benares, next in quality; the third is Rungpore; and the fourth and last quality is Boggulpore (or Bogglipore opium).

The best opium in the world is said to come from Patna, (where it is made in great quantities,) and allowed by the Malays and Chinese to be better than that which is called Turkey opium, and carried to Batavia and China by ships from Europe.

I have already mentioned (under the head of Batavia) that opium is prohibited to be imported or sold by individuals, being a monopoly of the Dutch Company; nor are individuals allowed to make or export opium in or from Bengal, except such as is bought at the Company's sales; for which quantity, being limited, they have contractors who furnish the supplies. But notwithstanding the prohibition, there are large quantities of opium made and exported from Bengal, exclusive of that sold by the East India Company.

Opium is an inspissated juice, partly resinous and partly gummy, and brought to us, at Calcutta, in cakes of from one to five pounds weight, packed in chests, (in the leaves of the poppy,) covered with hides.

It

It is very heavy, of a denfe texture, and not dry, much refembling pitch in a half fluid ftate, eafily receiving the impreffion of the finger, its colour is a very dark brown yellow, fo dufky that until held up to the light it appears black; it has a dead faint fmell, and its tafte is very bitter and acrid. It fhould be chofen moderately firm, and not too foft, (as that of the years 1789-90, which was quite in a fluid ftate, and univerfally rejected by the Malays, as unmerchantable); its fmell and tafte fhould be very ftrong, and care fhould be taken, when rubbed between the fingers and thumb, that there is no roughnefs; for if there is, the article is thickened and adulterated with duft or ftoney matter.

Opium is the juice of the poppy, with which the fields (where the article is made) are fown, as ours are with corn. When the heads begin to ripen they cut or make incifions in them, with an inftrument made for the purpofe, and from thefe wounds the opium flows; and the next day a perfon takes off what ouzes from them, making another incifion on the poppy head at the oppofite fide, which completes the fcarification all round. What he collects he puts in a veffel which is faftened round his waift; and he thus goes round the field wounding the poppy and collecting the juice.

After they have collected the opium they moiften it with water or honey, (the latter is the beft, not being fo fubject to evaporate or dry,) and work it a long time upon a flat fmooth board, with a thick and ftrong inftrument, made for the purpofe, until it becomes of the confiftence of half fluid pitch; it is then worked into rolls or cakes with the hands, and packed in the withered leaves of the poppy in chefts for fale. Each cheft fhould contain two factory maunds (of feventy-four pounds ten ounces each), or one hundred and fifty-nine pounds four ounces avoirdupois.

Thofe who take opium to excefs foon become enervated, and look old; when deprived of it, they are faint, fpiritlefs, and dejected, and experience the fame languor as thofe who are in the habit of drink-

ing

ing ardent fpirituous liquors to excefs, nor (like thofe) is it removed until they take a repetition of the dofe.

In fine, opium contains gum, refin, effential oil, falt, and earthy matter; but its narcotic and fomniferous qualities have been experimentally found to refide in its effential oil.

Indigo has lately become an article of great export from Bengal to Europe; it is therefore much cultivated in the provinces, and the foil agrees particularly well with the fhrub; it grows to the fize of a rofe-tree, but has a fmooth rind. The leaves, when ftripped off at the proper feafon, are laid together, when a vegetable dew exhales from them; they are then immerfed in water, contained in veffels adapted for the purpofe. After the water has extracted the blue from the leaves, it is drained off; the fediment is then expofed in broad fhallow veffels to the fun-beams, through the heat of which the moifture evaporates, and the indigo remains in cakes at the bottom.

Bengal produces the *Sugar Cane* in great abundance, of which they make excellent fugar and rum. The filk-worm is alfo reared in that country, and their fabrics of filk are excellent; but thofe of cotton are fuperior to any in the world.

Cochineal, or *Cocheneel,* has within thefe few years drawn the attention of many of the gentlemen of Bengal, and it has been reared by them with fome degree of fuccefs, although not in fufficient quantities to make the exports confiderable. As it doubtlefs will in a fhort time become an object of confiderable magnitude to the merchant and planter, a fhort account of it may not be thought improper in this work; I will therefore attempt to give the beft account I could collect from thofe gentlemen who had the plant and infect.

It

It is generally underftood to be a drug, and ufed by dyers for giving red colours, efpecially crimfon and fcarlet, and for making carmine; and likewife in medicine as a cardiac, cordial, fudorific, alexipharmic, and febrifuge.

The infeĉt was firft fuppofed to be brought to Calcutta, by fome gentleman, from Manilla, about the year 1788; fince which time it has been attended to, though not in the manner fuch a valuable article of commerce feems to deferve. Several famples have been fent to Europe; but whether it really is of an inferior quality, or a want of knowledge in the collecting and preferving of it, I do not know, nor could I learn; but the account received of it did not anfwer the (perhaps too fanguine) expectations of the perfons who tried the experiment.

The cochineal, in the ftate it is brought to us, is in fmall round bodies of an irregular figure, ufually convex, and ridged and furrowed on one fide, and concave on the other.

The colour of the beft fort is a purplifh grey, powdered over with a fort of white duft.

All that Europeans knew of this for a long time was, that it was gathered from certain plants in Mexico, and therefore it was naturally fuppofed a feed; until, in the year 1692, Father Plumier gave Pomet an account of its being an animal; and this, though difregarded at the time, has been confirmed by fubfequent obfervations. Indeed, to confirm the point, we need feek no further than the means now in our hands; but if it required further proofs, we need only moiften and foak in water or vinegar, a number of cochineals until they are fwelled and diftended, to know that every one is more or lefs the perfect body of an infect. The moft imperfect and mutilated fpecimens always fhew the rings of the body; and from obferving others, it will be eafy to find the number and difpofition of the legs; parts, or even whole ones, being left on feveral, and often

complete

complete pairs. In this way, the legs, antennæ, and probofcis, may be difcovered.

This infect much refembles what we call the lady-bird (or lady-cow), and is called by the Manillians, Vacca de Sant Antonia (or St. Anthony's cow). They gather it in the woods, where it lives, grows, and multiplies exceedingly, upon the uncultivated nopal prickly pear, or milk bufh; which grows all over India in great abundance. As they gather it, they brufh it from the leaves with a feather into an earthen pot, and afterwards kill it, by fpreading it upon fheets of heated copper: by this procefs the beautiful colour is prevented from evaporating, of which it lofes much by being allowed to die naturally in the earthen veffel or upon the leaves. And although that which is collected dead from the leaves is fold cheaper, there is no advantage in ufing it, as it requires a greater quantity to give the dye.

A PLAN,

FOR A SHIP ENGAGED IN THE RICE TRADE FROM CALCUTTA TO MADRAS.

THE beft fized fhip for this trade is a long, low, broad fhip, that will carry about ten or twelve thoufand bags of rice; and draw only feventeen or eighteen feet water, by which means fhe might occafionally load all her cargo at Calcutta. And fuch a fhip may be navigated with very little additional expence, on the fame terms of a fhip carrying only feven thoufand bags.

The reafons for having a fhip particularly built for this trade, muft appear obvious to every perfon who knows the trade of India, the

qualities

qualities a ship should have, and the navigation she has to engage with, as well shoal water in Calcutta (or the Hoogly) rivers, as short seas, and sometimes violent blowing weather, when beating against the S.W. monsoon, in the Bay of Bengal.

To answer the queries that naturally arise from the described qualities of the ship I propose, I would first have her a long ship; by which means she becomes proportionally a broad ship. She must, for the above reason, be a long ship, which will also add very considerably to her facility of sailing, and make her easier in those short chopping seas, which she invariably meets with in the Bay of Bengal, when beating against the S.W. monsoon.

I would next have her a broad ship, proportionable, or rather exceeding the proportion of her length, that she might carry her cargo easy, and load well; for rice being nearly as heavy as sand, ships do not require such an extraordinary quantity of room as if they were to take on board gruff goods as cargo, which would require more room for stowage; with this advantage, also, her breadth adds to her stiffness; she will consequently require a smaller quantity of ballast, which for large ships costs a great deal of money, reduces considerably the profits of the voyage, and invariably occasions much delay in Madras-roads, (as well as much trouble in shifting ship *), there being but

---

* Shifting ship, is a technical term used for changing cargo for ballast, or ballast for cargo, keeping a sufficient quantity of either, or dead weight, in the ship's bottom, to prevent her liability to overset, as very few ships will stand upon their legs (or upright) without some considerable weight in the bottom, particularly sharp fast-sailing ships. The Company's ships all carry a proportion of kentledge (or iron ballast) to make them stiff, and to shift easier, though I only think it useful to their China ships, who load all gruff goods home. The coast and bay ships can be made sufficiently stiff with saltpetre from Calcutta; and the Bombay ships, which fill up with pepper on the Malabar coast, might have saltpetre sent to Bombay by the country ships, at a less expence than the Company pay the ship owners for carrying useless, unprofitable kentledge. The Bencoolen ships might be supplied with saltpetre by the same mode upon country ships.

a proportion of Mafoola boats allowed to each fhip, according to the number of fhips in the roads.

I would have her a low fhip for thefe reafons:

By being low it adds to her ftiffnefs, not expofing fo much top-hamper (as it is called) above the bends to make her crank, (liable to heel or overfet eafily,) being the reverfe of ftiff. She will, therefore, require little ballaft, perhaps none, which will facilitate difpatch both in loading and unloading.

She will confequently be more weatherly, which is particularly requifite in a fhip which has to make four or more beating paffages againft the monfoons annually.

There are many other good qualities attached to a long, low, broad fhip, which, from what has been obfetved, muft be obvious to the difcerning navigator.

But fuppofe we have a fhip every way fuiting the plan, for a rice fhip; the voyage fhould be fo planned as to make her carry four rice cargoes anually from the Hoogly to Madras.

To effect this, we fuppofe the fhip capable of loading ten thoufand bags of rice, at feventeen feet draft of water, all of which fhe may take in at Calcutta; or eleven thoufand, at eighteen feet draft of water, which fhe may take in at Kedjerree.

In peaceable times I would navigate her, if poffible, with Euro-pean feamen, by the run, as the colliers are navigated to the Thames; but fuppofing thofe kind of feamen are not to be had, we muft have recourfe to the native lafcars; who I truft, before this time, are better regulated than hitherto, as none would go a voyage of one month, unlefs they received four months advance; and upon their arrival, they confider the extra wages forfeited, and their time ex-pired. Cuftom in fome meafure made this a law; they never worked the time out, and if detained, they found opportunities of deferting, to the lofs of the owners, and frequent detention of the fhip; for it requires from a month to fix weeks to collect men for a fhip of any

confider-

confiderable burthen; and longer time if many fhips are fitting out together.

But we fuppofe that we have our fhip loaded and manned the 1ft of January, and that fhe leaves the pilot the 5th, and arrives at Madras the 10th. I will endeavour to allow fufficient time for every thing to be done in this voyage; and, barring accidents, have time to fpare.

This being a dead feafon of the year at Madras, and few (if any) fhips in the roads, fhe ought to fail from thence the 1ft of February; at which time the foutherly winds and northerly currents begin to creep along the Coromandel and Golconda coafts; and the fhip fhould, in confequence, keep clofe along the fhore, without going into Petapolly or Mafulapatam bays; and fhe will make her paffage in ten days, arriving the 10th of February, fay the 15th. This ends the firft, and probably the quickeft voyage.

The lafcars are now to be well-looked after, to prevent defertion. For the reafons given before, and as a further fecurity, the fhip fhould not go above Coxe's Ifland; or fay Kedjerree, on the oppofite fhore.

Her cargo being down in floops, or burrs, (at this fine feafon,) fhe ought to be loaded in fifteen days, and leave the pilot on the 5th of March. By taking the eaftern range, prefcribed in my Directions, fhe will be at Madras in ten or twelve days, fay fifteen, that is on the 20th of March. We will now (as there are more fhips in the roads) allow her one month to unload and take in ballaft and water, when fhe will fail the 20th of April, and get to Kedjerree the 25th of April, (ending her fecond voyage), where her cargo is to be in floops, and a frefh crew of lafcars ready to go on board. The weather now begins to be bad for loading of fhips, and probably the river floops will not be fond of coming out of Kedjerree; we will, therefore, allow her one month to load, and fay fhe will leave the pilot the 1ft of June, which is allowing great time.

P p

She

She has now to work againft the S.W. monfoon, and will therefore require time. I may fay, with confidence, fhe will arrive the 20th of June, but fay the 1ft of July, at Madras. Our European fhips will probably be there at this time, and boats will be difficult to be had; we will therefore allow her to the 5th of Auguft to leave the roads; and having a fair wind fhe will be at Kedjerree the 10th of Auguft, ending her third voyage. The weather being pretty well fettled, her cargo ought to be on board and leave the pilot the 15th of September; and keeping clofe along the fhores of Orixa, Golconda, and Coromandel, in the ftrong foutherly currents, occafioned by the rivers emptying themfelves after the inundations, particularly the Ganges and Kiftna rivers, fhe will make a paffage to Madras in ten days, arriving the 25th of September. Every difpatch is to be ufed now to get the fhip clear, as the monfoon changes upon the full moon in October, which is generally attended with a gale of wind, and frequenty does much damage in Madras-roads; but fhips attending to the weather, fea, and furf, may always avoid it; as the gale comes firft off the land, which enables fhips to run a few leagues off to fea, and there heave too, until the gale is over. In confequence of thofe heavy gales at the change of the monfoon, upon the Coromandel coaft, the underwriters in India, viz. Calcutta, Madras, and Bombay, have agreed, and the cuftom is admitted, though omitted and not entered in the policy, that all rifk ceafes from the 16th of October to the 15th of December upon thefe coafts, from Cape Comorin to Point Palmiras.

I think, with difpatch, the fhip may be cleared in one month, and leave Madras in fufficient time to fave her infurance (the 16th of October): and as fhe has now to beat up againft ftrong currents and the N.E. monfoon, fhe muft take a large eaftern range, though I would not advife her to go farther than three and a-half or four degrees to the eaftward of Point Palmiras; for about the meridian of the point, and three degrees to the eaftward, you generally find an

eddy,

eddy, from the great current which fets along fhore to the fouthward, or counter current, draining up to the northward; which, when fhe has found, by increafing her latitude more than the log will give, fhe ought to keep in by fhort tacks, that fhe may not overfhoot the limits (which are narrow) in which this favourable ftream runs.

Having left Madras, probably with light breezes, fhe will be fet far to the fouthward before fhe lofes this foutherly current; we muft on that account allow her to the 25th of November to get to Calcutta, (as fhe ought now to go up to town,) fay the 1ft of December; and not having in this bufy voyage time to examine the rigging, there fhould be extra, or batta, lafcars employed to overhaul it. Take in the cargo, and prepare the fhip for fea, while the Serang (or native boatfwain), whofe duty it is to fhip and provide lafcars, is getting your crew; and ought to be ready to fail again on the 1ft of January, commencing your voyage regularly.

By this Plan, a fhip (as defcribed) would land anually at Madras forty thoufand bags of rice, which, at two and a-half rupees per bag freight (or profit), and which is a low average upon the Calcutta and coaft prices, would amount to one lack (or one hundred thoufand rupees); which, fuppofing the fhip to fail at two thoufand rupees per month, leaves a nett profit to the owners of feventy-fix thoufand rupees, which, at two and fixpence the rupee, is nine thoufand five hundred pounds fterling.

The bufinefs of buying and felling is done by a fet of people, called fircars, who are immediately connected with, and fubordinate to, a richer man of the fame clafs, who is complimented with the name of banyan, fhroff, or banker.

Their characters I will ftate under the general name of their tribe.

THE

THE HINDOOS

Are effeminate and luxurious, and, by education, taught to affect a grave deportment. This naturally initiates them early into the arts of diffimulation; fo that they can carefs thofe they hate, and even behave with the greateft affability and kindnefs to fuch as they would wifh to be deprived of exiftence.

Thus educated, they feldom fcold or wrangle; and I never remember to have feen two Hindoos fight, or even ftrike each other.

Their common method of falutation (the falam) is performed by lifting one or both hands to the head, according to the quality of the perfon faluted; but they never ufe the left hand fingly, as that is a mark of the greateft difrefpect.

Their manner of drinking is remarkable—they religioufly avoid touching the veffel which contains the liquor with their lips, but pour it into their mouths, holding the veffel at a confiderable diftance above their head. Their idea is, that they would be polluted by drinking ftagnant water, which they do not confider to be fuch while it runs from the veffel; they will therefore drink from a pump or running ftream, but not from a tub, a cafk, or a pool.

From their temper and tenets, as well as from the authorities of antient hiftorians, it appears more than probable that the fame kind of garments, food, furniture, building, and manners in general, which prevailed among their progenitors fome thoufand years ago, actually prevail among the Hindoo tribes to this day; fo little are thefe people flaves to fafhion.

To fum up their general character in few words; they are gentle, patient, temperate, regular in their lives, charitable, and ftrict obfervers

of

of their religious ceremonies. They are fuperftitious, effeminate, avaricious, and crafty; deceitful and difhoneft in their dealings, void of every principle of honour, generofity, or gratitude. Gain is their predominant principle; and as a part of their gains, beftowed in gifts to their priefts or charities to the poor, will procure their pardon, they can cheat without fearing the anger of their gods.

Such is the character of the fircars, who principally tranfact bufi-nefs for all the European merchants in Bengal.

A PLAN

A PLAN

OF A

V O Y A G E

TO THE

PEDIR COAST,

FOR A VESSEL ABLE TO CONTAIN 2000 OR 3000 BAGS OF RICE, OR FROM 150 TO 200 TONS.

FIRST, let us suppose the ship to be fitted-out from Calcutta, and ready to fail (immediately after the Company's first opium sales) the 15th of January, and leave the pilot the 20th, supplied with a choice investment for the coast, and say twenty chests of opium.

She has a prospect of getting the Company's freight opium to Pinang, and perhaps to Batavia: the latter pays thirty, the former ten rupees per chest, and would be an object for a ship of the above size, equal to foregoing her coast voyage.

But suppose that the owner has not interest to get these freights, let us pursue our original plan. From Calcutta, let her push for Junk Ceylon, where she will fell her rice (ballast to advantage; and, perhaps, receive one or two hundred bloars of tin. But

she

she is not to lose time if she cannot get assisted by country boats, (which is seldom the case,) but push on to Pooloo Pinang (the inside passage), and endeavour to supply that island with any Bengal goods that are in demand and they want; using every means to find what goods are in demand on the Pedir coast, and reserve them for your own purchase (or barter). For the goods you dispose of at Pinang, take equal quantities of dollars, and Acheen gold-dust (if to be had, if not, take the best you can get, Jambie is the next quality). Sail from Pinang, and go directly to Tellosomoy; send one boat to Courtoy, and you will soon find out what goods they want, and what they have to give in return: chickney and pepper are the things you want. Play them off, and ask for white beetle-nut, (as you may be assured there is not one hundred bhar on the coast at this season); then ask for red-nut, which is not so scarce; but demand sufficient to load your vessel: if you get it, return to Pinang and sell, or send it to Pegue, by chartering a large ship to bring your returns: yet this defeats the intent of the Plan, and I only mention it eventually, to shew you cannot be disappointed in the returns the coast may supply; and as it is very improbable, the getting nut gives you the advantage of the staples they have. Suppose you succeed in getting chickney and pepper, with some red-nut, you try every other place on the coast to complete your cargo, and if you do not at Acheen, run round to Sufoo, and Labon Hodgee; there are many other places of trade between Acheen Head and Labon Hogee; but as I suppose the executive agent to have a knowledge of them, as well as the places on the Pedir coast, I omit particulars, where we are to close the first returning cargo, and proceed to the weathermost port on the coast of Coromandel, say Negapatam, for a market, or say Porto Nova, Pondicherry, or even Madras. The agent, or commander of your ship, wants no memorandum to remind him of the necessity of finding what coast goods are in demand, and supply himself with them, as returns for his chickney and

pepper:

pepper; and leaving the coaſt with all poſſible diſpatch, get to Soofoo or Labon Hodgee, or any port on the weſt coaſt; and as the object of your voyage is now changed, you are to ſupply yourſelf with gold, pepper, and white-nut. Should you find any difficulty in fetching far enough to windward on the weſt coaſt, loſe no time, but puſh for Acheen, where you will, in all probability, ſell goods and receive gold (or cargo). If you are ballaſted with ſalt from the Coromandel coaſt, endeavour to ſell it before you go on the Pedir coaſt. I now ſuppoſe you have left Acheen and arrived at Pedir, and having tried the place of trade on that coaſt, as far as Tellofomoy and Courtoy, run over for Pinang with your nut, pepper, wax, &c. &c. ſtaples for the China market.

Now let us ſuppoſe the market at Pinang will not admit of an advantageous ſale, and you have little, perhaps no funds left. You ſhould have a credit at that place for as many dollars, to be inveſted in gold and goods, as will re-load your ſhip with the articles you know, from experience, to be in greateſt plenty; and as you have little time to loſe, go over, as before, to Tellofomoy, and run that coaſt down to Pedir, only inveſting, as before, for the China market. You muſt go back to Tellofomoy, for the purpoſe of fetching over to Pinang, by which you will have an opportunity of filling up, and finding what remains on the coaſt, as well as getting the neceſſary information of what they want for your Pinang inveſtment. Let us ſuppoſe, on your arrival at Pinang, that none of the Indiamen bound to China have paſſed, and that your firſt cargo is on hand; you muſt land your ſecond, and borrow money on the depoſit. For your re-turn to the coaſt loſe no time, as the ſale of this trip depends on diſ-patch. Go to Tellofomoy and down to Pedir; return again to Tel-lofomoy, and if not full run for Battabarra, and fill up with canes and rattans, and again to Pinang, where we may now ſay you have three cargoes for the Indiamen; wait their arrival and ſell them yourſelf;

3

you

you will fave five per cent. commiffion on the fales, which you will find is an object.

Having fold your cargoes, paid your debts, and releafed your credit, keep no more funds than you want to load nut for Bengal, and remit the remainder to difcharge your bonds; or purchafe opium in the event of being late on the coaft, and go once more to Tellofomoy and down the coaft of Pedir; and if you do not fill up, keep on to Acheen, and round to Soofoo, &c. &c. for wax, pepper, benjamin, and elephants teeth, for Bengal. Having filled up, proceed to Bengal; but, if not full, firft to Pinang. Fill up with what you can get on account or freight, and run to Bengal; if early, call into Junk Ceylon, if not, run by and fave time.

Now, fuppofe you leave the Bengal pilot the 20th of January, and arrive at Junk Ceylon the 5th of February, 15 days, (a great allowance); fay you are here five days, and fail the 10th, arrive at Pinang the 15th, and fail the 20th; arrive at Tellofomoy the 25th, and having a fair wind, I will allow you to the 15th of March to get to Acheen, and the 25th to Soofoo. Sail for the coaft the 5th of April, and arrive at any port on the coaft the 20th; fail the 1ft of May, and get to Tellofomoy the 15th of June, to Pinang the 20th, and fail the 25th; arrive at Tellofomoy the 1ft of July, and arrive at Pinang the 5th of Auguft; fail the 10th, and going over the fame track, and to Battabarra, arrive the 20th of September; fail the 1ft of October, going down the coaft, and to Soofoo, and returning to Pinang, arrive the 5th of December; fail the 8th, and arrive at Calcutta the 1ft of January, this leaves you 15 days to fhip your lafcars, and purfue the fame track.

JUNK CEYLON.

Being bound into Junk Ceylon, you may go to the northward of Pooloo Raja. Between Pooloo Raja and the Brothers, or to the fouthward of the Brothers, keep along the iflands to the northward, and pafs any where within three quarters of a mile from the fhore, having no danger but what is above water. Having Pooloo Raja S. three-quarters W., fteer in N. or N. half W. until Point Capall bears E. half S.; then haul in W. half S. for Junk Ceylon Roads, and anchor in four fathoms; or having Pooloo Capall N.E. three-quarters E., Pooloo Tullore S.E. by E. three-quarters E., haul up for the Roads N.W. half N. keeping along the white fandy beach of the Great Lolland.

This is fo inconfiderable a place of trade, fince the eftablifhment of Pooloo Pinang, or Prince of Wales's Ifland, that it is not worth the attention of a merchant to call here. All their trade is taken away by the prows and fmall craft belonging to that ifland.

The bhar of this place fhould be 509 lbs. avoirdupois.

QUEDA

Was formerly a place of confiderable trade, before the eftablifh-ment of Pooloo Pinang, fince which time the prows and fmall craft of that ifland have carried all the trade there, for the euro-pean and country fhips going to China.

When going on fhore you land on the ftarboard hand, or eaft fide of the river, and the Captain Chinaman will report your arrival to the Shabundar, who will introduce you to the King. You muft not neglect to carry a prefent with you, according to the quantity of

goods

goods you expect to fell; which will be but fmall, as Queda is conftantly well fupplied from Pooloo Pinang. However, your prefent
fhould be genteel, and do not forget the Captain Chinaman and Shabundar, as they can be of great fervice to you, and inform you of all
the cuftoms, as well as the markets; and whether any thing is likely
to be done.

They weigh here by the dotchin (or wooden fteelyards), and four
hundred and twenty four pounds avoirdupois is the bhar; but they
have fcales and weights; or you may weigh by your own.

The duties here are two and a-half per cent., and the moft reafonable of any port on the Malay Coaft, or to the eaftward; and the
feweft impofitions.

Beware of dealing with the Malabars who refide here, for they are
invariably cheats; and not only here, but in every port to the eaftward where they are found.

The produce of Queda is, tin, pepper, elephants teeth, wax, &c.;
and the imports the fame as to other Malay ports; opium and
Spanifh dollars forming the principal part of your cargo: for the
latter you are certain of procuring a cargo, if it is to be had; and
frequently a few chefts of opium will bring a good price.

I would advife a fhip, on her returning voyage to Calcutta, to call
at Salangore, Pooloo Pinang, Queda, and Junkceylon, if fhe has any
time; for fometimes, at the end of the feafon, fhe may collect fome
tin, pepper, wax, beetle-nut, elephants teeth, and rattans, for the
Bengal market. I would even recommend her to leave the coaft of
Pedir a fortnight or twenty days fooner than fhe otherwife would,
in order to try thefe places.

It is to be obferved, that I fpeak of the veffel trading from Calcutta
to the Pedir Coaft; and whofe Plan, for a trading voyage, I have
already laid down.

POOLOO

POOLOO PINANG; OR PRINCE OF WALES'S ISLAND.

Since the eftablifhment of this ifland, as a place of trade, by the Englifh, it having been granted to them by the King of Queda, it is become a very confiderable market for every produce of the Malay coaft, particularly for fuch ftaples as anfwer the Chinefe market, and has nearly ruined the Malacca merchants, whofe principal trade is gone.

Almoft all the country fhips bound to the eaftward, particularly thofe for China, touch here, where they refrefh and purchafe fuch articles of trade as they have room for, and they think will fuit the market.

The Eaft India Company's fhips from Bombay and the coaft of Coromandel, (bound to China,) touch here, and take in great quantities of tin, canes, rattans, fago, pepper, beetle nut, tripong, (beech de mar, or fea fwallow), birds nefts, &c. &c. for the China market, as well as dunnage for their teas to Europe. The trade being chiefly in the hands of Britifh merchants it requires little defcription.

The harbour is large, fafe, and clear of dangers; the accefs to it eafy; and there is an excellent outlet to the fouthward; but it will be neceffary to have a pilot for this channel from the ifland.

In this place, fince the eftablifhment of the colony in the year 1785, by Captain Francis Light, to whom it was given by the King of Queda, centres all the trade of the Straits of Malacca, from Junkceylon even to Tringano, and from Acheen to Palambang along the coaft of Pedir on the ifland of Sumatra.

SALANGORE.

SALANGORE.

Having recommended the ſhip from the Pedir Coaſt to call at Salangore, it is neceſſary I ſhould give ſome account of it.

It is one of thoſe places whoſe trade (as well as **Queda** and **Junk-ceylon**) chiefly centers in Pooloo Pinang; yet after the ſhips for China leave the latter iſland late in the ſeaſon, they may have ſome trade collected: at all events it is worth the trial, and nothing of conſequence out of her way, particularly if from Battabarra or Tello-ſomoy.

Upon your arrival at Salangore, your firſt viſit (as in moſt places upon the Malay coaſt) is to the Shabundar, at his houſe on the right-hand ſide of the river as you go in; from thence he introduces you to the Rajah, and alſo to the Rajah Syed. The next day you bring your muſters on ſhore, and having made your bargain (to ſell), you may bring your veſſel into the river, for the convenience of re-ceiving your returns, (if you have any time to ſpare), and moor off the Shabundar's houſe. You are perfectly ſafe in this port, while in the river; and it is the only port upon the Malay coaſt, except Tringano, where you are free from apprehenſions for your life and property. But lying in the roads, it will be neceſſary to be alert, and ready to repel any attack made by the ſtraggling prows that are always about, and ready to take advantage of any inattention; you ſhould not therefore ſuffer any prows to come near after dark. It never has been known that any accident happened in the river of Salangore by a ſhip being cut off, as the Rajah finds it his intereſt to eſtabliſh a good name to the port.

Coming into the river of Salangore, ſteer for the look-out houſe, keeping it rather on the larboard bow, and the river's mouth fairly open. The ſoundings are mud; and if you ſhould touch the ground you have nothing to fear.

Since

Since writing the above, I have been told the Dutch have funk large ftones acrofs the entrance of the river, which fhould be guarded againft.

The fifhing ftakes you may run between, only obferve to keep clear of thofe to which the nets are attached, as they being pretty ftrong may hurt your copper; and befides you do the fifhermen a wanton damage, which they will not eafily forget.

Should there be any buggefs prows in the river, avoid making any private bargains with them, as the king does not allow any to trade with them, or the Chinefe. He monopolifes all this trade himfelf, and if he finds it out, which he is certain of doing by his informers, he will ever after give a preference in trade to any body elfe than you.

The buggefs prows import, at Salangore, pepper, cloves, wild nutmegs, wax, nutmeg oil, rattans, dammer, wood, oil, &c. &c.

From a large river near Salangore, called Burnum, are brought great quantities of long rattans. Choofe your rattans long, thick, and clear, and rejeft all that are black or fmall; for though you purchafe by tale, or number, you fell them at Canton by weight.

In choofing your tin, at Salangore, Queda, or Junkceylon, give the preference to the tompong, or fmall piece, as the flabs are frequently adulterated with drofs, ftones, lead, and iron fhot.

The prefents at Salangore are many, though not fo valuable as at Acheen; and you will find it much to your intereft to keep on good terms with the Shabundar, and Mette Motta (or Weighmafter).

The bhar at this place is only three Chinefe pecul, of one hundred and thirty-three and one-third pounds, or four hundred pounds avoirdupois.

In making your bargain infift upon having your tin weighed by your own weights; as their dotchin is generally fhort of the weight you ought to receive: and agree for fo many bhar per cheft of opium, at fo many Spanifh dollars per bhar. Endeavour to find out which

is

is moft plentiful, tin or dollars; and agree, if poffible, to be free from all duties.

Should you fell for gold, be very cautious, as it is generally very bad. I would not advife you to receive any but what is examined by a touchadore, and then have the king's chop upon it.

Of opium, if frefh and new, they will not weigh above a cheft or two; if it is not frefh they will weigh every cheft; and it ought to be one hundred cattys (or a Chinefe pecul). Should it be dry and weigh lefs, the deficiency muft be made up; though if three or four cattys more (which frefh opium will fometimes weigh), they do not fuffer you to take the exceeds.

MALACCA,

Before the eftablifhment of Pooloo Pinang, was the principal place of trade in the Straits of Malacca, (from which place the Straits take their name). All fhips paffing for China ufed to call here, as well for the purpofe of trade, as to fill up their water and take in refrefhments.

This place is fupplied with grain from Bengal, Java, and Sumatra; but it has the fineft yams of any produced in India. It has a variety of fruits, and particularly the mangofteen, which is a very delicious one.

The trade of this place is fupplied by all the produce of the Straits and eaftern ports, fuch as tin, pepper, tripong, fago, rattans, canes, elephants teeth, &c.

Sheep and bullocks are fcare here, but there are buffaloes, hogs, poultry, and fifh, in great plenty; and in general very cheap.

The roads are large and fafe, and the beft in India; but you go into the river to land, the entrance of which is rendered intricate by

a bar,

a bar, over which boats cannot pass before first quarter flood, nor after last quarter ebb, except with much difficulty.

The Price Current of the China market should be your guide in making your purchases here, as it will not be worth the risk and trouble if they will not yield from fifteen to eighteen per cent.

There are a few private merchants here, but the Governor, Fiscal, and Shabundar, are the principal dealers; and should you deal with the private merchants, agree with them to pay the duties, customs, boat hire, and all charges to the ship.

The measure at Malacca for grain is a ganton (or forty peculs); but for sago, the ganton will seldom weigh more than thirty-two peculs: this difference is a great object, for though you buy your sago by measure here, you sell it by weight in China.

Should you purchase any beetle nut here, or at any other place, observe that it is new and free from holes, dust, or worms; and have good bags to put it in if for the China market, as those you get here are mat bags, made of bulrushes or flags, and soon fall to pieces by handling and moving: the same caution is to be used in packing your sago.

Should you purchase baroose camphor, commonly called native camphor, you should pack it closely in boxes, or it will evaporate and lose much of its weight: but, before you send it on shore at Canton, let it be packed in fine light stuff, as the Emperor allows ten per cent. discount upon the weights: and goods in these kind of packages have the same allowance as if packed in wine chests.

The East India Company's ships used formerly to call here to refresh and purchase trade for China; but our own settlement of Pooloo Pinang has effectually superceded the necessity of their continuing to do so; as they find, upon their arrival at the latter place, that their trade is more certainly provided, and in larger quantities; the merchants not being cramped by the monopolizing spirit

of

of the Dutch; who allow no competition in trade if the government officers can manage the whole.

The country fhips from Calcutta to the Malay coaft, (with opium, piece goods, and dollars,) ballaft with rice, which, if they do not difpofe of at Junkceylon or Pooloo Pinang, they fell here, and ballaft with fand, or a gravelly red ftone. This is a great market for piece goods; but opium is fold to the Governor (only), for the Company's account; any fold to private merchants was delivered to their boats, and generally landed on one of the water iflands (called Blymbing), for which you are paid in Spanifh dollars before it is delivered, as the merchant fmuggles it at his own rifk *.

SIAM.

The Englifh know fo little of this place and its trade that it will require a particular defcription, as the traffick may be much improved, particularly for the import and confumption of Britifh manufactures, fuch as broad-cloths, cutlery, ironmongery, jewelry, and toys.

The Portuguefe have principally enjoyed the trade and profits of this place. There have been fome fpeculations made by Britifh merchants from Calcutta, and which always turned out to advantage.

The Menam (the chief river) by which fhips enter Siam, difcharges itfelf into the Gulf of Siam, and is rendered difficult of accefs, on account of a bar; to crofs which it is neceffary to have a pilot.

The winter here is dry, and the fummer wet, occafioned by the different monfoons, which act here as in the Bay of Bengal, viz. the north-eafterly monfoon bringing in dry, and the

* For an account of TRINGANO, fee page 124.

R r

fouth-wefterly monfoon bringing in heavy clouds, thick weather, and rain.

The foutherly monfoon is therefore the feafon for fhips to go to Siam, as it is a fair wind to crofs the bar; and the northerly monfoon to leave the bar, and proceed to India through the Straits of Malacca.

Bankafoy, fituated on the river near the bar, is the principal place of trade; and the King is the chief merchant, for his revenues are paid in elephants teeth, fapan, and aquilla wood. This is the beft part of the Malay coaft for procuring that exquifite fauce, called ballichong, which the eaftern epicures fo much feek, value, and regale upon: it is made of a compofition of dried fhrimps, pepper, falt, feaweed, &c. &c. beaten together to the confiftence of a tough pafte; and then packed in jars for fale, ufe, or exportation.

Siam, near the fhores, (the only places where European traders have accefs to,) is very unhealthy. The land feems to be formed by the mud defcending from the mountains; to which mud, and the overflowings of the river, the foil owes its fertility; for in the higher places, and parts remote from the inundation, all is dried and burnt up by the fun, foon after the periodical rains are over.

The arts have been in more repute, and better attended to formerly, than at the prefent time. Few travellers will omit noticeing the many cafts at this place, both of ftatues, and cannon of an immenfe calliber and length, as well as many other curiofities, many of them in gold.

The mountains produce diamonds of an excellent water, (little if at all inferior to thofe of Golconda, though not fo large,) fapphires, rubies, and agates.

They have tin of a very fine quality, of which they make tutenague; fteel, iron, lead, and gold: they have copper alfo of a fine quality, but not in great plenty.

The low grounds produce rice in great quantities; and on the

higher

higher grounds, that are not inundated, they raife wheat. They have many medicinal plants and gums, oil of jeffamin, lack, benzoin, cryftal, emery, antimony, cotton, wood oil, varnifh, cinnamon, caffia, caffia buds, and iron wood, which is much ufed by the natives, Malays, and Chinefe, as anchors for their veffels. They have alfo a great quantity of white beetle nut, which is exported to China, by the junks and Portuguefe fhips, who have enjoyed almoft uninterruptedly the whole trade of this place, and the coaft of Cochin China, from the Ridang Iflands to Macao.

They have alfo the fruits known in India, as well as the durian, mangofteen, and tamarind, which are remarkable for thriving here.

The animals are, horfes, oxen, buffaloes, fheep, and goats, tygers, elephants, rhinocerofes, deer, and fome hares.

There is poultry in great abundance, with peacocks, pigeons, partridges, fnipes, parrots, and many other birds.

They have infects and vermin, as peculiar to other parts of India.

The fea yields them excellent fifh of all kinds, particularly flounders, which are dried and exported to all the eaftern ports; and they have extraordinary fine lobfters, fmall turtles, and oyfters. Here too are very fine river fifh, particularly the beatie (or cockup), filver eels of a very large fize; and mangoe fifh, fo much efteemed in Calcutta

From the humidity of the foil, it is almoft unneceffary to obferve, that the chief diforders, to which Europeans are fubject, are, fluxes, dyfenteries, fevers, and agues.

No private merchant here dare trade in tin, tutenague, elephants teeth, lead, or fapan wood, without leave from the king, which permiffion is feldom granted; as he monopolifes thefe articles to himfelf, and pays in them for any goods he purchafes, at the higheft prices they will bring at moft markets in India.

R r 2

The

The following are the general prices for elephants teeth from the king in payment:

2 teeth to the pecul, equal to 120 ticalls.
3 ditto   ditto   112 ditto.
4 ditto   ditto   104 ditto.
5 ditto   ditto   96 ditto.
6 ditto   ditto   88 ditto.
7 ditto   ditto   80 ditto.
8 ditto   ditto   72 ditto.
9 ditto   ditto   64 ditto.
10 ditto   ditto   56 ditto.
11 ditto   ditto   48 ditto.
12 ditto   ditto   40 ditto.
13 ditto to 20 or 30 ditto   32 ditto.

thus falling eight ticalls in each pecul, as the number of teeth increafes. But if you purchafe with ready money, inftead of receiving them in barter (or payment) for goods, you will buy each quality eight ticalls per pecul cheaper than the above prices; and ftill lower, if you have permiffion to trade with the Xtiams, or private merchants.

In purchafing fapan wood, it is cuftomary to allow five catty per pecul for lofs of weight; and as each draft is weighed by the large, or five pecul dotchin, you are allowed 525 catty; which, if it is the firft fort, fhould not be more than 16 to 18 pieces: fecond fort runs 22 to 24 pieces; and as the number of pieces increafe, the price falls in proportion.

After you have fettled with the minifters what part of your cargo the king is to have, (which is commonly called a prefent, unlefs he afks particularly to buy any thing,) fome of the principal merchants of the place are called to value them; and as they are valued, you are paid, by the king as a prefent, in the forementioned goods, at the higheft prices they will bear.

It

It may not be deemed fuperfluous here to obferve that a complaifant behaviour, and a cheerfulnefs of difpofition, are abfolutely
neceffary, particularly if you have (as all traders muft have) a point
to carry. Prefents, (as they are called,) but in groffer language
bribes, properly applied, gives the officers of government and people
in power the true tone and relifh to ferve you, as you will have frequent occafion to call upon them in their official capacities.

Every application for a permit to purchafe any defcription of goods
cofts ten and a-half ticalls: this permit only ferves for one houfe,
and one time of weighing: fo that, if you are about receiving any
quantity of goods of the fame quality from different merchants, agree
with them to fend it all to one houfe, and make one day for weighing off the whole in the merchant's name at whofe houfe it is
weighed. This mode will fave the expence of a multiplicity of permits, and quicken difpatch. Upon each of thefe weighing days you
muft have three of the King's writers, the firft and fecond Shabundar,
and the Linguift: to each of thefe, daily, you pay one-quarter ticall;
but it will be your intereft to give them fome trifling prefents.

Elephants teeth, tin, fapan wood, and lead, purchafed from the
King, are free of all cuftoms; but if bought from private merchants
they pay as follows:

Elephants teeth, (any fort), 4 ticalls per pecul.
Tin,   —   —   2 ditto per bhar.
Sapan wood, —   4 ditto per 100 pecul.
Lead,   —   —   2 mace per bhar.

If from any part of India, (as Bengal, the Coromandel, Malabar,
or Guzerat coafts, Bombay, Surat, &c.) you pay the following cuftoms before you fail:

Meafurage, if above three fathoms, or eighteen feet beam, to the
King, 10 ticalls.

To the Barcola, (or firft Shabundar,) 10 ticalls.

To

To the fecond Shabundar, 10 ticalls.

For your arrival at the bar, 10½ ticalls.

To pilots, and entrance, 10½ ticalls.

To pafs the two tobangoes (or chop-houfes) each 10½ ticalls.

To each permit, 10½ ticalls.

To a permit to meafure, 10½ ticalls.

To a permit to open your bales, 12 ticalls.

To a permit for leave to fell, 10½ ticalls.

And on going away, to each of the two tobangoes, 20 ticalls.

At the place where they infift on your landing your guns 20 ticalls; with fome other charges which are trifling.

The duties upon your imports are eight per cent., except dates, kiffmiffes, almonds, and fome other trifies which are excufed.

Veffels from Malacca, Palambang, Banca, Batavia, Tringano, Cambodia, Cochin China, and their coafts, pay neither duties nor cuftoms on their goods; they only pay,

For regiftering inwards, 1½ ticall.

Two permits to pafs the tobangoes, each 10½ ticalls.

If the veffel has no goods fhe will pay one ticall per covid (of 14¼ inches) for her breadth of beam; but if fhe has trade fhe pays two ticalls per covid.

I would advife all veffels from India, going to Siam, to take a frefh port clearance from Malacca; as it muft appear obvious the great indulgences fhe will enjoy, and the faving in the meafurement and charges.

GENERAL

GENERAL INSTRUCTIONS

REGARDING EASTERN VOYAGES.

THE principal plan of a voyage to the Malay coaſt and the eaſt-ward, being to procure tin and pepper for the China market; and Banca being the only place which produces tin in ſuch quantities as to inſure ſuccefs, though not ſufficient to load all the ſhips which ſpeculate in opium and piece goods to the Malay coaſt and the eaſt-ward; it may, therefore, be thought requiſite to lay ſome other plan, that all the ſhips which carry thoſe articles of trade (being ſtaples of Bengal) may not meet at the ſame market.

I have already laid before the merchant a Plan for the Coaſt of Pedir; a Plan for a Banca voyage; and ſpoken of the opium ſhips running down the weſt coaſt of Sumatra, where Bencoolen will be her laſt port upon that coaſt. From thence ſhe proceeds to Batavia, where, if ſhe does not meet with a ready ſale, ſhe ſhould go on to Boetan; failing of a ſale here, ſhe ſhould go to Barroos, in Buggies Bay; from hence to Sambava, where there are many articles for the China market; from hence ſhe may go on the north-weſt coaſt of Borneo, and calling at all the different ports, ſuch as mentioned in my former Plan, taking the ſouthern ports firſt, viz. Succadanna, Pontianna, Momparva (or Mompava), Sambafs, and Borneo Proper.

Momparva is one of the beſt markets to the eaſtward for opium, the conſumption of which place, and its dependencies, being at leaſt five hundred cheſts of opium per annum. Sambafs is the next beſt place for a certain ſale, the conſumption being rather more than at Momparva. Succadanna is alſo an excellent market, particularly if you happen to be an early ſhip.

At

At all thefe fouthern ports you will get gold, fome pepper, and rattans for your opium; and, in barter for your piece goods at Borneo Proper, you will receive pepper, wax, rattans, mother of pearl (teapoy) fhells, with many other articles of trade for the China market, which will return a very handfome profit.

While upon the coaft of Borneo, be particularly cautious, and always ready to repel an attack, for your fhip is never fafe; and when at Borneo Proper, be careful of venturing on fhore; and upon no account whatever be perfuaded to take your fhip into the river. They will anxioufly wifh you to go in for the purpofe of difpatch in loading your veffel; but it is doubtlefs (and has been too often proved) for the purpofe of difpatching you and your officers, and getting poffeffion of your fhip and cargo: the former of which they difpofe of either to the Spaniards at Manilla, the Javans, or burn her to procure the iron; the latter they ufe and difpofe of among themfelves, the Rajah having the largeft proportion for conniving at their infamous practices.

Having finifhed your trade upon the coaft of Borneo, proceed to Canton, and follow the directions already given for your conduct.

Should your fhip be fmall, or your pepper, rattans, &c. not in fufficient quantity, fo as to make it an object, (having no particular inveftment to take from Canton), I would advife you to lie about Linting Fora or Large Bay, until fome of the Eaft Indiamen from Europe arrive in Macao-roads, and load your cargo for the Canton market upon them; as the commanders will carry it to Whampoa for one per cent., and you will thereby fave the duties, cuftoms, meafurement of your fhip, and Emperor's prefent, which will be a very confiderable faving to the voyage.

Your long-boat equipped, as before. defcribed, and prepared as for the Malay coaft, except that fhe need not be fo abundantly armed, may go to and from Whampoa at any time, to bring you, from Lark Bay, fuch ftores as you or your fhip may be in need of; only ufing

the

the precaution of paffing the Bocca Tigris (or Mouth of the Tigris) by night, as this will fave trouble and anxiety; though I never knew of any fhip's boat being ftopped by the Chinefe paffing or repaffing the Bocca. In the year 1790, when three veffels lay in Lark Bay, with opium and furs, boats ufed to go to and from them every week, unmolefted and unnoticed.

Let us now fuppofe that merchants have employed fhips with full inveftments for thefe different tracks already mentioned. There is ftill a good market for one or more early fhips with opium. Let us fuppofe, inftead of going by any of the foregoing ports to Banca or Batavia, they try the fouthern ports mentioned, upon the weft and north-weft fide of Borneo, and then crofs over to Tringano, where two or more fhips will fill with pepper; or that towards the latter end of the feafon, fuppofe we fay the 10th of September, they run over to Borneo Proper, and fill up there with pepper, &c. &c., and then proceed to Canton; all, or any of thefe, will turn out profitable voyages if they are well conducted; and the merchandife, particularly the opium, is good. In the year 1790, the opium carried out by the different fhips was univerfally complained of; and Capt. Canning, in the Nonfuch, (built in or about the year 1780, by Colonel Henry Watfon, at Calcutta), a faft-failing and well-appointed fhip, particularly calculated for the Malay coaft and eaftern trade, was near two years effecting his fales; and although well acquainted with the eaftern trade, made a lofing voyage: But the Eaft India Company, from their well-known liberality to deferving individuals, whether in or out of their fervice, have appointed him (as a remuneration) Mafter Attendant, at Calcutta. It was extremely fortunate for my employers that year, that I had fuch good connections at Batavia; as by that means I fold the whole of my cargo, when every other of the five fhips in the roads were obliged to fail, having their opium rejected, as damaged and unmerchantable.

SOME

SOME ACCOUNT OF SUCCADANA.

WHEN you arrive at Succadana, your firſt viſit muſt be to the Shabundar or Cuſtom-maſter, who will introduce you to the King, and the male part of the Royal Family. It is the cuſtom here, and at all eaſtern ports, to give a preſent at your firſt audience, which you muſt proportion to the rank of the people you viſit. The King's preſent ſhould not be leſs than 50 dollars, Raja's about 30, and Shabundar's and agents 20 each. Theſe are the only preſents abſolutely neceſſary to be made at this place. The perſons of the greateſt note are, the King, Raja Ally, Raja Samatt, and the Shabundar; the latter two in particular are not much to be depended upon or truſted. The Shabundar will inquire what you have brought for ſale, and will be inquiſitive about the quantity; to the latter give him an evaſive anſwer, to make them more and more eager after your goods, and give yourſelf time to find out the market prices, and what articles are moſt in demand.

It has hitherto been the cuſtom of this place for the Raja's family to engroſs all the opium trade. No ſtrangers are allowed to purchaſe from the Europeans, nor are the Chineſe. All other trade is open; but permiſſion of the Shabundar, by way of compliment, will be neceſſary, as alſo to keep on good terms with him.

Cuſtoms.

Five per cent. on all ſales. Should you have dollars to purchaſe pepper, gold, or tin with, you pay the ſame for them as on goods.

Anchorage.

Anchorage,

250 dollars, fhould you fell goods to that amount; if under that fum no anchorage is to be paid.

Prices of Exports in 1786.

Tin 16½ Spanifh dollars,⎫ per China pecul of 100 catty, or 133¼
Pepper 14 d° d° ⎭ pounds Englifh.

Tamby Gold, ⎧ 26 Spanifh dollars, per tale of two dollars weight,
Siac d° ⎨ of which 20 tale make a catty, or 40 dollars
⎩ weight.

Mompowa d° 20 to 22 per tale weight, this gold is of an inferior quality.

Should you take gold in your returns, you muft truft to the King for its finenefs, by having it in your agreement that he is to feal on it, and be anfwerable for the quality. This is the only fure way to take gold at any of the Malay ports; but if you are going to China, the lefs gold you take the better.

When you bargain for your opium, or other goods, you muft fettle what returns you are to receive. This is generally fettled according to what demand the goods are in: if in great want of them, infift on having all tin; if otherwife, in proportion, half tin, half pepper, or one-third tin, and two-thirds pepper; or elfe a proportion of tin, pepper, and gold. Be fure to agree about the price, and let your agreements be in writing, and figned by the party agreed with, whether king or fubject, to prevent them flying off and evading payment, which they will do if poffible.

Tin was purchafed here for 15, and pepper for 13 Spanifh dollars cafh; but this was in October, November, and December, before the arrival of the Chinefe junks. Thefe people always keep

up

up the price of tin and pepper during their ftay, which is from January to the month of Auguft. All goods are weighed here with Englifh beam fcales and half hundreds, and afterwards turned into cattys and peculs of 133⅓ Englifh.

CHARACTER OF THE MALAYS IN GENERAL.

As the Malays have the character of a treacherous fet of men, I would advife all people to be on their guard while in any of their ports; and when on fhore never to be without a hanger in their hand. Every one of them go armed with a creafe, (hanger,) or a weapon fomething like a chopper, and very fharp. When they fee you are prepared, they will not be fo apt to infult you, which the vulgar are ready enough to do.

It is in the power of any man to kill his own flave with impunity; and they are fuch a daftardly fet that they have not courage to refent an affront perfonally, but will drefs their flaves, and give them orders to kill any man they pitch upon, who, after being intoxicated with opium, is infenfible of any danger he runs into, being equally at the rifque of his life to return without executing his mafter's orders, or to be cut to pieces in the attempt.

I have always made it a rule of having my guns loaded with round and grape fhot while on the Malay coaft, with a cheft of good arms upon deck, lighted matches and hand grenades in the tops, two fepoys at the gangways, two lafcars on the forecaftle, and two more on the poop. The officer of the watch and feaconys go round the fhip at leaft every half hour; and centinels and lafcars to call " all's well" every quarter of an hour during the night. Thefe regulations to commence at eight o'clock, and to continue till after the reveillie is beat in the morning at day-light.

Rice,

Rice, fifh, and fruit, are the common food of thefe people, who eat very little flefh, or animal food. They drink water, toddy (a diftillation from the palm-tree), and coffee; and they chew beetle conftantly. They eat but two meals a day, one in the morning, and the other about fun-fet, the latter of which is the principal: in the intermediate fpace they refrefh themfelves by chewing beetle, or fmoaking tobacco mixed with opium. They fet crofs-legged on the floor at their meals, and the better fort have very low tables for their provifions, which are fet on them in china plates, or difhes made of wood highly japanned; but they ufe neither knives or fpoons. They have veffels for the purpofe of fpitting in when they chew beetle or fmoak tobacco; and are particular in keeping their perfons and the infide of their houfes clean. They have but little furniture, except the neceffary utenfils for cooking their provifions, and carpets to fleep and fit upon; but they are very oftentatious of difplaying a great number of pillows, the ends of which are richly embroidered, and the whole covered with the richeft filks.

Thefe people are fo little addicted to litigious difputes, that they have neither lawyers, attornies, nor bailiffs. If any difputes or differences arife, the parties apply perfonally to the Judge (or Carrangue), who determines the matter with expedition and equity *.

In fome matters, particularly of a criminal nature, they are permitted to do juftice to themfelves. If a man detects another in the commiffion of adultery, murder, or robbery, he has a right to exe-

---

* How different, in this refpect, is the jurifprudence of our country, *where the law's delay* and uncertainty deprive the fuppliant of more than half his due; while its voracious retainers overwhelm whole families in mifery and ruin. Happy will it be, as has been juftly obferved, " when a fyftem of legal reform fhall diminifh the number of wretches who fubfift on the vitals of their fellow-creatures; and, by feparating the unworthy from the deferving, protect the profeffion of the law from the indelible reproach produced by its worthlefs practitioners."

cute

cute juftice himfelf, by deftroying the culprit; the weapon in thefe cafes is invariably the creafe or dagger.

The Malays are all ftrict mahomedans; which religion they are particularly tenacious of infringing. Many of them are great pretenders to magic, and carry charms about them, on a fuppofition of their fecuring them from every danger.

The common people have no other covering than a fmall piece of linen faftened round the waift; but the better fort wear a kind of waiftcoat made of filk or broad-cloth, over which they throw a loofe garment of filk that reaches to the knees. They alfo wear a pair of drawers, but wear neither fhirt, fhoes, or ftockings; and when they go abroad they always wear a creafe or dagger, and a handkerchief tied in a peculiar way round the head.

The falem, or lifting the hands to the head with the palms joined together, until the thumbs touch the forehead, and bending the body, is their mode of falutation. When they appear before their fuperiors, they raife their hands above the forehead; and if before a prince, they proftrate themfelves on the ground, with the forehead refting on their hands, which are ftill joined, and retire backwards on their knees.

The natives pay great homage to their princes and rajas, and it is difficult for a ftranger to get accefs to them: the readieft means to effect this is, by complimenting them with fome valuable prefent; and the ftranger will be treated with refpect according to the prefent he makes, avarice being their ruling paffion. The return is generally made in fruit, and a few fowls; but if the ftranger, at the time of making the prefent, is a great diftance from his fhip, or living on fhore near the palace, for the convenience of trade, he is fent fome rice, pillaw, and fifh, from the prince's table.

It is an univerfal cuftom, both with men and women, to bathe in a river, at leaft once a day; this makes them all expert fwimmers;

which

which not only promotes health, but prevents that contraction of filth, which would be otherwise unavoidable in a hot climate.

They are so proud and revengeful, and so indolent, that they will neither endeavour to improve themselves in arts, sciences, or husbandry; but suffer their manufactures to be neglected, and their lands to lie without cultivation.

The Dutch have a proverb, which signifies

> They are ugly and strong,
> And will bear malice long.

Caution.

I beg leave to mention a remark, which I have made on board different vessels trading to the eastward, which is, the commanders of them neglecting to exercise the great guns; and when Malay prows are alongside, instead of keeping one watch, or division of the crew, at the guns, with lighted matches, and the guns pointed into their boats ready to sink them, they are either all at work, or running about the deck in perfect security. I have no doubt but such security has been the loss of many vessels; when, with this precaution, the dastardly rascals dare not think of attacking you. I could enlarge upon this subject, but think, the person not capable of profiting by what has been already said, is not fit to be entrusted with any man's property, and the lives of people under his command. When commanders trade with their own capital they have only to consider the lives of their crew; their own lives and property they have the best right to dispose of.

DIRECTIONS

FOR SHIPS LEAVING CALCUTTA LATE IN MARCH, BEING
BOUND TO MADRAS OR THE SOUTHWARD.

LEAVING Bengal late in March, and bound to Madras, ſhips generally leave the pilot with a freſh gale between S. and W.S.W., with which, in ſtanding two or three days, cloſe hauled, between the S. and E.S.E. as the wind will permit, they commonly run into light breezes from the N.E. quarter; and with them ſteer away S., S. by W., S.S.W. and even S.W., until they ſee Ceylon, about Trincomale, or more to the ſouthward; taking care not to go to the weſtward of Point Palmiras until they are to the ſouthward of 12° N.

The reaſon of keeping ſo far to the eaſtward is to avoid the weſterly and ſoutherly winds, which at this ſeaſon prevail along the Coromandel coaſt, and the current which now creeps to the northward along all the weſtern ſhores of the Bay of Bengal; therefore if you leave the pilot with a fair wind, it is beſt to ſteer S., or even S. by E., or S.S.E.; than ſhape a direct courſe down the Bay for your port of deſtination. On the other hand, ſhould the S.W. winds force you ſo far to the eaſtward, that before you are in the latitude of 15° N., or to the ſouthward of Cape Negraiſe, that you have made 3°, or 3° 30 E. from Point Palmiras, I woulo rather adviſe a ſhort tack, of a degree, or a degree and a-half, to the weſtward, than run out of the track of the N.E. winds, as they are not yet done ſo far to the eaſtward, and ſtand back again until the wind comes fair; at which time ſhape a courſe for that part of Ceylon

which

which you mean to make your landfall, or (as most of the ships are now coppered, and sail superior to what they did when I first went to India) shape a course for that point in the latitude of 12° N. which lies exactly in the meridian of, or due south from, Point Palmiras. It is absolutely necessary for you to fall in with the land to the southward of your intended port; for the winds and current are setting so strong to the N.E., that if you get to leeward of your port a few leagues you will have much trouble and delay in working up; and, probably, be obliged to stretch off shore again, and go to the southward as far as you should have originally gone, in order to secure your passage without this waste of time.

DIRECTIONS

FOR GOING IN AND OUT OF MASULIPATNAM-ROADS.

Going into Masulipatnam from the southward, observe in rounding Point Divy (which lies in latitude 16° 6′ N.), not to come under six or seven fathoms, in order to give the Divy Flat a good birth. You will be then seven or eight miles from the point, which is very low, without any distinguishing mark.—In that water, steering N.N.W., you will shoal in gradually to five or four fathoms, by borrowing, as you get to the northward, a little to the westward. Take care to keep the lead going, and not to come into hard ground, as you will be on the edge of the Flat, where it is hard sand; but, with a commanding southerly wind, you can immediately keep more to the northward and eastward upon shoaling your water. However, I think no ship should go under

T t

four

four fathoms going in, be the wind as it may; for in that water you are very near the Divy Bank. If you are to the northward of the flag-ftaff, or even with the flag-ftaff weft, and a little to the north-ward of it, you may come as near as you pleafe, the water gradually fhoaling to any depth you think proper to lie in. From what I have feen, I find there is more than four fathoms feven miles from the fhore; all over the roads ftiff mud.

This month (September) the currents fet very ftrong to the fouth-ward, and the winds quite unfettled.

Sailing out of Mafulipatnam-roads, you muft fteer Eaft, and no-thing to the northward of it until you are clear of Narfepore-point, until you deepen to 10 or 11 fathoms, when you may haul a point or two to the northward, according as you have the wind; but be fure you give Point Guardewar a good birth, which bears about E. half N. from Mafulipatnam, diftance 27 leagues; and as there are many fhoals betwixt it and Narfepore, it fhould be ap-proached with care. When at anchor in Mafulipatnam-roads, the flag-ftaff bore N.W. by W., the extremes of the land from S.W. by S. to N. by E., diftance off fhore four miles, in two fathoms and three-quarters at low water.

THE MALDIVES.

Some years back one or two fhips ufed to go to the Maldive Iflands to load cowries, a fhell which paffes current in Eengal as the fmalleft fpecie of money; but, from the delay they ufed to meet with, the difficulty of getting full cargoes, and the unhealthinefs of the climate, added, I fuppofe, to making indifferent returns, the profits not being equal to the rifk of health and lofs of time, there has been no fhip there for fome time.

The trade of thefe iflands is now principally carried on by the
Maldivans

Maldivans in their own boats, which are very awkward, being fomething in the form of a Portuguefe bean-cod, but not fo well calculated to endure bad weather, and conftructed of the trunks of the cocoa nut-trees, which are cut down between Balafore, at the weft entrance of the Hoogly (or Bengal river), and their own iflands, where they do not diminifh the number of that valuable tree.

The Maldive boats arrive at Balafore in fleets of twenty or thirty, or upwards, in the months of June or July, (when the S.W. monfoon is fteady in the Bay of Bengal,) loaded with coir, cocoa-nut oil, together with all the other produce of the cocoa-nut tree, cowries, falt-fifh of different qualities, turtle-fhell, &c. &c.; and return about the middle of December loaded with rice, fugar, hardware, broad cloth, cutlery, filk ftuffs, coarfe cottons, tobacco, &c. &c.

They appear to be a quiet inoffenfive people; they profefs the mahomedan faith, but are not very rigid. Their complexions are a yellow copper colour, and are in general about the middle ftature. They drefs after the manner of the Mahomedans (or Moors) of India.

DIRECTIONS

FOR SAILING THROUGH THE STRAITS OF CHEDUBA, ON THE COAST OF ARACAN.

COMING up the coaft of Ava, and bound to the northward, and defirous of going through the Straits of Cheduba, you muft endeavour to make the land about Foul Ifland. If you make this ifland,

it

it is the beſt landfall; it lies in 18° 20′ N. and is about five leagues to the ſouthward of Cheduba. Being about three leagues to the eaſtward of this iſland, you will ſee ſeveral iſlands to the northward of you, the three weſternmoſt of which make the Straits of Cheduba.

Cheduba is known by its being the weſternmoſt of the iſlands: it is of a moderate height, with ſeveral hummocks on it; but the ſouthernmoſt head makes a high bluff, which at a diſtance may be taken for the ſouthernmoſt extreme, until you have riſen the lower part of the iſland, which appears like iſlands ſeparated from it; but when you are near you may ſee them from the maſt-head, that they join to the high bluff land that was at firſt taken for the ſouthern head of Cheduba.

The next iſland to Cheduba is round, and of a moderate height, though not near ſo high as Cheduba, the upper part black, and the lower part white; this lies almoſt in the middle of the Straits, and which you leave on your left hand going through. To the eaſtward of it are the iſlands which form the Straits; they are four or five in number, though they appear when you are abreaſt of Foul Iſland to be in one.

In nearing theſe iſlands, you will perceive a rock in ſhore, called The Commodore, from its reſemblance to a ſhip under ſail, with a broad pendant flying. This rock you muſt not borrow on; for, when open to the ſouthward of the above iſlands, which form the ſouthern-moſt extreme of the Straits, the ground is foul above one mile and a-half off; for which reaſon give it a birth of two miles to the eaſt-ward of you. As you draw near to Cheduba, you will ſee an iſland under the high land, ſurrounded with rocks; it appears ſo cloſe to Cheduba, that you will take it to be on the beach, though it lies four miles off Cheduba. This is dangerous, as there is a reef extends one mile and a-half from it, on which the ſea continually breaks; ſo that I would adviſe no perſon to come nearer than four miles, or not at all, if poſſible to keep the eaſtern ſhore on board.

I

From

From this low land there are innumerable rocks ftretching to the fouthward as far as Foul Ifland, through which, if there is a paffage, it muft be a very dangerous one.

The White Ifland, (which I have called the Round Ifland,) lying in the Straits, is rather more than one-third channel over from Cheduba to the eaftern ifland. Keep rather on the eaftern fhore than on it, on account of a reef of rocks running near two miles to the N.N.E. from the N.E. part of it. After you bring the ifland to bear S.W. by S. you will fhoalen your water to five or four and three-quarters fathoms, which depth will continue until you have brought it to bear South. You will have five fathoms regular found-ings until near the N.E. end of Cheduba, off which you muft be very careful, there being a fandy point ftretching near one-third over to feaward, conftantly breaking on it. It is oppofite a bluff point on the eaftern fhore; for which reafon endeavour to keep one and a-half or two miles off the eaftern fhore. This is the higheft land to the northward, and what you will take to be the northern extreme of the eaftern iflands when you enter the Straits; but you will find them continue further to the N.W. than the Cheduba Iflands do to the W.N.W.

When you have rounded the fandy point of Cheduba before-mentioned, and deepened your water to fix and a-half or feven fathoms, you will be about two miles off the eaftern fhore. Hav-ing the northernmoft extreme of Cheduba W.N.W., and the north-ernmoft extreme of the iflands N.W. half N., keep mid-channel be-tween the two points, on account of a reef of rocks extending from each. If you have the two points in one (or the fame bearings) fteer N.W. by W., on which courfe you will carry fix and a-half or feven fathoms until you have failed about four miles; then you will fhoal gradually to five and a-half fathoms, which will be the leaft water you will have through the Straits. By keeping two and a-half or three miles off the eaftern fhore, you may carry this water, perhaps, for one mile and a-half or two miles, and will then deepen gradually to what depth you pleafe to run out into.

I would by no means advife hauling up to northward of N.W. by W. until you are in 22 fathoms, on account of the Terrible Rocks, near which we had 20 fathoms. The body of them lies in latitude 18° 28′ N. extending to the northward and fouthward for feveral miles.

Thefe rocks are the more dangerous, as neither The Englifh Pilot or French Directory give any account of them. They lie fix or feven leagues to the weftward of the Coaft of Aracan, and bear from the Broken Iflands about S.S.W. diftance feven or eight leagues.

Both Cheduba and the eaftern iflands are inhabited; for which reafon, I think, perfons paffing thefe Straits fhould be upon their guard, as the people are of a hoftile difpofition.

ARACAN AND CHEDUBA.

The kingdom of Aracan and the ifland of Cheduba are both fituated upon the eaftern fide of the Bay of Bengal. They both produce great quantities of grain, which I believe was not generally known in the year 1780 and 1788, when the fcarcity of rice happened in Bengal. I mention it here, as fhips of any burthen may load at Cheduba; and veffels, which do not require a greater depth of water than from 16 to 18 feet, may load in Aracan river at any time of future fcarcity.

THE

THE MOST ELIGIBLE TRACK FOR SHIPS TO KEEP IN, BEING
BOUND FROM EUROPE TO INDIA OR CHINA, TO OR ROUND
THE CAPE OF GOOD HOPE.

In the latter end of September 1797 I failed from Torbay, and,
being under convoy, we made the island of Madeira; which I would
by no means recommend, but to keep a greater offing, and be
thereby more remote from the regions of calms, and have the advantage of a current constantly setting to the southward, as well in
the summer as in the winter or autumnal equinox.

Captain Forest (who found the same disadvantages I did, and
who seems to have experienced what I afterwards benefited by, viz.
currents and a scant wind, which obliged the whole fleet to make
more westing than they originally intended) has so exactly coin-
cided in my opinion, that I shall here give the account in his own
words; and I trust I shall not be accused of plagiarism, when I do so
for the benefit of the navigator, as I do not believe such are given
in any of the present Directories. I shall therefore quote the whole
passage from his valuable work.

" If a ship bound from Europe to India in the winter, i. e.
from the autumnal to the vernal equinox, keeps a good offing, and
does not come near Madeira, she will have the advantage of not
being so much in the region of calms as if she keeps further east,
and will also be favoured with a current setting to the southward.

" There are also other reasons why I would advise a ship bound
to India to keep well to the westward, even at all times.

" It is obvious that leaving the Channel with a north-east wind,
and having got so far south as abreast of the coast of Portugal, if the

ship

fhip does not keep well to the weftward, the high Pyrenean mountains, and others on the weft quarter of the continent of Europe,
may, in all likelihood, check a wind, which a hundred leagues further off blows in force*.

" Being further advanced abreaft the great continent of Africa, if
the navigator does not keep well to the weftward, the retardment
he will meet with may be more confiderable; for the continent of
Africa being very broad, its middle part full of fandy deferts, may
retard or ftop the general eafterly wind in a very confiderable degree.
The Pyrenean mountains can only check, but the Deferts of Africa
may almoft extinguifh, that wind. And it is remarkable that
the region of calms, rains, and tornadoes in the Atlantic, are oppofite to the broadeft part of Africa, being nearly in the fame latitude:
and this is not to be wondered at, when we confider that Africa is
the broadeft piece of land upon the globe, that paffes under the
Equator. No wonder then if the wind that blows from the Indian
fide is heated, cooled, and almoft extinguifhed in paffing over that
vaft heated peninfula.

" And although in the fummer monfoon the winds off the eaft
promontory of Brafil may be from S.S.E., yet from an apprehenfion
that fuch are foul winds to get on with into a high fouth latitude,
I would by no means have the navigator be againft ftretching that
way, becaufe he will thereby efcape the calms that prevail further
eaft near Africa; and fhould the wind come fo far to the weftward
as S.S.W., a good ftretch may be made S.E., to where more in the
middle of the South Atlantic the S.E. trade may be expected. At

* " So fhips, bound from the low latitudes of America to crofs the Pacific to India,
are often baffled for weeks together, and feen at a good diftance from the land; which
certainly is owing to the interruption the mountains left behind give to the wind.
Farther on, fairly in the South Sea, this feldom or never happens.

" Commodore Anfon experienced this when he left the coaft of America; he was
many days becalmed in the Centurion."

the

the fame time I would not advife to make fo free with the coaft of Brazil during the fummer monfoon as during its oppofite, for then, their winter, the current off the eaft promontory of Brazil affuredly fets to the fouthward; but I fufpect it fets fo all the year round, for reafons already given.

" Having got into the South Atlantic, I would have the navigator pay more regard to getting fouth than eaft, that is, to fteer rather S.S.E. than S.E., fuppofing the wind enables him to do either.— I know to this advice will be objected, Why not fteer S.E. rather than S.S.E., it cuts off fo much diftance? I fee the force of this objection; but let the navigator reflect, that this fair wind, on which there can be no dependence for continuance in fteering S.E., and by which it would feem he coveted eafting as well as fouthing, at the fame time may leave him in the lurch, by the expiration of the favourable fpirt, in a parallel far fhort of where he might have got, had the getting fouthing at this time been his principal object; letting the eafting come in only as a collateral or fecondary confideration.*

" Having got well to the fouthward, I would by no means advife coming near the Cape of Good Hope, if the navigator intends going without Madagafcar, but to keep in thirty-fix or thirty-fix and a-half degrees of latitude. The variation of the compafs determines the longitude nearly, though not fo well as the lunar obfervations; and it is not unadvifable to make Gough's Ifland, whence, who knows, but refrefhments may be had, and a harbour difcovered †. In this

---

* " In the Lively Brig, in 1780, I got from Falmouth to the latitude of the Cape in thirty-one days. I kept a good way to the weftward of Madeira."

† The Author had, in India, a MS. which gave an account of a Dutch fhip being driven off the Cape in a heavy gale of wind, and found an ifland with a good harbour, where they hauled the fhip on fhore, repaired fome injury in her bottom, and found buffaloes, goats, and poultry in great abundance; and the fea full of fifh in or about this latitude. The MS. is loft or left behind.

U u

high parallel the winds are more fteady, and the currents fetting weft near Africa are avoided.

" If bound without Madagafcar, I would now advife the navigator to pay his chief regard to getting eaftward, and not covet northing too foon. Never to keep his fhip right before the wind (unlefs indeed fhe fails beft that way), but to rembember that E.S.E. and E.N.E. courfes combined, differ not from E. And here I would have him ftudy the eafe of the fhip and her mafts, in the courfe he fhapes; always giving his officers a latitude of altering the courfe two or three points, as far as fo doing makes the fhip eafier, or enables her to go fafter; and by no means to confine his courfe to a certain point, as if deviating therefrom could be of any bad confequence here in the wide ocean.

" From the longitude of 10° E. beyond the meridian of the ifland of Madagafcar, the wind will frequently veer from W. to S.W., S., S.S.E., and S.E., and in the courfe of forty-eight hours, or three days, come round to the weftern quarter again. When this happens, let him keep his fails rap full, and rely chiefly on his variation or obfervations for making Ceylon or the Straits of Sunda.

" If, during the S.W. monfoon, but efpecially in May, June, or July, he is bound for the Straits of Sunda, let him fall in with the Coaft of Java, as S.E. winds prevail there in general during thefe months, at the fame time attended with revolutions from the oppofite quarter; remembering that the current, generated by the wind at N.W., on the north end of Sumatra, in fummer, though it drains in fhore as far as the fouth part of that ifland; the draining eaftward goes not beyond the Straits of Sunda to the Coaft of Java; it being already exhaufted on the Coaft of Sumatra."

A TABLE

A TABLE

OF

LATITUDES and LONGITUDES of PLACES;

TAKEN FROM

ASTRONOMICAL OBSERVATIONS.

THE PRINCIPAL PART OF THEM BY THE AUTHOR:

Many of which have not hitherto been laid down.

NAMES OF PLACES.					Latitudes.	Longitudes.
		A.			° ′	° ′
Acheen roads,	-	-	-	-	5 35 N.	95 35 E.
Afcenfion ifland,	-	-	-	-	7 57 S.	14 19 W.
Amfterdam ifland,	-	-	-	-	38 42 S.	77 22 E.
Andamans, north end,	-	-	-	-	13 30 N.	92 30 E.
—— bank, fouth end, ⎫ Leaft water on this				-	13 4 N.	91 45 E.
—— bank, north end, ⎬ bank five fathoms				-	13 26 N.	91 56 E.
——, port Cornwallis, ⎭ with overfalls.				-	13 20 N.	92 54 E.
Avarilla, cape,	-	-	-	-	12 55 N.	109 E.
Armegon fhoal, north end,	-	-	-	-	14 11 N.	80 28 E.
Alguado point,	-	-	-	-	15 29 N.	73 45 E.
Anjengo roads,	-	-	-	-	8 40 N.	76 55 E.
Ampats,	-	-	-	-	3 39 S.	116 40 E.
Arnol,	-	-	-	-	19 34 N.	
Agullas, cape,	-	-	-	-	34 50 S.	20 1 E.
Aracan river,	-	-	-	-	20 17 N.	93 5 E.

U u 2

NAMES OF PLACES.	Latitudes.	Longitudes.

B.

	° ′	° ′
Batavia, - - - - -	6 10 S.	106 51 E.
Balafore, - - - - -	21 20 N.	86 1 E.
Bencoolen, Fort Malbro', - - -	3 46 S.	102 E.
Bombay, - - - - -	18 58 N.	72 38 E.
Bourbon ifland, - - - -	20 52 S.	55 33 E.
Barn ifland, - - - - -	1 9 N.	103 55 E.
Bimliapatam, - - - -	17 57 N.	83 32 E.
Billiapatam, - - - -	11 54 N.	75 10 E.
Barren ifland, - - - -	12 18 N.	94 9 E.
Banguey-peak, - - - -	7 18 N.	117 18 E.
Bajadore, cape, - - - -	18 30 N.	120 15 E.
Boliano-fhoal, - - - -	16 12 N.	118 18 E.
Barroos, - - - - -	1 57 N.	98 23 E.
Banjack, - - - - -	2 14 N.	97 20 E.
Baffes, India, - - - -	21 28 S.	40 8 E.
Black Pagoda, - - - -	19 52 N.	86 12 E.
Boucanjeeree-point, - - -	2 50 N.	98 6 E.
Brothers, off Pooloo Lout, - -	4 30 N.	116 15 E.
Brace, weftern foot of the, - -	21 4 N.	87 45 E.
Bancoot, - - - - -	17 56 N.	73 20 E.
Bufforah, - - - - -	30 31 N.	47 30 E.
Banca, north point of, - - -	1 35 S.	105 58 E.
———, fouth point of, - - -	3 4 S.	106 14 E.
Bralla, - - - - -	4 45 N	103 32 E.
Borneo, fouth point of, - - -	4 12 S.	114 36 E.
———, north point of, - - -	7 N.	116 50 E.
———, eaft point of, - - -	5 15 N.	118 57 E.
———, weft point of; or Pointeanna, -	0 0	108 45 E.
Balambangan, - - - -	7 30 N.	117 2 E.
Banguy-peak, - - - -	7 17 N.	117 30 E.
Bergen's fhoals, on the weft coaft of Sumatra, -	2 47 N.	96 36 E.
Bintang, - - - - -	1 N.	103 50 E.
Barcelore, - - - - -	13 45 N.	74 15 E.
Batacolo, - - - - -	7 55 N.	81 5 E.
Beetlefackie, - - - -	15 40 N.	57 20 E.
Borneo, city of, Proper, - - -	4 55 N.	112 2 E.

NAMES OF PLACES.	Latitudes.	Longitudes.

C.

	Latitudes.	Longitudes.
Calcutta, Fort William, - - -	22 35 N.	88 30 E.
Canton, - - - -	23 8 N	113 2 E.
Cochin, - - - -	9 58 N.	76 27 E.
Cape Comorin, - - -	7 56 N.	77 59 E.
Chittagong, - - -	22 20 N.	91 55 E.
Calaboot, Ifland Banca, - -	1 33 S.	105 53 E.
Condore-harbour, - - -	8 40 N.	106 18 E.
Callingapatam, - - -	15 29 N.	84 10 E.
Cocoa's iflands, weft coaft of Sumatra, -	3 15 N.	96 52 E.
Corringa, - - - -	16 58 N.	82 30 E.
Carrimon, Java, - - -	5 54 S.	109 34 E.
Counfel's fhoal, China Sea, - -	8 54 N.	114 15 E.
Ditto Ditto - -	7 52 N.	112 32 E.
Cocoa iflands, Bay of Bengal, north end, -	14 16 N.	93 22 E.
Ditto Ditto fouth end, -	14 3 N.	93 11 E.
Cheduba, north end, - -	19 3 N.	93 56 E.
Carnicobar, north end, - -	9 13 N.	92 55 E.
Cape St. Jaques, - - -	10 15 N.	106 35 E.
Cape Avarilla, - - -	12 55 N.	109 E.
Cape Bajadore, - - -	18 30 N.	120 15 E.
Cecir de Terre, Pooloo, - - -	11 11 N.	108 22 E.
Chriftmas ifland, - - -	10 35 S.	104 49 E.
Cecir de Mar, Pooloo, - - -	10 30 N.	108 30 E.
Cape Negrais, - - -	15 30 N.	94 27 E.
Cocoas iflands, Indian Ocean, north end, -	11 50 S.	97 13 E.
Ditto Ditto fouth end, -	12 33 S.	97 24 E.
Cape Felix, - - - -	3 48 N.	96 3 E.
Cape l'Agullas - - -	34 50 S.	20 1 E.
Cape of Good Hope - - -	34 29 S.	18 23 E.
Cape Hanglip - - -	34 16 S.	18 44 E.
—— St. Mary's - - -	25 33 S.	44 59 E.
Comoro, - - - -	11 33 S.	43 33 E.
Celebes, fouth point, - - -	5 42 S.	120 16 E.
———, north point, - - -	2 N.	124 2 E.
Cape Howe, - - - -	37 24 S.	149 54 E.
—— Dromedary, - - -	36 21 S.	150 4 E.

NAMES OF PLACES.	Latitudes.	Longitudes.
Cape Hawke, - - - - -	32 13 S.	152 28 E.
—— Danger, - - - - -	28 7 S.	152 28 E.
—— Morton, - - - - -	26 57 S.	153 22 E.
Cumberland ifland, - - - -	20 30 S.	148 45 E.
Cape Cleveland, - - - -	19 10 S.	148 5 E.
—— Flattery, - - - - -	14 52 S.	145 10 E.
—— Conway, - - - - -	20 44 S.	148 10 E.
—— York, - - - - -	10 44 S.	141 37 E.
—— Falfe, - - - - -	8 40 S.	136 30 E.
—— Babelmandel, - - - -	12 38 N.	43 47 E.
—— Frio, - - - - -	12 35 S.	41 10 W.
Crokatoa, - - - - -	6 8 S.	105 36 E.
Cranganore, - - - - -	10 N.	75 5 E.
Cuddalore, - - - - -	11 30 N.	79 56 E.
Colombo, - - - - -	7 N.	80 25 E.

D.

Diew point, - - - - -	20 44 N.	70 3 E.
Denis's, St., ifland Bourbon, - - -	20 52 S.	55 30 E.
Diego Garcia, - - - -	7 28 S.	72 28 E.
Diamond ifland, - - -	15 15 N.	94 22 E.
De Breto's, Matthew, reef, - - -	10 32 N.	107 23 E.
Danifh rock, - - - -	28 20 S.	98 30 E.
Dangers iflands, - - - -	5 27 S.	71 55 E.
Dwalder, off Pooloo Lout, - - -	4 16 S.	
Donder head, fouth point of, Ceylon, - -	5 47 N.	81 2 E.
Damaun, - - - - -	21 5 N.	72 35 E.
Dabul, - - - - -	17 30 N.	73 55 E.

E.

Entrance, port Cornwallis, - - -	13 20 N.	92 54 E.

NAMES OF PLACES.	Latitudes.	Longitudes.

F.

Falfe cape - - - - -	34 16 S.	18 44 E.
Fort Marlbro', - - - -	3 46 S.	102 E.
Fort Victoria, Bancoot, - - -	17 56 N.	73 20 E.
Fort St. George, Madras, - - -	13 5 N.	80 25 E.
Felix cape, - - - - -	3 48 N.	96 3 E.
Foul ifland, - - - - -	18 47 N.	93 23 E.
Fernando Noronha, - - - -	3 56 S.	32 24 W.
Fyal bay, - - - - -	38 32 N.	28 39 W.
Falfe point, Palmiras, - - -	20 17 N.	86 45 E.
French flat, buoy of the, - -	21 21 N.	87 56 E.
Fairway, buoy of the, - - -	21 28 N.	87 58 E.
Fort St. David's, - - - -	11 29 N.	79 58 E.
——— Dauphin, - - - -	25 S.	47 10 E.
Funchal, - - - - -	32 38 N	17 5 W.
Frio, cape, - - - - -	12 35 S.	41 10 W.

G.

Goa, - - - - - -	15 38 N.	73 45 E.
Goat ifland, - - - - -	13 55 N.	120 2 E.
Good Hope, cape of, - - -	34 29 S.	18 23 E.
——————— town of, - - -	33 56 S.	18 23 E.
Grand Ladroon, - - - -	22 2 N.	113 53 E.
Gafper ifland, - - - -	3 17 S.	107 8 E.
Ganjam, - - - - -	19 23 N.	85 7 E.
Galle, point de, - - - - -	5 55 N.	80 16 E.
Gheriah, - - - - -	16 36 N.	73 19 E.
George's, St., ifands, - - -	15 26 N.	73 20 E.
Gallegos, - - - - -	10 25 S.	56 45 E.
Gelolo, north end of, - - -	2 13 N.	126 15 E.
Gibby, - - - - -	0 6 S.	126 24 E.
Glaffes, H., coral bank, eaft fide Borneo, - -	2 10 S.	
Gambaroon, - - - -	27 18 N	56 6 E.
Ganjam, - - - - -	19 25 N.	85 20 E.
Guinea, New, eaft part of, - - -	6 20 S.	148 E.
Gough's ifland, - - - -	40 3 S.	2 30 W.

3

NAMES OF PLACES.	Latitudes.	Longitudes.

H.

Hanglip cape, - - - -	34 16 S.	18 44 E.
High mount, Junkceylon, - - -	7 54 N.	98 25 E.
High peak, on the eaft end of Pooloo Boutan, -	6 30 N.	99 24 E.
———— on the weft end of Pooloo Boutan, -	6 30 N.	99 15 E.
Holland's, Van, bank, - - -	10 42 N.	108 20 E.
Helena, St., James' valley, - - -	15 55 S.	5 51 W.
Hainan, north part of, - - - -	20 2 N.	110 15 E.
—— fouth part of, - - - -	18 12 N.	109 20 E.

I. & J.

Java head, - - - - -	6 49 S.	106 50 E.
Iflamabad, - - - - -	22 20 N.	91 55 E.
Johanan, - - - - -	12 17 S.	44 30 E.
Jarra, Pooloo, - - - - -	3 57 N.	100 15 E.
Invifible fhoal, - - - - -	11 8 N.	93 25 E.
Ifkapilly, - - - - -	14 39 N.	80 20 E.
Invaldoona, - - - - -	14 46 N.	80 18 E.
India, Baffes de, - - - -	23 23 S.	40 8 E.
———————— north extreme, - - -	21 28 S.	39 59 E.
Ingellee Pagoda, - - - -	21 40 N.	87 57 E.
Jagrenaut Pagoda, - - - -	19 48 N.	85 57 E.
Junkceylon, fouth end of, - - -	7 54 N	98 25 E.
Judda, - - - - -	21 30 N.	39 30 E.

K.

Kedjerree, - - - - -	21 48 N.	88 2 E.

L.

Ladroon, the grand, - - - -	22 2 N.	113 53 E.
Louis, port St. - - - -	20 10 S.	57 28 E.
Leema, the grand, - - - -	22 4 N.	144 5 E.

NAMES OF PLACES.	Latitudes.	Longitude.
Lincoln's fhoal, - - - - -	16 30 N.	112 32 E.
Lagullas, cape, - - - -	34 50 S.	20 1 E.
Lucepera, - - - - -	3 12 S.	106 15 E.
Lacadives, north-weft part of, - - -	12 38 N.	72 30 E.
M.		
Madras, Fort St. George, - - -	13 5 N.	80 25 E.
Macoa, - - - - -	22 12 N.	113 34 E.
Miroe, Sombrero channel, - - -	7 29 N.	93 41 E.
Macaffer, - - - - -	5 9 S.	119 42 E.
Malacca, - - - - -	2 12 N.	1 2 5 E.
Manilla, - - - - -	14 36 N.	120 53 E.
Mauritius, - - - - -	26 10 S.	57 29 E.
Mons, cape, Guzarat, - - -	24 58 N.	65 49 E.
Macclesfield fhoal, - - -	15 45 N.	114 39 E.
———— north-eaft fide of, - -	16 2 N.	114 42 E.
———— fouth-weft fide of, - -	15 28 N.	114 36 E.
Marlbro' fort, - - - -	3 46 S.	102 E.
Manapar point, - - - -	8 29 N.	78 5 E.
Mount Dilly, - - - -	12 6 N.	75 24 E.
Mangalore, - - - -	12 50 N.	75 6 E.
Manado, Pooloo, - - - -	2 2 N.	124 3 E.
Myo ifland, - - - -	1 31 N.	125 50 E.
Morintay, - - - - -	2 50 N.	126 33 E.
———— north cape of, - - -	3 2 N.	127 22 E.
———— fouth end of, - - -	1 40 N.	128 6 E.
Marfingola fhoal, - - -	15 23 N.	118 36 E.
Monday, or Barren Ifland, - - -	12 18 N.	94 9 E.
Matthew De Britto's reef, - - -	10 32 N.	107 23 E.
Momparva, - - - - -	23 N.	109 17 E.
Monopin hill, - - - -	2 3 S.	105 18 E.
Monaviffa, - - - -	4 22 S.	115 45 E.
Mocho, - - - - -	13 17 N.	43 17 E.
Mafulipatam, - - - -	16 16 N.	81 27 E.
Mayotta, - - - - -	12 49 S.	45 35 E.
Mohilla, - - - - -	12 32 S.	43 55 E.
Madeira, eaft point of, - - -	32 50 N.	16 46 W.
———— weft point of, - - -	32 30 N.	17 26 W.

X x

NAMES OF PLACES.	Latitudes.	Longitudes.
	° ′	° ′
Maldives, fouth-eaft part of - - -	40 S.	74 55 E.
———— north-weft part of, - - -	7 15 N.	73 40 E.
N.		
Nafhe's fhoal, New Holland, - - -	12 29 S.	123 56 E.
Ditto Ditto - - -	13 58 S.	122 21 E.
Negrais, cape, - - -	15 30 N.	94 37 E.
Nicobars, Quoin Ifland, - - -	8 49 N.	93 5 E.
North Watcher, - - -	5 14 S.	106 32 E.
Negapatnam, - - - -	10 38 N.	80 2 E.
Norcandam, - - -	13 26 N.	94 13 E.
Natal, - - - -	32 N.	98 57 E.
Nicobar, fouth end of the, - -	6 48 N.	93 34 E.
———— body of the, - -	7 5 N.	94 92 E.
Northernmoft Ampat, - -	3 38 S.	116 27 E.
New Holland, fouth-weft cape of, - -	43 42 S.	
——————— fouth-eaft cape of, - -	43 46 S.	147 5 E.
New Guinea, eaft point of, - - -	6 20 S.	148 E.
O.		
Oyfter rock, - - - -	14 55 N.	74 8 E.
Oujong Raja, Pedir, - - -	5 33 N.	96 36 E.
Ormus ifland, - - - -	27 20 N.	56 25 E.
P.		
Point Palmiras, - - -	20 44 N.	87 2 E.
Paul's, St., ifland, - - -	37 51 S.	77 48 E.
Pondicherry, - - -	11 42 N.	79 53 E.
Pooloo Condore, - - -	8 40 N.	106 56 E.
———— Timoan, - - -	3 N.	104 25 E.
———— Jarra, - - -	3 57 N.	100 15 E.
———— Perah, - - -	5 46 N.	99 12 E.
———— Rajah, - - -	7 35 N.	98 27 E.
———— Boutan, eaft end of, - -	6 30 N.	99 24 E.

NAMES OF PLACES.	Latitudes.	Longitudes.
Pooloo Boutan, weft end of, - - -	6 30 N.	99 15 E.
—— Pinang, fort Cornwallis, -	5 27 N.	100 26 E.
—— Roundo, - - -	6 7 N.	95 13 E.
Parflar hill, - - - -	2 52 N.	101 30 E.
—— low point, - -	2 52 N.	101 21 E.
Pedro Branco, in the Straits of Malacca, -	1 18 N.	103 30 E.
Pooloo Auro, - - - -	2 30 N.	103 58 E.
—— Piffang, on the weft coaft of Sumatra, -	58 N.	99 55 E.
—— Cecir de Terre, - -	11 12 N.	108 22 E.
—— Cecir de Mar, - -	10 30 N.	108 30 E.
—— Sapata, - - -	9 56 N.	109 10 E.
—— Domar, - - -	2 49 N.	105 20 E.
Pratas, north-eaft fide of the, - -	20 51 N.	116 50 E.
—— fouth-weft fide of the, - -	20 37 N.	116 40 E.
Pedro Branco, Leemas, - -	22 20 N.	115 15 E.
Paffage ifland, on the weft coaft of Sumatra, -	2 23 N.	97 28 E.
Point de Galle, - - - -	5 55 N.	80 16 E.
Porka, - - - -	9 21 N.	76 28 E.
Parmira rocks, - - -	13 17 N.	74 46 E.
Pigeon ifland, - - -	14 4 N.	74 35 E.
Pooloo Manado, - - -	2 2 N.	124 3 E.
Priaman, on the weft coaft of Sumatra, -	47 S.	99 40 E.
Padang, ditto -	58 S.	99 59 E.
Paffier roads, - - -	1 49 S.	116 30 E.
Preparis ifland, - - -	14 56 N.	93 41 E.
—— fhoal, - - -	14 50 N.	93 55 E.
Port Cornwallis, entrance of, - -	13 20 N.	92 54 E.
Pontianna river, - - -	13 N.	108 45 E.
Pooloo Lout, - - -	4 11 S.	115 58 E.
Point Pedro, - - -	9 57 N.	80 42 E.
—— Gardwar, - - -	16 45 N.	82 40 E.
—— Romania, - - -	1 15 N.	103 42 E.
Paracels, north part of the, - -	16 30 N.	110 5 E.
—— fouth part of the, - -	13 39 N.	109 5 E.
Pooloo Racket, - - -	6 1 S.	108 3 E.
Porto Santo, - - -	32 58 N.	16 20 W.
Point Divy, - - - -	16 6 N.	81 30 E.
Prince's ifland, in the Straits of Sunda, -	6 24 S.	105 20 E.
Pooloo Tingy, - - -	2 30 N.	105 8 E.
Pulicate, - - -	13 34 N.	80 1 E.

NAMES OF PLACES.	Latitudes.	Longitudes.
Q		
Queda roads, - - - -	6 11 N.	99 50 E.
Quilone, - - - - -	8 58 N.	76 37 E.
Quoin ifland, Nicobars, - - -	8 49 N.	93 5 E.
R.		
Rio Janeira, - - - - -	22 54 S.	42 44 W.
Roderigos, - - - - -	19 41 S.	63 10 E.
Round Arroe, - - - - -	2 50 N.	100 48 E.
Rajapore, - - - - -	17 3 N.	73 33 E.
Ragged point, - - - - -	1 24 S.	116 20 E.
Rocky ifland, off Pooloo Lout, - - -	4 7 S.	
Racket, Pooloo, - - - -	6 1 S.	108 3 E.
S.		
Saldanha bay, - - - -	33 10 S.	17 59 E.
Sapata, Pooloo, - - - -	9 56 N.	109 10 E.
Siam, - - - - -	14 18 N.	100 55 E.
Sooloo ifland, - - - -	5 57 N.	121 16 E.
Speaker's bank, - - - -	4 55 S.	72 57 E.
Surat, - - - - -	21 10 N.	72 34 E.
Sombrero channel, - - - -	7 30 N.	94 12 E.
Slipper ifland, - - - -	7 12 N.	99 9 E.
Songy Booloo, - - - - -	1 44 S	105 28 E.
St. George's ifland, - - - -	15 26 N.	73 20 E.
Seyers, northernmoft, - - -	8 44 N.	97 35 E.
—— largeft, - - - -	8 37 N.	97 26 E.
—— fouthernmoft, - - - -	8 31 N.	97 19 E.
Salatan point, - - - -	4 12 S.	114 36 E.
Siao, - - - - -	2 41 N.	124 49 E.
Samonbouangan, - - - -	6 58 N.	122 28 E.
Soofoo, on the weft coaft of Sumatra, -	3 41 N.	95 59 E.
Sinkell roads, - - - -	2 10 N.	97 38 E.
St. Jaques, cape, - - - -	10 15 N.	106 35 E.

NAMES OF PLACES.	Latitudes.	Longitudes.
Succadanna, - - - - -	1 16 S.	109 18 E.
St. Helena, St. James's valley, - - -	15 55 S.	5 51 W.
Sambas roads, - - - -	1 15 N.	108 15 E.
Sand banks, on the eaſt ſide of Borneo, - -	2 27 S.	
Southern Ampat, - - - -	3 41 S.	116 53 E.
Suez, - - - - -	29 50 N.	33 27 E.
Socatra, eaſt point of, - - - -	12 18 N.	54 25 E.
St. Auguſtin's bay, - - - -	23 35 S.	43 35 E.
St. Julian's, - - - - -	45 N.	106 45 E.
Scarbro' ſhoal, - - - -	15 N.	117 12 E.
St. Maria's iſlands, - - - -	43 20 S.	148 10 E.
St. Patrick's head, - - - -	41 44 S.	148 20 F.
Salvages, - - - - -	30 8 N.	16 4 W.
St. Paul's, - - - - -	37 51 S.	77 48 E.
St. Salvadore, - - - -	12 46 S.	38 40 W.
St. Jago, north part of, - - -	14 54 N.	23 25 W.
———— ſouth part of, - - -	14 18 N.	23 26 W.

T.

Timoan, - - - - -	3 N.	104 25 E.
Tringano roads, - - - -	5 23 N.	103 16 E.
Tapanooly, - - - -	1 44 N.	99 33 E.
Trichindore Pagoda, - - -	8 37 N.	78 14 E.
Tellicherry roads, - - -	11 45 N	75 31 E.
Tanjong Salatan, - - - -	4 12 S.	114 36 E.
Timontangis, - - - -	5 57 N.	120 54 E.
Triangles, ſix rocks in the China Sea, -	16 17 N.	112 2 E.
Timlee point, - - - -	14 52 N.	80 14 E.
Telingchon, (or Telican), - - -	8 33 N.	93 43 E.
Telloſamoy, - - - -	5 15 N.	97 10 E.
Triſtan de Acunha, - - -	36 27 S.	13 17 W.
Tombenjoa, - - - -	3 47 S.	114 37 E.
Tanjong Lapar, on the eaſt ſide of Borneo, -	2 8 S.	
Trinidad, - - - - -	20 15 S.	30 30 W.
Trincomale bay, - - - -	8 35 N.	81 27 E.
Turon bay, - - - -	16 4 N.	106 42 E.
Tingy, (or High Peak iſland) - -	2 30 N.	105 8 E.

NAMES OF PLACES.	Latitudes.	Longitudes.
U. & V.		
Vanſittart's ſhoal, (where ſhe ſtruck), - -	2 11 S.	106 48 E.
———— wreck, (upon Pooloo Panjang), -	2 9 S.	106 22 E.
Vingorla rocks, - - - -	16 N.	73 37 E.
Victoria fort, Bancoot, - - - -	17 56 N.	73 20 E.
Van Holland's bank, - - - -	10 42 N.	108 20 E.
Vizagapatam, - - . -	17 46 N.	83 35 E.
Victoria iſland - - - -	1 28 N.	105 55 E.
Van Diemen's bay, - - - -	10 30 S.	130 15 E.

F I N I S.

N O T I C E.

CAPTAIN ELMORE, confident there are many Gentlemen, both in Europe and India, of fuperior merit to himfelf, and whofe opportunities of acquiring nautical knowledge have been at leaft equal to his own, (but who, perhaps, from delicacy or apprehenfion of bringing their names before the fcrutinizing eye of the Public, or that they have not matter fufficient to form a publication,) will thankfully acknowledge the receipt of any remarks, additions, or fuch matter as may enable him to improve this Work. He therefore requefts, that any Gentleman who may have any manufcript inftructions, remarks, or charts of particular places, within any of the Honourable Company's limits of trade, will do him the favour of tranfmitting them to his Publifher, and they fhall be added to the foregoing Work, with the party's name to whom he may be indebted for the obligation.

T. BENSLEY, Printer, Bolt Court, Fleet Street, London.

For EU product safety concerns, contact us at Calle de José Abascal, 56–1°,
28003 Madrid, Spain or eugpsr@cambridge.org.

www.ingramcontent.com/pod-product-compliance
Ingram Content Group UK Ltd.
Pitfield, Milton Keynes, MK11 3LW, UK
UKHW012200180425
457623UK00020B/318